Fine Cuts

MW00856764

Fine Cuts:
The Art of European
Film Editing

Roger Crittenden

AMSTERDAM • BOSTON • HEIDELBERG • LONDON •
NEW YORK • OXFORD PARIS • SAN DIEGO • SAN FRANCISCO •
SINGAPORE • SYDNEY • TOKYO
Focal Press is an imprint of Elsevier

Focal Press is an imprint of Elsevier
Linacre House, Jordan Hill, Oxford OX2 8DP
30 Corporate Drive, Suite 400, Burlington, MA 01803

First published 2006

Copyright © 2006, Roger Crittenden. All rights reserved

The right of Roger Crittenden to be identified as the author of this work
has been asserted in accordance with the Copyright, Designs and
Patents Act 1988

No part of this publication may be reproduced in any material form (including
photocopying or storing in any medium by electronic means and whether or not
transiently or incidentally to some other use of this publication) without the written
permission of the copyright holder except in accordance with the provisions of the
Copyright, Designs and Patents Act 1988 or under the terms of a licence issued by
the Copyright Licensing Agency Ltd, 90 Tottenham Court Road, London, England
W1T 4LP. Applications for the copyright holder's written permission to reproduce any
part of this publication should be addressed to the publisher

Permissions may be sought directly from Elsevier's Science and Technology Rights
Department in Oxford, UK: phone: (+44) (0) 1865 843830; fax: (+44) (0) 1865 853333;
e-mail: permissions@elsevier.co.uk. You may also complete your request on-line via
the Elsevier homepage (http://www.elsevier.com), by selecting 'Customer Support' and
then 'Obtaining Permissions'

British Library Cataloguing in Publication Data
A catalogue record for this book is available from the British Library

Library of Congress Cataloguing in Publication Data
A catalogue record for this book is available from the Library of Congress

ISBN-13: 978 0 240 51684 4
ISBN-10: 0 240 51684 2

For information on all Focal Press publications visit
our website at: www.focalpress.com

Typeset by Charon Tec Pvt. Ltd, Chennai, India
www.charontec.com
Printed and bound in Great Britain

Working together to grow
libraries in developing countries

www.elsevier.com | www.bookaid.org | www.sabre.org

ELSEVIER   BOOK AID
            International   Sabre Foundation

Contents

Contents

Acknowledgements

In the first place I have to express my sincere thanks to all those who have contributed to this book, especially the editors from all over Europe who are represented here. For one reason or another some of those I wished to include are missing. There is a modesty about editors which inhibits them from developing any self-importance, and I did not possess the powers of persuasion or sufficient charm to convince some of them to be part of the enterprise.

This was especially true of Martine Barraqué – who worked for François Truffaut in the last phase of his career and is still an active editor. Martine was on my original list because she was my first contact when I wrote a book on Truffaut's '*La Nuit américaine*', and I have considered her a friend ever since. It was Martine who introduced me to Yann Dedet and the conversations between the three of us in Martine's Paris apartment made me aware more than any other encounter of the passionate dedication of editors to their craft, and of my own lifelong fascination with that passion. Although Martine would not be persuaded to be in the book, Yann has been a wonderful supporter of the idea from the beginning, and his own conversations with me set the tone for all subsequent encounters.

It is a similar case with Roberto Perpignani. Of all the interviews I conducted the one in Rome with Roberto was the most intensive. It lasted three days and could have gone on forever. In recent years Roberto has combined editing with teaching at the Italian National Film School and his desire to communicate the magic of the editing process gives us a mutual agenda that I am so happy to share.

But all my contributors share that passion and I hope the reader feels that it is communicated in these pages. Where I was unable to travel to the country of a contributor in some cases the interview was conducted by a mutual friend, in others the response was by letter and e-mail. Often it involved translation, either by colleagues in England or before the text was sent to me.

With Agnès Guillemot I was lucky enough to have Sarah Hickson with me and Arlette Kendall kindly translated from the tapes. Although Yann Dedet and I talked in English I have used part of another interview and that was translated for me by Elizabeth Hardy. Virginie Langlais was good enough to translate some of François Gedigier's interview.

I have to thank Alan Griffin for his research on my behalf and making contact for me with Julia Juaniz in Spain and Eleni Alexandrakis for performing similar services for me in Greece and making the time to interview Takis Yannopoulos in Athens.

Sylvia Ingemarsson's original text was translated for me by Päivi Overend. Sylvia's interview was conducted during a particularly pleasant day at her home. Andrej Mellin set up my contacts with the two Polish editors, and Gaby Prekop acted as intermediary for the Hungarians. 'Bara' Kastakova performed a similar service vis-à-vis the Czechs. I have also to thank all other translators including Eva Cieszewska and Emiliano Battista.

At Elsevier, Jenny Ridout was the one who believed in the concept for the book, and I thank her for putting her faith in me, even though it has been a struggle to deliver the MS. Christina Donaldson and Georgia Kennedy couldn't have been more helpful.

Lastly I wish to record my deep sense of loss at the death of Sabine Mamou. Sabine welcomed me into her home and immediately moved me by her open and honest attitudes. Her moral stance and her political and social commitment stood as an example to us all. She served to remind me that although editing can be a very rewarding role it can also involve questions of morality and of good and evil. I am sorry Sabine will not see this book but I think and hope her words represent her well.

Foreword: The Transformation of Chance into Destiny

Film is the only art whose birthday is known to us.

Béla Balázs

The motion picture was born in Edison's New Jersey laboratory in 1889 and spent an innocent childhood at fairground sideshows around the world, amusing and astonishing audiences with its one trick – single-shot representations of events like *The Sneeze, The Kiss, Train Arriving at the Station, Workers Leaving the Factory.* Then around 1903, at age fourteen, it unexpectedly discovered the intoxicating and almost sexual power of montage. What emerged out of this adolescence, as a butterfly out of its chrysalis, was cinema. The construction of a coherent and emotional story from discontinuous and sometimes conflicting images is the fruitful paradox that lies at the heart of the equation: MOTION PICTURES + MONTAGE = CINEMA.

We have the testimony of Edison and the Lumière brothers, American and European inventors of the mechanisms that made motion pictures possible, but the voices of those who invented the art of montage, which made *cinema* possible, are long lost. And they were largely European, anticipating developments in America by a couple of years. How did G.A. Smith, in 1900, arrive upon the idea of the closeup in *Grandma's Reading Glass*? Or James Williamson, in 1901, the idea of action continuity across various locations in *Fire*! We simply don't know. How were these basic ideas elaborated and refined by Meliès, Mottershaw, Haggard, Porter and others? There are some interviews with the American director D.W. Griffith, and the books on theory written years later by Russian directors Eisenstein and Pudovkin. But as for what actually took place in the editorial trenches in the first two decades of the 20th century we have only the most fragmentary circumstantial evidence, and in 1924 Balázs was already mourning the lost opportunity. 'It was the first chance to observe, with the naked eye so to speak, one of the rarest phenomena in the history of culture: the emergence of a new form of artistic expression. But we let the opportunity pass.'

All the other crafts of film – acting, photography, painting, drama-turgy, architecture, music, costume, make-up, dance – are based on long-established arts, with roots extending down through mil-lennia of development and tradition deep into the fecund secrets of humanity's prehistory.

But the defining craft of cinema – montage – seems to have quickly invented itself in a cocoon of silence, and to have continued that reticence as part of its protective colouration. Perhaps this is due to the personality of film editors themselves, or to the nature of their role as seconds to forceful and articulate directors. Or to the work itself, which most often aspires to burnish the efforts of others and to remain itself unnoticed. Perhaps it is simply priestly discretion: there is something of the confession booth to the editing room, where the omissions and commissions of shooting are whispered and discretely absolved by concealment or alchemically transformed into discoveries. Or maybe it is due to the very lack of deep-rooted tradition: there is not (yet) a rich vocabulary to describe *what goes on* as moving images mingle and fertilise each other, so we remain mute. Or cryptic: 'Why did you make that cut?' 'I don't know – it just felt right.'

Whatever the cause, this reticence is thankfully – after more than a hundred years – beginning to disappear. Several compilations of interviews with American film editors have been published in the last decade, but *Fine Cuts: The Art of European Film Editing* is notably the first collection to focus on European editors with their inspiringly diverse ways of assembling film. It also features illumin-ating guest appearances by a number of European directors – Godard, Varda, Tarkovsky, Truffaut, Mackinnon, Tarr – offering their insights into the editing process.

Many of the interviewees belong to cinema's fourth generation – those who began their careers in the 1960s and 1970s, as does the author Roger Crittenden – and as do I. Many of us consequently share the same inspirations, though I was born in New York. Like Roger, I was electrified by *The Seventh Seal* when I saw it at age fifteen – Bergman's vision was so distinctive that I left the theatre shaken by the thought: *somebody made that film*. As obvious as it might have been, this had never occurred to me before – Hollywood movies seemed simply to *appear*, like the weather, or landscapes glimpsed from a train. The unspoken corollary was that if *somebody* made that film, *I could make a film*. But the idea was too much for a fifteen-year old with no family connections to the film industry, and so it lay dormant.

Dormant – until I saw Truffaut's *Quatre cents coups* the next year, and Godard's *À bout de souffle* the year after that. As those two films confidently broke rules to which I had been oblivious, they allowed me my first glimpse of the power of montage, and it was consequently a great pleasure to read Roger's conversation with Agnès Guillemot, the only editor to work with both Godard and Truffaut.

What gives all of these interviews their complexity and warmth is not only the ten different nationalities, but even more so the richly diverse and 'uncinematic' family backgrounds of the editors collected here. Had they followed in their parents' footsteps they would have instead become teachers, pilots, tailors, doctors, farmers, chemists, vegetable sellers, astronomers, bookkeepers, salesmen, road workers, dry cleaners, dentists or civil servants. Luckily for the readers of this marvellous book, and for world cinema, they took another route and – to use Godard's evocative description of film editing – *transformed chance into destiny*, making the varied circumstances of their lives a reflection of montage at its most sublime, when accidental moments are propelled by structure into inevitability.

Walter Murch
London, June 2004

Introduction

The fascinating odyssey of investigating and appreciating the lives and careers of more than two dozen editors from across Europe has reminded me of my own initiation into the craft. Many of my contributors entered the cutting room by accident rather than intention. Certainly the majority did not choose editing as a career until after their initial experiences. Their innocence at the outset, even their naivety, may in some cases have made them better candidates for the job since, in my opinion, a lack of preconceptions gives the aspiring editor certain advantages.

Ironically, by the time I had graduated from university with a degree in sociology, which had been a strange diversion from reality, I knew categorically that I had to work in film and moreover that I wanted to be an editor, despite having never entered a cutting room or even read a book on the subject – the pleasure of discovering Karel Reisz's '*The Technique of Film Editing*' came later, and if I had read Eisenstein and the other Russian theorists I might well have been put-off the idea all together. However I had fallen in with a group at college who shared a passion for the cinema and I became obsessed with the medium which could deliver such a spectrum of pleasures from '*Singin' in the Rain*' to '*The Seventh Seal*'.

After a dreadful autumn and winter trying and failing to break into the business, I got my first job as a dogs-body in a small film company in London's Soho, just as I had resigned myself to the idea of working in a processing laboratory to get a Union ticket – an essential passport to the industry in those days. Just as important as the job was enrolling in evening classes at The London School of Film Technique which was housed in a run-down Victorian house in Electric Avenue, Brixton.

The course taught me next to nothing: the lecturer in direction, a veteran of the Berlin Studios of the 1930s who claimed to have worked with G.W. Pabst, whose '*Pandora's Box*' had transformed the career of Louise Brooks, only appeared twice. His unfortunate wife usually substituted for him and amongst other subjects coached us in how to make the best goulash outside of Hungary.

The axiom of the editing tutor, who was very articulate about coping with the privations of cutting in the inhospitable climate of West Africa, from where he had just returned, was that in cutting 'if it looks right, it is right'. The one skill I acquired was to make cement joins in 16mm film which stood a fair chance of holding together when projected. For our final project groups of us were given hundred feet of black and white 16mm film, which lasts two-and-a-half minutes, to make a silent film. It was hardly a step to Hollywood or even Pinewood.

But over the six months, on two evenings a week, I made two wonderful friends – an Indian, Durga Ghosh, and an Australian, Ron Porter. Their knowledge of cinema was far greater than mine and their passion had brought them to this institution from the other side of the world – much to my embarrassment. Durga was to gain some success as an editor for German Television in Stuttgart before he succumbed to kidney failure. He was one of the most cultured and stimulating men I have ever met. I still have a copy of the film he made about Rabindranath Tagore, that remarkable writer and thinker.

Ron, on the other hand always wanted to be a director, and the following year sunk all his savings in a modest film which I helped to conceive and subsequently edited. It was a simple story of an encounter between a young man and a young woman, set against the background of London's Portobello Road Market, which we shot over several weekends with a crew of volunteers. The cast were Norman Mann, an aspiring actor, and Niké Arrighi, a trained ballet dancer who was to go on to some success in movies including the role of the make-up girl in Truffaut's '*La Nuit américaine*' (*Day for Night*).

The film was shot silent and often took advantage of the passing parade which is the life of the Portobello Market. As it was silent and the narrative was only loosely predetermined, we had to find the shape and rhythm in the editing. Ron and I met of an evening in a Soho cutting room and experimented with juxtapositions – placing reactions of the two characters against each other and the environment they moved through.

We were playing with the form without having learnt any conventions or rules. I can't say we lacked anxiety, but we possessed a nervous energy born of ignorance and a concern that we would not be able to make the best of the material. After all if the film worked at all it might lead to other opportunities for one or other of us. Eventually we completed a twenty odd-minute final cut and '*The Market*' was chosen to be shown in the London Commonwealth Film Festival, an honour that I like to think was not entirely due to Ron being Australian. My involvement merited a short article in the Kent Messenger, the local paper where I grew up. More importantly it helped me to get one of twenty places on the newly launched BBC trainee editors scheme in competition with twelve hundred other applicants.

In the next few years I developed as a 'proper' editor, acquiring the language and the rules to deliver an efficient cut of conventional narratives, almost as if my initiation with Ron had been a shared self-deception. Yet when we cut our film Godard had already made '*Breathless*' and the Nouvelle Vague had challenged conventional film-making fundamentally, including the way editing functions.

To put my editing experience in perspective, although many of the films I cut were run-of-the-mill drama and documentary for TV, I also had the good fortune to work on some of Ken Russell's best films for the small screen, including '*Song of Summer*' and it was extremely liberating to be given material that allowed, even invited the use of less hidebound editing techniques.

I now realise that the naivety with which I had approached working on '*The Market*' made me open to using editing as a remarkable tool without the shackles of ridiculous rules. Many of the editors in this book had to reach the point of a crisis of confidence before they could work without the safety net of conventions. Often this was associated with developing a working relationship with a remarkable director. In some cases the revelation was a shared journey. For others the editor benefited from a journey in film-making that the director had already made.

You can sense the excitement experienced by these editors as you read their testimonies. They share an involvement in the variety which European cinema represents. None have had an ordinary predictable career. I have brought some of these 'cave dwellers' out of their normal, abnormal habitat, blinking in the light of day, despite a shared fear of confessing the details of their voluntary commitment to a closed world. It remains to be seen whether future generations can look forward to a similar richness of cinematic forms emerging from the edit suites of Europe.

Agnès Guillemot with Roger Crittenden (© Roger Crittenden)

1 Montage, Mon Beau Souci

(Montage My Fine Care, Jean-Luc Godard – Cahiers du Cinéma, December 1956) © Les Cahiers du Cinéma, 1996

This is an extract from the article referred to by Agnès Guillemot in our conversation where Godard says 'If direction is a look, montage is a heartbeat'. Considering that when he wrote this piece he had yet to make a full-length film, it is a surprisingly elegant insight.

. . . montage is above all an integral part of mise-en-scène. Only at peril can one be separated from the other. One might as well try to separate the rhythm from the melody. '*Eléna et les hommes*'[1] and '*Mr Arkadin*'[2] are both models of montage because each is a model of mise-en-scène. 'We'll save it in the cutting room': a typical producer's axiom, therefore. The most that efficient editing will give a film, otherwise without interest, is precisely the initial impression of having been directed. Editing can restore to actuality that ephemeral grace neglected by both snob and film-lover or can transform chance into destiny. Can there be any higher praise of what the general public confuses with script construction?

If direction is a look, montage is a heartbeat. To foresee is the characteristic of both: but what one seeks to foresee in space, the other seeks in time. Suppose you notice a young girl in the street who attracts you. You hesitate to follow her. A quarter of a second. How to convey this hesitation? Mise-en-scène will answer the question 'How shall I approach her?' But in order to render explicit the other question, 'Am I going to love her?' you are forced to bestow importance on the quarter of a second during which the two questions are born. It may be, therefore, that it will be for the montage rather than the mise-en-scène to express both exactly and clearly the life of an idea or its sudden emergence in the course of a story. When? Without playing on words, each time the situation requires it, each time within a shot when a shock effect demands to take the place of an arabesque, each time between one scene and another when the inner continuity of the film enjoins with a change of shot the superimposition of the description of a character on that of the plot. This example shows that talking of mise-en-scène automatically implies montage. When montage effects surpass those of mise-en-scène in efficacity, the beauty of the latter is doubled, the unforeseen unveiling secrets by its charm is an operation analogous to using unknown quantities in mathematics.

Anyone who yields to the temptation of montage yields also to the temptation of the brief shot. How? By making the look a key piece in his game. Cutting on a look is almost the definition of montage, its supreme ambition as well as its submission to mise-en-scène. It is, in effect, to bring out the soul under the spirit, the passion behind the intrigue, to make the heart prevail over the intelligence by destroying the notion of space in favour of that of time. The famous sequence of the cymbals in the remake of '*The Man Who Knew Too Much*'[3] is the best proof. Knowing just how long one can make a scene last is already montage, just as thinking about transitions is part of the problem of shooting. Certainly a brilliantly directed film gives the impression of having simply been placed end to end, but a film brilliantly edited gives the impression of having suppressed all direction. Cinematographically speaking, granted the different subjects, the battle in '*Alexander Nevsky*'[4] is in no way inferior to '*The Navigator*'.[5] In other words to give the impression of duration through movement, of a close shot through a long shot, is one of the aims of mise-en-scène and the opposite of one of those of montage. Invention and improvisation take place in front of the Moviola just as much as it does on the set. Cutting a camera movement in four may prove more effective than keeping it as one shot. An exchange of glances, to revert to our previous example, can only be expressed with sufficient force – when necessary – by editing. . . .

. . . . The montage, consequently, both denies and prepares the way for the mise-en-scène: the two are interdependent. To direct means to scheme, and one says of a scheme that it is well or badly mounted.

That is why saying that a director should closely supervise the editing of his film comes to the same thing as saying that the editor should also forsake the smell of glue and celluloid for the heat of the arc lamps. Wandering on the set he will discover exactly where the interest of a scene lies, which are its strong and weak moments, what demands a change of shot, and will therefore not yield to the temptation of cutting simply on movement – the a b c of montage, I admit, provided it is not used too mechanically in the manner of, say, Marguerite Renoir,[6] who often gives the impression of cutting a scene just as it was going to become interesting. In so doing, the editor would be taking his first steps in direction.

Notes

1. *Eléna et les hommes* – Jean Renoir (1956) with Ingrid Bergman.
2. *Mr Arkadin* – Orson Welles, 1955.
3. *The Man Who Knew Too Much* – Alfred Hitchcock, 1955.
4. *Alexander Nevsky* – Sergei Eisenstein, 1938.
5. *The Navigator* – Buster Keaton, 1924.
6. **Marguerite Renoir (born Houllé)** – She was Jean Renoir's partner and edited all his films in the 1930s from '*La Chienne*' in 1931 to '*La Règle du jeu*' in 1939. I think this remark is a little harsh on the person who, for instance, cut '*Ume partie de campagne*' (1936).

2 Agnès Guillemot

The only editor to work with both Godard and Truffaut, Agnès Guillemot's career spans from the beginning of La Nouvelle vague in the 1960s to the sexual radicalism of Catherine Breillat at the turn of the century. I talked to Agnès in her home in Paris, where she was then living with her husband Claude, a film-maker in his own right. My friend, Sarah Hickson, joined me to lubricate the conversation for which I am immensely grateful. I started, as usual, by asking Agnès about her background.

Agnès Guillemot and Jean-Luc Godard in the cutting room (© les cahiers du cinema, 1985)

I am a war child from a modest background in the north of France, Roubaix. During the war there was not much cinema. Our studies were done in the cellars with air raids in the background. I did not feed on films when I was young. I went on studying. I read a lot and went on to study philosophy. But the arts were revealed to me, not by the dialecticals or intellectuals, but by the poets and their world and philosophy.

The art that appealed most to me was music. Unfortunately I had been unable to learn it. I would have liked to become a conductor and I discovered that cinema is music and that editing is like being a conductor. I would not be able to invent themes, to be a composer, but I can produce orchestrations – I can adapt things therefore I can edit.

In fact I did not have any manual dexterity. I could not draw – editing gave me all that. It did not come from the head – it came through the rhythm, the music, the poetry, which brought me to the meaning of things. One had to listen, feel, receive and then transmit. This is how I came to it – not through my family.

We lived in the north during the textile crisis, during the war. My mother was a maths teacher. I had an unhappy childhood. It does not prepare one for the cinema. I was a student in Poitiers. Then I discovered music (discovering something late has many good points), what music meant. A discovery in depth – music in its entirety, its vastness – as well as an analytical approach – it engulfed me from all directions.

I had not been brought up with the radio on all the time – I never had a gramophone (record player). I was addicted neither to films nor to music. You can count on your fingers the number of films I saw as a child. One day the school took us to the cinema. It makes me laugh because of '*Les Carabiniers*'.[1] It was a film on animals: a bear was disappearing at the bottom of the screen – I got up to see it go! It always reminds me of the shot in *Carabiniers* where the young actor, Michel Ange, goes to the cinema and wants to touch the woman at the bottom of the screen and tears it. It was the same naivety. His discovery was like mine, but I was young.

Nothing prepared me for it but then I discovered the role of the conductor. When I saw a film on Roberto Benzi, who was a child prodigy conductor in the 1950s, I said to myself this is what I want to do. Not with music – with what I did not know – but I would find out.

I had finished my degree, in philosophy, and I thought about the cinema – its role, its meaning, its ethos – all that, and I wanted to write a thesis on this. But I went to IDHEC[2] and editing seduced me. It was not out of an inability to do anything else – it was a deliberate choice. It was meant for me.

I could not have been a director – I cannot invent stories. Editing has one marvellous thing – you are alone with the material and you listen. I use many metaphors, metaphors you use when talking about painters and sculptors. They look at a landscape, a stone; the stone inspires them to do this or that. Editing is the same. The material is given by somebody else, but I listen to it afresh. I do not try to make it mine, I try to make it produce what it can do. The object is inside – it must be made to come out. It is exactly this – I listen, I look a long time with all my being and I extract what the director wants.

I do not rush and produce some mechanical cuts – all this is not what is real. Everybody can do this but it does not make a film. To give birth to the true film is my passion. I am very lucky, I am very modest and I do not mind doing this for somebody else. On the contrary, I can 'be' the other person – enter his skin, feel what he wants to say, empathise completely, be one with the other. I can go very far in that direction – it can become like an addiction, but it is instrumental in the formation of a good editor.

When I edited my first Truffaut after having edited for Godard, some friends of Truffaut said, but she is going to do a 'Godard'. Completely idiotic – it was too much praise and at the same time not being understood at all. I deliver a Truffaut from Truffaut, a Godard from Godard. I do not mix things up. Film buffs recognise a film edited by me not because of some special seal but through sheer research and attention – I reach a certain truth, a strength. You could think of such and such a piece of music conducted by such and such a conductor and you recognise the conductor's hand. I have not written the music, but I conduct it.

I have been very lucky. Of all the films I have edited, I only regretted doing one (I will not tell you which one) and it is not the worst of all the films I edited. Some were very good, others more indifferent, but in all of them I thought it was worth giving something of myself. Some films I refused to take because the directors do them so as to be 'somebody' in social circles. They do not care a damn about their films. I am not at the service of the director – I am at the service of the film. Otherwise I quit. People who want to shine in society alongside a director are legion: I can't.

* * * * * * * * * * * * *

When I arrived in Paris, my degree in philosophy in my pocket, I thought I would do some work in depth on the cinema, its aims and responsibilities, its meaning, its ethics. To be right in it I did IDHEC. My parents were all for it, my mother being herself in teaching. It was a good place to learn, to be in the middle of things. I preferred the way IDHEC was run in those days. Some said it did not let students' genius develop. This is wrong. Genius is not given by any school – either you have it or you don't.

At IDHEC we knew that the cinema is a team effort. At La FEMIS[3] I saw the director on his own in the cutting room, editing his own film. It is not right. The director is not the best person to deliver his film. He delivers what he thinks is best, but he does not know it all. The greatest directors have always worked with editors.

It is true, later on, Godard with his sense of humour said 'I edited my films myself when I saw how easy it was', but this was after having edited a dozen films with me. I was his only editor, although there had been some substitutes when I was pregnant or editing another film. But even in his first political films he had an assistant – an assistant not a partner in editing. After he did it on his own when he discovered video and he meditated at length on virtual editing thinking one could mix film and video. For years he pondered about this and I could not follow him on those tracks. In the end he again separated one from the other. In Telerama he said: 'He who makes films like they were video is a dunce; he who makes video as if it were film is also a dunce'. From then on he separated the two.

He did try to make films where he mixed both. '*Passion*' despite being a success is not completely a film. The first he did really with his own money and which meant a lot to him was '*Je vous salue, Marie*'[4] on film. This year of reflection led him to see that different methods give different results. I am not saying that you must not do any videos but you must not think that if you make video instead of a film, on film you will have the same thing. The thinking time (*during editing*) does not take place in the same way. It is a solitary work that has no transmission of knowledge. It is terrible; the constant work at night – abnormal working conditions. On top of that the producer thinks it's easy.

On my last film, '*Selon Matthieu*',[5] I fell ill. When I was getting better they sent me a cassette of the film. The director and the producer had done a version to ask me what I thought. Abominable! There is no distance. You must take the audience on a voyage of discovery, whereas in their version they knew everything before the end, and I do not think that films can be edited like this. In France the Cinema is being invaded by the power of TV. If TV does not want such an actor you do not shoot the film. It is frightening.

I am glad that the end of my career coincided with the compulsory use of video. In 1966 I cut '*Mémoires d'un jeune con*'[6] on Avid and they then printed it on 35mm. The director, Patrick Aurignac, spent seven years in prison and wrote a script based on his experiences. I found this worthy of interest. The producer, to save money, made him direct his film and it went to his head. He was not up to it – it would have been a worthy film but he was badly advised. He committed suicide. It was worth breaking my beliefs for, but I wish it had a better ending.

Since I retired I have been working as an adviser on films shot on video. I always use the same technique. I will not say straight away after looking at it, it's fine or no, something is wrong. I will say – we watch the film together and then you go and have lunch. I think and then two hours later I will tell you the result.

When I watched a film I would treat it as I would a music manuscript – I would divide it into movements. I can tell you that timing the pieces made it obvious, allowed a dialogue with the director, showed why it did not work – a question of rhythm. If you try to explain to them, make speeches, they do not understand. If you tell them you have two sequences lasting exactly the same and which say more or less the same thing they understand. Even working in Avid I did some scenes like this to be able to discuss them.

* * * * * * * * * * * * *

Agnès then decided to show me the way she prepared her dubbing sheets – using music manuscript paper horizontally instead of the industry norm of vertical.

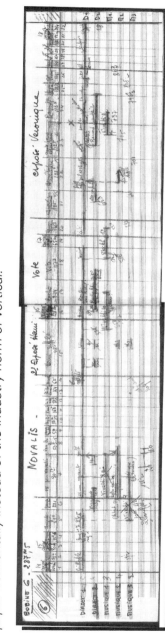

Example of dubbing chart designed by Agnès Guillemot (Courtesy of Agnès Guillemot)

My first 'score' was with Godard on 'Le Petit Soldat'[7] and he called them 'my little trains'. In France we used to prepare mixing sheets vertically. Why vertical – they used to answer me – because the film unthreads vertically. I do not see the relevance. On my 'score' I would indicate the main shots (i.e. the image), direct sound, dubbing and all similar effects – played on the same 'instrument'. It allowed us to divide it up in a more musical way.

My husband who did some editing – he is not an editor he is a director – used to say, you are not going to do like everybody else, with vertical sheets, it is ridiculous. Together we realised it was much more 'crafty' to do them horizontally. In the vertical sheets we had big long columns and to know what was happening in parallel made very difficult reading. Moreover one would not prepare the charts in advance. I prepare in advance where my assistants must put the sound. Before they put it where there is an empty column. There was no planning. In 'Virtual' they found out what I used to do, the horizontal way (timeline), it is obvious.

Godard said I should give them to the Cinémathèque.[8] This one is 'Le Mépris'[9] (shows me example). Everybody speaks of the shot in this film – so beautiful; 'Do you like my feet, etc.' In fact it is not the original version; before we went straight from the cameraman, Raoul Coutard,[10] who arrived with his camera, to Jack Palance, who was coming out of the studio. The Americans said there is not enough sex. Godard added the scenes of Bardot naked. The scenes are peppered here and there. He added that travelling shot on the bed – everybody thinks it is superb. I get cross – it was superb to go directly from the credit to the film in one shot. Now one speaks about the splitting up of time but it was not like this – it was a much more linear, simple film. When he had to put things for the Americans he did his best (superb shot where they are sitting on the settee and he strokes her legs, interspersed with shots of her on a carpet, red, white and blue). It was a long shot (continuous) but it was cut to put in these censored shots. It was painful – I have the proof in these documents.

Agnès shows me the various versions.

With 'Vivre sa Vie':[11] when he shot he knew exactly what he was going to do – no discussion. He was the only one (and even his friends of the Nouvelle Vague were astounded by this) who knew. He 'saw' his film before actually shooting it. There were very few things he did not know. We hesitated a few little times but for most things it was a logical continuation of what preceded it. It was in his head.

We spoke very little. We were two shy guys. We understood each other's body language. I was on the editing machine – he was next to me. I run the film – when he thinks we should stop, I stop. We look again – we stop at the same point. We spoke very little. When there were doubts – it happened once or twice on some travelling shots in relation to the music – he would say 'underline the strong beats in white – I will sit down and mark them' – he used a yellow marker. When we looked at the film the yellow and white coincided. He said 'it won't be possible to say we did not get on'. Sometimes things would surprise me, but I would listen.

In the book 'Godard by Godard'[12] in the piece '*Montage mon beau souci*' (*Montage my beautiful concern*) he said 'To direct is a look to edit is a beat of the heart'. Our hearts beat at the same rhythm – we did not need to speak. Take '*Les Carabiniers*'. There is a scene in the woods; the partisans are ambushed by the so-called soldiers. One of them removes a partisan's cap and fair hair falls to her shoulders. The gesture is done twice – in closeup and again in a wider shot. We tried to do a classical link, but it did not have the same import as it did when we used both shots.

I put them both together again and Godard said 'How are we going to justify this?' and I said 'we can say, he did it and when he did it he asked himself why he did it – he does it again to know how he did it'. It is the only thing I said to Godard. It was a bit twisted – not an explanation, only a word here and there. For the sake of equilibrium we needed other 'double raccord' (repeat actions) in the film, but they were less moving than this first one.

Godard's films are impeccably constructed. The only time that censorship came into his films was in '*Le Mépris*'. He was furious because he knew that if you take off a beat the whole thing may fall. I learnt this with him: equilibrium. What I learnt with him is that genius is caring passionately. I told this to Nicole Garcia[13] who did not understand at first, but saw the truth of it later on. One reacts differently as an actress than as a director. Her films are good. She was good. I ended my career as an editor with '*Romance*'.[14] Good film – great dignity of female sexual pleasure – not pornographic.

'*Vivre sa Vie*' is a masterpiece. There are different categories of film in Godard – for instance contemplative films, of which '*Vivre sa Vie*' is the prototype. '*Bande à part*'[15] is something else. I worked with Godard in the first ten years of his career. He then stopped to make his political films and then his research. When he started again he did not want an editor. He was not sure of himself but he was sure he had 'perfect pitch' as far as films were concerned.

He could not stand people talking on the set. They prevented him from listening. He looked at everything with an open eye. His films were not expensive – he shot very quickly – he knew exactly what he was going to do. He extracted from things all that could be extracted. I see him walking in the location of '*Masculin, Feminin*',[16] a bistro. He sent all the team to the next bistro to be in peace, and he 'felt' the set. When he asked people to come back he knew exactly where to put them. It was not as things were done then – we are going to do a shot here and there – he would do long tracks. He did not change things without a reason. He found things in the workplace – no known recipes.

* * * * * * * * * * * * *

Jean Douchet[17] in his book on the *New Wave* said we were not aware of what we were inventing or discovering – we lived it intensely but without saying to ourselves we are inventing new things. On the whole people do not like it when I say this. Anna Karina[18] in an interview describes Godard as an intellectual, but I do not think this is the right term. He is marvellously intelligent but not an intellectual. The other day I was asked why did he want to do a science fiction film with '*Alphaville*'.[19] I answered, he did not decide to do a science fiction film. He went looking for locations for '*Ume Femme Mariée*'[20] – he was looking for locations in Orly airport, which was being built. He saw the basements, the odd buildings – at the time the atomic bomb was in the headlines. He saw the swimming pool in the airport – a new thing at the time. The film was to be called, '*A new adventure of Lemmy Caution*'. When he saw all these settings it all crystallised and became the elements of what became a science fiction film, linking the swimming pool and the interrogations, as in certain countries at the time. At the time and even now people do not realise that it is a 'true' science fiction – there are no special effects. Here it is the daily routine, which creates the science fiction.

Godard looked at everything with passion. He found things in everyday life when he walked, listened, found things for his scripts. He listens. It is while walking in the street, seeing the girls in the street, that '*Vivre sa Vie*' started. There is an expression of a novelist – 'Sculpture came up from his feet'. Inspiration came from his feet to the heart. It is tactile, physical. Intellectuals would talk at conferences on Godard, but when Godard came they did not ask him any questions. Vampires, they live off Godard's films but the person does not interest them.

I divide people between the earthly and the pure spirit. Godard told me he was visual/audio and I was audio/visual. I was an audio tactile. This is why I could not work in virtual. I have to touch the film. In the last film of Godard, a reflection on the cinema, he edits a film with a female assistant who is blind. He gives her a piece of film and asks her to put the sound on it.

A producer once said, he hasn't done any splicing for three days. He spends his time looking at the film backwards, looking at the same scene. I am sure this is how one should edit ones film – not by rushing to do the first splice. I had to fight with the producer at first. They wanted me to edit the first sequence to find the results, but it does not mean that the final editing will be the same. You have to see the whole film – I have to explain this to directors.

Once Catherine Breillat called me to come to her aid. She had told her editor to edit the first sequence between two characters. She said the editor had sabotaged the sequence. When I came I saw why it did not work. We saw the characters later on – we discover their tempo – their dialogue. She had edited this tac/tac/tac quickly. Whereas it was two characters that took their time to speak; the editor must see the whole of the film.

In French films music is used as an illustration – not a good use of music and sounds. Godard always uses direct sound except in '*Le Petit Soldat*' because of Anna Karina's accent. He wanted to show the sound level. We are not conscious of the sound level we hear.

(He was in the editing room for the image but not for the sound – he was in the bistro downstairs.) In '*Le Petit Soldat*', at the beginning, a car arrives silently, one does not hear the brakes, sound of a match, car goes, one hears nothing – then music.

By the way, I did not know Godard before I worked with him. He had asked one of my former pupils in IDHEC if she knew somebody who was not deformed by traditional films who could edit his film.

In '*Ume Femme est ume femme*' Anna Karina gets up, goes to the bistro. She is inside, asks for a 'green' crème – goes out in the street, lots of noise, the shot after – no more noise. It was to make us hear the sound level that you normally do not hear, like abstract music. With the Italians we sent them an International copy (*sound mix without dialogue*) with the cut. They thought there was a mistake and they reintroduced the sound everywhere – put sound in the 'hole'.

He sees it as his rhythm that he adds to the music. He always said that he is not a musician himself and discovered music later on. He had a tremendous ear – he did not want to use music to illustrate things, to accompany. He wanted music that would talk with the other sounds in the film – a dialogue – not music to make things smoother, easier to understand, to create false emotions. Sometimes I hear people say here it is not too good, let us put some music.

'*Le Mépris*' was the only time when he used a score – Delerue[21] – good collaboration. He did not cut it. In the scene in the music hall, normally you would lower the music when people talk – here he cuts it: no half-measures.

****

I worked with Truffaut from '*Baisers Volés*',[22] because Claudine Bouché[23] was not available. We got on well with '*Baisers Volés*', the way one got on with Truffaut. Truffaut was not bothered by how one makes a film, how one puts things together. He is the spectator – he wants to see the result, not the know-how. I was completely puzzled. Godard never shot a scene from different angles saying we will choose, but Truffaut did it. Naively I thought he was going to say I want this or that in closeup on such characters. He said nothing, do what you like, disconcerting but exciting.

'*Baisers Volés*' was edited in quite a new way. For instance the scene where Lonsdale[24] comes to see the private detective and says nobody loves me, when you sell shoes you are a shoe-nick twenty-four hours a day. In principle one puts a wide shot then one gets nearer, then closeup. Looking at the film I thought this is ridiculous – why do this? Lonsdale was fantastic in medium closeup and closeup. I went from one to the other to take the best.

Truffaut asked why did you do this? I said I do not want the best things to stay in the rushes, discarded. He accepted the principle of the thing after we projected it. When it was alright he would not say much but when it did not work he would say so. He was jealous of Godard. I suffered from having worked with Godard but I was proud of it. Truffaut did not use me without letting me know – it was his way. During '*Domicile Conjugal*'[25] one scene with Claude Jade[26] was causing problems. He said we should not edit it this way. I said I had tried everything – can you come to the editing room. Then he was mad. He did not know what to say – he hated it.

'*Baisers Volés*', '*L'Enfant sauvage*'[27] and '*La Sirène du Mississipi*'[28] are his three best films. '*Domicile Conjugal*' I like least. Truffaut was very susceptible. Jealousy and his unfaithfulness were his worst defects. He needed to love and be loved. His films went by fours. Of his editors only Martine Barraqué[29] did more.

When I was on the dole I went to see a director – a lover of film – Pierre Tchernia.[30] He was making a film that I do not like – '*Le Viager*'.[31] He told me 'I do not do Godard'. Later on when somebody said that to me I would reply 'it is a shame you don't'. There is a very poignant article by Godard in Telerama. After his accident he tried to start again. 'I have to start from scratch, as if I had not done anything before'.

Truffaut shot in a more traditional way. His trademark is his sensitivity. There is a charm that is Truffaut – it comes from the way he learnt about the cinema when he was very young – he likes cliché. With Godard it was the opposite so for me it was sometimes difficult. The cliché which may cost me my work with him was in '*Domicile Conjugal*'. Claude Jade has a child. Léaud[32] comes home late – meets his in-laws at the bottom of the stairs. Truffaut shot two versions: one where the in-laws said, 'Be nice to her, she had a lot of pain, she went through a lot' the other 'You have a lovely little boy, be happy and nice with her'. Earlier in the film we had been told that she was listening to a record about childbirth without pain – automatically I chose the second version. Truffaut said to me 'why did you choose this one?' I said 'If you shoot her listening to the record, you are not going to traumatise generations of young women'. It was bad faith. In the scene where Claude Jade and Leaud meet again she says 'now you are proud of your son, but before, you dropped me'. He betrayed her with the Japanese girl – it was bad faith.

Godard says 'the cinema is a question of morality'. It was contrary to my belief to put the first version. For Truffaut it was better to put the more hackneyed idea. Women suffer and to hide the fact she was putting on a face because her partner had betrayed her. He took my version but he was not a moralist. I was nearer to Godard.

With Truffaut there was no joy in the cutting room. Once I had a big bouquet and a telegram for '*Baisers Volés*': 'make the film how you like, I shot it thinking of other things (it was 1968) I trust you completely, do as if I were dead' I found this note after Truffaut's death. In June 1968 all the technicians were on strike. He had asked me if we could go and do one projection without saying anything to anybody. I said no. I did not like it, it was contrary to my principles. I do not see why I should have given in.

I am very severe on '*La Nuit américaine*'.[33] It presents the cinema to the public in the same way that Cinémonde[34] would show it to the reader. This is why I share Godard's view who wrote to him: 'From a cineaste who is such a film buff you should have been more faithful'. One could have done better on a film about film. When I saw it, it annoyed me.

I did not like this line in '*Baisers Volés*': 'politeness is better than being sincere' – I do not think so. In the scene when Delphine Seyrig[35] comes in the room it was not easy. The frame when he is clowning in his bed – it was not very well directed – and hard to find some reactions. She is superb – I love the scene when he is on top of the ladder in the shoe shop and sings.

In '*Le Sirène du Mississipi*' there were lots of aphorisms: 'I love you because you are loveable'! One could not discuss with him.

Not even Suzanne Schiffman[36] – she was wonderful – she just died. She understood Truffaut. She had worked with Godard too. When they split it was very painful. I do not like to speak too much of my work with Truffaut. It is good to admire and I do not admire him that much. At first it was possible when he was in love with Catherine Deneuve.[37] He went to Brittany and left the film with me, in full confidence. Then when he broke with Deneuve – I knew he would not take me again. He had an extraordinary wife, Madeleine Morgenstern.[38]

Yann Dedet[39] and Martine Barraqué went on the set. I never did – or I went out of politeness. Truffaut liked people to go. When I see a film being shot it has not the same mystery for me as when I discover it in the projection room. It is fantastic, the editor seeing it for the first time. This does not happen in video – everybody has seen everything as it happens. One's eyes are polluted by so many shots.

Anna Karina says in an article 'to make films one has to take everything seriously' – I add to this 'except oneself'. One has to be modest:

Shall we drink a coffee now?

Agnès Guillemot with Roger Crittenden (© Roger Crittenden)

Notes

1. *Les Carabiniers* – Film by Jean-Luc Godard, 1963.
2. **L'IDHEC** – L'Institut des Hautes Etudes Cinématographiques, French National Film School, established after the 2nd World War in Paris.
3. **La FEMIS** – Fondation European des metiers de l'image et du son, successor to the above institution.
4. *Passion* (1982), *Je vous salue, Marie* (1985) – Jean-Luc Godard.
5. *Selon Matthieu* – Xavier Beauvois, 2000. Edited by Christophe Nowak.
6. *Mémoires d'un jeune con* – Patrick Aurignac, 1996.
7. *Le Petit Soldat* – Jean-Luc Godard, 1960.
8. **Cinémathèque** *(Francaise)* – This refers to the institution established by Henri Langlois where many of the French New Wave gained their cinematic education by full immersion in screenings and discussions of films from all places and eras. Langlois became a *cause celebre* when the government closed the Cinémathèque, provoking violent demonstrations which were a precursor to the unrest of 1968, only in France!
9. *Le Mépris* – Jean-Luc Godard, 1963, based on a novel by Alberto Moravia and starring Brigitte Bardot, Michel Piccoli and Jack Palance.
10. **Raoul Coutard** – Along with Henri Decae the leading cinematographer of *Le Nouvelle Vague*, to whom much credit must be given for the visual style developed during that period.
11. *Vivre sa Vie: film en douze tableau* – Jean-Luc Godard, 1962.
12. **Godard by Godard** – Fascinating book where Jean-Luc Godard chronicles his career including many examples of his working documents. Partial version available as *Godard on Godard* translated by Tom Milne.
13. **Nicole Garcia** – Brilliant actress, born in Algeria, who in recent years has successfully turned to direction.
14. *Romance* – Catherine Breillat, 1999, a frank and, for some, disturbing examination of female sexuality, which this director has further explored in other films.
15. *Bande à part* – Jean-Luc Godard, 1964.
16. *Masculin–Féminin: 15 faits précis* – Jean-Luc Godard, 1966.
17. **Jean Douchet** – Actor, director, writer and former professor at L'IDHEC.
18. **Anna Karina** – Actress born in Copenhagen, was Godard's muse in the early sixties and also played leading roles for Jacques Rivette and Agnès Varda.
19. *Alphaville: une étrange aventure de Lemmy Caution* – Jean-Luc Godard, 1965.
20. *Ume Femme mariée: Fragments d'une film tourné en 1964* – Jean-Luc Godard, 1964.
21. **Georges Delerue** – Eminent music composer for well over 300 films including many for Truffaut.
22. *Baisers Volés* – François Truffaut, 1968.
23. **Claudine Bouché** – Editor who cut for Truffaut and is still active. Most recently – '*Water dropping on Burning Rocks*' for François Ozon.

24. **Mich(a)el Lonsdale** – Prolific actor, including for Luis Buñuel.
25. *Domicile Conjugal* – François Truffaut, 1970.
26. **Claude Jade** – '*Baisers Volés*' was her first screen appearance. She reprised the role of girl friend and then wife to Antoine Doinel in two subsequent Truffaut films, '*Domicile Conjugal*' and '*L'Amour en fuite*'.
27. *L'Enfant sauvage* – François Truffaut, 1969.
28. *La Sirène du Mississipi* – François Truffaut, 1969.
29. **Martine Barraqué** – Editor for François Truffaut on his last eight films.
30. **Pierre Tchernia** – Actor, writer, director.
31. *Le Viager* – Tchernia, 1972 (there are three editing credits).
32. **Jean-Pierre Léaud** – François Truffaut's alter-ego as Antoine Doinel from '*Les Quatre-cents coups*', 1959 to '*L'Amour en fuite*', 1979. Also acted for Godard.
33. *La Nuit américaine* – François Truffaut, 1973. Truffaut's tribute to the magic of filmmaking.
34. *Cinémonde* – A popular film magazine.
35. **Delphine Seyrig (1932–90)** – Born in Beirut, became an eminent actress in French films and theatre. Worked with, amongst others, Truffaut, Resnais, Buñuel and Akerman.
36. **Suzanne Schiffman** – François Truffaut's right hand woman, from script girl to co-writer. Also worked with Godard.
37. **Catherine Deneuve** – Worked with Truffaut and Buñuel, amongst many other credits, still the Diva.
38. **Madeleine Morgenstern** – Ran Truffaut's company, Les Films du Carrosse, after his death, having been his wife at the start of his directing career. A remarkable woman.
39. **Yann Dedet** – Film editor – see interview next. . .

3   Yann Dedet

Yann's first films as editor were with François Truffaut. He subsequently became the editor for amongst others, Maurice Pialat and later Cédric Kahn. He has recently directed his first feature length film, 'The Land of the Singing Dog'.
  We talked in his Paris apartment and at a nearby café.

I was born in Paris in 1946. My father was a publisher, including for instance the last three books by Antonin Artaud.[1] My mother was an 'antiquaire' (antique dealer). I was very 'moyen' (average) at school, but I developed an early interest in the theatre (Shakespeare, Strindberg).

My father took me to see my first film when I was eight. It was *'L'homme des vallées perdues'* (*Shane*) by George Stevens.[2] I ran out of the theatre, crying, when the dog howled to death at his master's funeral. Later *'Peter Pan'*, *'Snow White'* many *peplums* and westerns and then the first Chaplin films that I saw (*'Les temps modernes'* (*Modern Times*)[3] and *'The Great Dictator'*)[4] made a bridge to reality by such a mixture of joy and sadness. From where, I think, I got the idea of making films myself; a hope materialised by my grandfather when I was eleven, by the gift of a Paillard-Bolex eight millimetres[5] and the making of 'movies'. Other early films that made an impression on me were *'La Prison'* (*The Devil's Wanton*)[6] by Ingmar Bergman, Fellini's *'Eight-and-a-half'*[7] and Visconti's *'Il Gattopardo'* (*The Leopard*).[8]

Culturally, my first loves in music were Vivaldi, Moussorgsky, Prokofiev, Tchaikovsky, Varese and Léo Ferré; in literature Julien Green, Henri Bosco, André D'hotel and Ionesco.[9]

My first passion was really theatre, maybe more serious because nearer to literature. The shock was the sight, in an editing room of the two 'celluloids', the brown sound and the grey (black and white) image, falling together in a box under the Moritone,[10] mixed together like two snakes, and the nazillard, direct sound making its way above the strong noise of the motor and the celluloid splices passing *en claquant* through the wheels of this magical and physical machine.

But at the time the pleasure of holding my little camera and the fact of choosing what was to be filmed was stronger than the idea of editing, less instinctive for the moment than framing. So I want to go to the Vaugirard[11] School of Photography to learn framing. But studies went worse and worse because of the awakening of adolescent 'pulsions' (urges) which pushed me to make with my Paillard-Bolex a very destructive and auto-destructive little movie in the mood of '*Erostrate*' by Sartre.[12]

* * * * * * * * * * * * *

So no Vaugirard and instead one month in London to improve my English (and for my parents to put me far away from a very pousse-au-crime friend I admired very much) and six months in a film laboratory where I spent half my time synchronising dailies; another shock coming from my 8mm to this huge 35mm and even more when one day I touched 70mm from 'Playtime' of Tati.[13]

But I only really knew what editing was when I edited myself the sequences that were reshot for the – very bad – movie I made my first *stage* (trainee-ship) on. Happily there were a lot of bad sequences reshot and, coming in at around six in the morning, I tried all sorts of stupid cuts, and even splicing the film upside down, drawing on the film, etc. At the time it was only a game and now it is real work but happily the pleasure of playing is still there. As Pialat[14] says, 'Its only when you have fun that you work well'.

The editor I saw working on this first *stage* was so bad that I could begin by learning, what not to do, a very important step. Afterwards, Claudine Bouché,[15] whom I assisted on '*La Mariée était en noir*' (*The Bride Wore Black*)[16] confirmed in me that playing in work is essential, and Truffaut was so incredibly easily changing the meaning of the material, of the shots, twisting, reversing them and placing them so freely out of their first place that once again I felt the *ludique* (play) side of editing.

Then Agnès Guillemot,[17] edited the next four Truffaut movies, and he asked her to keep me as assistant. Agnès has two enormous qualities; firstly, she tries nearly every solution, even the ones which look logically bad, and secondly, she lets the movie breathe, almost by itself, waiting very often for the solutions to become obvious.

She puts shots, *not* cuts, next to each other to try to see what is the effect between the two shots, but not the splice, the interior of each shot, what it says, the meaning, the colour, the pace of the shot. Then she cuts entire shots out and suddenly there is something obvious between the shots that remain and then she makes the *raccord* (match) between the shots but not before. It's like you don't take the skin off the chicken until you know it is a good piece. So Agnès has a good way of attacking the work, which is waiting–looking–thinking–hearing the music then *tout à coup* this piece can be out because its not the mood of the whole thing. It's very delicate work.

For me it is different. I replaced this method by being very *presse*, always a guy in a hurry. So very quickly I focus on a centre – the shot from the rushes which speaks to me – and little by little I extend, maybe too fast but sometimes it has good results because it provokes interest in the rest of the rushes.

François (Truffaut) hated the cut on action, like the Americans always do. A gesture should be complete and not interrupted by a cut and/or change of angle. Rather the rhythm should dictate the moment. Also I don't like *champ-contre-champ* (matching two-shots), with a piece of somebody on the edge of frame. It's like a stupid proof, just for what? It wastes the energy of the image; putting technique before art.[18]

I don't remember this kind of thing in silent cinema. I think it is the demand of sound, suppressing the character of ancient cinema.

* * * * * * * * * * * * *

I had an entirely different experience with Dusan Makevejev on '*Sweet Movie*'.[19] The structure there is not essentially narrative but essentially *emotive*; that a scene follows another by opposition or

Yann Dedet (on left) cutting with Jean-François Stévenin (Courtesy of Yann Dedet)

by similitude is the important thing. At the wall of the editing room on the list of the sequences, each sequence is characterised by a little coded sign which means: 'something violent', 'something sweet', 'something sexual', 'something animal', 'something horrifying', 'something tender', 'something historical', 'something childish', etc. The way he chooses the pieces to edit is very special too; totally un-narrative at first, just putting cut – cut the pieces he likes without any apparent idea of construction.

But the greatest editor for me is the director Jean-François Stévenin,[20] always chasing the '*défauts*' (flaws) in each shot. I like imperfection; things should be seen and heard that are *défaut*. Films need arrhythmic things, too long or too short. Stévenin's movies are full of *ellipses*. He has a certain pleasure, and talent too, for breaking the logic of a scene, and mixing the ups and downs of an actor in so complete a disorder that he amplifies the trouble – that the actor was trying to express – ten times more than expected.

Then I worked with Patrick Grandperret[21] who is in some sort the opposite of Stévenin, framing himself, shooting his movies in a total disorder, rewriting the script every night, and changing direction the next day. In all this mess editing is the moment when he really writes, cutting one shot to another so that the movie looks like one long sweet movement (Stévenin on the contrary shoots very controlled *plan-sequence*s and editing is the moment of putting everything in 'living-disorder').

With these four directors, Truffaut, Makavejev, Stévenin and Grandperret, I must say that this period was my school time, I was learning and learning.

* * * * * * * * * * * * *

Maurice Pialat was the second director to choose me '*against*' Truffaut (the first was Makavejev) having respect but no approbation for Truffaut's style. In fact, as often as not, opposition was the game, the idea being to compare and oppose one idea of cinema to another, for the purpose of refining his style. Or by using methods from other styles, or not using them, by discovering something which improves and goes further in his own style. Very drastic, very radical solutions are found this way, often by leaving the problem *without solution*.

After that I worked with Philippe Garell:[22] with him each time you cut five frames, you check the entire twenty-minute reel to feel whether the *inside music* of the film has been broken or not. Then with Cédric Kahn,[23] who is an incredible mix of instinct and reflection; with Manuel Poirier[24] whose dream would be (as for Pialat in fact) not to cut; the less shots there are, the better it is to let time flow.

With Claire Denis[25] we spoke a lot, but it is as if words couldn't be of any use. Only listening to the film counts. The important thing about Claire is that she never wants to say what she wants; she is suspicious of words. So our dialogue is always going around the subject. Like Stévenin, they both don't want the words to come before the act of building the film.

It is the opposite with Pialat; the talk is nourishing the film; a way of liking life. He believes you will never have a good movie if you don't have fun with it. He is suffering because you have to cut, so is trying to cut by playing with cutting. It is a magical moment when the '*réalisateur danser devant son film*' (the director dances in front of his film).

My key experiences as an editor have been Truffaut for learning (he was my cinema father – I never read Bazin[26] who was the grandfather), Stévenin for the feeling that everything can be tried, even what seems impossible, and Pialat who seems totally untechnical, who is as free as life.

For example, in '*Van Gogh*',[27] in the cabaret sequence, I remember a savage cut in the music, surely unbearable to a musician, a savage cut which, *en rapport avec* the other cuts and jumps of image and sound in this sequence, was something which gave *équilibre* (balance) to the whole thing, as if life lay in the erratic cuts more than in the logical cuts. For me this kind of thing is impossible to replace by another *figure de style* (stylistic device).

* * * * * * * * * * * * *

What seems to be apparent in most of American Cinema is a very important rational thinking at work: everything has to make sense, and to be precise, like subtitled, the sound saying the same thing as the image, and shots explaining and saying again and again the same idea, which is already over-expressed by the intentional face-playing of the actors, the endless repetitions of the dialogues. The American ideal of cinema is an infinite continuity of *pléonasmes* (emphasising the obvious).

In European cinema you can sometimes see *un plan pour rien* (literally a shot for nothing) different, elsewhere, out of the movie, but which is in fact the movie. Sometimes when I'm very glad for a movie I say, '*un film pour rien*' it was just like a part of life, or a good dream. There is no story, no thesis to defend, there is no purpose, just doing music, letting time flow. Show it how it flows, marvellously. This is *un film pour rien*.

In the storytelling process European editors have to work like musicians, like rowers in rapids, trying to listen to the sound of the falls, not to be pulled towards them by the flow.

Maybe the biggest utility of an editor is to be like a mirror, but one who gives back another image to the director. Often, just listening to what someone says makes the 'sayer' aware of the fact that he just said something wrong or incomplete or stupid or . . .: and this is part of the role of an editor and this quality – just being there to receive, even saying nothing – helps the one who creates to 'see' as he never saw his work.

For the editor, arriving first at work is very important, to take possession of the film as much as working alone on it sometimes. The editor is coming late to the film: he didn't dream, didn't write, didn't direct the film and he has to take the film, to touch it, break it and splice it to understand how the film is thought and how it reacts.

The ideal editor is a humble director.

The difficulty in everything is **not** *to be perfect.* An editor must be half-intelligent–half-instinctive, half-romantic–half-logical, half-imaginative–half-*terre à terre* (down to earth), half-here–half-dreaming . . . . This makes a lot of halves and I would say that such a mess is more a gift of nature than something that can be worked and built.

The first reason for choosing to work on a movie is the director, and most of all how he speaks about cinema – or about life. All those who are very aware about techniques or about the business world of cinema are very repulsive to me. The best is, as Pialat does, to speak music, sex, painting, mountains, sculpture, love . . . (Although the most revealing thing for me was when he asked me ten years before we worked together: 'Do you like films in which the guy says "lets go to the sea", and the next scene is on the seashore?')

Very seldom scripts are good enough to really imagine how the movie will be, what I mean by good is poetic without being literary, giving the *envie* (desire) to see images and hear sounds of a special universe, like 'not really belonging to this planet' as John Boorman said about '*Passe-montagne*'.[28]

* * * * * * * * * * * * *

On the question of whether I prefer to read the script before committing to a film, the best thing is **not to read** a script and to judge a film only by seeing the images and listening to the sounds, in order to edit, not with the ideas but with the filmed material.

Sometimes when I am asked for I read the script very fast never reading over to try to have the screening-feeling; incomprehensible things staying incomprehensible.

My best editing machine was the Moritone, something like a Moviola but a little bigger, on which I edited standing up, thus improving the physical pleasure of editing. Flat-bed machines give less pleasure.

What is very difficult in actual editing rooms – not conceived by editors – is the totally stupid place of windows (even on the ceiling! I often have to bring curtains from home) and the horrible noise of air-conditioning (as in movie theatres nowadays it is quite impossible to listen to *tenu* (weak) sound or to really see a night scene because of the exit or toilet lights).

I always need a big board on which I can change the place of the sequences, written in several different coded colours, depending on the kind of narration: a colour by character, place or period or any essential point of view regarding the nature of the particular movie. And like a real cowboy, I can't have a door at my back in the editing room.

I try to be very near to what I think the film must be when I am editing, as if the mix would be the day after, except for **very enormous errors**: much too long or too short shots, bad takes, holes in the *narration* (storytelling), objectionable repetitions, which I think are necessary to the deep thinking about the film. Sometimes the question asked by the film is so huge that you have (I have) to make the proof by the contrary, and it can happen that one or several of these mistakes leads to an idea which fits the film. Or that this attempt to be like the opposite of the film, it leads to express by opposition that the direction of the rest of the film is confirmed by the obvious contradiction of this solution.

I can spend, like everybody I guess, between one second and one hour on one cut, but I'm very confident on instinct; a first instinctive *raccord* (link) tells something precious.

The interaction between image and sound is essential in cinema. The sound must lead half of the film; it must be the guide alternatively with image. It is very interesting to check how the image can be forced to get (synchronised or de-synchronised on purpose) into a sound cut, even if the image cut is hard, brutal and the sound cut imperceptible. It can be an instinctive desire which leads you to cut the sound first, or it can be a very cold thinking like: 'lets try this kind of thing now'. In fact, I am sure the film itself forces you to think for and with it. You are not the one who decides, and if you let yourself go in this *esclavage* (slavery) it is pure *délice* (delight) to be half-master, half-slave of the film.

The new technology can be very efficient to try immediately sound ideas, but I keep a certain nostalgia for sound on one track, because it forced you to try and find the good cut. The good idea of cutting in regard to what this cut should **mean** and **bring as emotion**.

* * * * * * * * * * * * *

To begin with, I must say I don't much like music in movies. It is too often used as a means of underlining, or is pleonastic or heavy or *complaisant* (indulgent).

But we sometimes have to dare to make this fault. For instance, when music is obviously something completely different than the scene, in complete *décalage* (separation), but I must say I nearly always have this feeling of *décalage* when there is music, even when it seems to be in the same mood as the scene. Music always says:

'I'm here!'

The right *adéquation* ('accord') is hard to find. I have a few good souvenirs of adequate music. One is on Pialat's '*Under Satan's Sun*'.[29] The reason I think is because he had lived with the idea of putting Dutilleux's[30] music on the images of his film before having shot them, and that the shooting was carried by this strong thinking.

Another good souvenir is the opposite *démarche* (process). It was after many tries (Wagner, Strauss, two composers who wrote or improvised something after having seen the cut of '*Passe-montagne*') and by an enormous work of cutting in the music itself and repeating the notes he wanted to hear more and more among other things we made a *boucle* (loop) several times repeated, that Stévenin was able to use the music written for another movie ('*Barrocco*'[31]), and forced the accord between this music and his image by two very difficult hours of mixing sound in the auditorium.

This is the total opposite of the experience with Pialat. The first time I placed '*a la volée*', Dutilleux's music on the sequence where Depardieu gets lost in the countryside, Maurice told me to make a synch-mark very fast on the sound with a white pencil and never touch it again; it was good and he didn't want to risk losing it.

Very often I will choose the music against the sense of the director. I think the music brings more sense than the sense itself, and I was fighting, I remember, a lot of times with directors. Although never with Stévenin for instance whose films are pure music, for him the base, everything comes after, if it can, because it doesn't always fit with the pace. This is the difficult work with Stévenin, learning what not to do: not to listen only to the sense; not to listen only to the horrible logic; not to listen only to the story as it was written, because the physical shooting has changed all that – in time and space – in that I mean time and space have to be reconsidered within a (the) frame.

It is difficult to analyse the relationship between rhythm and meaning. Take for instance the idea of suppressing dialogue. Very often when you cut out dialogue and put a look which is after or before you have the 'music' which is not entirely explanative but which is *comme un piste*, as a track, as a direction in which you can ask the spectator to go. Something like an aspiration or inspiration of something; the feeling rather than the explanation. I think here the 'music' stands, and here, maybe, the more profound sense stands. The sense unexplained.

With the great directors this comes very simply. With Truffaut for instance, he did it himself. Just cut out the last phrase and put a *plan muet* (mute shot), just a face. With Pialat too, a long held look is easy between the sentences, but with others I have to struggle, I have to be a traitor, not to say its cut but just let them see it in a screening.

* * * * * * * * * * * * *

With the new technology I try to keep things the way they were with film. I try to limit the number of versions of scenes and resist the fact that the Lightworks[32] can keep as many as I want. I try to keep these things on a human scale. The machine is not the editor, as producers tend to believe and I have to decide how I want to be organised and not let the machine usurp my control.

First of all – headache – the computer is obliging you to think with its methods, which is a coded method, not a physical method, which obliges us to transfer our thinking into another form. It's very painful for me to be obliged to use a code that I didn't invent, which I find very stupid, very badly named. There is a very beautiful sentence by a famous French author which is 'Naming things badly adds to the unhappiness (misfortune) of the world', because it doesn't fit with the emotions.

I am very impulsive and I think I wouldn't dare do foolish, insane or even stupid things if I was more wise, more careful. This can serve the picture by pushing the search for solutions very far. Also I can't bear being beaten by a failure and up to the last day of editing I will try and try again to look for solutions, going back to the dailies, and trying to invent another point of view to overturn the problem which made us fail.

Definitely, variety is the gas for my engine. Documentaries to enrich the capacity of *fictioning* reality; fiction to enrich the capacity to *documentarise* fiction; short films to breathe and meet new blood. TV things to know what not to do.

* * * * * * * * * * * * *

The following extracts are from an interview with Yann Dedet in 'Cahiers du Cinéma' No. 576, February 2003, part of a tribute to Maurice Pialat. Yann's comments add weight to his analysis of the special qualities that he admired in the work of Pialat.

The common link between all the great directors that I have known is the total freedom which they allow the people that work with them, actors as well as technicians. With Pialat, this is particularly true. I already had a tendency to build a sequence around a central point, on a basic fact and this was developed even more with him. What first appears is not necessarily how the sequence will start nor how it will finish. It is this that frees you from the emphasis and the specifics of the film, which differentiates between pure narrative and emotional narrative.

The thing about Pialat is that he didn't hesitate to throw away scenes essential to the narrative, if they were not good enough. Whatever he was not satisfied with would be thrown out. In all the

Maurice Pialat (on right) when shooting 'Van Gogh' (Courtesy of Artificial Eye)

films that I edited, I think there is only one single scene which he kept in – forced and constrained by the narrative – because what followed would have been incomprehensible without it. It was the scene in the parlour between Marceau and his lover in '*Police*'.[33] He did it voluntarily but he didn't like doing it. When the film was finished, he said 'Next time, I'm going to take on a real director, or I'm going to learn how to direct properly. I'm fed up with films full of holes!'

He would take a shot again and again, and very long shots. For the five minutes of the lunch in '*Van Gogh*', there are six hours of rushes. That makes for a very long editing process. For two months we had a special room reserved for editing this sequence of the lunch.

There were some sequences which we edited entirely together, like the cabaret in '*Van Gogh*' some when he was never there at all, some sequences where we spent hours together talking about other things. Once, we had stopped on an image in '*Van Gogh*'. There was a sort of bizarre shadow, very strange, which turned out to be that of the clapper-boy, who was standing in the field. He (Pialat) stopped at that image and said to me: 'If all film images were like that, you could keep account of what you would have done.' I believe that he talked for an hour and a half. It was very enlightening, it summed up everything that he does: the intervention of chance, the lack of pure logic of light, a mysterious beauty . . . . And then he left, because he was tired of talking for an hour and a half, because he realised that that was enough. He knew very well what he had done: he had filled you full of the mindset of Pialat. He was no longer actually there but I continued to work with him. He's the kind that can give you an injection of himself by telephone.

We played lots of games over the question of the order of scenes. We were even going a little far with '*Loulou*'[34] as we had finished by making him die. A knife cut at the end and then finished. The scene order in '*Van Gogh*' was also very varied. I had even found a way of making the film in flashback. The end was at the beginning, the woman saying: 'This was my friend . . .' and then, with the opening of the mists we put on the beginning of one of the 'Nuits d'été' by Berlioz: 'Open your closed eyelids . . . .' We had all of the song and then the train. Maurice said: 'It's out of the question that we keep it this way but today we can begin the edit'. He used this as a jumping-off point. It was very beautiful in itself, but it wasn't his way to make films in flashback; on the other hand, it laid open the belief that you could have this in a film. You told yourself: 'The film is do-able.'

(There was an) enormous amount of work on sound editing, particularly on '*Van Gogh*', changes in phrases, small sounds taken from other takes. He was not one of those who makes the image and then the sound. He refused dubbing as much as possible. There are some scenes that are incredibly empty of sound, almost unrealistic. He made a complete mockery of the rational approach of the technicians, and of their way of doing things. If one of them said to him: 'At that time of day, you can't have so few cars', he would look at the image, listen to the actors talking and say: 'What, isn't there enough ambience there?'

Recorded on 17 January 2003 in Paris by Patrice Blouin.
Translation: Elizabeth Hardy.

Notes

1. **Antonin Artaud (1896–1948)** – Playwright, actor, director and theorist. One of the surrealists in the 1920s his most famous text is '*Le théatre*

et son double' 1938 (The Theatre and its Double). Created what has been termed 'The Theatre of Cruelty'. Immensely influential on post-war theatre.

2. **George Stevens** – First worked with Hal Roach on Laurel and Hardy films. Apart from '*Shane*' (1953) he also directed '*A Place in the Sun*' (1951) and '*Giant*' (1956). His earlier work is more interesting, including two Katherine Hepburn films, '*Alice Adams*' (1935) and '*Woman of the Year*' (1942).
3. *Modern Times* – Charles Chaplin, 1936.
4. *The Great Dictator* – Charles Chaplin, 1942.
5. **Paillard-Bolex eight millimetres** – Before portable video, eight milli-metres was the gauge for home or amateur movies and the Bolex was the Rolls-Royce of this medium.
6. *La Prison (The Devil's Wanton)* – Ingmar Bergman (1949). Original title '*Fangelse*' and a very early work.
7. *Eight-and-a-half* – Federico Fellini (1963) was the examination of his own fears and anxieties as a director, played by Marcello Mastroainni, struggles with a film he seems unable to bring to fruition.
8. *Il Gattopardo (The Leopard)* – Luchino Visconti (1963), epic film from the novel of the same name starring Burt Lancaster as an Italian aristo-crat who is powerless to stop his world disappearing as Garibaldi strives to unite 19th century Italy. Visconti at his operatic best.
9. Yann's taste in music and literature is interestingly varied. The composers are mostly well known though the writers less so.
10. **Moritone** – This editing machine was a European version of the Hollywood Moviola, which was originally put together from projector parts, with an intermittent and very noisy movement. I learned to cut on the Moviola.
11. **Vaugirard** – School of photography which gets its name from the part of Paris where it was situated.
12. *Erostrate* – It is a story by the existentialist philosopher and writer Jean-Paul Sartre, based on the myth of Herostratus.
13. *Playtime* – Jacques Tati (1967). His third great film after '*Jour de fête*' (1949) and '*Monsieur Hulot's Holiday*' (1953).
14. **Maurice Pialat** – Director, with whom Yann Dedet worked five times and whose work he particularly admires. His elliptical style tends to occlude his staunchly humanist philosophy.
15. **Claudine Bouché** – Editor for early films of the 'New Wave' and still cutting.
16. *La Mariée était en noir (The Bride Wore Black)* – François Truffaut (1967), which reunited the director with Jeanne Moreau.
17. **Agnès Guillemot** – See previous interview.
18. **Cut on action/matching two-shots** – Part of the essential style of 'con-tinuity editing' where the cut is made essentially to achieve smooth tran-sitions, rather than for other aesthetic purposes or to serve the narrative or emotional line of the film.

19. ***Sweet Movie*** – Dusan Makavejev (1974). A Yugoslav director who figures in the careers of three of the editors in this book: see also Tony Lawson and Sylvia Ingemarsson.
20. **Jean-François Stévenin** – Has made a varied career in French cinema from assistant directing to acting – notably the school teacher in Truffaut's '*L'argent du poche*' and more recently as a director of his own very particular films which at their best treat of everything but narrative thus evoking a world which hardly acknowledges the camera since it is so self-contained and sufficient to itself. I totally concur with Yann's admiration for this other kind of movie.
21. **Patrick Grandperret** – Yann cut his '*Mona et Moi*' in 1989 in which he acted alongside Jean-François Stévenin.
22. **Philippe Garell** – Yann cut '*J'entends plus la guitare*' in 1991 and '*La Naissance de l'amour*' in 1993 for him.
23. **Cédric Kahn** – Yann has cut four times for him notably '*L'Ennui*' in 1998, '*Roberto Succo*' in 2001 and most recently '*Feux rouges*' in 2004.
24. **Manuel Poirier** – Yann has been involved in three of his films, notably '*Western*' in 1997.
25. **Claire Denis** – Yann cut '*Nenette et Boni*' for her in 1996. A very interesting director from her first film, '*Chocolat*', 1988 to more recent work like '*Beau travail*' 1999.
26. **André Bazin (1918–58)** – The father of the French New Wave through his writing (notably in *Cahiers du cinéma*) and thought which fed the passion of a whole generation of aspiring filmmakers and thus (with Henri Langlois and the Paris Cinémathèque) the begetter of modern cinema.
27. ***Van Gogh*** – Maurice Pialat's wonderful film which almost alone amongst biographies of artists, manages to evoke the true spirit of its subject, 1991.
28. ***Passe-montagne*** – Jean-François Stévenin. Yann also edited '*Double Messieurs*' 1986, for Stévenin (1978).
29. ***Under Satan's Sun (Sous le soleil du Satan)*** – Maurice Pialat, 1987, for which he won the Palme d'or at Cannes, which he promptly handed to his star Gerard Depardieu. The latter returned it to Pialat's ten-year-old son at a screening in Cannes to commemorate the directors death.
30. **Henri Dutilleux** – Composer born in 1916, originally inspired by Debussy and Ravel, but developed his own style. Became professor at Paris Conservatoire in 1970.
31. ***Barrocco*** – Directed by André Téchiné, 1976.
32. **Lightworks** – Name of a digital editing machine which until a few years ago was the machine of choice of many famous editors.
33. ***Police*** – Maurice Pialat, 1985.
34. ***Loulou*** – Maurice Pialat, 1980.

4 François Truffaut on Editing

(From Truffaut by Truffaut, Courtesy Harry N Abrams New York, 1987)

It is Truffaut's discovery of the need to 'mistreat' the film in the cutting room that intrigues me. It is one thing to put the rushes together efficiently. It is quite another to transform the rhythm and form. He was always afraid of boring the audience and perhaps was too severe on some of his films as Yann Dedet suggests, but the willingness to be disrespectful of your own film is a healthy attitude in the edit suite.

I began to get really interested in editing with '*Shoot the Piano Player*',[1] because it was a pretty special film in which there was a great deal of improvisation. At the end of the shooting, after the first rough cut, it gave the impression of being unusable, because of a too jerky story, especially compared with that of '*The 400 Blows*',[2] which was simple and in a straight line. I spent several months on the editing of '*Shoot the Piano Player*', I came to think of it as passionately interesting work, and for the first time I began to mistreat the film, to knock it about. In that work there was also influence from '*Breathless*',[3] finished a few months earlier, and whose editing had been quite revolutionary, really free.

In '*Jules et Jim*'[4] editing likewise plays an important part because there were many improvised scenes that could be placed here or there; I had thought up many short skits for the chalet scenes, and with the script girl we classified them as scenes of happiness, scenes of unhappiness. The editing of '*Jules et Jim*' consisted in finding a kind of equilibrium; will this bit of film go better after a scene of happiness or after a scene of unhappiness? That was another work, special, exhilarating.[5]

* * * * * * * * * * * * *

I get to understand certain things only at the editing table: in '*Day for Night*'[6] e.g., important decisions were made rather late. So when you see Jean-Pierre Léaud firing several shots one after the other at Jean-Pierre Aumont, that came out of the montage because normally there was only one take but here, because we shot the scene six times, I realised we needed this sort of ballet at the end and I mounted all the gunshots one after the other.

Editing is a very creative period because, as a rule, you can't afford to blunder. A film can get ruined in the editing, but generally you do it a lot of good. One of the montages I regret is that of '*Two English Girls*'[7] because I edited it as if the film had turned out rather well. I did an optimistic montage that I regretted later, because the film

François Truffaut and Jacqueline Bisset during the shooting of '*La Nuit américaine*' ('*Day for Night*') (Courtesy of Les Films du Carrosse)

was too long. And I likewise regretted not having been as strict and severe as in other montages: it should have had two more months' work tightening etc.[8]

Notes

1. *Shoot the Piano Player – (Tirez sur le pianiste)* – Truffaut, 1960.
2. *The 400 Blows (Les Quatre cents coups)* – Truffaut, 1959.
3. *Breathless (À Bout de souffle)* – Jean-Luc Godard, 1959.
4. *Jules et Jim* – Truffaut, 1961.
5. Interview by Pierre Billard, Cinéma 64 no. 87.
6. *Day for Night (La Nuit américaine)* – Truffaut, 1973.
7. *Two English Girls (Les Deux Anglaises et le Continent)* – Truffaut, 1971.
8. Interview in Jeune Cinéma, no. 77, March 74.

5   Sabine Mamou

I talked with Sabine in her Paris apartment, the morning after a preview of 'Ma Vrai vie à Rouen', the delightful film which was the third she edited for Olivier Ducastel and Jacques Martineau, who both joined us for lunch. Sabine's career began when she knocked on the door of the cutting room of Abel Gance and that was the first of many wonderful experiences. Sabine's death at the end of last year made me realise how privileged I felt to have met her. I hope this interview will stand as witness to her commitment and passion.

I was born in Tunisia in 1948 and my mother died at my birth. My father had a garage, which pleased me very much because I could share something with Jacques Demy: we both had a father who owned a garage. Movies and reading were the two things I liked most. I have to remind you that TV did not exist at that time. I remember a movie I saw which was called something like '*Geneviève de Brabant*',[1] and it was the story of a catholic saint who got burnt. My step-sister was Geneviève, and it was something wonderful to imagine that she could be burned too. I must have been very young – three or four – because it's one of my first memories: being at the movies and thinking it was true.

Going to the movies was a joy, a reward, a passion; movies would magnify life, with actors being bigger than us. There was Asmahane, Farid al Atrache's[2] sister, even more beautiful than '*Gilda*',[3] there were Burt Lancaster and Kirk Douglas, and Jerry Lewis, who have remained my favourites. There were Victor Mature, the Indian musicals, and a very strange film called '*Goha le simple*' by Jacques Baratier,[4] the first film where they spoke Tunisian, starring Omar Sharrif. Goha, called Ch'rah in the Maghreb and Eddin Hodja in Persia, is a character loved both by Jews and Arabs when they used to laugh together. Jacques Baratier filmed Goha joining his lover at night, crossing a street from a village and entering the street of another village. In the eyes of a little girl so curious about love, it was a secret unveiled.

Life passed by, I wanted to be a movie star, have my name and my image big on the walls. It happened once, as I have been the star of Agnès Varda's '*Documenteur*'.[5] First in Los Angeles (LA), then in Paris, and I was ashamed when I warned my father that I was naked on the poster. I was then living in LA, full time in love and didn't come to Paris.

As a teenager I discovered the Italian neo-realists, and the 'angry young men' whom I loved so much. A movie newspaper printed an article I wrote on '*The Loneliness of the Long Distance Runner*'[6] when I was fifteen, I became a woman with '*Family Life*',[7] '*I pugni in tasca*',[8] Godard, Demy, Varda, Satiajit Ray, Woody Allen, Nanni Moretti, Chantal Akerman.[9] I was a very lonely person, and their works were the only ones speaking to me.

Going to movies is still a feast. Living in Paris is lucky. Although a lot of cinemas have disappeared I guess it has remained the capital of

Sabine Mamou in Agnès Varda's '*Documenteur*' (Courtesy of Sabine Mamou and Agnès Varda)

movies. I remember the Styx where we used to see horror movies seated in a coffin; the Luxuor where we'd see Indian films like '*Mandala Fille des Indes*'[10] or '*Mother India*';[11] the Delta which was showing kung-fu films and the Japanese '*Baby cart*'.

There are directors, and the list would be long, that fill me with admiration. I'd adore to be Soderberg's[12] cutter, to participate in the discovery of the sense created by two shots. Being able to see how a film is done, in terms of movement of camera, cuts, voice on or off, multiplies my pleasure and my admiration in looking at films. It's a pity not to be allowed anymore to stay in the cinema for the next performance. I remember having booked a whole afternoon for Alan Rudolph's '*Remember My Name*'.[13]

It is also important for me to go to movies when I am editing a film. When the film director with whom I am working is a friend, we go together with other friends. The first Kitano[14] I saw was with Olivier Ducastel and Jacques Martineau and we solved a problem we had in '*Jeanne et le Garçon Formidable*'[15] thanks to that film. Funnily enough, it again happened with another Kitano when we edited '*Drôle de Félix*'.[16]

Going to movies helps me stay alert. '*King of Marvin Gardens*',[17] '*Safe*',[18] Douglas Sirk,[19] Jean-Claude Guiguet's '*Les Passagers*',[20] Alain Guiraudie,[21] '*Bloody Sunday*',[22] any Kaurismaaki,[23] they all wake me up, ask me to pay attention.

* * * * * * * * * * * * *

Now back to chronology. I passed my baccalaureate when I was sixteen and a half, entered university, graduated one year and decided not to carry on. Though I had developed other passions than going to movies, as literature theatre and concerts, I wanted to work in the movies and I had to earn my living as I had left home and had no place of my own. The sister of my parents' best friends was a famous editor for trailers and that's how I started. I entered a cutting room and really loved it: the smell, the noise of the 35mm perforations on the Moviola, the white gloves, the taste of the film. You remember, Roger, the feeling of the film in your mouth, there was the shiny side and the matt side, and the matt side is the one that sticks to the lips. In winter, if you had dry lips, it would take off a little of your skin. It was enough to forget to check once and be called to the screening room because all the emulsion was scratched on 'la tete de lecture' (playback head), and shame on you!

When I look back on those times we would work ten hours a day, six days a week. As an apprentice I was not being paid as I was supposed to be learning. I earned money working in dubbing theatres. I remember a long summer when I subtitled 'zarzuelas', Spanish musicals. I also worked in laboratories which did opticals.

* * * * * * * * * * * * *

In one of these laboratories Abel Gance was working on a new version of '*Napoléon*',[24] I was a fan of Abel Gance and so I knocked on his door and told him. 'Admiration bien placée' he answered (admiration well placed), and he accepted me in his cutting room. I worked there for six months, in great admiration. I loved him and would imitate him in every gesture, trims around my neck sweeping the floor and smoking two packs of Gauloises a day. You may shudder as we were working on inflammable film that could ignite instantly.

When Gance shot '*Napoléon*' in 1926, sound in movies had not yet been invented, but he insisted that the actors should say their lines. So when sound was invented he could dub the film. This is part of his genius. So he re-cut the film and dubbed it. Now, in 1970, he wanted some of the mute sequences that had not been inserted in the 'version parlante' to be part of the new version. For example the little boy on the battlefield beating his drum and when he is killed the sound of hail pouring on the drums replacing him. He also inserted some of Napoleon's speech and I was able to see Albert Dieudonné in the theatre, dubbing himself over forty years after the shooting.

There was no money for me but it seemed fair as there was no money at all: Abel Gance had to stop till a few years later Claude Lelouch[25] came by and helped him out. By that time, I was engaged on, God knows what and couldn't work on the last version of '*Napoléon*'.

* * * * * * * * * * * * *

Then, one day, I was hired as an apprentice on a 35mm fiction film. Spares and trims and trims and spares; after three of those six months apprenticeships, you'd earn a card from the National Centre of Cinema that said that you were an assistant. By that time, I was fed up with the editor working behind a black curtain and the films I was working on (films I would never go and see in the cinema). So I quit editing for good and started travelling in a small truck with my lover, his basset, my Newfoundland dog and a library. Gone my dream of working with Agnès Varda, Mai Zetterling and Jean Schmidt. It was even more than a dream, it was what I had sworn to myself. The first two names were the only female film directors – apart from Paula Delsol[26] – of those times and Jean Schmidt[27] was a director of documentaries I admired.

I travelled for almost a year, reading Beckett, Joyce, Proust, Bashevis Singer, Flaubert, Manes Sperber, Cervantes, Forster, Koestler, Tanizaki, Nemirovskis.[28] Time didn't count. The future didn't count.

I came back on the day a friend was looking for me to edit a short film by Mai Zetterling, who was looking for an editor who spoke English. We met, I was an admirer, having seen the films she had performed in, when she was Bergman's actor,[29] and the film she had directed. I guess my enthusiasm made up for my total lack of experience, she trusted me and I edited her film '*La Dame Aux Oiseaux*'.[30]

Then another friend offered to introduce me to Agnès Varda, to finish '*One Sings, the Other Doesn't*'.[31] Imagine, it was on the phone that she told me she'd meet me in the cutting room on Monday, 10:00 a.m. I asked her, 'Don't you want to see me before?' She replied that she was going away for the weekend and that there was no problem. I spent more than ten years working with her. Till now, I have problems with directors who cast editors. I have problems with 'frileux' which translates into English as 'sensitive to the cold' and 'unadventurous'. In French it is one word. The problem with 'frileux' is that you tend to be 'frileux' as well. All I know, I have learned from her and the other film directors I have worked with.

Just like Claude Accursi[32] in 1973 – I was twenty-four years then – who chose me to edit his 35mm film. He asked me: 'Tell me, mademoiselle, why you want so much to edit my film?' I answered: 'Sir, because you took the greatest actor in the world, Roger Blin'.

[Roger Blin was above all the director of Beckett and Genet, and an incredible theatre actor. Imagine I didn't even know his film was about Dadaism! – Sabine]

So when Claude Accursi told me that, I rejoiced and when he told me the difficulties he had finding the poem, 'Dada au coeur' I said 'Its simple, it's in the book published by Seghers'.[33]

Comforted by the fact that I had worked with those two, I wrote to Jean Schmidt, it was good timing – he had just finished shooting '*Comme les Anges Déchus de la Planète Saint-Michel*',[34] and he hired me as the editor. So now that I look backwards I see a twenty-nine-year-old woman having coffee with Jean Schmidt who had responded to her love letter. My knowledge of his work and my admiration for it – documentaries were not so fashionable then – made him decide to choose me. It was my first work on documentaries and I realised we had to invent the structure, how you start, how you associate, how you finished the film. Nothing was taken for granted.

* * * * * * * * * * * * *

In 1980, Agnès Varda phoned me from LA and asked me to come and assist her on the preparation and the shooting of '*Murs Murs*'[35] and then edit it. My love for her is inextinguishable. Does such a word exist? Though I was overwhelmed with joy, I still made one phone call as I had heard that a man had recorded hundreds of hours with survivors of the Shoah. I didn't know then that it was Claude Lanzmann, author of '*Why Israel?*'[36] the first day of the screening of which was the first day of the Iom Kippour War. I phoned the cutting room and learned that Claude Lanzmann already had two editors, so I flew to LA and Agnès.

'*Murs Murs*' took us nine months, from preparation to the end of the mix. We finished at Christmas. For Christmas I offered Agnès a copy-book where I had written down all her day-dreams about a film being the shadow of '*Murs Murs*'. She later on said in 'France Culture' that it was what made her decide to shoot the film, which was called '*Documenteur*'. She said to me 'I saw you play with my son Matthieu yesterday and thought you could act in the film'. I was very aware of the risk she was taking as I was not an actress, but I trusted her. She wanted to do a home movie: the characters of the film were her son, and friends of hers or mine. We would shoot and edit and shoot. What I lived through this film was being very close to the process of creating. Seeing Agnès shooting a feature film without any scenario.

The editing machine, a 16mm Atlas, was at her place. I was living very close; my lover was an actor in the film and the assistant of the Director of Photography (DP). The DP was one of my best friends, Nurith Aviv.[37] Those times were among the happiest in my life; filled with wit and joy, laughter, energy, tenderness and passion.

* * * * * * * * * * * * *

Jacques Demy was something else – Jacques Demy was the impossible dream – he was very English – to me what is English. Like he would say 'Oh, I am late' and not move faster and say goodbye and be very polite. I remember him when there was a big discussion in LA, everyone was talking and he was translating very, very peacefully and very slowly to someone who couldn't get the whole thing and he was translating everything. This for me was incredible. I was always hanging around at Agnès production and she was looking for an assistant speaking English for 'Lady Oscar' by Jacques Demy.[38] So I asked Jacques if I could be the assistant and he said: 'Sabine you can't because now you are a young editor and you can't now just go down and be an assistant'. I said: 'Oh but Jacques I'd rather be an assistant with you than an editor with anyone else'. So he started smiling – he was a little perverse really, and I got the job – the editor was Paul Davies,[39] because he wanted an English person to edit the film. I liked very much the sound editor, Alan Bell.[40]

I was living in LA and I was starting to edit some small documentaries, some small shorts out of the Union. In 1982 I was thirty-four years old, Agnès Varda was back in Paris and I was still living in LA and full time in love. Jacques Demy called me and asked me if I would edit his film, 'Une Chambre en Ville'.[41] He had always been one of my favourite film directors. So I said 'Yes, right away'. He said 'Is there nothing to restrain you?' He amused me as he was offering me the castle and at the same time he was giving me the price to pay: a separation from my love.

Jacques Demy wanted me to begin before the shooting. We had to figure out the preparation for playback. I remember being jet-lagged and understanding nothing. So I said 'I have never edited a musical in my life and I am lost'. You could feel all the stress, which filled the mixing room, flying away, as in fact it was what everyone was thinking.

'*Une Chambre en Ville*' was pure happiness – what can I say. For example I remember that '*Lady Oscar*' was in the era of John Travolta. It was the time of the Palace, a nightclub, which was a kind of paradise on earth. Fortunately it would only start opening on Thursday – so from Thursday – we were three girls in the cutting room – we would arrive at work at 10:00 a.m. already dressed for the Palace. It was disco time, all glitter, and at 7:00 p.m. we would leave Jacques Demy and his editor, and we could see in the eyes of Jacques Demy that he would have just loved to come with us. He would say, 'Thursday Night Fever!' But we would also go out with him a lot at night. It was very nice to spend the whole day with people and then call your lovers and all go out together.

* * * * * * * * * * * *

Just after that, a friend of mine named Claude Weisz, with whom I was a political militant, arranged a meeting for me with Yilmaz Guney,[42] who was looking for an editor. Instead of asking Costa-Gavras,[43] whom he knew very well, he asked this old friend from old times when he was not yet a prize winner at Cannes. Yilmaz Guney was hiding – the Turkish police were looking for him. So it was like during the occupation moving from one appointment to another one – I entered the room and I saw a very beautiful man looking at me. It was Yilmaz Guney. I went to the kitchen with him and his translator, and we started talking and the translator started laughing. Yilmaz Guney asked the translator why he was laughing and the translator said because we were supposed to get acquainted and he saw that Yilmaz Guney and I were talking as if we had known each other for a long time.

'*Le Mur*'[44] was extraordinary – to work with someone with whom you have no common language. What a pity that sometimes nowadays, like in a fairy tale, you have to show 'white hands' to prove I don't know what. You had to prove nothing before. People are free or not – you feel you're accepted and then it's extraordinary – you feel you could die for them! You trust them, you admire them and then you want to go beyond yourself.

I met a girl – a very strange girl in LA. She asked me if I could see her short film. The film was very good. I said why is this shot upside down? She said because Jim Morrison says 'Head upside down'.[45]

I told her: 'The film is perfect, I have nothing to tell you, but you have twisted the leader for the sound and it's difficult to adjust because the sound is cut diagonally. So I am going home, phone me and I'll come and fetch you, you'll sleep at home or I'll drive you downtown'. I never heard from her again that night.

When for '*Une Chambre en Ville*' I needed an apprentice, I remembered that girl. I was anxious, never having edited a musical in my life. I was phoning her everyday telling her I needed an apprentice who had already worked on a musical, and then I made up my mind and asked her to be my apprentice. This girl is Patricia Mazuy.[46] After being my apprentice on '*Une Chambre en Ville*' she was my assistant on '*Le Mur*'. She was very original. Later she directed '*Peau de Vaches*',[47] which was a very good film with Jean-François Stévenin.[48]

We edited '*Le Mur*' in Pont Sainte Maxence which is about one hour drive from Paris, where Yilmaz Guney turned a convent into a prison. I have loved Yilmaz Guney immediately: he was an oriental prince to me. He had problems with the French crew. I loved the dinners, with the Turkish crew, the workers, the painters, all the kids and the women. We had Greek food. I just loved it. I was with Patricia while the crew would eat outside.

At one point there was a strike of the French crew. They couldn't cope with waiting for Yilmaz Guney to start shooting. They couldn't cope either with his attitude to the kids. I remember him slapping a boy because he was late for the shooting. So the boy cried and said he went to the village because it was his birthday. Yilmaz Guney did not reply, but that night there was a super birthday party for the boy. I didn't go on strike with the French crew. I remember they were not happy with the script in Turkish, on which Yilamz Guney was still working.

We finished the editing in Paris. We immediately fired the translator who was too slow and what he'd say would make no sense. We went on working, Yilmaz Guney not speaking French and I not speaking Turkish, but we understood each other.

Patricia was an incredible first assistant on '*Le Mur*'. I remember at a point there was no reel one. I said to her: 'How come there is no reel one? So just call the reel two reel one'. So she said: 'No, reel two is reel two'. 'Well where's reel one?' 'Reel one is not yet made – it's made of all the shots that are in reel three, four, five, six –' She was incredible: I had total confidence, but for weeks we had no reel one[1]!

Somehow I just communicated with Yilmaz Guney. He had a court around him – men around him – a lot of men. You would hear them speaking Turkish and then pronounce Marx or Engels or Lenin and then go back to Turkish. I didn't know which International they were preparing. Every night Yilmaz Guney would give dinner – every night we would go to a restaurant. I was invited with whoever I wanted and could bring as many friends as I wanted. He was very gentle and very generous.

Maybe I'm talking about love instead of talking about editing, I hope it's okay with you. After that film he got sick, and I remember he had learnt French a little. He told me he would bring me to Istanbul at the crossing of the three seas after the Revolution. We would be there and drink and eat grilled fish. I still have this dream of something I will never do.

There were thousands of people at the burial of Yilmaz Guney[49] – the burial of Victor Hugo must probably have been the same. They had come by bus – Turks from Germany as well as from Turkey itself. A lot, a lot, a lot, of people. Sometimes I still meet one of the Turkish crew. I still have a few friends. I made very, very nice friends there.

Once a crew from TV came to film him in the editing room. Yilmaz Guney asked me: 'What do I do?' I replied: 'As usual, you press my shoulder when you want the shot to finish.'

For his birthday we decided that we were all going to learn a piece of the script of '*Le Mur*'. We knew it was insult. All the editing crew dressed in white and red, the colours of Turkey, and we played the part. He was crying with laughter. When we got the answer print with subtitles, we realised that what we had said was even worse than we had thought. Things like: 'I fuck the garage of your mother for generations'!

* * * * * * * * * * * * *

I was from time to time asking about Claude Lanzmann's film '*Shoah*'[50] until one day Catherine Zins,[51] a friend of mine, told me that she was offered to edit part of the sound of his film and couldn't do it as she was directing her own first film '*Matura 31*'.[52] So I went to Claude Lanzmann's cutting room and was hired right away. This incredible and daring trust that creators give you allows you to surpass yourself. '*Shoah*' was the film I was expecting. It signified the end of my nightmares.

RC: Tell me why you hated Resnais' film '*Night and Fog*'.[53]

SM: '*Night and Fog*' is obscene. I don't think you should be allowed to show a corpse unless you get the permission of the corpse. No one wants to be shown dead or even in such a state of degradation. All the more because we found out afterwards that Alain Resnais accepted the cutting of photos in two to hide the participation of the French police. The legend of the French only being resistant had to be created. France had to sit around the table of victims!

I felt offended and humiliated by the silence that was made around the Shoah. I did all my classes for fifteen years and the Shoah was never taught. I remember saying once that Second World War had been a war against the Jews and being thrown out of the class for saying such absurdities.

'*Shoah*' for me is a masterpiece of structure and of form. Claude Lanzmann said something which I like very much: 'Without form you don't inform'. Form creates sense, it imposes a way of seeing.

While I was editing the sound for '*Shoah*', TV showed '*Documenteur*', where I play a love scene and a nude scene. Lanzmann came in the cutting room and said, 'So you are an editor too'. This man who has made the masterpiece of the movies doesn't freak out to see that an actress is cutting the sound of his film. Such confidence! Of course he doubts. He's the man who works with doubts, but doubting has nothing to do with trust.

When Claude Lanzmann asked me to edit '*Tsahal*',[54] you can imagine what a gift it was. Even if sometimes afterwards I would quote Thérèse d'Avila: 'Que de larmes versees pour des voeux escauces' ('how many tears you shed for wishes that are granted'), because the editing lasted three years and the film is five hours long! He was shooting in Israel – I was getting the rushes in Paris. I had to tell him things and at one point he said: 'Why are you telling me that?' I said: 'I just thought this would be really great to start with'. He said: 'Oh it's strange I thought the same'. With Lanzmann, who is probably the man I admire the most, I am not afraid to sound silly. This is his freedom.

After '*Tsahal*' we edited '*The Living from the Dead*'.[55] There was something written in Czech on a wall and he said he wanted the translation. I immediately phoned a Czech friend. When he returned my call I was busy, so I asked my daughter, Rachel, who was seven to write the French translation down. I brought it to Claude – with no time to check it and realised there was at least one fault in each word! Claude read it and said, very gently: 'But, Sabine, how are you writing French?' I sometimes feel this is how love can last forever, with a man accepting you write like a seven-year-old kid.

Of course it was hard and of course it lasted a long time, but it's so interesting to edit a documentary with several characters. How and when does one appear? When are you going to find him again? Will you see him again? And when you are ready to treat a new theme, who will talk about it?

* * * * * * * * * * * * *

RC: When you talk about finding freedom from people, how does that relate to your development as an editor?

SM: I'm not afraid to make mistakes: I invent an association – I invent a structure – I invent a form – I am free even with sync – I hate sync! Its something I have worked on a lot with Agnès Varda. How a voice over can come in and be out and be in again. You cheat with the sync. You can invent a silence when there is none. This is absence of fear of making mistakes. They have to allow you that. When a director is petty or mean or when he is waiting for you to make a mistake, it's impossible to work. I have to work with directors with whom I'm not afraid to sound silly, to have no solution, to say I don't know.

RC: Is it harder in fiction film, because of the conventions?

SM: No, there are no real conventions in French films. In fiction the more I respect the director, the more I feel free to take a sequence and throw it in another place and see what sense comes out of this change of structure. The director changes your changes and at the end you don't even know who thought what. Claude Lanzmann said a very beautiful thing. When I decided to take a weeks holiday after three years the producer said 'Well, as long as the film can continue', and Claude Lanzmann replied: 'She can't edit without me and I can't edit without her'. I thought it was so beautiful to say that. It relates to what is born in the

49

unique relation between the film-maker and his editor. The miracle can happen from film to film.

* * * * * * * * * * * * *

Now I can talk about Olivier Ducastel and Jacques Martineau. Olivier Ducastel was a student at IDHEC (Institute des Hautes Etudes Cinematographiques); being a fan of Jacques Demy he asked me to be his teacher. He had directed a short musical, a very beautiful one called '*Le Gout de Plaire*'. He finished School and I chose him to be my assistant on '*Trois Places Pour le Vingt-Six*', by Jacques Demy in 1988. He was a wonderful assistant – I adored him. When we finished the film he asked me: 'Who is going to trust me like you did?' I replied: 'If there is someone for whom I don't worry it is you'. I decided that I would not keep him as an assistant. So I gave him all the jobs I wouldn't do. He became an editor very quickly and then a sound editor.

Then Olivier Ducastel met Jacques Martineau who had written a musical: '*Jeanne and the Perfect Guy*', he introduced me as the editor of Jacques Demy. I saw in Jacques eyes that I was like a goddess. Olivier asked me to edit the film and I accepted gladly.

They came in the cutting room on a Sunday. I didn't even know how to make the machine work. So Olivier Ducastel turned to Jacques Martineau and said: 'I told you she would have stage fright but you didn't believe me!' That was set! It was just like he had always known me, sick, physically sick on the first day. Whether Olivier had been my pupil or my assistant had not changed anything.

It's extraordinary to work with both of them – '*Ma Vrai vie à Rouen*' is already the third film. I cut with Olivier Ducastel then we turn to Jacques Martineau and Jacques is le 'garant', he guaranties.

* * * * * * * * * * * * *

RC: Then you worked with Catherine Corsini.

SM: Yes. I first edited '*La Nouvelle Eve*'.[56] Catherine Corsini is a very beautiful woman – a sort of savage cat in black leather and hair upside down – very beautiful. The first day she told me: 'I don't understand why we leave a shot to go to another one' I replied: 'You are right' – it came from my heart. She looked at me and asked: 'What makes you cut here and not there?' I said: 'I don't know – its something deep inside, which I cannot name'. It was then that I thought I will be able to work with this woman. It was laughter for three months with tears running down. The film was very good, very funny, great actress, Karin Viard,[57] first commercial success in my life. We had no idea it was going to be a success. A little film produced by Paulo Branco,[58] a daring man.

* * * * * * * * * * * * *

RC: So the fear when you start a film . . .

SM: It's just a fright that I have to overcome.

RC: And does it happen every time you start a film?

SM: Oh yes, and sick for a week.

I haven't read many books on cinema. The book which taught me a lot was Jerry Lewis's book.[59] First I adore him, always adored him. He says things like: 'When I am very bad tempered and I come to the stage I tell people, "Look, it has nothing to do with you, I am very bad tempered because the plumber fucked the toilet". Then every one on the stage is working peacefully and smiling'. This kind of thing he tells you is true because when you are bad-tempered your assistant and your apprentice start to wonder: 'What have I done?' You just have to say: 'It has nothing to do with you it's just this sequence – I don't know how to edit it', and you see how they keep on working calmly.

RC: When you moved from cutting on film to the Avid – do you have any feelings about that, and the effect it has on you as an editor?

SM: Working on film we would go to the screening room and discover the film on 35mm on the screen, and then we would cut on the machine. Now, in France you discover the film on a video monitor, so you don't recognise what you have seen on the big screen. The first thing I edited on Avid was the pilot for '*Jeanne and the Perfect Guy*'. I didn't edit the long shots, the master shots, because I couldn't see anything. We went to the screening and I said I was sorry. I went back to the cutting room and we edited the master shots. How can you choose which is the best master shot, when you discover it on your Avid screen? This is stupid. We have to have more money to be able to print the rushes and then you recognise it on Avid. We need more money – the rest is no problem.

There are no more apprentices and you have no chance to meet your assistant except if he or she overslept when digitising! It's a pity. I think that you don't learn editing, you practice it. An apprentice, an assistant learns by watching you deal with the most difficult thing in editing: the relation with the film director.

The only really excellent thing is the sound. Whereas you had to choose between cheese or desert (as they say in French restaurants), with Avid, or whatever, you can have both; words, music and even effects. Also you can raise or lower a sound or the entry of a sound. How many times did we have to redo a cut, just because the entry of the sound wouldn't match! And remember when we had to fill a piece of a sound shot. It would start by a phone call to the sound department! And now, copy, insert, it's done. Numerique (digital) was born last century, so what's new?

How much I loved to enter the film cutting room and smell fresh coffee, fresh smoke from English tobacco, the ink of the numbering machine and Guerlain. I had forbidden the use of tolluène[60] long before doctors did and changed it to some Eau de Cologne by Guerlain; it wipes false numbers just as good.

* * * * * * * * * * * * *

A donkey can edit. However long it will take, it will be good in the end, if the rushes are good. Maybe it will take him ten years but the donkey will manage. But how do you deal with the director, with his anguish? I'm not even talking about how you deal with yours, but how do you deal with theirs. How can you be in sympathy with him, not suffer too much from his anguish. Make silence so he can say what he thinks of what you did. Who knows if the cut is good – who knows? It's fashion, and it's not only the director. It's the producer. Even if the producer is right, how do you behave? You can listen but you don't start speaking with the producers saying: 'How right you are!' I've seen editors doing this. That's stupid. And now it's not only the producers, it's the distributor who come along. So you have to deal with all of that. To keep calm – this is the difficult part of editing – the rest is pure joy.

> **RC:** You can say this now after thirty years but you still had to learn and to find the freedom as you put it. To feel as an editor that you can have the trust and have the freedom to work with the material and find the form.
>
> **SM:** Maybe because I was a very young editor with film directors who had already done several films and were at ease with

themselves. I can't take this out of my experience. I would rely on them – they taught me everything.

RC: Something Agnès Varda said when she came to the Tate Modern. She talked about the fact that she didn't know cinema before she became a film-maker. But she knew painting, she knew literature and she said she knew that the form did not have to be conventional storytelling, especially in the linear sense – that there are other ways of representing life than just telling a plot. Therefore the form could be free from what happens next in a story. So her mind was free of that convention of telling stories the way Hollywood does most of the time. Do you know what I mean? That freedom is so important for there to be a cinema which is not just about plot.

SM: I listen to you and I think maybe something that helped me a lot is having been born in different cultures and different languages. In Tunisia we would have Maltese, Italian, Jewish, Arab – you had five or six languages in the playground. There were differences between the plot of an Indian film or an Egyptian film or a French film. I remember seeing '*Les Quatre-Cents Coups*'[61] and turning around at night in my room and understanding suddenly that this was what people call 'having the blues', and then going to bed because I could put a name to what happened to me.

RC: But what gives you the freedom to explore beyond conventional cinema?

SM: For me it's the relation with people. For example, there's a man I like very much, called François Barat who has always made underground films. I have edited maybe ten of his films. When I edit he comes. He speaks about editing. I swear I have never understood what he said and my apprentices look at me – they feel silly because they haven't understood. I tell them I haven't understood either, but his words put me to work again. Since it's underground we are very free to explore. No distributor is here to give us recipes.

Agnès Varda made some conventional and some unconventional films. '*Sept Pieces, Cuisine, Salle de Bains à Saisir*'[62] I like very much. I don't know what it is – I like things that look like nothing.

RC: Yann Dedet said to me that he likes a film 'for nothing' which is why he said he likes working with Jean-François Stévenin. '*Passe-montagne*'[63] is not like anything.

SM: Yes, '*Passe-montagne*' or '*Le Bonheur*'![64]

* * * * * * * * * * * * *

RC: The reason for doing this book is because I feel that – not just European cinema – but other kinds of cinema are so import-ant to preserve and develop because otherwise we are totally swamped by the deluge of the conventional cinema. It scares me because working in a film school where it's sometimes very difficult to get young film-makers to have the courage to do something different. Many of them are just imitating what they think is cinema that works for them and they are often ignorant of other kinds of film-making.

SM: I would like once to see an African film with an African that would tell me if this is the normal way to tell a story. In a film there's a woman who goes to market, comes home, enters her home and you never see her again in the film. I don't know in Africa if this is the normal way to tell a story or is it just this person who decided that he would tell the story that way.[65]

Conventions are normal with young people. You have to work to go beyond convention. There are very few innovators. You think of Abel Gance. He invented the travelling, he invented the subjective, he invented the 'montage-parallele', he invented almost all techniques – flashbacks; in 1910, he had already done it all. Students have to go beyond admiration and start to be themselves, start to express and explore.

RC: Is it good for you to go from documentary to fiction?

SM: Yes, it's perfect. One nourishes the other. There is no such thing as documentary – they are both mise-en-scéne. Shooting a documentary, a director decides to shoot this person in this place doing this and that, in that specific light. Remember Claude Lanzmann shooting Bomba as a hairdresser though Bomba had retired? The difference from fiction is that in docu-mentaries the structure has to be invented. Even then in fiction when the script is not strong enough you may have to re-organise the structure by changing the order of sequences.

'Documentaries' were the very boring films we had to see before the film in the cinema fifty years ago, but you may see films like 'Sabotier du Val de Loire' by Jacques Demy[66] which is pure poetry.

RC: Do you like poetry itself?

SM: Yes I do. For the concision for the raccord, for the form, and especially for the construction.

RC: When you are not editing, what do you do if it's not cinema?

SM: In my daily life? I'm a great reader. I am a translator too. I trans-lated into Spanish a book on Talmud, by Marc Alain Ouaknin, with my best friend, Julio Maruri. Now there's a book they've published in Madrid, both in Spanish and in French, called '*Promenades Avec Julio Maruri*'.[67] It was originally a script abandoned because I never found a producer. The manuscript was lying on the floor of my brother in Madrid. A young man got crazy about it and decided to publish it as a book. So he asked us to translate it into Spanish, which we did. I have spent for ten years about three or four evenings learning Talmud with Marc Alain Ouaknin, the book of whom we decided to translate after as an homage of admiration. I write short stories which have been published in '*Le Temps Modernes*'. I have directed a few documentaries on my best friends.

I take Kung-fu lessons for my love of Kung-fu films. My teacher is a beautiful woman named Xiao Yan, which means 'Little Nightingale'. I practice three days a week. So does my daughter who is fifteen years old and Champion of France.

* * * * * * * * * * * * *

RC: Can you recognise who has cut a film by the style?

SM: There are films you don't even have to read the credit – you know who has edited the film. This is what I hate most. This idea that they have a style and whatever they cut they cut exactly the same way – I can't stand it. Can you imagine a hairdresser who would give exactly the same cut to everyone because it's his style!

French movies have an old tradition of being talkative, (I'm not being pejorative). Think of Louis Jouvet or Jean Eustache.[68] Words are important and loving words helps. Sami Frey directed '*Je me Souviens*' by Georges Perec.[69] It was his first experience as a director. He asked Agnès Varda to give him the name of an editor who loved reading. You'd think: what's the importance, it's a play, we won't take a word out of it? Yet, that was – to my luck, as he's my favourite French actor – his demand. Not an editor with a sense of rhythm, an editor who loves reading.

As for your question if life changes radically when I'm not working, well, no. When I'm working, I need to be kept awake; I need to go to movies, to concerts, to read. Even more, filled with the energy of work, I have often been able to create short things, a short story published here, a short film shown there. While I can be really lazy when I don't work and stay at home and read without any make up on and let my daughter come home with the smell of English cigarettes welcoming her, whereas I'd be more careful that she gets a good dinner when I work.

RC: How do you choose to do a film?

SM: At the worst, 'l'occasion fait le larron' (literally 'opportunity makes the thief'). At the best, I was there the moment of the birth of the first sprinkle of the scenario.

RC: How does the script relate to the editing?

SM: I just read the script, sometimes I have been given all the versions of the script. Then I edit. The first duty is to edit the film as the script goes. Then I often go back to it after the first cut, after having worked on new structures . . .

RC: What is important for you in the cutting room?

SM: Fortunately, my favourite landscapes do not change. I'm thinking of the faces of my favourite film directors, Claude Lanzmann or Olivier Ducastel and Jacques Martineau.

RC: Do you start by doing an assembly?

SM: The first cut is the final cut till I change it or till I'm asked to change it. Even if I know that there is little chance that it lasts till the answer print! And yet some have.

RC: How important is sound?

SM: It's the sound that makes me cut the picture, with questions like how much silence should I give her before she replies or how many frames before the sound of the spoon against the cup? I edit everything that concerns speech. The sound editor adds the additional effects.

RC: And music?

SM: You know that in France, the film editor cuts the music, we are the music editors as well. You choose with the film director the spots where you desire music. In the dubbing theatre, you're the one to discuss with the film director to mix it or not. Yet I think that how music is used and the type of music used remains the most boring and conventional aspect of movies.

RC: Do you value your assistant?

SM: Have you ever noticed how important it is to be three in order to understand one another, two talk and one listens and strangely enough, the two that talk understand each other. Being a very unorganised person, having almost never been an assistant, I have always let my assistant organise the things for me. Till now, my favourite assistants are still working with me logging and digitising and putting in order and I rely on them. Technology bores me: four Avid ways to make a cut bore me, what excites me is where to make the cut.

RC: Does your personality affect the way you cut?

SM: I wouldn't speak of personality, as I don't think you are the same person whoever you deal with. Unless you're hysterical! I have no cutting style, let's take three of the films I'm most proud to have edited: *Une Chambre en Ville, Tsahal, Ma Vrai vie a Rouen*. I have edited more than one film of those film-makers. An editor needs just one quality: the ability to listen.

Notes

1. *Geneviève de Brabant* – or *'Genoneffa di Brabante'*, Italy, 1947.
2. **Asmahane** was a talented singer who starred in two films and her brother **Farid al Atrache** had a long and successful career in movies.
3. *Gilda* – Directed by Charles 'King' Vidor starred Rita Hayworth in her most celebrated role, 1946.
4. *Goha* – Directed by Jacques Baratier, 1958.
5. *Documenteur* – Agnès Varda, 1981.
6. *The Loneliness of the Long Distance Runner* – Tony Richardson, 1962.
7. *Family Life* – Ken Loach, 1971.
8. *I pugni in tasca* – Marco Bellochio, 1965.
9. These directors are largely familiar except perhaps Nanni Moretti, *'Dear Diary'*, 1994, and *'The Sons Room'*, 2001 and Chantal Akerman who has made an impressive number of films which challenge our perceptions both of life and cinematic form. I recommend *'Les Rendez-Vous d'Anna'* as a starting point, which features a stunning performance by Aurore Clement and *'Jeanne Dielman'* which is riveted together by Delphine Seyrig's disturbing presence.
10. *Mandala Fille des Indes* – I can find nothing to remotely match this title.
11. *Mother India* – Mehboob Khan, 1957.
12. **Stephen Soderberg** – First made a strong impression with *'Sex, Lies and Videotape'*, 1989, and has since established a solid reputation with films like *'Erin Brockovich'*, 2000.
13. *Remember My Name* – Alan Rudolph, starring Geraldine Chaplin, 1978.
14. **Takeshi Kitano** – Japanese director whose films usually have a violent edge which is mediated by acute human insights. For instance *'Sonatine'*, 1993 and *'Hana-Bi'*, 1997.
15. *Jeanne et le Garçon Formidable* – 1998.
16. *Drôle de Félix* – 2000.
17. *King of Marvin Gardens* – Bob Rafelson, 1972 with Jack Nicholson.
18. *Safe* – Todd Haynes, 1995.
19. **Douglas Sirk** – Born in Germany in 1897 he had already established himself before the Nazi takeover in the thirties. It was in Hollywood in the

fifties however that Sirk became the king of melodrama – his films drenched in rich colour and high emotion.

20. **Jean-Claude Guiguet's** *Les Passagers* – 1999.
21. **Alain Guiraudie** – French director, born 1964.
22. *Bloody Sunday* – Paul Greengrass, 2002.
23. **Aki Kaurismaaki** – Born Finland, 1957. With a very deadpan style: For instance '*Drifting Clouds*', 1996.
24. **Abel Gance** – '*Napoléon*', 1926. Its restoration has revealed the true extent of his genius.
25. **Claude Lelouch** – French director perhaps most famous for '*A Man and a Woman*', 1966.
26. **Female directors** – The numbers have grown since then but not as much as they should have done. Agnès Varda has sustained a significant output over more than fifty years but the other two did not produce a significant body of work.
27. **Jean Schmidt** – Maker of political documentaries.
28. **Writers** – Three are less familiar. Sperber (1905–84) was a disciple of Alfred Adler in Vienna, a communist for many years he wrote a three volume biography entitled 'All Our Yesterdays'. Tanizaki was a Japanese novelist and essayist whose exquisite 'In Praise of Shadows' is of tangential relevance to cinema. I have found two 'Nemirovskis', one a mathematician and the other a pianist. Sabine may have been thinking of a third.
29. **Mai Zetterling and Ingmar Bergman** – Interestingly this impressive actress was only directed by Bergman once in '*Musik I Morker*' (*Music is my Future*) in 1948. She did however star in a film written by him, '*Hets*' (*Torment*), directed by Alf Sjoberg in 1944.
30. *La Dame Aux Oiseaux* – No trace of such a film.
31. *One Sings, the Other Doesn't* – Agnès Varda, 1977.
32. **Claude Accursi** – Best known as a screenwriter.
33. *Dada au Coeur* – 1974.
34. *Comme les Anges Déchus de la Planète Saint-Michel* – 1979.
35. *Murs Murs* – Agnès Varda, 1980.
36. **Claude Lanzmann** made '*Why Israel*' in 1972.
37. **Nurith Aviv** was an accomplished Cinematographer who worked many times with Agnès Varda.
38. *Lady Oscar* – Jacques Demy, 1980.
39. **Paul Davies** – British editor – worked a number of times with Mai Zetterling and also for Sam Peckinpah.
40. **Alan Bell** – Highly esteemed sound editor especially amongst his peers, has worked with Joe Losey, Lindsay Anderson and Nic Roeg amongst many others.
41. *Une Chambre en Ville*, Jacques Demy, 1982.
42. **Yilmaz Guney and Claude Weisz** – The latter made a film about Guney in 1987 after his death called '*On l'appelait le roi laid*' (*We called him the ugly King*). Sabine was not alone in finding Guney a very special person.

43. **Costa-Gavras** – Maker of films with a political edge, for instance, '*Z*' in 1969 and '*State of Siege*' in 1973.
44. *Le Mur* – Yilmaz Guney, 1983.
45. **Jim Morrison** – Lead singer of the legendary group '*The Doors*' – he always wanted to make films but died tragically in 1971.
46. **Patricia Mazuy** subsequently edited '*Vagabond*' for Varda.
47. *Peau de Vaches* – 1988.
48. **Jean-François Stévenin** – See also in Yann Dedet's interview.
49. **Yilmaz Guney's burial** – There is no doubt that he remained a rallying point for exiles from the oppressive regime in Turkey even after his death.
50. *Shoah* – Claude Lanzmann's epic of nine and a half hours of survivors living testament to the holocaust remains unparalled in cinema history, 1985.
51. **Catherine Zins** is a film editor.
52. *Matura 31* no trace of such a title.
53. *Night and Fog* (*Nuit et Brouillard*) – 1955 is, however considered by many to be an eloquent, poetic though devastating film.
54. *Tsahal* – Claude Lanzmann, 1994.
55. *The Living from the Dead* – Claude Lanzmann, 1997.
56. **Catherine Corsini** – Director, '*La Nouvelle Eve*', 1999.
57. **Karin Viard** – Popular actress born in Rouen.
58. **Paulo Branco** – Prolific producer born in Portugal.
59. **Jerry Lewis** – The book Sabine refers to is hard to find, but I am sure it is invaluable.
60. **Tolluène** – Chemical fluid for cleaning film.
61. *Les Quatre-Cents Coups* – François Truffaut, 1959.
62. *Sept Pieces*, *etc.* – Agnès Varda, 1984.
63. *Passe-montagne* – Jean-François Stévenin, 1978.
64. *Le Bonheur* – Agnès Varda, 1965.
65. **African Storytelling** – The differences in narrative form in different cultures is too little recognised and needs protecting from the homogenisation process.
66. *Sabotier du Val de Loire* – Film about a clog maker made by Jacques Demy in 1955, produced by Georges Rouquier of '*Farrebique*' fame.
67. **Julio Maruri** – I would like to hope that Sabine's admiration for this estimable person results in his work being more widely known.
68. **Louis Jouvet** – 1887–1951 – 'a living glory of the French theatre'. **Jean Eustache**, director, 1938–81, for example: '*La Maman et la Putain*', 1973.
69. **Sami Frey** – a splendid french actor who was in a television documentary about Georges Perce the author of '*Je me souviens*'. I am unable to trace the *film* Sabine refers to.

6 Agnès Varda and Alain Resnais

In 2001, after the release of her film 'Les Glaneurs et la Glaneuse' (The Gleaners and I) Agnès Varda was invited to the Tate Modern in London to talk about her career.

In describing her entry into cinema she emphasised that she had no training or background in the medium and drew on other forms for her inspiration and approach: She emphasised that: 'Literature – Joyce, Faulkner, Dos Passos – showed that linear narrative was not the only way' and therefore her films from the beginning have not embraced linear narrative. 'Not A to B to C even if "the guilty one" is identified at the end'.

She said that 'A film should offer something to everyone – images, sounds, emotions, maybe a story, but above all the chance to feel something' and that she wishes 'to project real things but not to make realistic films'.

Even the making of films should be non-linear: 'Write–shoot–edit–shoot–edit–write: an integral process'. To begin a film neither script nor even idea is necessary. You can 'start with an image' which itself can be surreal for instance 'If my aunt had wheels she would be a beautiful bus'.

She believes in 'the accidents or chances of cinema' and 'narrative by association – both instantaneously and predetermined'.

By returning to film the people who are her subjects in 'The Gleaners and I', two years after the original shoot, Varda added another dimension to this non-linear and reflexive cinema. The subjects are part of the dialogue with the filmmaker and her audience. In all this *her editing is informed by a different consciousness of the why of filmmaking. To her 'The audiences are witnesses'.*

* * * * * * * * * * * * *

In 1954 Agnès Varda made her debut film, '*La Pointe Courte*'. She knew virtually nothing about cinema or filmmakers. Literature and painting were her passions. Her ignorance of filmmaking included the editing process. This is how she describes what happened after the film was shot.

RESNAIS MONTEUR

Alain Resnais editing (Courtesy of BFI)

Back in Paris, I needed to find an editor who was willing to work without wages, as part of the co-operative, like the other technicians. People mentioned Resnais of whom I knew nothing. I write to him. He replies requesting my scenario. I send it to him.

His next letter was discouraging: 'Your research is too similar to mine . . . I am sorry'. I ring and insist. He agrees to look at the rushes. We meet at the Éclair Laboratory in Epinay.

There are ten hours of silent images. We are planning to show him only four. He sits in the middle of the room towards the front and me four rows behind him. We don't exchange a word whilst the film passes in silence, although I could have spoken the dialogue to him out loud. After two hours he stands up and says: 'I have seen enough, I don't believe I could work on that film'.

He is smiling but distant. I am demoralised and ask him what I should do. He says: 'In any case to edit a film you need to number the material, one number each foot. If you wish I will lend you a rewind with a crank, a rewind without, a piece of film marked up for the length of a foot, and a small *synchro*'. I had the distinct impression he had spoken Javanese![1]

He brings everything to the rue Daguerre.[2] I screw the rewinds on a table and start numbering the film outside of the perforations with white ink and a tiny nib. I turn once, tick, then write down the numbers: one for the shot, one for the take (1st time, 2nd time, etc.). I was on a treadmill.

After ten days of working with almost no break, I ring Resnais: 'I have finished what you asked me to do'. 'You have numbered 10,000 metres in ten days! You are mad! Okay, I will come and do your editing but on my conditions. I agree to the co-operative salary, but I want my lunch paid for each day. Also I stop at 6 p.m.'

In short, working for nothing but no overtime!

I hired a CTM editing machine and fixed up the rest of the installation. Resnais was living in the 14th arrondissement like me. He came on his bike with clips on his trousers. He was punctual.

I will never forget his generosity, the way he worked for months on this editing without any wages, nor the lesson I retained from it. Noticing that '*La Pointe Courte*' was shot at a slow pace without safety shots (no cutaways, no alternative angles, no safety close-ups), he was saying that we needed to keep the rigidity of the film, its slowness and its bias without concession.

But he also made remarks like:

This shot reminds me of Visconti's '*La Terra Trema*'.[3]

'Who is Visconti?' I would ask.

'There is in Antonioni's "*Il Grido*"[4] the same taste for walls'

'Who is Antonioni?'

Resnais did not try to use his talent as an editor to transform the film, re-arrange or adapt it to a simpler form, more lively or rapid. He was looking only for the right rhythm of this film.

I also remember the dazzling laugh of Anne Sarraulte, Resnais' trainee assistant, the wrinkling of her eyes and her cascading giggles.

The 'Estro Armonico' records which I had listened to when writing the film also influenced the rhythm of the editing. When Resnais was riding home on his bike, I listened to Brassens, Piaf, Washboard Sam and Greco when she was singing Queneau:

'If you think little girl, little girl, that it will, that it will, that it

Will last forever

You got it wrong little girl'.

FROM INNOCENCE TO RULES OF THE GAME

Resnais talked to me about Renoir, Murnau, Mankiewicz, all strangers to me. He led me to discover that a Cinémathèque existed in Paris, Avenue Messine, advising me to start with '*Vampyr*' of Dreyer.[5] He came as well on his own. We talked on the pavement afterwards. He led me to know the names of the great filmmakers, if not their films. Apart from my evolution from rough cineaste to debutante, it was through him that I discovered an exotic Paris, its Chinese restaurants, its Jewish district, the green path where the circular train used to run, and the mound of the Buttes Chaumont.

He astonished me one day that he knew the number of spectators for a film. He told me how one could read every morning – as for the stock exchange – the number of entries in the cinemas, by film, by day, by week, etc. There I was thinking that a film was like a painting, viewed by a few and going from gallery to gallery, and I discovered the commercial controls of the industry, certificates, the committee of censorship, the agreement files. How funny life was, to be taught all this by Renais, the cineaste of '*L'Année Derniére à Marienbad* and of '*La Chante du Styrène*',[6] always searching for an inventive cinema, sincere and structured. Nowadays beginners, both talented and untalented only know Cine-Chiffres, the CNC,[7] the Box Office and Audimat!

From:
'Varda par Agnès', Cahiers du Cinéma et Ciné Tamaris, 1994. © les cahiers du cinéma, 1996.

Notes

1. **Javanese** – Resnais was describing the process which is used to identify each foot of the film rushes and to keep it in sync during the editing process. In France this was done by hand at that time – a painstaking and laborious job.
2. **rue Daguerre** – Where Varda had her home. She made a film about the shopkeepers on her street *'Daguerrotypes'* in 1978.
3. *La Terra Trema* – Luchino Visconti, 1948.
4. *Il Grido* – Michelangelo Antonioni, 1957.
5. *Vampyr* – Carl Theodore Dreyer, 1932. The **Cinémathèque** run by Henri Langlois was where whole generations, especially that of the 'New Wave', discovered world cinema.
6. *'L' Année Derniére à Marienbad*, 1961, and *La Chante du Styrène*, 1958 – both Alain Resnais.
7. **CNC** – **Centre National (de la cinématographie)** – The public body in France charged with supporting and regulating the Industry. Despite much criticism from filmmakers it has been a major reason that cinema has maintained its strong cultural and economic base in France.

7 François Gédigier

I talked with François over coffee and croisants in a hotel just off the Place d'Italie in Paris. It was not long after he had cut the controversial film, 'Intimacy' for Patrice Chéreau whom he has been editing with since 'La Reine Margot'.

François Gédigier (Courtesy of François Gédigier)

I was born in Paris in 1957. My father was a commercial salesman in the clothing industry and my mother was a secretary. I have a brother who is three years older than me. He works as a teacher in a centre for young disabled people.

I left school when I was seventeen, a year before the baccalaureate, but from the age of sixteen I was already working in a small theatre near Montparnasse. I was so happy to be there – I had arrived there by chance and spent my time acting, assisting, helping with the lighting. I was convinced I had found my vocation. The director of the theatre was a woman with a very strong personality and it took me two to three years to realise that the environment of the company was rather sectarian and I left. But I still love theatres, especially when the stage and seats are empty before the show – it is really beautiful.

At the same time I was acting in short films. I had a friend at INSAS[1] and he called me to play in his film. I discovered something that was really like an empty theatre – the set. I was a mediocre actor but I was fascinated by the work of the whole team – the lights, the sound – all these people who knew what they had to do.

So I tried to work in film and the first door to open was the editing room for 'Diva',[2] where I was offered the role of trainee assistant. Beineix[3] was full of nervous energy (it was his first feature film) and Philippe Rousselot[4] did the lighting (that blue light). All the team were new and young. The producer was Irene Silberman, the wife of Serge Silberman,[5] who produced for Buñuel and Kurosawa.

> **RC:** Were you cutting on the Steenbeck?[6]
> **FG:** Yes, I was numbering by hand,[7] but I was so happy to be there. I didn't understand much about editing but I would have done anything for the film with the same pleasure, like searching the whole of Paris for pumpkins. Beineix had read that Hitchcock had used them to imitate the sound of being stabbed with a knife.
>
> After that nothing; I tried to work on the set, but I didn't like having to deal with so many people. So I was ready to leave with my father, take the suitcase and sell clothes. We had just put the suitcase in the car and we were coming back to close the house and the phone rang. It was Gaumont who were looking for a trainee to work on a comedy film called 'La Chèvre' by Francis Weber.[8] Marie-Josephe Yoyotte,[9] who was the editor that I assisted on 'Diva' had given my name. So there I met Albert Jurgenson.[10]

RC: Who was an editor and who was also a teacher?

FG: Yes, he was professor at INSAS in Brussels and then he was head tutor for the editing department at La Femis.[11]

RC: And he wrote a book on editing – so did you learn from him?

FG: Yes a lot and first because he was an active supporter of the function of editing in the whole process of filmmaking. He was editing on the Moritone, which is a bit like the Moviola.[12] He was making marks, quickly and precisely, so cutting it at the assistant's table I was able to follow his editing, step by step. He was famous for his bad humour, but he was respected and devoted to his work.

The second film with him was '*La Vie est un Roman*' by Alain Resnais.[13] I had already seen and liked '*Muriel*' and '*Providence*'[14] – and I met a man who in a certain way is still a bit of a teenager. When people think about Resnais they think he is very intellectual and serious and he's really funny. He's really courteous and attentive to people working with him.

RC: Because in a strange way his films have become lighter too. When you think of *Marienbad*[15] or *Muriel* – they are heavy films – as he's got older the films have got lighter. Because he was an editor first, was he very much there all the time?

FG: No, he came by arrangement and worked with Albert for two or three hours, and then would come back three or four days later, which I think is a good way to work.

Then thanks to Juliet Berto,[16] I worked with Yann Dedet[17] for Jean-François Stévenin film, '*Double Messieurs*'.[18] It was absolutely the opposite from what I had experienced with Jurgenson, except that they both gave the same importance to the function of editing. Where Albert had worked with an apparent total absence of doubt, Yann would everyday question the structure of the film, and I learned that everything had to be tried that might serve to support the story or the emotion.

Yann Dedet moved things forward during the 1970s and 1980s and his influence on the way of editing is visible today. The term 'Yannerie' invented by Stévenin, designates a form of editing that is particularly strange and elegant. I also did the sound editing on '*Double Messieurs*' Stévenin has a real taste for sound. For instance, a washing machine becomes a plane or an ambulance at night in the mountains becomes a wind – it's really beautiful. So I decided to become a sound editor. I worked on Peter Brook's '*Mahabarata*',[19] creating sound from scratch, but not being totally realistic.

RC: What about music, you were once in a rock band?

FG: Oh! That was in 1978, at that time everyone was doing it. It felt like the real thing – singing and writing songs – groupies – the whole scene! Then I went to Brussels to sing in 'Der Dreigrossenoper'[20] – a small part – that was fun.

RC: Is music still important to you?

FG: In the film yes – I spend a lot of time choosing music and cutting it, but live sound can be as effective. One can choose a take because of an accidental occurrence in the sound which allows you to make a connection to the next shot. I struggle a little to understand why there is a division between picture cutting and the rest. I try to ensure that the cutting copy is as close as possible to the final version. This applies of course to the kind of films that I cut.

RC: Then how did you make the leap from sound to picture editing?

FG: I was doing short movies at night or during the weekend with Pascale Ferran.[21] She was at IDHEC[22] with Arnand Despleschin[23] and he was looking for an editor for his first one-hour movie called 'La Vie des Morts'.[24] It was a really good film with a lot of young actors, some of them coming from the Chéreau school.[25] It was a real pleasure the whole time – no pressure, no money and I learned so much. The film was released and it was a success.

* * * * * * * * * * * * *

After 'La Sentinelle'[26] with Despleschin, the first full-length feature for both of us, Chéreau called me for 'Le Temps et la Chambre'.[27] I remember that someone who was living with me at the time took the call and told me 'Patrice Chéreau called you!' and I said 'Oh – the real Patrice Chéreau?'

I knew him before when I assisted Jurgenson on a film in 1987. I left the film half way through, because I had been called to New York to do sound editing with Robert Frank. I'm still not very proud of that to this day, but we all make mistakes.

However when we met again it was like for the first time. I worked very hard, because it was my first time on Avid and I learnt as I did it. 'Le Temps et la Chambre' was a play by Botho Strauss.[28] Chéreau had created it at the Odeon Theatre and then re-staged it in the film studio. Chéreau was quick and fast and the first rough-cut I showed him was very close to the decoupage and he said 'Okay, so that's the rushes and now?!' In fact he wanted something to react to and I understood very quickly that I had the freedom to suggest my own vision.

Then when we were mixing the film he said what are you doing after, and I said nothing, and he asked me to do '*La Reine Margot*',[29] and I was really surprised, to be asked to cut such an expensive and important film, after having cut only two features.

>**RC:** Was there a lot of material?
>
>**FG:** A lot – they shot for six months and the film had to be ready for Cannes. It was hell. Added to the pride that I felt in working on a film of that scale, and the pleasure of editing such images and the collaboration with Chéreau, nobody could say now that I was a beginner. When you've done a film like that you've done it!
>
>There was this strange experience after the release of the film. Miramax bought the film and they wanted to make some cuts. I began to work with their editor in New York, a specialist in re-editing foreign films, but it was unpleasant to work without Chéreau. Back in Paris with Chéreau we suggested *our* cuts. Of course because time had passed we found re-editing easier and we had a certain amount of pleasure. Editing is all about time and sometimes determination.
>
>**RC:** Going back – what was your first experience in New York?
>
>**FG:** The film called '*Candy Mountain*' with Robert Frank and Rudy Wurlitzer.[30] I was the sound editor. It was a road movie, and the artifice of sound montage was not needed. But Robert Frank was nice and relaxed – teasing me a little.
>
>Later, when I did '*La Captive du Désert*' with Depardon[31] I had the same problem of the lack of necessity for sound design. On the first day of the mix he said 'Wah! I'm not Sergio Leone – I don't want to put flies – I don't want *more* sound'.

∗ ∗ ∗ ∗ ∗ ∗ ∗ ∗ ∗ ∗ ∗ ∗ ∗

In 1999, thanks to Humbert Balsan,[32] Vibeka Vindelow[33] contacted me and I went to Denmark to edit the musical scenes in '*Dancer in the Dark*',[34] shot with one hundred DV cameras. It started with a meeting at which we were shown a random montage of scenes. Then Bjork[35] explained what she was trying to say with the music and the choreographer was talked about the dance routines and Lars von Trier[36] was saying nothing – he didn't want to say anything.

There was a young film student type there too and another guy who was working on the set with the hundred cameras, who was also an editor of music videos. Lars said 'Okay, each of you will do your own version of the train scene'. I thought what am I doing here – am I supposed to make a competition with those people – shall I stay or go? I had a contract so I thought let's stay and see what happens. I had read the diary von Trier wrote when he was making '*The Idiots*'[37] and I knew already that he was special.

It took two weeks to have something to show. For one take of six minutes you had ten hours of rushes. For five takes, fifty hours, and there was no indication from Lars.[38]

RC: So these other two were also making their versions – how extraordinary.

FG: The reason given was that the approach was so new that they needed to gather every possible idea. There was something mystical about this one hundred camera idea. It took quite a while to accept that there were just scenes with a lot of material. Lars needed to know the trajectories of the characters in the film before being able to concentrate on the songs. After three weeks, we presented our work and then my relationship with von Trier became more normal. We stopped the comparing game and started to work seriously. Von Trier is funny and charming together with a fear of losing control.

RC: Then you came back to Chéreau – to '*Intimacy*',[39] which I enjoyed very much. Was that a hard film to cut?

FG: In the beginning, yes a little – sex scenes are not my favourite, it's a bit like killing – you know it's not true – also it's not particularly pleasant to watch and there was a lot of material, but the scenes were so precisely shot that after a while it became just a question of rhythm – like a conversation in fact. Chéreau had so much pleasure with the actors, because they were so generous in their playing, which is not so common in France.

There is also the pleasure of working with Chéreau – after several films. As time goes by he gains confidence in himself and in cinema; he knows how much he can ask of those who work with him and that for the technicians there is no question that he is the leader – the author.

RC: Do you think that cutting is instinctive?

FG: That's why it's very hard to explain why you have cut something the way you have. The answer is likely to be because I preferred it that way – a bit brief but no less true. As an editor you develop some habits – even if you try not to. I remember when we were cutting '*La Vie des Morts*' the aim was never to cut back to the same shot – just because it seemed to us so boring and it's still something I resist even if, when you are doing champ-contre-champ,[40] you are obliged to.

As for European cinema and American cinema, I don't know if the frontier is situated there or between those films which believe in the existence of an audience, which comes with intelligence and sensibility and those products which are looking for the maximum return at the box office.

Notes

1. **INSAS** – French speaking Belgian film school in Brussels.
2. *Diva* – Jean-Jacques Beineix, with Wilhelmina Fernandez in the title role, 1981.
3. **Jean-Jacques Beineix** – director, born 1946, also '*Roselyne et les Lions*', 1989.
4. **Philippe Rousselot** – eminent cinematographer, born 1945. Also shot '*La Reine Margot*' for Patrice Chéreau.
5. **The Silbermans** – Serge was born in Lodz, Poland in 1917 and died in 2003. He produced '*Ran*' (1985) for Kurosawa and several Buñuel films from '*Le Journal d'une Femme de Chambre*' (1964) onwards. Irene produced a handful of features apart from '*Diva*'.
6. **Steenbeck** – The most successful German table editing machine – as reliable and long lasting as a BMW.
7. **Numbering by hand** – Literally stamping the film rushes at foot intervals with a different number for identification in editing. Common in France for many years when other countries had moved to a mechanical device.
8. *'La Chèvre'*-**Francis Weber (or Veber) 1981** – Weber was famous as a writer of comedy film scripts, notably '*La Cage Aux Folles*', 1978.
9. **Marie-Josephe Yoyotte** – Film editor from late fifties – e.g. '*Les Quatre Cent Coups*' (1959), François Truffaut. '*Le Testament d'Orphée* (1960), Jean Cocteau and '*Léon Morin, Prêtre*' (1961), Jean-Pierre Melville.
10. **Albert Jurgenson (1929–2002)** – Film editor, notably for Alain Resnais.
11. **La Femis** – French national film school in Paris which replaced IDHEC.
12. **Moviola** – Upright editing machine which was originally constructed by the adaptation of projector parts – notable for their noise and small viewing aperture. Beloved of a whole generation, before the table machines took over. The **Moritone** was one of a number of imitations.
13. *La Vie est un Roman* – **Alain Resnais**, 1983.
14. *Muriel* (1963), with Delphine Seyrig, '*Providence*' (1977) with Dirk Bogarde, both directed by Resnais.
15. *'L' Année Dernière à Marienbad* – Resnais, 1961.
16. **Juliet Berto** – Writer, also actress. Co-wrote '*Céline and Julie Go Boating*' (1974) directed by Jacques Rivette, and played in several early Godard films.

17. **Yann Dedet** – Editor, see interview in this book.
18. **Jean-François Stévenin** – *Double Messieurs* (1986), most recently directed *'Mischka'* (2002). Acted in many films. Was assistant director for Truffaut and others.
19. *Mahabarata* – Peter Brook, adapted from the great Indian epic, 1989. Brook is a legend in the theatre – see *'The Empty Space'* his book on the nature of theatre.
20. *Die Dreigroschenoper* by Berthold Brecht based on John Gay's *'The Beggars Opera'*.
21. **Pascale Ferran** – writer *'La Sentinelle'*, 1992.
22. **IDHEC** – The original French national film school.
23. **Arnand Despleschin** – Director, also *'Esther Kahn'*, 2000.
24. *La Vie des Morts* – Directed by Despleschin, 1991.
25. **Chéreau School** – Patrice Chéreau, born 1944, is a theatre and opera director of enormous standing in Europe, from Shakespeare to Wagner. He is fast establishing an equivalent standing in the cinema.
26. *La Sentinelle* – Arnand Despleschin, 1992.
27. *Le Temps et la Chambre* – Patrice Chéreau, 1992.
28. **Botho Strauss** – Writer, also adapted Gorky's *'Summer Folk'* for the screen in 1975, directed by Peter Stein.
29. *La Reine Margot* – Patrice Chéreau, with Isabelle Adjani, 1994.
30. *Candy Mountain* – Robert Frank and Rudy Wurlitzer, with Harris Yulin and Tom Waits, 1988. Robert Frank made a film in 1958, *'Pull My Daisy'* which, apart from featuring the major 'beat' poets, included the first screen appearance by Delphine Seyrig, later to be Resnais' leading lady in several films.
31. *La Captive du Désert* – Raymond Depardon, starring Sandrine Bonnaire as the 'captive', 1990.
32. **Humbert Balsan** – Very experienced producer who worked several times with Robert Bresson early in his career.
33. **Vibeka Vindelow** – Producer, notably von Trier and other Danish 'Dogme' directors.
34. *Dancer in the Dark* – Lars von Trier, 2000.
35. **Bjork** – Born in Iceland, singer, composer, actress.
36. **Lars von Trier** – Danish director. First international success with *'Breaking the Waves'*, 1996.
37. *The Idiots* – von Trier, 1998.
38. **'One Take of Six Minutes' etc.** – Having worked on material shot on three cameras I find it hard to conceive getting my head around one hundred alternatives. I'm not even sure I can imagine how such a number could be useful.
39. *Intimacy* – Patrice Chéreau, with Mark Rylance and Kerry Fox, 2001. Based on the book by Hanif Kureishi.
40. *Champ*-Contre-Champ – Literally 'field-counter-field'. Used to describe inter-cutting matching shots, most commonly close ups of two people facing each other.

8 A Conversation with Nino Baragli

(This interview was conducted a few years ago by Stefano Masi and was published in the book 'Nel Buio Della Moviola'. It is printed here with his kind permission and that of Gabriele Lucci, to whom I am most grateful. The translation is by Emiliano Battista.)

At the time of this interview Nino Baragli was the President of the Italian Association of Film Editors (AMC). He has, in the course of his career, cut thousands of miles of films: he is one of the undisputed old masters of this craft. His contribution to Pasolini's filmography was enormous: *Accattone, Mamma Roma, Uccellacci e uccellini/Hawks and Sparrows, Il Vangelo Secondo Matteo/The Gospel According to Saint Matthew, Teorema/Theorem, Porcile/Pigsty, Medea, Decameron, I racconti di Canterbury/The Canterbury Tales, Il Fiore delle Mille e una Notte/The Arabian Nights, Salo' or the 120 days of Sodom.*

He had recently worked for Sergio Leone on *Once upon a time in America*: a truly monumental task with more than six months of work in the cutting room. For Leone he has also edited *Il buon, il brutto ed il cattivo/ The Good the Bad and the Ugly, Once upon a time in the West* and many other films. He had worked for a host of other directors from Mauro Bolognini[1] to Bernardo Bertolucci. More than 200 films cut in thirty-five years.

Baragli is a man with a big deep voice, he couldn't be from anywhere else than Rome. He wears a shirt open at the neck and sports a thick golden necklace. His skin is dark: he looks tanned. But how is it possible for an editor, always stuck in a cutting room, to get a suntan?

Nino Baragli (left) with Roberto Perpignani (Courtesy of Roberto Perpignani)

I meet him at the CDS Studio on a hot mid-May afternoon. Roberto Perpignani was there with me. His support has been crucial in my investigation about editors in Italian film history. I am slightly late and I find them in the middle of a discussion with another editor, Raimondo Crociani.[2] The three of them are all governors of the AMC. They are talking about producers and how editors are paid. It is rather an interesting issue as there are two different positions within the Association. Young editors like Cruciani insist that the Association should fix what is the minimum fee editors can claim for a film. On the other side Baragli argues that this wouldn't really solve anything as producers always find a way to avoid regulations and do things in their way. But young editors with little contractual power feel that they are not being protected when facing producers and they are forced to accept very low fees.

Stefano Masi: Mr Baragli, I would like you to help me solve a little mystery about the origins of this craft. An old Italian DOP, Otello Martelli, told me that in his early days the camera operator and the editor would sometimes be the same person. Does that make sense to you?

Nino Baragli: It does actually sound a bit strange. But it is not impossible.

SM: Let's put it like this: on the one side you had the intellectual. He would have the idea, write the script and direct the movie. On the other side you had the technician who would be in charge of photography and editing. So that the technician, editor and camera operator, was the manual worker, the one who would physically handle the film.

NB: Now that I think about it, it is not so strange after all. My uncle Eraldo worked for a while as a camera assistant before turning to editing. I don't really know why and how he went into editing . . .

SM: Your uncle Eraldo, Eraldo da Roma,[3] is the greatest Italian editor of all times . . . . .

NB: His real name was Eraldo Judiconi. He started in the 1930s. I remember that when he was working on *Addio Kira* and *Noi Vivi* I was already there, as close as possible to his moviola, to see how the film is spliced together and how the image moves . . . .

SM: Why did he decide to be called Eraldo da Roma?

NB: He used to be a tenor and Eraldo da Roma was his stage name as a singer. He was really great. He used to perform a lot, mainly operas. I remember him in *La Tosca*. I still have a picture of Eraldo playing as Cavaradossi. But his real surname was Judiconi: he was my mother's brother.

SM: So he moved into cinema and he kept his stage name. Why did he stop singing?

NB: He never had the big break in that world. Once he had an audition at the *Teatro dell'Opera*. Rita Gigli, the daughter of the great Beniamino Gigli, heard him singing and thought that he was her father. Eraldo had a great voice, but it was really difficult to make it as one of the top singers. That's why he decided to quit and started working as a camera assistant.

SM: And what about you, did you start working as your uncle's assistant?

NB: No. I actually started in cinematography, even if just for a short while. So what you were saying at the beginning about the connections between editor and cinematographer is probably right. I started in the camera department myself.

SM: When, and how?

NB: In 1944 my sister moved up north to join her husband Carlo Bellero. He was the camera operator in films like *Alfa Tau* and *La Nave Bianca*. During the times of the Salo' Republic[4] they were still in the north, in Venice. I hadn't seen my sister for a

SM:

long while and decided to join her in Venice. It was a rather adventurous journey . . . .

SM: And what about your uncle Eraldo? Had he moved to Venice as well to join the Salo' film industry?

NB: No. He stayed in Rome. The production company Scalera had resettled in Venice. They were trying to complete a new film directed by De Robertis.[5] It was called *Marinai senza stelle*.

SM: How old were you at that time?

NB: No more than sixteen or seventeen years old.

SM: And what was a seventeen years old kid doing on the stage of Scalera-film in Venice?

NB: I was the apprentice with my sister's husband. He was the camera operator. I started as his assistant and camera loader. Arriflexes weren't too difficult to load. Then, since De Robertis would cut his own films, I joined in to help out in the cutting room as well.

SM: So De Robertis was a director without an editor but with an assistant editor?

NB: I have to say that in the 1940s there was still not a great awareness of how crucial the editor's role is. Then we had some great editors, like Serandrei[6] and Eraldo, who showed how important this profession is.

SM: Straight after the war the editor's role was really obscure.

NB: Sure, the layman wouldn't know anything about the existence of editors and editing. But people in the industry knew how important editors were. De Sica[7] knew my uncle was an extraordinary man. And Visconti[8] knew he owed a lot to Serandrei, that his editor had really given him a lot.

SM: Do you know if De Robertis would always cut his films on his own?

NB: I don't really know. But from what I saw he would do everything by himself. He would sit at the moviola and do the whole thing: he would cut and splice just like an editor. He had a girl assisting him. I can remember that cutting room being a real mess: they didn't use rubber numbers, they could never find trims and so on . . .

SM: After that film you went back to Rome and started working with your uncle. Is that right?

NB: Yes. He was cutting a film called *Eugenia Grandet*, directed by Mario Soldati.[9] I only did a couple of films with uncle Eraldo. And I wasn't even his main assistant, I was the second assistant. Then after that I started to cut myself.

SM: On which of the films edited by Eraldo did you work?

NB: The first was *Eugenia Grandet*. Then there was something called *Premio di Roma*: a very strange experience. It was one of the first times the Americans came to work in Italy. The whole thing was a joke: these people claimed to have great actors, they were pretending to be really big names, but none of it was true. They had this Montgomery[10] guy, but he wasn't the famous one. These kind of things would happen at the end of the war . . . .

SM: So we are talking about the period between 1946 and 1948.

NB: That's right. And straight after that I cut the first film that was just 'mine'. It was in 1950. It was an American production and the whole crew spoke only English. I couldn't understand a single word. The film was called *Dark Road*[11] and the producer was Mike Frankovic. We would all call him 'Big Cigar' because of this long thing constantly hanging from his mouth. A couple of years later he became the President of Columbia Productions. *Dark Road* was also Tonino Delli Colli's[12] debut as a DOP.

SM: How would an editor get to cut his first film feature in the late 1940s?

NB: As far as I can tell things haven't changed at all. You had schools before and they are still here. Take the Centro Sperimentale di Cinematografia[13] for instance: it is still working. And just like today you would have nepotism which you see everywhere in the industry: I have a friend, you have a friend, he has a nephew . . .

Nepotism is part of our cinema as much as it is part of the rest of our culture. I don't think anything has changed. From the way I see things, Film Schools don't really produce editors. I guess there is something wrong in the way things are structured. For instance I have two nephews who work as assistant editors. Roberto Perpignani has a daughter who does the same. Montanari[14] got his son into the industry. You see, that is how it works.

SM: And you are saying that forty years ago it was exactly the same?

NB: Maybe things are just a bit different. Forty years ago there was a rather small number of editors around. They formed a closed circle probably even more than now. Sometimes it was very difficult to make it even if you had somebody in your family who was an editor.

I remember that when I started my uncle Eraldo told Camillo Mastrocinque[15] not to hire me as an editor. Eraldo was

Mastrocinque's editor and instead of supporting me, he told him I was still too young and inexperienced and that he would have to cut the new film as well. It was a very tight 'clan' you see . . . .

SM: Why do you think that is?

NB: Take Eraldo and Serandrei. I remember that, if they met in Cinecitta', they would avoid eye contact and literally look away. They never said hi to each other. Things are very different now and there is a strong bond between all of the editors in the Association. Those who accuse us of not allowing enough space for newcomers are very much mistaken. They should rather realize that it was much tougher for us who made our debut thirty or forty years ago.

SM: How many of you came from the Centro Sperimentale di Cinematografia?

NB: As far as I know nobody did, and it is still the same today.

SM: Silvano Agosti[16] is the only exception then?

NB: Well, he studied editing but now he is a director . . .

SM: So why do you think there is such a bad connection between School and Industry?

NB: Schools are a good thing but they have their limits. Learning how to cut a film is not the same as learning that 2 plus 2 equals 4. Sometimes, in film editing, 2 plus 2 equals 3. Do you know what I mean? It has to do with your ability to be inventive. Being able to cut a film . . . it is something you either have or not. There are certain things that cannot be taught at school.

SM: Yes but don't forget that you need the right chances and connections if you want to make it. Otherwise you can't be as talented as you want . . . .

NB: As Eduardo De Filippo[17] said 'exams never end'. It is like that whenever you work with a director you are being examined by him. Same thing with the producers . . . so all the time we constantly are trying to pass exam.

SM: Would you say that about a low-budget film?

NB: As far as I am concerned, there is no difference between one film and the other. There is no such a thing as class A-movies and B-movies. They all matter in the same way. Think of the director of a low-budget film: that little film is nonetheless going to be his 'Ben Hur'.

SM: Do you still work with young and first-time directors?

NB: Of course I do. A couple of days ago I met Cinzia Torrini[18] about a project she has that I might cut for her. Actors like

Robert Duvall and John Savage are expected to be on board. She wrote the script and asked me to have a look at it. So we sat together and started revising it. I had never done it before. This is her second film. It has been a wonderful experience. I didn't ask for money, I didn't want anything. She said: 'Let's wait and put everything on the final bill!'

SM: Is it normal for an editor to start collaborating with the director at the script stage?

NB: It almost never happens. But it would actually be a very good thing to do. Editing means reinterpreting the script after it has been filtered by the director. Sometimes you really do change the film in the editing. See that film on the shelf: *L'Attenzione*[19] by Giovanni Soldati.[20] Well . . . you should read the original script and then look at the film. Things have changed so much.

SM: To have the editor cooperating on the script is actually a sort of Utopia, in strong contrast with the attitude most directors have. Perpignani told me that Orson Welles used to tell him: 'You are not supposed to think!'[21]

NB: It is true that at the moment there are very few directors who are up for a real and full collaboration.

SM: Looking at the editor's work, what are the main differences between contemporary cinema and yesterday's cinema?

NB: From what I can see, one of the main differences is in the amount of footage that is shot for a single film. Forty years ago, editors would not sit at the moviola struggling with the incredible amount of footage we are faced with nowadays. For Leone's *Once Upon a time in America*[22] I had something like three hundred kilometres* of film from which to chose. Forty years ago, you would never have more than ten kilometres of film in the cutting room.

SM: You can't really make a comparison with *Once upon a time in America* . . .

NB: It is true that Leone's is a rather special case . . . but even for other films you are always have around 70,000 metres of film. You should also bear in mind that in the past things were normally shot more in continuity. People tended to do a certain amount of editing work at the shooting stage, editing 'in camera'. Take Germi,[23] for instance, he would always know beforehand where he was going to cut. Now they have second and third cameras . . . what a waste of film stock.

*A 100-minute film is approximately three kilometres in length.

SM: Can you think of any directors who is not following this new trend?

NB: Recently I had a chance to look at the rushes of Ferreri's[24] new film. He doesn't shoot that much. He still makes cinema the way people used to many years ago.

SM: Let's go back to 1950, the year of your debut as a feature editor. If I were to walk into a cutting room from 1950 would I see anything different compared with the cutting rooms you work in today? Different kind of tools maybe?

NB: No doubt about that!

SM: Can you describe me these different tools?

NB: As far as I can remember at the time moviolas were built on a wooden base and we only had four plates. No hand controls, we would use pedals to run the film backwards and forwards. Right pedal to go forwards, left backwards. And you had to lift your feet from both pedals to 'brake' and stop the film.

SM: And did you have the Catozzo splicer (Tape joiner)?

NB: No, and that was the real problem! In the 1950s you really had to be good to make a cut. Now it is much easier: you can actually see the joins and you can try things over and over; if it isn't working you can actually try and add two more frames. Nothing terrible is going to happen. There is no way you could have worked like this in the olden days. With the cement splicer you would lose a frame for each joint.

SM: Did that imply a different way of working?

NB: Before making a cut you would examine the frame very carefully with a magnifying lens.

SM: Did your uncle Eraldo have one?

NB: Oh yes, he had a magnifying lens in a golden frame, he got it as a present from Vittorio De Sica, or maybe it was from Rossellini.[25] I can't remember now. Anyway, I inherited from him when he died. With this lens Eraldo would carefully analyze the movement in the frame, check the position of the head or the arm of the character. He also used a lamp, he would look, check, make his marks. Then he would go back, look at the frame again and change the marks. So you can see that it really took a long time to make a single cut.

SM: Did you also work like this in your early days?

NB: Not really . . . honestly I wasn't really worried about making mistakes because I would use a little bit of black spacing on every cut. But then of course you had a black flash on each joint of the film.

SM: What was the black spacing for?

NB: To fill the gaps created when you had to remove little slices of the frame in order to make the joint.

SM: I can imagine it must have been quite a lengthy procedure.

NB: It would take ages.

SM: Practically, who was in charge of doctoring the film like this? Was that the assistant's job?

NB: No. Editors would do that by themselves. The assistant was in charge of the sound tracks. And that was a very delicate task, since at the time we would cut what used to be called 'the standard' (*master*). The sound was already printed next to the picture but with a 19-frame offset. So you had to cut in a very particular way.

SM: It must have been like cutting a positive married print!

NB: More or less. This is how we did it: we had to cut the picture first and then pulled the handles of each shot for the dialogue to be dubbed. We basically had to cut the film twice: it was an endless process. And I'll tell you something more: straight after the war the dub was done on a half-band optical negative (and I am almost sure that FONO-ROMA kept working this way till very recently). It is actually 35mm stock cut in half, they would use both sides in order to save money. Once I had to sync up a film with the negative of the sound track.

SM: What does that actually mean?

NB: Well, say that you break the film as you are working on it, then you have to call the actor and have him rerecord his lines form scratch.

SM: So was the syncing up part of the editor's duties?

NB: At the time there was a lot of sync sound. You would have departments in charge of this, but sometimes the assistants would do the syncing up for the editors. Editors would never do it themselves. I did it sometimes as an extra job when I was working as an assistant, just to earn a little bit more money. I did syncing up for Cinquini[26] when he was cutting *Il diavolo bianco*.

SM: So you were working as an assistant and doing night shifts syncing up?

NB: Exactly. After a day of work in the cutting room I would sit at another machine and do syncing up till midnight.
    You do these kind of things only if there is a great passion!

SM: So you didn't have much time left for other things or other people?

NB: You have to love this job to the point that you become completely obsessed by it. I don't trust those people who go around bragging about being able to cut a film in ten days. Let's say: it might even be possible . . . but then you have to spend an other ten days watching it over and over because there is always something that is not quite working. I don't like rushing things. You have to be committed to what you do.

SM: And do you believe in this regardless of what the shooting ratio is?

NB: It doesn't really matter that much, you know. Sometimes, when people are trying to convince me that they are talking about a rather easy project, they will say: 'He's the kind of director who doesn't shoot that much!' But not having a lot of rushes doesn't necessarily simplify the editing. When there is a lot of material it might take a lot to find the right stuff, but at least I know I'll find it eventually. When the shooting ratio is really low, you might not have what you need at all.

SM: Could you talk about a project you worked on which you think is particularly interesting from an editing point of view?

NB: I think *Accattone*[27] did something to slightly change the way we approach editing, the system behind it. The film was initially produced by Federiz (Fellini and Rizzoli). Pasolini went out shooting for two weeks. Then Catozzo, the editor, told the producers that, from his point of view, it was impossible to put together the things Pasolini was shooting! The production came to a halt. Everybody who has been involved with Pasolini knows very well how emotional and passionate he could be. He felt shattered at the time (He seriously wanted to kill himself after *Mamma Roma*,[28] because he didn't like the film.) Then a new producer, Alfredo Bini, stepped in and we went through the rushes together.

SM: And what did you think of Pasolini's rushes?

NB: I was shocked! Pasolini would film a man running out of frame, then all of a sudden you would find him standing perfectly still. We, the editors, were used to people leaving and entering frame, while Pasolini would film a shot in Frascati (Suburb of Rome) and the reverse angle in Venice. But I manage to understand exactly what he wanted. Pasolini was a silent type and it was very difficult to understand his way of working.

SM: His background was mainly in literature. Maybe he didn't have a good relationship with technology.

NB: I would always ask him the same question: What is the point of this sequence?' Since you wouldn't understand anything by the way his scripts were written. His scripts were rather short but with a lot of things in them. I would ask him: 'What are you trying to say?' At that point he would take his glasses off, put them on his lap and then start to explain.

SM: But how would he explain himself: on the intention, the narrative content or the metaphorical one?

NB: He would explain a sequence as if it he was talking about a book. Even shooting for him was like writing a book. He didn't have any kind of fixed rules: he always had to be interpreted.

SM: And how did your colleagues react to such an unconventional way of editing?

NB: Serandrei came to congratulate me after he watched *Accattone*. He told: 'What I just saw was something truly wonderful!'

SM: When you were younger, did you ever work in the sound department?

NB: Yes I did because getting into editing was really difficult and so all the youngsters would work doing syncing up and mainly wait for the right chance to come up.

SM: Why was it so difficult to get into the big time?

NB: Since there were a few big names in the industry that were doing all the available films preventing anybody else from working on anything serious. They would cut four or five film at the same time. Serandrei was even able to work on eight projects at the same time: he was the number one at Titanus.

SM: How could they possibly cut four, five or even eight films at the same time?

NB: They did manage. I have done it myself. In the golden days I would really cut four films at the same time.

SM: But how could you work in four different cutting rooms, dealing with four different directors?

NB: Obviously it wasn't easy! I remember that once I was working on four different films, all of them in the studios of the old Istituto Luce.

One morning I got there and I saw all four directors, Montaldo, Vancini, Caprioli and Gregoretti standing in the courtyard, all four waiting for me. As soon as I spotted them I just said 'I am going to the bar!'. And so I ran away. Then I rang each one of them to arrange different appointments.

SM: But don't you think there is something wrong in working on four films at the same time?

NB: I try not to overlap projects. I try at least. But editors have many clients and we have to make them all happy. At times I have to say no to somebody. I remember that Scola wanted me to cut *Riusciranno i nostri eroi.*[29] I was approached by the producer first and then Scola himself rang me at home. I wasn't in so he spoke with my wife: 'Tell Nino I'll be delighted to work with him. I am about to go away to shoot now. I'll let him know something later on'. At the same time Pasolini was about to start *Porcile(Pigsty)*[30] which was not a big production but struck me as being quite an important film. So I had to make a choice. And I went for *Porcile.* Of course, I never worked with Scola again after that! You see, that is why sometimes we are forced to say yes.

SM: So you spend most of your time in the cutting room?

NB: Do you know how I cut Bolognini's *La notte brava*?[31] He'd been working with Cinquini up to that point. That was my first film with him. We were running out of money during the editing. So I spent four days and four nights working without a break on a version of the film to be shown to people who were interested in investing in it. I had a little nap on a couch from time to time. I barely washed my face and never left the cutting room for those four days.

SM: When things are so difficult what can an editor rely on?

NB: Your instinct mainly. Some editors have it, others don't. Instinct tells you what to take out of the film and what to put in. You can spend your entire life on a sequence that maybe is never going to work. Other times you immediately know what you have to do.

SM: But what about working on more projects at the same time. How can your instinct keep shifting between different narrative situations? How can you cut a war drama in the morning and a romantic comedy in the afternoon?

NB: You have to think you have different airtight rooms in your head, you know what I mean? Think of a submarine ready to go on a mission. If you don't make sure all the rooms are airtight it is going to sink. The brain works in just the same way. In one place you have one film, in a different place you store another one. At any point you can lock one room and go into another one.

SM: Has it happened to you to try and find a shot that actually belonged to a different film? Don't you ever get confused?

NB: That would be a sign that I am losing the plot.

SM: So you really need an extraordinary memory for this job!

NB: What really matters is that you have to respect your film and your craft. If you get into a film there is no way you are going to be confused. It can only happen if you are not focused on what you are doing.

SM: Editors have their own professional association. What are its aims?

NB: I would like to stress the importance of promoting a new image of who the editor is. We created the Associations of Italian Editors because we want people to know and understand who editors are and what they do. Sometimes even in the industry people don't know that much about editing. My uncle Eraldo, the great Serandrei and all the other wonderful editors have passed away before somebody realized the importance of collecting and treasuring their experiences. When people talk about editing they never go beyond Eisenstein and Griffith.

SM: Have you already achieved something with the Association?

NB: Yes. We managed to finally have awards for editors, so now there is a *Donatello* (*Italian equivalent of the Oscar*) for the best film editor of the year. And we are hoping to have more awards next year.

SM: How did the producers react to your Association?

NB: Some of them might believe that we are joining forces against producers. But they are wrong. We only work towards the best for the film.

SM: Do you ever as an editor have to negotiate between director and producer?

NB: Sometimes you are caught between two fires: the director wants something and the producer wants the opposite of it. But you have to understand the producer's reasons and point of view. Sometimes the producer comes and says: 'We are going to be in trouble with the board of censorship unless we cut that scene out!'

SM: And what if the director really wants the scene in?

NB: I have to find a way to make them both happy, mainly for the film's sake. Things like this happens all the times. I remember cutting Comencini's *Tutti a casa*[32] produced by Dino De Laurentis.[33] De Laurentis almost convinced Comencini to cut out a very beautiful scene which was not in the script and had been invented during the shoot. I was the only one that still wanted that scene in. We had a test screening in Florence and I persuaded the producer to leave the scene in at least for that occasion. The audience's reaction was very strong, there was loud applause and so that the scene never went out again.

SM: Ruggero Mastroianni[34] told me about a very curious technique used by Serandrei before the tape joiner was introduced and editors were still using cement splicers. He would make a cut but then, instead of scratching the film and joining it with cement, he would spit on it and overlap the two frames on each side of the cut. The saliva would hold for a while and then his assistant would do the proper joint later. Do you know of anybody else who used to work like this?

NB: I would never spit on the film because that is where what I eat comes from . . . I've never seen anybody doing it. I can say for sure that my uncle Eraldo didn't do it.

SM: Serandrei was the top editor in Italian pre war cinema. Still his colleagues didn't know anything about his way of working. I assume there is not a real flow of information amongst you editors!

NB: Every editor has a different way of working. I work a lot at the editing machine. Some editors only mark the film at the machine. Then the assistant makes the cuts and they check the final result in the projection room. My approach is different. I sit at the machine till the whole sequence has gone from the left to the right plate and I can say that I am satisfied with the result. On top of that, I start from the assumption that cinema was originally silent so everything should make sense even without sound and dialogue.

SM: Are you saying that you edit without sound?

NB: No. I cut picture and sound at the same time. But when I finish cutting a sequence I rewind the film and check it without sound: it has to work even silent. Otherwise it means that it isn't perfect.

SM: Do you ever cut without sound?

NB: Only in special circumstances. You can't really do it all the time: if you don't really master the language, for instance, you have to cut the sound. The first film I ever cut, *Dark Road,* was in English. In cases like this you have to cut the sound by yourself.

SM: Was it difficult to cut *Dark Road*?

NB: Very complicated. Everything was done in the American way: the director would shoot and then leave. The producer had the last word on the final cut. I didn't even know it at that time.

SM: Are you saying that the director was not in the cutting room?

NB: Never! That is a typical American thing. They have three different stages in the editing. The editor does the first cut. The second is the result of the discussion between editor and director. But they don't work together in the cutting room: they watch it in a theatre, taking notes and using a projector that can play the film backwards as well. Then for the final cut, it is the producer's call. He can always impose his will. Of course things are different if the director is called Coppola or Scorsese or Spielberg.

SM: In Italy we don't really have this idea of the Final Cut, do we?

NB: No: it is an American thing. I've met many American editors, like Peter Zinner who cut *The Godfather*. They have a completely different system. Sometimes they even have a little editing machine on the stage. For *Lady Hawk*,[35] for instance, I've seen that they had a Moviola in Cinecitta' Studio 5, where they were shooting. They would use it to check some effects and camera angles.

SM: In America the editor's work is much more respected.

NB: In the American film culture the editor is a central figure: he is the most important man. He starts working on the film when the shooting begins. He is alone in the cutting room and he is completely autonomous. The Americans know well how the film comes to life in the dark of the cutting room.

Notes

1. **Mauro Bolognini** – Director (1922–2001), e.g. *'La Dame aux Camélias'* with Isabelle Huppert in 1980.
2. **Raimondo Crociani** – Editor, born 1946, still active.
3. **Eraldo da Roma (Eraldo Judiconi)** – Editor whose post-war career covered most of the films now labeled Italian neo-realism from *'Rome Open City'* (1945), *'Paisa'* (1946), *'Bicycle Thieves'* (1947), *'Germany year Zero'* (1949), *'Miracle in Milan'* (1951), to *'Umberto D'* (1952). He subsequently worked frequently with Michelangelo Antonioni.
4. **The Salo' Republic** – (1943–5), The Italian Social Republic which was a fascist puppet state formed in German occupied Northern Italy.
5. **Francesco De Robertis** – (1902–59), Director.
6. **Mario Serandrei** – Editor, notably for Visconti including *'The Leopard'* (1963). Also cut *'The Battle of Algiers'* (1965).
7. **Vittorio De Sica** – Director, crucially associated with neo-realism including *'Bicycle Thieves'* (1947) and *'Miracle in Milan'* (1951).
8. **Luchino Visconti** – Director, was assistant to Renoir before making his first feature *'Ossessione'* (1942) the essential harbinger of Italian neo-realism to which he made a crucial contribution. He had a long career as director of films and opera, the latter medium becoming more and more an influence on his films e.g. *'The Leopard'* (1963) and *'The Damned'* (1969).
9. **Mario Soldati** – Director (1906–99), notably *'Woman of the River'* (1955) with Sophia Loren.

10. **Montgomery** – possibly Robert of that name.
11. *Dark Road* (1948), directed by Alfred Goulding.
12. **Tonino Delli Colli** – DOP on most of Pasolini's films.
13. **Centro Sperimentale di Cinematografia** – The Italian National Film School in Rome.
14. **Sergio Montanari** – Editor, including several Hercules epics.
15. **Camillo Mastrocinque** – (1901–69), Director.
16. **Silvano Agosti** – Director/editor, who has managed to juggle the two roles during his career.
17. **Eduardo De Filippo** – Actor, writer, director, theatre and film.
18. **Cinzia Torrini** – Director, film and TV.
19. *L'Attenzione* (1984).
20. **Giovanni Soldati** – Director/writer.
21. See interview with **Roberto Perpignani**.
22. **Sergio Leone/*Once upon a time in America*** – (1984), This was Leone's last film as a director. He started as an assistant director, notably on *'Bicycle Thieves'* in 1948. Instrumental in the invention of the Spaghetti Western, he died in 1989.
23. **Pietro Germi** – (1914–74), Director/writer e.g. *'Divorce Italian Style'* (1969).
24. **Marco Ferreri** – (1928–97), Director, notably *'La Grande Bouffe'* (1973).
25. **Roberto Rossellini** – Director from *'Rome Open City'* (1945) to *'The Rise of Louis XIV'* (1966), he was an intrepid explorer of film form, frustrated that most movies are mere illustrations of their subject.
26. **Roberto Cinquini/*Il diavolo bianco*** – (1947), Editor, cut *'For a Fistful of Dollars'* (1964), Sergio Leone's first Spaghetti Western.
27. **Pier Paolo Pasolini/*Accattone*** – (1961), was Pasolini's first feature. His style, which ignored the rules of conventional film language, appeals to many filmmakers, especially editors, who admire its vitality, and roughness.
28. *Mamma Roma* – (1962), written by Pasolini – we should not forget that he contributed enormously to the writing of many Italian films, apart from his own.
29. **Ettore Scola/*Riusciranno i nostri eroi a ritrovare l'amico misteriosamente scomparso in Africa?*** – (1968) Scola was a prolific screenwriter and director this one is a contender for the longest title. It means 'Will our Heroes be able to find their friend who has mysteriously disappeared in Africa?'
30. *Porcile* – *'Pigsty'*, 1969.
31. *La notte brava* – Mauro Bolognini, 1959.
32. **Luigi Comencini/*Tutti a casa*** (1960), war drama.
33. **Dino De Laurentis** – Producer, both in Italy – several of Fellini's films (with Carlo Ponti) and in USA – *'Ragtime'*, *'Blue Velvet'*.
34. **Ruggero Mastroianni** – Editor (1929–96), cut often for Fellini and Francesco Rosi amongst many others.
35. *Lady Hawk(e)* – (1985), directed by Richard Donner, with Michelle Pfeiffer.

9 Meeting the Tavianis

I met Vittorio and Paolo Taviani with Roberto Perpignani during a lunch break at Cine Citta Studios in Rome.

Roberto had told them about my project and they launched immediately into their feelings about editing. I was immediately impressed by the way each of them respected the other when speaking. They never interrupted each other, but when one had finished, the other took up the subject without repeating what the other had said or contradicting his brother. Instead they each took the discussion to a new level as if there was a secret or instinctive dialectic going on between their two minds. It was magical and immediately explained to me why they have been able for more than thirty years to share the direction of their films. From the start they have taken turns not with each scene but with each shot. Their films are wonderfully coherent, but the structure of scenes and the cutting between scenes is often scintillating in their surprising juxtapositions.

But I must let them speak for themselves.

'It was seeing "*Paisa*"[1] that led us to think either cinema or nothing, and abandon cultural studies. We were interested in working with Roberto because Bertolucci said how calm he was, but then he learned karate so that he could explode and return to the calm state immediately!

The emotion during the film dictates the rhythm more than the story. Editing is an important moment because we are finally in control.

This moment is shared with the editor who is the first spectator. We are three in the cutting room.

The rhythm of the story already exists, but the scene as filmed gives the real suggestions in editing, but always respecting the inner rhythm.

The screening of rushes is a crucial moment. We are never again virgin spectators. Choices made at this moment are vital because they are instinctive in face of that first experience of the material.

After thirty-three years there is a risk of too much mutual understanding, a risk that we can assume what the other is thinking and not challenge each other and the film enough. Roberto is there to keep us on our toes. He will hide things from us that we can rediscover.

Back then "*Padre Padrone*"[2] was a provocation. It has been difficult to sustain that quality but the new film, which is extremely long feels like we have found our old fluency.

The Taviani Brothers during the shoot of '*Kaos*' (Courtesy of Filmtre, Italy)

Roberto has a natural feeling for musicality, which allows us to connect with him because we conceive musically. It was André Delvaux[3] who when admiring one of our films mentioned a feeling of Stravinsky. Since then we have called Roberto "The Stravinsky of the Moviola".

For us music is a big father of cinema. Our new film has a quartet structure, but the editing must support the musical form.

Roberto is finally "the third way".'

Notes

1. **Paisa** – Roberto Rossellini, 1946.
2. **Padre Padrone** – Taviannis, 1977.
3. **André Delvaux** (1926–2002) – Superb Belgian director, for instance; '*The man who had his hair cut short*' (1965), '*Femme entre chien et loup*' (1979). A passionate cineaste, admired by his fellow filmmakers.

10 Roberto Perpignani

The main conversation with Roberto took place over three days in June 2001. His career started through serendipity with Orson Welles, he matured as an editor with Bernardo Bertolucci and has cut for the Taviani Brothers for many years. We talked in his apartment in Rome where he lives with his wife Annalisa and their twin daughters.

I can't say how important the figure of my father was because he died when I was very little – I was five years old, but I remember perfectly that the house was full of photo machines, because he was a photographer. I realised after where my passion for images and photography came from.

My father had been Director of the Photographic Office of the Ministry of Public Education and it was he who took a large proportion of the photos of art in Italy so I grew up with the images of classical and ancient art.

When I was born he was sixty years old and he was waiting until the end of the war to restart the work, because all the art works were covered and stored during the fighting.

I have this precise memory of the photographic apparatus. He was doing his own processing and the darkroom was the kitchen (laughs). The tripods were enormous, how big I cannot say because I was very little and they were taller than me. Now my son is studying photography.

There is a Greek Venus – '*Callipigia*' – literally the Venus with a 'great arse', (laughs) and somewhere I have a photograph of it by my father. I think I started with my sexual imagination on the Greek proportions![1]

My mother I can say was a very nice person and very noble, but she always did simple work. Her mother was an 'Ironer', and she started when she was ten years old, taking the things that had been ironed to the customer. She ran a dry cleaners in Milano and then she went to South Africa, following a lyric theatre company as a wardrobe assistant.

She remained there six years and when she came back she met my father who was twenty-five years older than her. They were happy until he died. My father said – I was drawing all the time – 'this boy is going to become an artist'. When he died my mother thought that she had to realise this idea, but when I had to go to high school she said I have no money to buy books and I decided to go to night school, and I went for four years to study painting. It's very nice because they gave me the diploma *even* though the course was officially five years.

During the day I was working. I learned to do many things. At first I was attracted to working with children who had problems. I took part in some exhibitions with my paintings and I think I could have gone on. From fourteen I was involved in politics in the Communist Party, and I conceived my role with a lot of responsibility. If I wanted to be a painter I had to offer something with my work, but I didn't know how to absorb social problems and translate them into paintings.

(Roberto showed me one of his paintings. It reminded me of the work of Käthe Kollwitz; graphic, and uncompromising.)

* * * * * * * * * * * * *

When I was twenty a friend called me, actually Mariano, the son of one of my half-sisters, about joining him to assist Orson Welles. I was studying infant psychology and painting and I used to go to the cinema club as part of cultural and social engagement. I didn't know what to do and another friend said you must be mad, but I knew nothing about cinema. It was a very strange moment.

So I went there. In fact it was a garage where Welles had put two flat bed Prevost[2] editing tables. It was at a villa by the sea at Fregene; the Villa Mori which was the family home of his wife Paola Mori. They were working on the documentaries on Spain, which he made for Italian TV.

The young Roberto Perpignani working with Orson Welles (Courtesy of Roberto Perpignani)

He loved Spain – it seems he wanted to be buried there. He delivered this work without commentary. The TV directors didn't like Welles voice speaking in Italian – 'too much accent' – so stupid, and in the end not his words either. So we delivered the work. The material was mute and we made an international sound mix – wild tracks, voices and music – but without commentary. He made about ten different documentaries, e.g. Encierro de Pamplona, Feria de Sevilla, Catholicism, Spanish Art, amongst others. He conceived it as a diary. His eye plays an important part in showing us his Spain.[3]

When I started all I had to do was to compose the reels – the film was 16mm – whilst behind me were these two cutting tables and shadows moving. I couldn't understand what was happening there. After little more than a week, Welles said to the guys to teach me to use the cutting table. I started under his gaze. It was very embarrassing. I felt useless. He was not austere; he was leaving me the time to learn. In the first moments I made a lot of mistakes but I saw he was very, very patient. Gradually he became more and more demanding.

I didn't realise, but Welles' wife, Paola Mori, was the sister of Patricia Mori who was married to another nephew of mine, older than Mariano. So Mariano went to work there because he was the brother of the husband of the sister of Welles wife! So in a certain way I had a link with this strange person coming from somewhere in America called Orson Welles.

Six months went by working on the documentaries on Spain. When we finished there he left to shoot 'The Trial'[4] in Paris and we stayed to finish the mixing, Mariano and I. At a certain moment he wanted us to rejoin him in Paris with his two cutting tables; we went as a package! (laughs). Some months later Renzo Lucidi,[5] who cut 'Mr Arkadin'[6] was asked to help with the sound editing of 'The Trial' and he recommended Fritz Müller,[7] a nephew of his, who in fact is credited on the film. I cannot say if he was a young editor or a good assistant, but for sure he had more experience than us.

For a long while we worked in the Gare d'Orsay[8] where the film was shot, which was full of dust. At that time the station had fallen into disuse on the ground floor but was still functioning below ground level. We moved from 16mm to 35mm, from documentary to fiction and from claustrophobia to agoraphobia. Also there was an official French editing team who did nothing except keep a copy as the cutting went along, the same as Mariano and I who were the unofficial team although we were actually working with Welles![9]

At that time I was due to report for Military Service. As I was in Paris my mother went on my behalf. This was a risk because it was an obligation to appear in person. It turned out okay because I was the only child of an unmarried woman, and had her maiden name since my father could not give me his name because his previous wife would not give her consent. It was a sort of miracle and if the authorities had insisted on my return from Paris my life would have been changed forever.

I can say Welles was a fascinating person even if he was rude many times and although he was unpleasant, in a lot of small ways he was surprisingly sensitive. My personal crisis – a youthful insecurity, symptomatic of immaturity – was only resolved because of the intervention of such an imposing figure as Welles.

We have to be absolutely clear: during my work with him Welles did the editing himself. I remember watching him construct, and the manipulation of the pieces – watching him under the tension of finding his expression through choices. They are saying he is baroque – it's because he is always showing us what he means.

During the editing of the documentaries about Spain I remember Welles cast a dancer/choreographer called William Chappell as Titorelli[10] in '*The Trial*'. Welles put him up at the villa to be able to instruct him for the role. One day he gave him material of Beatrice (Welles 8-year-old daughter) dancing the flamenco to cut. When Welles saw what he had done after three demanding days of work he said 'You are a genius!' and then showed him the door. Immediately he left the room and shut the door. Welles said, 'Put it all back together again'.

Welles was a tireless worker and in following him you had to ask of yourself an inconceivable endurance. Before meeting Welles I was a little lazy and after, I changed my metabolism and could not work hard enough, with a rhythm so intense and my new way of life was totally conditioned by this experience. It was physical; his presence was so imposing. After I worked with him I couldn't say what I had learned because I had no ability to see myself from the outside. Only years later did I realise that I had absorbed Welles way of thinking by noticing that when selecting material I put the signs or marks on the film in the same way as Welles![11]

Bernardo Bertolucci once said: 'Nino Baragli[12] attacks the material but Roberto has to absorb the material first. Then he gives it back to you elaborated, giving form to a feeling – instinctively, involuntarily absorbed from the material'. Now I feel I use my brain more! In Portugal, where I was cutting a film in 1978, I did an interview and the headline was 'More to Feel than to Think'.

Of course Welles used to think a lot but during the editing in many cases he was more realising the reactions to the elements important because the connections you make with the reality (of the film) are not always the result of conscious research or work. Many times you discover things and you are attracted by what you have found.

This double experience with Welles (documentary and fiction) was very significant. I am writing now about that. In the first years of cinema there was a capacity to express the character of reality, and at a certain moment they discovered that they could use the medium to tell stories, having the opportunity to use the realistic pictures of cinema. It's a magical mélange, because you have the feeling that it is something true, objective in the photographic sense, and at the same time you are telling a story in your own way. It's the specific originality of cinema.

* * * * * * * * * * * * *

When I started to work in cinema I never took a pencil to draw or a brush to paint; never more. I also stopped my political activity. I think I lost something anyway but it was a sort of revelation. So it is right to say that Orson Welles gave me the answer to my instinctive research. And so I went on, allowing the work to absorb me, literally day and night.

Also I got married to the daughter of the owner of the hotel in which I was staying in Paris (laughs). I was twenty-one and my wife was nineteen, and two years later my first daughter, Allesandra was born. In fact it is very strange to reconsider one's own life.

Politically at a certain moment I had a discussion in the party, because they were asking me to be more present and I said to them you are really boring. I am sure I can do more by myself than you inside here.

In 1968 I didn't belong to that movement, except that my work was constantly committed. At that time I didn't feel directly engaged – also because the students were not my brothers. I was closer to simpler people. There was a distance between me and those guys.[13]

I restarted my subscription to the party in 1972. Why, because when I was married the first time it was to someone who was not engaged politically. When I remarried – went to live with another woman – she was more politically engaged – it was a sort of a pose – it's very important with whom you are living and sharing things.

RC: Were you provoked by the experience with Welles into treating cinema differently?

RP: At that time cinema was essential to the social context – to express, to represent and the quality of people working in cinema was very important. I thought that each of us had to give the maximum – it was like a mission you know, and as with all missions there was the problem of leaders. Welles was a leader. I was looking for leaders because I was unsure about myself. When I met Bernardo Bertolucci, he was a leader. When I met Bellochio[14] he was a leader. I remained very comfortable in my role as a collaborator because I thought my work could contribute.

When I went to see a film I was very demanding and it was not a job. But there was something very nice; I discovered I could be happy in my role because there was a space to offer yourself. I had been fascinated by Welles as an exemplar of a fine mind and that put me in the position to be enriched by each new encounter. Italian cinema was full of activity, both commercially and culturally, and it was involving all generations. Of course I belonged to the youngest but our work was giving us the feeling of being actually very present in the social context with our ideas, our engagement, our passion.

It's very strange – I remember that when making 'The Trial' I was not sure it was the best film of Orson Welles and it's exactly what I thought after. But if you go inside the film each shot is the maximum; the camera, the point-of-view, the acting, the editing and not least representing Kafka.[15] Welles never did a film 'with the left hand'. I can say for instance that I like more 'Othello'[16], and I think 'Falstaff'[17] is so full of poetry representing the authentic dichotimies of life. I'm not a blind fan of Orson Welles in any case. I don't like 'F for Fake',[18] but I love 'The Immortal Story',[19] where he gave us a lot of very precious emotions – despite the form sometimes being intentionally provocative or abrupt.

What I absorbed from him was a lot of sweat; sitting at the cutting table – back and forth – a cigar there – never we do it tomorrow, we do it now. If we are too tired it's a pity.

At that time I fell in love with my future wife. I had to come back to the hotel in time because she was closing the door at 2 o'clock in the morning. Once I was making a relay with Mariano at 10 o'clock in the evening and Welles was coming back from the hotel where he took a shower and he was ready for it! He had a big Havana in his mouth. I didn't know how to break his strength, but I started to work. He said do that – it was done. You know, after two to three hours he was destroyed because I was too fast, it's unbelievable. I was attacking him like a boxer in the liver, in the liver, in the liver; I have to break him, and at a certain moment he said to me 'Roberto, let's go home!' I jumped and I ran to the hotel, just in time. You know I was loving him but I was also loving my wife. It was really very funny.

I was so young, so impetuous. Once I left and closed the door with the handle and he is shouting 'Roberto' and I nearly broke his hand. His hands were quite big but '*molto delicate*' not a tough hand. Sometimes you need a break and once I went to the bar and I came back with an orange. He was at the door and he said 'why did you go?' Suddenly I remembered that he was allergic to oranges. 'To get this' I said. 'Go away!', he screamed. So I had fifteen more minutes. It's something very funny.

Another time he was working with Fritz Müller. I did not have a good relationship with Fritz, he was always upstaging me. Welles said. 'Roberto, did you do that?' I said, 'No, because you didn't tell me to do that'.

'No I told you'.

'No, I can say that if you told me, I would have done it'.

'No, I told you'.

By this time Fritz had gone out into the corridor.

'Perhaps you said it to Fritz in English, and you know you have to tell me in Italian'

I stood up and he came towards me. I was pushed against the cutting table and I was blindly looking with my hand behind me to grab the joiner; I remember I was prepared to hit him in the face.

Cross fade.

The next image I remember was being back at my editing table trying to cut and ten minutes after he turned to me and said: 'Roberto, do you want coffee?' I cannot say anything more expressive.

I was preparing for the mixing. He said let's see what you have to do for the music for the sequence of K, Anthony Perkins, running away from Tintorelli's studio and there is a big group of girls running after him. We had to prepare music with pieces on two tracks. He said 'take this and put it first' and so on. At the end it was very complicated, but I had my notes and I had my marks.[20]

'Can I count on that?' 'Sure' I said. 'I'll see you at the mix' he said, and left.

I started to work, but the notes and the marks were not matching, but I understood the meaning so I did it. I went to the mixing room. I said. 'Orson, you asked me to do something but there was a technical problem' and he said, 'Okay, don't worry'.

'But I did it, do you want to hear it?'

'No'

'I did it the way you asked me, do you want to hear it?'

'No'

At twenty years old you are too demanding and unyieldingly proud.

At the end of the reel he was standing in front of the screen. It was an image from '*Citizen Kane*'. 'Roberto, put your sequence on the projector!' I went to the projection box and laced the tracks myself. I explained to the engineer, in French, I asked him to be very attentive, we cannot make any mistakes. We started. It was like magic. The engineer was a magician and we arrived at the end. I was holding my breath. Welles turned round and said 'Bravo'.

I was so moved and confused so I said in his ear 'This time I had to think'. He turned towards me as if he was a pagan god who could burn me with his eyes. Why? Because all the year before when I did something not exactly as he asked, he was saying 'why did you do that?' To justify myself I used to say 'I thought that', and he would answer every time 'You don't have to think'. And now, after a year, I found the moment for demonstrating my involvement .

RC: Did you ever have any contact after that?

RP: No, and I'm very sad for that. (long pause) You are the first person I'm telling something which provoked in me a very big '*senso di colpa*' (sense of guilt). I was working with Bernardo on '*Before the Revolution*'[21] and in the same studio there were the Italian distributors for 'Citizen Kane'. They thought it was too long! So they said to me 'Could you cut "*Citizen Kane*"?' and I said 'No!'[22]

Bernardo said to me it's better you accept, because if you don't do it someone else will. It's better this person is you. You can understand it was like cutting my father! (laughs). They said to me the film has to be ten minutes shorter and I did it.

First I put the titles on the first sequence. Every time I had to consider a cut I felt a deep sense of guilt. I reduced many 'lengths' trying to be as 'soft', as invisible as I could. I had also to readapt music, because they didn't have the 'international' track. I met this guy who was originally supposed to do the re-cut, and I said it was very difficult, and he said it was not difficult at all – for instance the first reel is redundant. He was quite prepared to remove the documentary (*News on the March*).

After a while I started to hide the fact that I had done this, but I cannot die with this sense of guilt, it's too great a weight on me.

When, at the end of our work in Paris, I said goodbye to Welles, I was so moved I shook his hand so hard I nearly broke it. I cannot forget him screaming 'Wow!' It was a few days before Christmas and I realised that I couldn't work with him anymore. Why was that – because I was getting married. I had to be free if I was going to follow him. If I had a family it was not possible. When he came back to Rome I was already an editor. I was very happy, but in front of him, not because of *Citizen Kane*, I was really embarrassed to meet him as an editor, as a son comes in front of his father. I was not able to be proud in front of him – I remained his assistant. The relationship was never resolved, but really it was a form of love.

Once in the eighties, we were waiting for Welles to arrive in Rome for a lecture at the University. I obtained a lot of tickets for the students at the Film School. I was really anxious. He didn't come. It was what I expected but I realised I was hoping for it and couldn't help myself.

I wonder about Welles and *'Heart of Darkness'*;[23] I always remember his project: I = eye. Through the eye of the protagonist he wanted to capture the eye of the spectator, saying you are Marlowe. Coming from radio he could say that. ('*War of the Worlds*'[24] was so convincing). During all his life he was playing with the dichotomy of what's true and what's false. Kane had many points of view on something. Cinema can only take you to the window and the voice – 'Rosebud'. In *'Heart of Darkness'* Marlowe saw on a map of the Congo this river that was a snake with its head in the ocean and I'm sure Welles was fascinated by the snake, because he was betrayed. He was a Titan who was destined to lose! Someday I must write about him, but first I must understand him better.

* * * * * * * * * * * * *

RC: Remembering what the Tavianis[25] said yesterday when we met them at the studios, how did you come to music?

RP: It's very strange, because I cannot say that I have a good knowledge of music, but I have always had a very big interest

in popular music – all these records are popular music (*he gestures to the shelves behind me*) – and it's a political choice,
this preference. I have an intentional interest in this form.

I met a guy at the university who founded the department
of ethnomusicology, doing research and developing an archive
with Alan Lomax.[26] Professor Carpitella was also interested in
other forms of expression, '*non-verbale*', means of communication. For instance gestures. I worked with him making visuals for videos on body language – in Napoli, in Sardinia – total
contrast – fascinating. We were just working in Sicily discovering gestures not in synch with the words in a schizophrenic
way, that is, the opposite meaning between the gestures and
the words. We also made some research at the *Palio di
Sienna*[27] studying the collective rhythm reacting in a certain
way together. So I was thinking a lot about music and you saw
I have a harmonica and I play to feel lighter. There was a time I
had it in my boots while I was used to wearing a 'poncho'.

Speaking about how the Tavianis were talking yesterday, in
fact I am afraid about the non-sense of a certain way of using
music in cinema, because there is a big risk that the images,
the main expressive structure, along with all the other elements, although it seems the opposite, becomes poorer. The
forms have to be free to give an authentic contribution. If one
is not free then there is not the originality there could be. It's a
bad habit to consider the elements determined by virtue of
some principle of hierarchy; so you can call the composer
when the film is about to be finished to make it complete. You
feel you are dressing up the film. It's not exactly what we call
music, it's a signal – like they become painters for illustration.
I don't want to be excessive but in fact there are many things
to say on this subject considering a lot of different cases.

Morricone[28] is a great musician '*in assoluto*' (in absolute
terms) even if we are used to think of him in terms of cinema
but he has all his life been involved in research, taking part in a
group called *Nuova Consonanza*. He felt all his life that, in a
certain sense, he betrayed his master who said about him that
he could become a good musician. One day a friend of mine
who was a composer of *musique concrete* and electronic
music, Vittorio Gelmetti, met Morricone and the latter started
to complain saying 'You are free, you are the one', and Vittorio,
who had not a penny said 'What are you talking about? You
have everything you want. You have a house just in front of the
Piazza Venezia. Leave me free!' Sometimes it is difficult to be

objective. It is certain that everything has a cost, as much if you are free but poor, as it is if you are a prisoner in a castle.

There is a very good mood when I meet with musicians, because we belong to the same part of the movie, and we are used to collaborating. Nicola Piovani,[29] the Taviani's composer, in a meeting, when asked about his music said, 'I write it, I direct the recording *and then* Roberto is cutting it!' (laughs). Paolo or Vittorio said yesterday, 'I don't care if it's a perfect cut as long as it is what the film needs'. I cut following an emotion and it's the same way the musicians work.

Once we were talking about rhythm and I wanted to be more precise about this, as expressive, dynamic. You link the spectator to something and he is conditioned to be moved; it's *sedure*, taking with you, seduction. So I think it is a case of talking more of expressive scansions, and if we want to signify a sense closer to the term rhythm I prefer 'cadence'. The use of music needs research. Maybe it's been done but we don't know. A school is a good place for this to happen.

RC: When the Tavianis call you the 'Stravinsky of the cutting room' they mean you are deep in musicality. We don't want to be pretentious in cinema and it's very important to understand the popular idiom.

RP: Whenever 'Stravinsky' reappears I feel bad and I consider it an embarrassing, obsessive, ironic game. I have something to tell you about the role of someone who is not cultured enough – not structured at the beginning. In other words, someone who had a complex about not having the circumstances for going to high school and for that reason he studied all his life. It's as if I was looking for '*riemplire*' (to be fulfilled) I had a lot of holes and day by day in different periods of my life I tried to understand something more. I worked to fill the empty space but not always in a rigorous way. For instance, working so hard that I hadn't time enough to read but instead concentrated on watching images. Definitely it is good to be conscious of lacking something because you don't risk being pretentious. Moreover you are always studying, looking for something – there's always a ball to run after.

When I made these videos on Greek Philosophy I applied something without knowing. I was trying to give an image in an imaginative way – in the way that the audience could interpret. I became a sort of translator – trying to transfer the concepts from the verbal to the visual language – but in a very simple way, because I myself was fascinated and curious, so I was as the spectator, a role of someone who has to discover, to understand.

The cassette I made on Céline[30] is a case in point. The text was very interesting, but the writer was unable to resolve the problem of the images. At the end of my research I had 1200 images. I used everything, from Capa[31] to Cartier-Bresson.[32] So TV showed it twice, but couldn't sell it because of the rights. I spent a whole year on it, and it was enriching and revealing.

By the way, although in my not so rich family I could not have records, I did have a mother singing operas, because she worked at the opera. It is no coincidence that I was an extra at the Opera Theatre for a whole year. You should know that at an early age I played in '*Carosello Napolitano*', '*War and Peace*', '*Casta Diva*', '*Casa Ricordi*';[33] a lot of films she made wardrobe for. Also when I was following the studies about children I went to a course about popular dance because I had to dance with the children. You had to connect with the energy, but it was before my work in cinema.

****

RC: At some point you became an editor.

RP: We came back to Rome – my wife and I and I went knocking on doors for work, but nobody knew me, and anyway Welles was too exceptional for normal cinema. So I was on the list of people not working. Once I had a call to cut '*The Bible*' for John Huston;[34] it was true! I went but there were three Italians and three Americans; it seemed ironic that they had to invite someone from the unemployed list.

I did sound on archive films about German Wars. Then I synchronised the dubbing of an English film about a policeman named Norman, working day and night with my wife who was French and didn't understand a word. For instance she pre-pared 'tupid' for stupid and I had to look on the floor; 'where did you put the "s"?!'[35] The work was nearly perfect so I did it as a second job for some years for the money whilst editing for very little money.

Then I was introduced to Bernardo and he wanted to work with someone young rather than Baragli who was a classical editor. It was through a mutual friend – the teacher of child psychology – and we met in the Piazza del Popolo.

We started to edit at the beginning of December 1963 and we arrived at Christmas with something that was not clear. I was used to Welles saying cut here! I was used to following instructions but Bernardo wanted someone creating with him. Also I understood what he was looking for because we spoke about '*À Bout de souffle*', '*Les Quatre cents coups*', '*L'Année dernière à Marienbad*', '*Hiroshima mon amour*', '*Jules et Jim*'.[36]

Bernardo said to me when he was going home for the Christmas holidays, 'You have to share – I will leave you a sequence to do in the time that I am away. When I come back we will decide whether you stay as editor or as assistant, because I *need* an editor'.

I passed all the days watching the material, without the courage to cut. On New Years Day when everything was closed I went to the studio and persuaded the guard to open up and let me in. I started to cut and the next day I showed what I had done to Bernardo. That sequence is almost exactly the same in the completed film. I had to change my skin. I had to transform myself. I received the necessary shocks to be something, as someone who is thrown in the water and is faced with learning how to swim.[37]

Very soon I met Lattuada[38] and Bolognini[39] but they belonged to another generation and I felt proud to be young. Lattuada structured his films like an architect – nothing to change, nothing to learn. Bolognini was someone I loved so much – he was another extreme – but I did not have a similar mood and storytelling style. But when I met Bellochio – at that time he had done his first film – and others I became the editor of the young Italian cinema.

Returning to Bertolucci, you must remember the difference. He was culturally well prepared. His father a poet[40] and he was used to visitors to the family home like Pasolini[41] and Moravia.[42] Bernardo himself won an award as a poet when he was 20 and made his first film at twenty-one. But we connected through our knowledge of the 'New Wave'. French cinema gave us the space for creative freedom – it exists because you give it the form – the authority to dare.

We examined the sequence from 'Before the Revolution' which was Roberto's test, which interweaves several narrative/emotional strands – landowner – painter – young woman – landscape, and is a good illustration of the freedom in the cutting.

I was lucky that I had the tape splicer[43] for this film because if I had to use cement the responsibility of the cut was intimidating. There is a sort of style – a form pre-established – a sort of convention. It works this way, not another way. At that time I had to try and consider attentively what I was doing. With a lot of insecurity, although I felt free from conditioning and not tied to conventions. Each cut had six splices. It was my own personal challenge.

We watched other sequences in 'Before the Revolution': falling off the bicycle – rhythm of the falls, music, staging, lenses, and the cuts: a sense of 'now'. Also the woman in the bedroom: restructuring of action – neither in continuity or chronological – Keeping a shot – 'piece in bin' – habit formed with Welles of hanging up pieces he loved. Bertolucci went to see Pasolini and Roberto was left with a piece in the bin saying 'use me!' When she turns off the light Roberto is undercutting the linear nature of the sequence. It was illogical but the logic of a dream – freedom to dare.

I had many times the opportunity to be free in this way – the real richness of this experience – you have to be reached by something which is waiting to be discovered – if you recognise it – like out of the corner of your eye – please open the door. This kind of choice I am not sure I could make today. I can use my experience but I am not able to discover again. . . .

At this point in our conversation there was the most amazing clap of thunder, as though all Rome was shaking!

You see we need a shock like this otherwise you risk arriving at a certain point when you say I have done that before. When you have become just a harmoniser.

RC: The reason a shot is made is not always the reason you use it and that's such an important thing to keep telling yourself.

RP: I remember Miklós Jancsó[44] used to say; 'what you haven't got you don't need', you are not forced to use everything at your disposal. It is always a question of being open minded.

I am trying to understand if we can make ourselves free of naturalism, because the storytelling is established and we know that there exist many other ways to tell a story. Not telling a story as it happens but to interpret the emotions – what you have inside – so we can really dare, if our instincts have not become impoverished we can once more attack the system. In our system of perception and thought we are totally open to play with the elements. We are living a continuous time but we are also living a vertical time – with the memory, suggestion – everything we saved as significant and it's a continuous interaction – it's something to develop.

RC: There is something valuable in the conventional language which you can use for another purpose – because there is a conventional way of representing you can subvert it. For instance the way Buñuel does in *'Phantom of the Liberty'*.[45]

RP: Perhaps you have to accept that there is a level of imagination belonging in this case to the surreal – a game between realism and surrealism – and cinema forces you to find a balance. It is very provocative to deal with surrealism or un-realism along-side cinema's natural form which tends to impose a language that supports convincing storytelling. Also there is something to be learnt from comics, which incorporate a sophisticated graphic non-linearity, where you can discover things you have missed or only perceive out of linear order.

RC: Is this European rather than Hollywood? What elements are at work? What is the value of history?

RP: I proposed to do a sort of anthology of significant moments in the History of cinema through sequences, alongside examples from every form of expression. The problem is not to allow the memory to forget and to provoke.

'Have you ever seen that?'

'Yes, Pudovkin[46] did it in 1928'.

'Oh, really!'

Or why do I feel so moved in front of a Caravaggio[47] painting?

What's important is why the people ran from the room when the train entered the station – silent, black and white – so not real. It was an emotional response.

* * * * * * * * * * * * *

With Bertolucci's *'Partner'*[48] I shared his enthusiasm, but I was per-haps not critical enough to provide a dialectic of the form. I was not inside the literariness and the references to Dostoyevsky, Lautréamont and Artaud.[49] It was a provocative film. I felt that at least I could follow his mood, his way of being creative, letting it become mine. But I think that *'The Spider's Strategem'*[50] was a very interesting and more mature film – a very rich moment in Bertolucci's development.

I was convinced there was a cultural cinema for cultured specta-tors. I shared without concern that these kinds of directors could declare that they were the elite – and I've always been against elites so I don't know how I could take part in it so spontaneously! (laughs) Perhaps it was because I wanted to be accepted in the elite world. But there is another feeling – the Nouvelle Vague gave me this feeling – it was a cinema for a selected group made by a selected group, even if, in spite of that, I really appreciated their work.

But it is also true that they constituted an aristocratic world, in the cultural sense at first, and I normally don't feel at ease in sophisticated circles. It is the richness of contradictions. In cinema, as with everything, the problem is always a question of meeting the right people to nourish your interests. Possibly without sharing the snobbery.

It came at a moment when people began to call me 'the intellectual editor'. It was not a compliment – totally not – but I was recognised as someone who did his work not in the traditional or easy way. There was a very special meaning and that was that a film edited by Roberto is not earning a penny! (laughs).

* * * * * * * * * * * *

You know in 1968 I started with the Tavianis and they changed my way of conception enough, also despite or because their cinema was intellectual too. It was not a popular cinema. Also in their films they brought to the forefront a research on the language and the form and it was really very attractive to me.

In fact I was so happy to cut the first film with them, '*Under the Sign of the Scorpion*'.[51] At the time Italian cinema was full of interesting films: Antonioni, Fellini, Visconti and the younger ones. They came just at the right moment for me. Their 'research', which I shared in, went on obstinately into the middle of the seventies. I remember that there was a poster in the early seventies which had an inscription above a flock of sheep which said: 'Retour a la normale'.

When I met Jancsó in 1975 ('*Private Vices and Public Virtues*'[52]) I got the feeling he was very young. He was perhaps 55 but he seemed younger than a lot of people I knew. The first time he came to the cutting room he said: 'let's cut like Godard!' We invented a way – he was just trying to provoke himself because his previous films had been really great but with a progressive tendency towards formalism.

When Jancsó went back to Hungary he said he would call me, but he didn't because he married his editor! Later I took my partner Annalisa to Budapest and he was very hospitable. I've been very close to him because I feel there is a link. I was his assistant in the shooting on the programme he did at that time for TV.

With the Tavianis 'arrival' I couldn't have been more happy and sat-isfied. In fact in those years I was collaborating with many interest-ing 'authors'. In 1968 the year of '*Under the Sign of the Scorpion*' I also cut '*Partner*' and '*Tropici*', a film by Gianni Amico[53] telling about poverty and dignity in Brazil. Gianni was a very rich personality – even if not world famous in the commercial sphere he was a point of reference in France as well as Brazil and not least in Italy. Gianni and Bernardo were very close since '*Before the Revolution*' and events made me part of this very authentic friendship. We have to remember that those films were not supported by big investors, but in most cases from state funds, just sufficient to make the cre-ative work possible. Many of those films were made with 16 mm film – '*The Spiders Strategem*' is one of these, and I am happy, per-haps leaving aside timidity I can use the word proud, of having been part of this reality.

I was just starting to work on '*The Conformist*'.[54] The production office rang me and said you and Bernardo are just too close as friends, we have to realise this film for Paramount. We have to be sure the editor's contribution is a critical, a dialectical contribution. We prefer to propose someone else to him. Of course this had already happened. Bernardo had already met Kim Arcali,[55] who, by the way was a very interesting person.

I was disturbed of course. I had already started to watch the mater-ial, but at the same time I had the feeling that I could not fight this choice. Also very often directors are not able to tell you straight, face to face. They are using the production – it is far easier.

I remained shocked. I passed through a very big crisis. I said I have to show I could also cut commercial films for the big market. So I cut a film called '*The Police say thank you*' ('*Execution Squad*').[56] I thought it was a fascist film! I made a good job – very pro-fessional. This film was a big success – on the top at the box office. It was totally schizophrenic for me. I cut it under the producer's gaze, but I cannot repeat here what I said when he tried to convince me!

****

At that time the Tavianis were my salvation. I needed material that was challenging. We have arrived to today, after thirty-five years, without changing. One could say now it's too late! I am sure there was a moment they could conceive it, but they never made the decision.

Firstly I respect them both. They are similar and very different at the same time and I have formed a contact between them. I learned to consider their intentions and make a balance between them. On the set they direct one shot each alternately – in the cutting room they are two directors simultaneously.

We had a lot to discover until '*Padre Padrone*',[57] through the work on '*Under the Sign of the Scorpion*', '*San Miguel*'[58] and '*Allonsanfan*'.[59] For instance quick cuts to closeup and out again. Any moment, any style, any form must cross all the film – a structural symmetry.

From moment to moment, film-to-film, our work has gone on for thirty-five years, changing from time to time, following a natural evolution, but being faithful to the main inspiration. So far I have cut fourteen films with them, and it would be an enormous task to make an exposition of this total experience. Who knows, perhaps one day, but not just talking about the professional or human experience, rather analysing the films as I do when teaching in the School.
[This unique collaboration has included such delights as: '*Night Sun*',[60] '*The Night of San Lorenzo*',[61] '*Good Morning Babylon*'[62] and '*Kaos*'[63] RC]

Regarding '*Last Tango in Paris*'[64] it was Franco Arcali's original idea. The character is far closer to him than to Bernardo. Anyway Arcali fell ill and had to go to hospital. He had already cut five reels. Bernardo called me and said I am very embarrassed to ask you. I said I would do it with pleasure. After a long time I arrived to the end, fifteen reels, so you can say I cut ten reels. I stopped my work just before the last sequence. I waited for Franco to come, and so he cut the ending and retouched the whole film of course. But he was very disturbed. He could not accept sharing the credit. Bernardo suggested 'in collaboration with Roberto Perpignani' (*which is in fact the credit on the film*) but in fact, as we know, this is an objectively enigmatic expression. I wrote a letter to Arcali in friendship saying I did not want to take his place. I never had the temptation to be competitive, whether in an acceptable or unpleasant manner.

After this I proposed to be Bernardo's assistant on *'1900'*.[65] Unfortunately the start was put back. I was attracted by the chance to learn other things. The cutting room was too constricting. So instead I did the same thing with Maselli,[66] and then was just in time to cut the Taviani's *'Allonsanfan'*.

When I was twenty-six I learnt Karate – before I was too timid – although it was a bit stupid it was not a total waste of time since afterwards I was able to be more direct. I have never convinced myself to make a film. If asked why I answer, 'I prefer to be a good editor than a bad director'. I don't need a recognised and showy role in society.

I was thinking of a film on Van Gogh, especially the illness. I asked an intelligent psychoanalyst to do analysis on me. He said no, because you are not ill. You are just interested in conceptual analysis. It was also because of my wife and daughters suffering.

This psychoanalyst encouraged me to make the Van Gogh before I was fifty, but I consider this door still to be open. It is my choice. Perhaps it is not so important in my balance. Also you have to be not in need of money for a long time to be a director. Perhaps I would like to make cultural documentaries.

I dream about an archive of images to interpret things. I am looking for a meeting point of the visual arts, because cinema risks not exploiting enough what the image has to offer. Also the cinema has this tendency to be objective – reproducing what is before the camera. Representing things in a realistic way can involve excessive simplification.

This is connected to Welles. For instance he was also a painter. I am enriched staying with him for one year. Each picture showed a potential.

The courage of Bertolucci's ideas made me aware that expressive possibilities are limitless. We were so free from the naturalistic structure it was so fulfilling. I am grateful for the opportunity. You have to be lucky that this is offered to you.

Bernardo said once 'Kim Arcali showed me what's editing'. He forgot to specify *narrative* editing. He was a writer using editing to follow the narrative – I was more visual. But even if I know I was not complete, like a fruit I was not ripe, what we did we did together. And it wasn't just a matter of pure editing it had the specificity of poetry.

He also said 'Before Arcali editing was castration' – not true, we were constructing a visual dynamic of emotions. Arcali rationalised their creative moment. Was sharing their intention not autonomous?

The relation between what the film-maker says and what the audience receives or understands – the stimulation comes from ambiguity. Or you do a show for people expecting a show.

* * * * * * * * * * * * *

Gianni Amico, who found the money for '*Before the Revolution*', after that became a director in his turn and made a documentary on Afro-Americans representing in images the music of Max Roach.[67] We cut for five days and nights without sleeping. I slept for a couple of hours on the floor on the fourth day. Gianni had a crisis with his ulcer and they took him to hospital. As he left he said 'Roberto will finish it!' We worked so hard we didn't know if we were doing it right. Afterwards we had to re-cut for five days, but without the nights. In this way I thought I was involved in culture *and* politics in Italy. I was twenty-four. After that I cut almost all his movies.

Amico was also a friend of Glauber Rocha[68] who came to Rome and I helped him cut his first feature. '*Deus e o Diabo na terra do sol*'. It was a very emotional involvement. Rocha's cinema is so excessive it risks being out of control and losing sight of the message. What comes out is a mystery in some cases!

I was also very attracted by the Portuguese Revolution and in 1976 I cut a four-hour film on the subject. There were many things in this project which were very attractive to me: the political subject and the high level of anthropological documentation. Before starting I felt it was necessary to learn the language and only after was I in a position to take on a one year commitment. It was shown in Cannes in a reduced two-hour version. I totally disagreed because it was a question of giving up the authenticity and the balance of the big fresco. Worldliness has its costs.

Making cinema is sometimes such a compromise – nothing of yourself in the work. An editor can be more conscious of the weight of this compromise than the director, because you are the audience – receiving the material from the screen. You have to be critical in an active and positive way.

I said once to Grazia Volpi,[69] who was my wife at that time, when I read the script of a film she was producing: 'Why do you do that?!'

She said: 'because we have the money'.

I said: 'It's not a reason'.

She said: 'I am a producer'.

I said: 'You are a producer and you represent the choice at the maximum level'.

There was another experience. Someone was making a film on Pasolini's life including the murder. I was not sure at all but I accepted to cut this film. I discovered that I didn't agree with the director's way. So I started to organise a stylistic bluff, a le nouvelle vague – making a lot of 'free' cuts – it was such a misunderstanding. I gave a cultural form to something which was really poor.

We ended up going to the Cannes Festival. This was the first disconcerting thing. The critics were not able to attack the film openly; they were intimidated by the style. Just one of them said it's not a good film despite being well edited. That critic is the one you see in 'Before the Revolution', Morando Morandini.[70] At last, I realised someone can recognise the bluff. After that I stopped accepting films that I can't share in and in a meeting I declared that the young directors have to look for young collaborators to establish a balanced relationship.

* * * * * * * * * * * * *

So, I fell in love with the Tavianis with 'Under the Sign of the Scorpion'; a strange film, like a wall made without cement. It was considered an ideological film, both in the theme and also in the filmic expression. From then they went on with new kinds of stories and their obstinate investigation about the specificity of the cinematographic language. Such a committed cinema gave me the reason to feel involved, and much satisfaction. And it cannot be considered a contradiction if, over the years, the authors have mitigated their provocative tones. It is easy to understand how difficult it is to stay constantly on the edge of risk, especially in so critical a system as we have in Italy. In any case, year after year, my experience with them has gone on harmoniously, which is no small thing.

For instance I worked with Nanni Moretti.[71] He was interesting but very neurotic – very possessive about the film always fiddling with the cut. The last day I couldn't shut my mouth and I let go with a less than polite comment. He was offended – it was over a fade out – cutting three or four frames of black. He said 'one more frame'. I always conceived friendship and collaboration as belonging to the same tree, and editing can be really more creative if done 'a quattro mani'.

On the other hand working with Bellochio on '*Salto nel Vuoto*' ('*A Leap in the Dark*'), with Anouk Aimée and Michel Piccoli[72] was a very interesting and rich experience. Every decision was a result of our work together. Also, in the spirit of great collaboration, I had the opportunity to work with Susan Sontag on her very personal journal on Venice,[73] as well as other good memories regarding the editing of '*Empedocles*' by Klaus Gruber.[74]

RC: What about the question of Aristotle, Greek Drama and it's relation to cinema? For instance is a protagonist necessary?

RP: The protagonist in *Scorpion* is a collective. The Taviani's questioned the point of the protagonist. In '*The Night Of San Lorenzo*' the girl is the protagonist, but she is not a normal protagonist, but the story is built on her point-of-view. The Taviani's were not in many cases looking for the traditional form – and this is very difficult – with editing it is easier to follow the tradition than it is to conceive in a different way, even if the material is showing the way.

RC: The convention of the screenplay is an inhibition. The Eastern European idea of writing a story first, giving the feeling is potentially much more open.

RP: For instance '*Private Vices and Public Virtues*' – if you read the script it is completely different from the film. Why is that? Jancso needed to 'live' the set – the moment – the emotions of discovery day by day. He bases a lot on visual emotions – the meanings. The scripts are just a base to start from.

But with '*Under the Sign of the Scorpion*' the film is just like the script – not literally but everything is indicated. You would think many things are editing decisions but they are not.

This form is strange because it seems like a recording of pieces of reality put together to give the idea of a story. You understand that there is not a protagonist because the camera is always objective. With this objectivity you can reconstruct the main stories and at the time the form was not only provocative but very rich. When I worked on that film I was not used to considering cinema in the classical way, because my experiences, all of them, had been eccentric.

Any form is just one of a plurality of forms. It is funny to remember Griffiths doing 400 films in six years. So much development of the language in so little time! It is just as much of a shock to realise that Soviet Revolutionary Cinema lasted about six years as well.

* * * * * * * * * * * * *

More recently I worked with Michael Radford on '*Il Postino*'.[75] It was a very significant experience and we became friends. Then he had the courage to ask me to cut '*Dancing at the Blue Iguana*'.[76] I'm sad to admit this film needed an editor whose mother tongue was English, and I wasn't well enough prepared for that. But as usual I feel the need to react to my own inadequacies so I am working on closing the language gap.

Taking stock of my entire career, I would like to say something about the very strange fluctuating creativity of cinema. There is always hope for a balance but there is more often a conflict because management and authority represent the main dichotomy of the system. This should not be seen as scandalous if we consider that there has always been a problem between buyers or patrons and the artist, especially when there are considerable investments involved.

Actually cinema is just as much a cultural production, albeit mass culture, as it is an economic business. This confusion has ancient roots and, using the symbolism of conflict in the Middle Ages, we should remember that emblazoned on battle shields would be two feet on the ground and a head in the clouds. However it is not always recognised that creativity, the background of culture, is one of the essential motors of growth or human development.

But – and there are many 'buts' in cinema – there is one necessary clarification regarding the status of the collaborators who are so essential in cinema which allows the directors to make 'their' films and bring up the title of 'author'. It is evident that in the case of Cinema the quality of the creative product is totally open and that the contribution of collaborators is a crucial question.

In European cinema as elsewhere, 'A film by. . .' is the winning formula and although invented for the 'authors' it works in the commercial sphere as well. In addition it became a sort of 'caste' title, whether the directors deserved it or not. Returning to Welles, an undisputed author, he was inclined to say that the system had created a sort of protection for very good collaborators which allowed the weakest of them to feel at ease. So we are the only ones responsible for recognising where quality actually lies.

By the way, I've been teaching for twenty-six years now and have spent a large part of my life believing in a relationship with young people. Certainly I consider my own young years the time in which I defined my choices and tried to develop them through a series of fortunate encounters.

Perhaps, unintentionally, I tried to stay young while on the other hand the directors were gaining in years. So I sometimes feel younger than the young directors. In any case I prefer to play the father role with my children or the role of teacher when I'm in school but absolutely not in the editing room. I realise now that dividing my time between editing and teaching has allowed me to reach my aims to the highest degree.

Notes

1. **Callipigia** – This exquisite statue can be seen in the Museo Nationale in Naples. It once stood at the centre of a pool in Nero's Domus Aurea in Rome.
2. **Prevost** – An intimidating editing machine for those used to Steenbecks or now Avids, but once predominant in Italy and other parts of Europe.
3. **Orson Welles Spanish documentaries** – Series shown as '*In the Land of Don Quixote*'. Vivid and energetic in Welles passionate style – these should be re-issued.

4. **The Trial (Le Procès)** – Starring Anthony Perkins and Romy Schneider as well as Welles himself, 1962.
5. **Renzo Lucidi** – Also cut Welles' '*Don Quixote*' in 1992.
6. **Mr Arkadin** – Welles starred and wrote the script of this thriller in 1955.
7. **Fritz Müller** – Never established as an editor he later had a career as a film producer.
8. **Gare d'Orsay** – Opened as a railway station in 1900 but closed in 1939, partly because the platforms were too short! Before it was restored and reopened as a Museum and Art Gallery in 1986 it served as a parking lot amongst other things and was therefore available as a very credible setting for Welles' film of Kafka's masterpiece.
9. **Official editing team** – For many years, and not only in France, Film Industry practices led to doubling up of crews to satisfy national agreements. The true history of credits is therefore partly hidden.
10. **William Chappell** – Born 1908, dancer and choreographer who turned to theatre direction and design. Friend and/or collaborator with Noel Coward, Frederick Ashton and Agnes de Mille.
11. **Welles** – His work ethic was legendary – he stated to André Bazin that he didn't believe in something if it didn't have 'the smell of sweat'.
12. **Nino Baragli** – Extraordinary career – the first of his 180 plus editing credits was in 1949. Notable collaborations were with Pasolini and Sergio Leone. He retired in 1996 and turned his back on cinema (see interview before this one).
13. **1968** – The year of popular revolt in Europe, especially strong and violent in Paris. Now the backdrop to Bertolucci's '*The Dreamers*'.
14. **Marco Bellochio** – Distinguished director – first gained widespread recognition with '*Fists in the Pocket*' (*I pugni in tasca*), 1965.
15. **The Trial and Kafka** – Welles film has as strong an aesthetic as any of his films – several scenes are splendid exemplars of his particular signature, especially those involving Anthony Perkins and Romy Schneider. For instance there is a three-hander tense conversation with the actors physically touching and moving around each other which is like nothing else in cinema.
16. **Othello** – Winner Palme d'or at Cannes festival, 1952.
17. **Falstaff** – (*Chimes at Midnight*), 1965. Wells stars in the Falstaff story culled from Shakespeare and historical sources.
18. **F for Fake** – 'Documentary' about fraud and fakery – Welles the magician takes conjuring to another level, 1976.
19. **The Immortal Story** – Based on an Isak Dinesen novel, 1968.
20. **Sound tracks on magnetic film** – Imagine the complexity of modern sound design being carried out physically from hastily dictated notes from a director who has no idea how unclear his instructions are.
21. **Before the Revolution** – Bernardo Bertolucci, 1964.
22. **Re-cutting Citizen Kane** – It should not be imagined that this is an unusual occurrence. When the rights in a film are sold to particular countries, or 'territories' as they are called, the distributors will often make their

own version to suit their perception of what works for the local audience and to tailor the length to maximise the number of screenings in a day.

23. **Heart of Darkness** – Welles nursed the idea of adapting Joseph Conrad's novel even before he made his first film, '*Citizen Kane*'. The central character, Kurtz fascinated Welles – a genius destroyed by inner conflicts. The novel was to become an inspiration for Francis Ford Coppola's '*Apocalypse Now*', 1979 and was given a more direct transfer to the screen by Nicolas Roeg, 1993.

24. **War of the Worlds** – In 1938 Welles masterminded a radio broadcast of H.G. Wells novel about an alien invasion of Earth, which was so effective that many listeners believed that the invasion was real.

25. **Vittorio and Paolo Taviani** – See separate item before this interview.

26. **Alan Lomax (1915–2002)** – Folk song researcher and preserver and visionary, he believed in putting sound recording at the service of 'the Folk', and singlehandedly inspired a resurgence of folk song and its history and tradition in many parts of the world.

27. **Palio di Sienna** – Traditional horse race in the main square of the Italian city competed for by riders representing a dozen local groups.

28. **Ennio Morricone** – Classmate of Sergio Leone, who first gained fame for the scores of the latter's Spaghetti Westerns.

29. **Nicola Piovani** – Distinguished composer, who apart from his collaboration with the Tavianis also worked with Fellini.

30. **Louis-Ferdinand Céline (1894–1961)** – French doctor, writer – e.g. *Journey to the End of the Night (1932)* – a prophetic vision of human suffering. A supreme pessimist, but undoubtedly an extraordinary writer, he was accused of collaborating with the Nazis in WW2 and fled from France, returning after his pardon in 1951.

31. **Robert Capa (1913–54)** – Renowned war photographer who was born in Hungary and died when he stepped on a land mine in Indochina.

32. **Henri Cartier-Bresson** – Born in 1908 in France many of his photographs are classics of what he always preferred to be labelled 'documentary' pictures. Amongst his friends have been several famous film-makers including Renoir in whose '*Partie de campagne*' he plays a passing priest who is (not surprisingly) visibly disturbed by the sight of Sylvia Bataille on a swing.

33. **Carosello Napolitano** – Starring the dancer and choreographer Leonide Massine, 1954. **War and Peace** – With Audrey Hepburn and Henry Fonda, directed by King Vidor, 1956. **Casta Diva** – A biography of Bellini, 1954. **Casa Ricordi** – A history of the music publishing company starring Mastroainni as Donizetti, 1954.

34. **The Bible** – John Huston plays God, 1966.

35. **Dubbing** – It has been a particular habit and skill of the Italians to replace dialogue in films, preferring to get good images rather than compromise to get a good recording. Playing with words or as in this case an individual letter is part and parcel of this painstaking work.

36. *À Bout de souffle*, etc. films of the French New Wave by Godard, Resnais and Truffaut.
37. **Editors Baptism** – Most editors, in this book or not, will have experienced the moment when they confront their ability to cut creatively. It can be painful and prolonged, but is never forgotten.
38. **Alberto Lattuada** – Born Milan in 1914, he was co-director on Fellini's first film '*Variety Lights*'.
39. **Mauro Bolognini** – Fond of adapting classics, e.g. '*La Dame aux Camélias*', 1990, starring Isabelle Huppert.
40. **Attilio Bertolucci** – Eminent Poet father of Bernardo born near Parma in 1911, in a rural middle class family. Studied law but switched to literature. Wrote for many years for the newspaper 'Il Giorno'.
41. **Pier Paolo Pasolini (1922–75)** – Poet, novelist and controversial filmmaker. His loose cinematic style, with a free camera and the use of non-professional actors, has many admirers. Editors share an envy of those who cut his films.
42. **Alberto Moravia** – Italian writer whose work has frequently been adapted to the screen. Key to his life and work seems to be his suffering from tuberculosis from early childhood until he was 25. Kept at home and deprived of formal education he developed a very personal perspective on the world – as reflected in '*The Conformist*'.
43. **Tape Splicer** – For those of us who started in the cutting rooms with cement joiners the tape splicer was a liberating invention, since it meant you could try a cut without having to commit to it as the film could be restored and other cuts considered. However too much indecision resulted in the film being so cut and rejoined that the material was hard to see.
44. **Miklós Jancsó** – Sprang to international recognition in 1965 with '*The Round Up*', a bleak but compelling picture of 19th century Hungarian history. Remarkable because of his style, often choreographing complex moving shots that last six or seven minutes.
45. *Phantom of the Liberty* – Luis Buñuel, 1974. A surreal narrative, which challenges our belief in rational behaviour. Superbly structured in its illogicality.
46. **Vsevolod Pudovkin (1893–1953)** – Most notable films '*Mother*', 1926 and '*The End of St. Petersburg*', 1927. Perhaps now admired more for his theoretical writing than his films, in which he followed on from Kuleshov's experiments regarding juxtaposition of images and the control of meaning.
47. **Caravaggio** – 17th century Italian painter of riveting canvases often as much informed by the clearly vivid relationship between the painter and his models as the subject material. Derek Jarman made a beautiful film about the artist in 1986.
48. *Partner*, Bernardo Bertolucci, 1968.
49. **Dostoyevsky/Lautréamont/Artaud** – In this trio the Comte de Lautréamont (1846–70) is the least familiar. He only became well known after his death,

largely for his narrative prose poem '*Les Chants de Maldoror*', a macabre story of the outrageous exploits of the main character who celebrates the principle of Evil.

50. ***The Spider's Strategem*** – Bertolucci, 1970. Based on a short story by Jorge Luis Borges.
51. ***Under the Sign of the Scorpion*** – Taviani brothers, 1969.
52. ***Private Vices and Public Virtues*** – Miklós Jancsó, 1976.
53. ***Tropici*** – Gianni Amico, 1969. He also assisted Godard.
54. ***The Conformist*** – Bertolucci, 1970, based on a Moravia book, and starring Jean-Louis Trintignant.
55. **Kim Arcali** – Editor, writer – Died 1978.
56. ***Execution Squad (La Polizia Ringrazia)*** – 1972.
57. ***Padre Padrone*** – Taviani brothers, 1977.
58. ***San Miguel (St Michael had a Rooster)*** – Tavianis, 1972.
59. ***Allonsanfan*** – Tavianis, 1973.
60. ***Night Sun*** – Tavianis, 1990.
61. ***The Night of San Lorenzo*** – Tavianis, 1982.
62. ***Good Morning Babylon*** – Tavianis, 1987. Two Italians travel to Hollywood and build the elephants for the set of Griffith's '*Intolerance*'.
63. ***Kaos*** – Tavianis, 1984, based on several short stories by the Sicilian writer Pirandello (1867–1936).
64. ***Last Tango in Paris*** – Bertolucci, 1972 with Marlon Brando and Maria Schneider.
65. ***1900*** – Bertolucci, 1976 with Robert de Niro and Gerard Depardieu.
66. **Franco Maselli** – Born 1930, still active as a director.
67. **Max Roach** – Perhaps the most influential drummer in jazz history – collaborator with many leading musicians including Dizzy Gillespie, Charlie Parker, Miles Davis and John Coltrane. A living legend who went on to teach at Amherst College.
68. **Glauber Rocha** – Brazilian director who sprang to prominence with '*Antonio das Mortes*' in 1969 which caught the spirit of the revolt of May 1968.
69. **Grazia Volpi** – Producer mainly with Tavianis since 1990.
70. **Morando Morandini** – Intelligent and perceptive theatre and cinema critic who is still active – Also screenwriter.
71. **Nanni Moretti** – Popular director who once played water polo for Italy.
72. ***Salto nel Vuoto (A Leap in the Dark)*** – Bellochio, 1980.
73. **Susan Sontag**, was a superbly intelligent and perceptive commentator on political and cultural matters including many essays on cinema, e.g. Bergman's '*Persona*'.
74. **Empedocles and Klaus Gruber** – The former was a Greek philosopher who wrote 'On Nature' in which he expounded the theory of the four elements; earth, air, fire and water. Gruber is a stage and opera director.
75. ***Il Postino (The Postman)*** – Michael Radford, 1994.
76. ***Dancing at the Blue Iguana*** – Radford, 2000.

11 Simona Paggi

One of Italy's leading editors, Simona, has worked several times with Gianni Amelio, the award-winning director of 'Lamerica' and other superb films. Simona also cut the Oscar-winning 'Life is Beautiful' for Roberto Begnini. Her passion and commitment clearly spring from her background and upbringing, which comes across very strongly in her response to my questions.

I was born in Milan. My parents are Tuscan, from Pisa. At the end of the 1950s they moved to Milan to work there. My father is Jewish. His father was a surgeon who emigrated to Venezuela in the 1930s

Simona Paggi with her world map which always adorns the wall of her edit suite (Courtesy of Simona Paggi)

to escape the racial laws in Italy, while his mother fled to Switzerland with their six children and stayed there until the end of the war.

The difficulties created by the war forced my father to abandon his studies and go to work in the textile trade. With the help of some relatives, he moved to Milan with my mother.

My mother's father died when she was five-year old, struck down by tuberculosis, which in those years was an illness with a high mortality rate. She was brought up by an aunt and uncle who she lived with until the early post-war years. She studied bookkeeping. After her marriage with my father and the birth of my sisters and myself she followed a course in design and soon afterwards started to work as a stylist and designer. She set up a small dressmakers shop, for little girls clothing in fact, often subjecting us to agonising 'costume fittings'.

My father, who had to give up his studies, would have liked to become a journalist. He loved history and politics, maybe that's why he developed a passion for shooting in eight millimetres and he still has films of my mother, of our family and of the great political demonstrations, which date back to the early 1950s. He also has a magnificent collection of comic films starring Charlie Chaplin, Stan Laurel and Oliver Hardy.

I went to an experimental high school on a full-time basis to study photography and graphics. After graduating from school, I went to film school in Milan and specialised in editing. During my early teens I studied the piano, the guitar and the flute a little, as well as doing ballet dancing and acrobatic gymnastics. What I really loved was putting on shows with my friends in the neighbourhood.

I spent my time at secondary school surrounded by political demonstrations, by strikes, in the darkness of those years that saw the emergence of terrorism in Italy. I experienced a school that was at the mercy of political demonstrations, that at the time definitely involved the students. Lessons were continuously interrupted and this made it impossible to follow a real school syllabus.

So photography became the only school subject I had that offered a safe harbour. I would try to 'stop' something through the images, to focus on the stories of individual people and the political chaos.

* * * * * * * * * * * *

With regard to literature, amongst my favourite writers have been Morante, Calvino, Pasolini, Queneau, Salinger, Kafka, Hesse, Balzac, Bulgakov, Dostoyevsky, Stevenson, Hemingway, Marquez and Amado.[1] Musically, amongst the most famous rock groups and singers, I liked the Rolling Stones, the Doors, Lou Reed, P. Smith, K. Jarrett, Joni Mitchell. In jazz, Miles Davis, Dizzie Gillespie, John Coltrane, Count Basie. As far as classical music was concerned, Mozart was one of my favourites including some of his operas (Don Giovanni and The Magic Flute). Also Handel, Prokofiev, Stravinsky, Satie, Debussy, Ravel, Poulenc and Gershwin.

I have never been much of a theatregoer, and perhaps that is why the theatre has rarely filled me with enthusiasm. I have always found it hard to find a centre of attraction. The stage always seemed so far away, the actors style inevitably 'emphatic' and their voices 'projected' because of the need to be heard by the audience, to the extent that it has never managed to involve me emotionally as much as the cinema. It has always made me feel detached and maybe, in actual fact, I missed the closeups. On the other hand I like reading theatre – Brecht, Ibsen, Schnitzler[2] and Tennessee Williams are amongst my favourites.

As my great friend and teacher, Italian Director, Gianni Amelio[3] says, being born in the 1960s, I am a child of TV. It's true, I discovered the cinema through TV, apart from the endless Chaplin films that my father would project on the wall at home. Thanks to TV I discovered the *great* cinema of De Sica, Rossellini, Fellini, Visconti, Renoir, Carné, Godard, Buñuel, Bergman, Kubrick, Hitchcock, Lubitsch, Wilder, Capra, Houston, Kazan and Sirk.

But I was what you might call an eager spectator, wanting to see new stories set in epochs that I hadn't known, who waited for Monday night to come round – the only chance to see the great cinema on TV and it was also the only occasion when my parents would let us stay up late. I was, so to speak, just a spectator.

I would never have imagined that when I grew up I would have worked in films. I had no plans about what I would do when I was older. I was interested in everything – I thought that school was very important and that everyone needed to learn, to study in order to mature, to be able to have the means to understand things, not to be overwhelmed by life, by ourselves and by other people.

Maybe I wanted to become a primary school teacher . . . when I was ten I had tried to win a place in the corps de ballet of the Teatro alla Scala in Milan. Luckily, I was sent away after a month's trial, because I was too conditioned by the previous years spent studying ballet.

During high school I thought that photography would become my profession. I used to spend hours in the dark room first at school and then in the cellar at home. I experimented with developing and printing, re-framing and overlaying. I liked photography, but I couldn't visualise myself as a professional photographer. I didn't like photography in advertising because I couldn't stand consumerism. I couldn't see myself as a professional wedding photographer. Perhaps as a way of following my father's aspirations I could have tried to become a news photographer, but I didn't have enough cheek, as they say, I would never have had the courage to snatch people's moments of intimate happiness or pain – shoving a camera in their faces.

* * * * * * * * * * * * *

Then, during my last year of high school, as part of the preparation for the school-leaving exams, we had to shoot a film as an exam test. It was a commercial for Milan to be shot in super 8mm film or on video and so I dedicated myself to this little project, writing the screenplay, shooting and eventually editing the super 8 on a 'real' Prevost editing machine. It was an almost unique model created for work in super 8 and 16mm. It was a real revelation.

In that same year an entrance exam was announced to admit 25 young people from all over Italy into a school specialised in the teaching of film direction, photography, editing and sound. The course had to be attended full-time and a grant was assigned to each student. I sat for the entrance exam and in spite of my ignorance about the subject, I was admitted and that's how my new life began.

Film school was a fundamental experience. Apart from being the place where my basic cinematographic training took place, it was above all the revelation of a microcosm that anticipated everything I would come across in my future working relationships. I realised that making a film is the result of teamwork, of close co-operation between different departments and that editing in particular, would be influenced to a certain extent by acting, by photography, by sound, by the production design, by the production and lastly without any doubt by the direction.

Film school was where I met those who would become my teachers, who would contribute to my education – and not only in professional terms: Anna Napoli[4] and Roberto Perpignani. I remember Roberto when he used to come and teach us – Eisenstein and Orson Welles were his forte. He had worked with the greatest Italian directors – he was a kind of guru for all of us – after the screenings we would go into the cutting room to analyse and examine the structure of the film through the editing.

I studied, listened, tried to understand, but it was still early days for me. The real nature of editing I would have to deal with when faced with nothing but rushes in all their stark reality. It is something I understood only a few years later. His lessons returned to my mind, clear and comprehensible, when I started to put myself to the test on my own – to edit. Roberto had an extraordinary method: he would select everything that he thought could be used from every take – he discarded very little. He would make a big rough cut repeating actions and dialogues, with different shots of every sequence from which he would eliminate and reduce until he achieved the result he wanted to present.

Anna Napoli introduced us to the technical part of editing.

After finishing film school I worked for her for a few years. I can say that Anna has a great instinctive almost visceral talent. She would attack the dailies, looking at them again and again. In the end she would mark them in pencil, and hand me giant reels to assemble and add sound to. Anna liked to edit without sound – she started her career in the years when dubbing predominated in Italy over live recording. The sound was just a guide track which had no influence on the cuts, so therefore the definition of the final cut took place after the dubbing had been completed.

But the films Anna edited belonged by that time to the era of live recording and when she passed me the reels I had to add the sound to I discovered how sound could be astonishingly creative. I would polish the actors lines, shift the pauses in the off screen dialogue, add sound effects – in other words in my own little way I enjoyed suggesting almost a final version to her. For years I worked exclusively on sound editing and even now – when I'm editing a scene – I look for the best acted parts of the dialogue, the footsteps, the pauses, which in the context of a completely edited scene, can change and enrich the pace and the emotion of the scene itself.

Gianni Amelio is the person who introduced me to the cinema. He had come to the school in Milan, above all to prepare his film *'Colpire al cuore'* (*Blow to the Heart*)[5] and all us students took part in one way or another in the preparation, doing a bit of everything to help out. We were able to follow the developments and changes of the film from the sets to the actors. For many of us it was a unique and extraordinary training.

Amelio was and is a demanding director, every small detail is fundamentally vital. He has taught me above all never to be satisfied with an idea, but to insist to the point of exhaustion, to keep asking oneself questions, trying out extreme solutions. He has taught me that one has to be ruthless, able to give up entire sequences in order to privilege the story and the emotions. I have learnt *not* to cut with the intention of speeding up the film to favour a superficial pace and perhaps losing something in terms of dramatic truth.

It is always difficult to judge oneself and one's own work, to see oneself from the outside. What we are is the continuously evolving result of a long process, in which, in addition to one's own individual experiences, what has also counted enormously are the people we have known, with whom we have exchanged ideas – in order to compare them or perhaps even to discuss them. There is no point in denying it, each of us has had some 'teachers' in the profession, or rather some personalities who have predominated over the others, who have influenced us more than the others.

Having an aesthetic sensibility is part of a person's individual talent, but not everyone has an artistic vision. By artistic vision I mean an unmistakable way of expressing oneself, the capacity to interpret, that almost psychic ability of seeing what others don't see. This is what I think an editor should be. In the exchange with the director, with the original point of view, sometimes one can find oneself so close that you are actually a part of it.

How can one possibly not be influenced by this? Especially when that point of view appeals to you, when you feel it is congenial to you too. Assisting a director in the editing of a film is a complex and delicate operation. Apart from human sensibility and professional competence, what really counts is character. If there is a reason for the editor to be there, it is in order that he may look at the film with an independent gaze, external to the director's.

Unlike the shooting process, when it is necessary to seize a moment in time and act quickly, in the editing process there is time to think things over, which implies, – precisely – being patient. Everything can be seen from the opposite point of view. The time that one has in the editing stage is on our side and works in our favour. Little by little ideas emerge, things that before were invisible now become apparent and the solutions that are attempted reveal solutions that had previously not been seen. The most exciting moment occurs when one suddenly has an intuition; for example, by moving a shot or changing a fragment of dialogue, and the meaning or the pace of an entire sequence changes completely. And that seems to be the only possible choice which you hadn't seen before.

There is no doubt that my selection in editing is guided by the acting, the timing and the facial expression of the actors. The choice in the editing and the pace of the film are determined solely by the truth of their performances. The virtuoso feats of the camera leave me cold, except when it moves in an invisible way, drawing one into the story.

* * * * * * * * * * * * * *

I don't think one can talk in terms of a European cinema. Europe is made up of many different countries divided by different languages and cultures. Consequently Europe is the combination of many cinematographies, each of which expresses themselves in their own language and their own culture and which are difficult to consider as the expression of a single continent and especially difficult, for the same reasons, to export.

There has never been in Europe the slightest form of organisation able to compete with the United States Majors, or capable of making films all in the same language for every type of audience. In the early years of silent films Italian cinematography developed a strong competitiveness with the United States, creating big epic films and giving nourishment to the American cinema.

After the Second World War the neo-realist revolution imposed expressive forms in direct antithesis with the American star system, that had instead created stars and screenplays with an industrial philosophy of entertainment. In this way the United States, strong and united by a language and with a large internal market, has also succeeded to export and to impose its cinematography all over the world.

The European cinema failing to create an industrial form that is strong and powerful has though had space to express itself in a different way. In Europe openings emerged for the growth of the so-called power of the author. It has developed local cinematographies like Dreyer in Denmark, Bergman in Sweden and Buñuel in Spain.[6] That is why I think being an editor in Europe or in the United States is profoundly different.

The American editor is inserted in a production system in which he himself is a pawn – he is first and foremost a great technician at the service of the production of the film. While in Europe the editor is like the alter ego of the director, a watchful eye, a critical eye, the armed hand of the cutting room. He has to combine a rich technical knowledge with an open mind to be at the height of a day-by-day experimentation with new things.

* * * * * * * * * * * * *

I think I'm very lucky to belong to that generation that has learned and worked with the traditional system of film. When I started to work with the new technologies, I could boast an experience and a professional background which had been essential and unique.

I edited the first Italian film assembled with the non-linear system – it was a technical experience at every kind of level. I worked day and night, helped by an assistant and by a sound editor, to fully understand the new organisation of the footage. While with film footage we were surrounded by dozens of metal boxes divided according to scenes and tracks, nowadays everything is 'hidden' in a magic box that can swallow everything up and not give you back a thing . . . A real nightmare. I wanted to understand how all the procedures worked, before deciding on the real effectiveness of the new system. After various updates it is possible to say that it is extraordinarily effective.

I do not believe that the digital system has changed the way of editing a film. A revolution has undoubtedly taken place for so-called video editors, for whom it was impossible to cut, shift images, or to insert sequences after a rough cut – they could only copy or transcribe until they obtained a final cut. In the film-editing room however this has always been done.

The great advantage of digital editing in cinema is the opportunity to devote more time to creative work. Rushes appear in a split second, you can use the same shots for different possible editing versions, you can see the whole film in sequence. Without interruptions, without blemishes, without jumps in the splices, with a very high-quality provisional sound you can try out dissolves and fades in real time.

In spite of all these possibilities, I hardly ever keep several possible cuts of the sequence – in the end one choice only is the one that counts for me and allows me to proceed with my work. I really think this speed and easy access to the footage, calls for longer periods of reflection, it requires a more detached attitude. Also the electronic image itself is unfortunately 'cold' and the telecine machine does not transmit the 'warmth' of film, to the extent that at times, it makes you regret the passing of the old flawed optical projection of the editing machine.

As long as the cinema exists there will be editors – I don't think it will ever be possible to do without an editor. Maybe it's precisely the digital era, which has introduced the apparent ease with which the film seems to assemble itself on its own, that highlights the crucial role of the editor. More than ever faced with the 'endless' editing possibilities, directors discover the importance of the relationship with the editor, with whom they exchange proposals and counterproposals. Or even perhaps, just because the editor can represent the audience, have that first innocent and critical gaze which no director should do without. That is why I think the editor will always be needed.

When I start doing the rough cut of a film during the shooting, when I work on my own without the director, I love starting early in the morning. I create a semi-darkness effect that reminds me of the cutting room and send away my unique and irreplaceable assistant to be able to see the dailies on my own and start the editing with my mind fully concentrated. The more concentrated I am, the more

I immerse myself in the footage the better I select. A small light behind the monitor helps me to avoid destroying my eyesight, which unfortunately – contrary to what used to happen with the film-editing machine – tends to tire considerably. On good days I manage to stay seated, working on the film for many hours at a stretch. I never get up from my chair.

When I don't work I have to start all over again, to go back to the normal way of living, do the shopping, go to the cinema, read and get around. Perhaps people who work in the film industry always have to make an effort to regain an everyday way of living – artistic and production demands wipe out Saturdays and Sundays, Easter and Christmas holidays, there is no more time for friends. The film determines your new way of living.

The people you see are so often linked to the film that when the film finishes, I always experience an empty feeling, as if I have lost something – a little family perhaps that for months has enveloped you in a common fate that at a certain point no longer has any purpose. The film is finished and only the public will give you something back. Maybe that's why I tend to remain close to the directors and fellow professionals I have worked with. But when things go badly . . . everyone says, well, sooner or later all films come to an end.

To be able to excel in your work, you have to have ideas. The same goes for everyone – you have to have ideas, intuitions, imagination, you need to question what you're doing all the time and sometimes even to know how to wait. You must know how to listen, how to look, never be satisfied, to take risks. And in editing, which forces you to be in a state of constant evolution, this ought to be a dogma.

Frankly, I don't know whether anyone with all these qualities exists, but there is no doubt that experience, lived with a heavy dose of curiosity for life, can help you excel in your work, see further ahead and even to explain to others when your vision is the right one.

* * * * * * * * * * * *

If I could always choose which film to cut the target of my choice would be the director. I have so often had the experience of reading weak screenplays that have subsequently become great films, transformed by great direction. Conversely I have also seen great screenplays crushed by weak direction or even worse, by the wrong actors.

I always try to read the screenplay months before the making of the film, and the first reading is never sufficient. Normally I read it again making a sort of personal outline that I need in order to high-light the story – the story of the characters, the places and the passages of time. On this outline I jot down my queries and concerns and I discuss them with the director – sometimes with the screen-writers. The screenplay is the intermediary between the idea and the making of the film, it's a temporary instrument that often changes during the shooting and is often adjusted to suit the actors and the settings. In the end editing is a writing process too, basically it's the last chance to rewrite the film.

Once I have read the screenplay, only the film counts for me, the one that emerges from the rushes. I never read my old notes, the screen-play disappears, the only thing that exists is the film. For a time I thought I would like to edit a film without knowing anything about the story, but discovering along the way what the rushes proposed and subsequently editing to see whether – without knowing any-thing at all, without any influence whatsoever – I would have assem-bled a story that made sense.

I have started working with the Avid Media Composer and for the time being it's the system I like best. I am so automatic it would be an effort to change systems. In terms of editing I'm not very inter-ested in using special video effects or graphics, they're not very important. The basic Avid model is enough for me. I have heard people talk though about Final Cut Pro,[7] which many say is cheaper and inter-relates better with external software programs in situa-tions in which Avid is less flexible.

Having to spend many hours in the same place, I like the room to be clean and above all as empty as possible. For there to be a window, even though in the end it is darkness that I am looking for. For a few years now, I have always taken with me a big geographical map of the world which is like a second window for me.

My approach to the material is identical for every film. The aim is to achieve the maximum result that the material suggests, to reach the heart of the story, the best part. In the first cut I like leaving excerpts that are still not final, I leave some exaggerated pauses, I put together a first draft without looking it over. When I've finished a scene I look at it, correct it, and continue to leave some faults in it, perhaps because I'm not entirely sure yet and I leave my options open to having another view, another idea, maybe even to completely re-cut the sequence from the beginning. Ideas have to mature – if I perfectly defined every match cut I would stop thinking.

So I leave myself time to decide, to look over it the next day even, or at the end of the editing of the film. Working alone without the director is very important, because the tests I carry out will help me later in the work I do with him to rapidly demonstrate the course I have taken alone, without his influence. Proposing to him in this way an external view. I must have had the time to find the pace of the film in the pace of the actors, of the dialogues, of the gestures and of the internal pace of the takes. I must have the time to memorise all the material, to metabolise . . .

The sound, as I always say, is seventy per cent at the service of the scene. By sound I mean dialogues, rustling creaking doors, stones, footsteps, ambiences, music, silences – the pace of the scene changes completely according to the speed or the slowness of a sound that accompanies it, whether it is a line of dialogue or a noise – not to speak of the music which as well as changing the pace of the editing interprets and gives life to (or kills) entire sequences.

During the first stage of my work, especially when I select, even before doing the rough cut, I tend to memorise all the sound I could possibly use from the various takes to be able to enrich or even replace – dialogues, background noises and sound effects in the material that is eventually cut.

It is natural that the moment I focus on the sound occurs when I am fairly close to a convincing cut. In the first stage I only work on the original live sound tracks, choosing and editing everything that is necessary to the scene even subsequently as a guideline (an almost obligatory one, since I substitute words choosing from all the takes, not only from those printed by the director) for the sound editor. I very rarely use just any archive music, I prefer to work on the edited footage only with the original sounds. In a subsequent stage I start to think about where I should use music and where to create the sound atmospheres that serve to enrich and improve.

I think I have a feeling for music that derives specifically from the understanding of how much it can influence not just the overall pace of the film, but also the emotion of whole scenes. I don't particularly like the use of 'continuous' music except in the case of some 1930s cinema, in which the music track was almost a part of the acting. I don't like finding music loops prepared in advance estimated to the exact centimetre. I like knowing that even the music, after being recorded, will experience another moment of creative development during the editing.

Unfortunately, at least in Italy, technological changes have conspired against the training of fully qualified assistants. Initially most producers looked on the new technology as a major way of economising: they stopped printing the dailies and imposed the telecine of the footage directly from the negative, putting not only the negative at risk, but also the control of the quality of the shooting that for a certain period had been assigned to the laboratory. In this way they managed to eliminate the second assistant, leaving the unfortunate first assistant to carry the entire workload. Today, after various union campaigns, the second assistant has been reinstated, even though he or she comes rarely into physical contact with the film footage, leaving enormous gaps in their personal training as a result.

The new technologies haven't changed a lot in my way of editing or in my mental approach to the way I work. In a certain sense, when I worked with film footage, the decision to cut was more determined and well thought out. While nowadays I find myself working on the first cut never defining the match cuts one hundred per cent, the image on video seems less exciting to me and maybe this makes me regret the loss of the old editing machine a little. For this reason my dream would be to edit on the big screen. Luckily there's the sound editing to make up for it – however provisional, it has nothing to do with the old magnetic with which if you got a splice wrong, every time you ran it would cause a disturbance.

My personality is always at the service of the film. My cutting style varies because every film I edit is different. I would always like my style to be recognisable by the commitment and sensibility I put into my work to reach the heart that film may have. I have always dreamed of editing a musical, but perhaps I should have been born in America in the 1950s since in Italy unfortunately there has never been any tradition in that sense. There is no genre I prefer in particular: I would always like to have the chance to test my skills on films in which my contribution can always be more creative than technical.

Notes

1. **Writers** – Most are familiar: **Elsa Morante** (1912–85) author of '*Arturo's Island*', was married to Alberto Moravia. **Jorge Amado**, eminent Brazilian writer, translated into more than forty languages.
2. **Arthur Schnitzler (1862–1931)** – Viennese novelist and dramatist his '*La Ronde*' was filmed by Max Ophuls in 1950.
3. **Gianni Amelio** – Born in Calabria in 1945. Also made '*The Cinema According to Bertolucci* "a documentary about the making of" *1900*'.
4. **Anna Napoli** – Editor since 1980.
5. ***Blow to the Heart*** – Gianni Amelio, 1982.
6. **Dreyer, Bergman and Buñuel** – An impressive trio whose 'cinematography' is very individual rather than setting a style for others.
7. **Final Cut Pro** – Becoming the system of choice for many leading editors.

12 Julia Juaniz

Julia started her career as an assistant film editor in the mid-1980s. She is now one of the most eminent editors in Spain. She has worked a number of times with Carlos Saura, including 'Tango' and 'Goya'. She also cut Victor Erice's segment 'Lifeline' in 'Ten Minutes Older, the Trumpet'.

I was born in Arellano (Navarra), a village of about one hundred inhabitants located in the north of Spain. My father was a farmer and my mother was a housewife. In my youth I was interested in cinema, photography, reading, mathematics, painting, music and athletics.

Julia Juaniz in her edit suite (Courtesy of Julia Juaniz)

I used to go to the cinema every Sunday in the village where I was born. All our family liked it. We also saw films on TV. I think that from when I was very young I was happy in the cinema. I always wanted to study cinema, but at that time there was no film school in Spain. I began studying medicine but I did not finish my studies. I went to London to study English and nearly two years later I returned to Spain to learn about or work in film. I managed to get on to a film crew as an unpaid assistant to the director and following that I worked in the same capacity in camera and editing. After that I became a cutting room assistant and some years later I became an editor.

I have learned the craft from the editors I have worked with. Seeing interesting films at various times and studying them in detail have helped me a lot. Reading books of all sorts and especially ones about film had also helped me greatly. The editor who has most influenced me is Juan San Mateo.[1] Amongst directors the strongest influences have been Victor Erice[2] and Carlos Saura.[3]

With Carlos Saura I digitise the material that is shot each day and we talk together about the shooting. At the end of the shoot comes 'all the tomorrows' of editing. The atmosphere for cutting is good and the attitude to any problems that arise is positive. He has already made many films and knows that there is a solution to everything. We always have good communication right up to the finishing of the film.

With Victor Erice on '*Ten Minutes Older*'[4] I edited after the filming. There is a storyboard, but while we are editing things change because we think of a better way. I always intend that my relationship with the director should be cordial, and one of trust, in order that the director should be able to say everything that he wishes – and in the end we always become friends.

Other than these my list of directors whose films have had a strong effect on me includes Eisenstein, Chaplin, Griffith, Renoir, Rosellini, Godard, Murnau, Bresson, John Ford, Nicholas Ray, Dreyer, Buñuel, Robert Flaherty, Orson Welles and Hitchcock.

I think my work can best be seen in '*Goya*'[5] by Carlos Saura, '*Guerreros*'[6] by Daniel Calparsoro and '*Alumbramiento*'[7] by Victor Erice. They are three very different cutting styles.

* * * * * * * * * * * * *

European cinema is more a film-maker's cinema whereas Hollywood is more a producer's cinema. Due to its type of narrative, European editing takes more risks than American editing. Although it's well done they play safe.

I don't think that digital technology should have any influence on editing. It's just a question of comfort. Technology neither makes the technician nor the artist.

I think that advertisements and music videos are mainly responsible for the changes in editing style. There are advertisements that tell a story in twenty seconds, and the spectator can assimilate the information. Something that hadn't happened before, but for a film the shots have to be seen, not just transmit a sensation. Changes in how we edit are always for the better, if not now then later. The true editor will always exist, but perhaps in the future most people will only look for someone to stick the shots together. That's the way things seem to be going.

When I am editing I need to be in an ordered and agreeable place. More and more I need peace, silence and coffee. Normally if I'm not working my life is so different. The first two weeks are great, because you always have things to do. Then I need to be editing, if not I get anxious.

I think that being intuitive and sensitive is very good for being an editor. The important thing is to have the courage to do what you think you should do. Editors are born *and* made. Luck is a great help when it comes to finding interesting films and directors with whom you can continually learn.

* * * * * * * * * * * *

I choose what film I am going to work on by the script. It must strike me as interesting. If I know the director and how they work, it's better. If I don't know the director, I try to get to know them a bit, see what they are like, how they think, to determine if I'm interested in their film, but if I really like the script I usually do the film.

On the first reading, I read the script straight through, thinking about the story, finding out what I feel. Then I read it more slowly, thinking about other details – how it's structured, what the characters are like. Let's say I learn it and from then on I work with the shooting script (the marked-up script which shows how each moment has been covered in the shooting). I prefer to work on Avid and in a room that has all the equipment you need for editing – not to have things brought to you, when you need them, from another room.

I work on the emotional aspect of the film. I am guided by my intuition, my emotions and my sense of rhythm. In each film there exists a time which is intrinsic to that film and gives it cohesion. I look at all the takes several times and I note what I feel as I watch them. I think how I will do the first assembly, and I start doing it – usually a long assembly at first with various takes of the same shot so that I can make selections by seeing them several times. When the assembly is more organised I start doing a finer cut. I work on the sequences in the order they arrive from the shoot. I am continuously revising everything.

Sound has the same importance as image to me. As I edit I think about the image and the sound. Perhaps that's because in Spain the editor used to cut both picture and sound and I got used to working like that. The use of music depends on the director I am working with. Some ask your opinion more than others. For me the music must be just another ingredient in the film, which should accompany it, but not stand out from it. Music delimits the emotional space. Atmospheres delimit the physical space.

I have learnt that however a film ends up is the way it will be seen in future years and this always gives me sleepless nights because I want it to be the best it can be. When the editing of a film has been completed, there will have been only one way it could have been done at that moment; if I see it five or ten years later, I don't necessarily know if that was right. For me editing is enough of a burden and a challenge anyway, because I want to get the best I can offer at that moment. I have to say that I am sufficiently wilful that when I don't like a particular cut that we have done, I always say so and if necessary will keep saying so (more than once).

An editor believes that you have to be modest and humble enough not to want to make your own film with the material. What is essential is to maintain the spirit of the film itself. The thing that inspires me about editing is the unpredictability of the result and its capacity to manipulate or influence human emotions. The desire

Ana Torrent the magical child in *'Spirit of the Beehive'* by Victor Erice (Courtesy of Optimum Releasing)

not to explain (predetermine) everything allows one to work from the point of view of the spectator and to resist answering all questions.

To get all this right in some films can be more complicated than in others; one suffers more and the work takes longer, but in the end you want to believe that you have done everything possible to get it right for this particular film at this particular time.

Notes

1. **Juan San Mateo** – Assistant Editor for Victor Erice on *'The Spirit of the Beehive'*, 1973, and Editor on the same directors *'The Quince Tree Sun'*, 1992.
2. **Victor Erice** – Born in 1940 he has made only a few films but each is exquisite. Apart from those mentioned in the previous note he made *'El Sur'* in 1983.

3. **Carlos Saura** – Born in 1932. First major success, '*Cría cuervos*', 1976. Also '*Carmen*', 1983 and '*Ay, Carmela!*', 1990. His narratives often incorporate dance.
4. ***Ten Minutes Older, the Trumpet* (2002)** – A fascinating collection of ten minute film by internationally renowned directors of which Erice's '*Lifeline*' is easily the most affecting and its precise montage contributes greatly to this.
5. ***Goya* (1999)** – Carlos Saura, the life of the painter Goya in Bordeaux.
6. ***Guerreros* (2002)** – Daniel Calparsoro. Story of a Spanish platoon in the Kosovo war.
7. ***Alumbramiento (Lifeline)* (2002)** – Victor Erice.

13 Takis Yannopoulos

Takis Yannopoulos has worked with most well-known Greek direct-ors during his forty-five years in the Industry, including Theodoros Angelopoulos. Like many of the individuals in this book Takis exem-plifies the total preoccupation with the work, which characterises the dedicated editor.

He was interviewed by my good friend, the distinguished film director, Eleni Alexandrakis.

I was born in Athens in November 1940. My family was very poor – my father had a small shop at the wholesale vegetable market. My mother was not working – she brought up my brother, sister and myself. I finished primary school at a central Athens neighbourhood and secondary school in the suburbs. Afterwards I went to study law at the University of Athens. In the third year I had to decide whether to continue my studies or find a job, and because we needed the money I left the university. I turned to the cinema thanks to my mother's brother, who was a successful film director.

As a child I couldn't have any pastimes apart from playing with other children in the street. School was the only outlet; ancient Greek mythology and Homer's epics were taught very thoroughly at the time, and for us they were like fairy tales. Our financial situation did not allow trips abroad, neither could I afford to attend expensive shows. However I went to the cinema as often as I could – some-times even twice a day. I really loved cinema.

I started working in the cinema in the summer of 1958, as soon as I finished secondary school at the age of eighteen. As I said, my mother's brother was behind it all. He was a producer and film direc-tor named Andreas Lambrinos.[1] In those days most films were shot 'silent' and the crews consisted of seven or eight technicians who did everything. I served as assistant director, continuity, best boy, runner, boom-man, if needed, and whatever else was necessary for the shooting. I'd buy lunch, or paints or whatever was needed for props. This is how my life in the film industry began.

From morning till afternoon I worked on location and in the evening I would go straight to the editing room as I was also the editor's assistant. My job was to put the rushes in order, and gradually, because of the dubbing that was common in those days, I learned how to synchronise image and sound. At the same time I was studying all the little details that make up this magic invention of the twenty-four frames a second.

✳ ✳ ✳ ✳ ✳ ✳ ✳ ✳ ✳ ✳ ✳ ✳ ✳

Those were my first experiences with cinema. Two years later in 1960 I met a great editor of that time. His name was Aristidis Karydis-Fouks.[2] Sadly he died four years ago. He took me at his side and I worked as his assistant for ten years. To him I owe the most important things I have learned. I believe that Karydis was a master craftsman who influenced me greatly. Of course I must also acknowledge the contribution of my uncle, Andreas Lambrinos – who however died early – and the other important editors of the time who influenced and helped me a lot. Nevertheless the person to whom I owe most is Aristidis Karydis-Fouks.

My initial experiences as a film editor came about in 1959 and 1960. My uncle urged me to start editing, just like that. He showed me the Steenbeck and made me start editing although I didn't know the first thing about it. Knowing me well all my life he insisted on my becoming an editor. I as a youngster preferred the noise of the shoot and the socialising of the crew to the lonely darkness of the editing room. Abandoning my studies, I found myself in the glamorous world of cinema, which had nothing to do with the misery of post-civil war Greece. Nevertheless, my personal attitude is that I examine very carefully everything that I have to do and test it in every possible way before I feel ready to get on with it. At first editing seemed a bit boring to me. It is the way that great love stories begin, those that determine a person's life. After the first two films I edited in 1959 and 1960, I realised that film editing is a very demanding and serious job and that spending my life doing it would be a challenge. I find exciting the process by which the rules of editing are subconsciously carried through in your daily life, your relationships, and the way you set up your own reality. As if your life is a film, only instead of working on it on the editing machine you live it through.

After those two films I stopped editing and became an assistant to Karydis for the next ten years. I believe that film-making is an art that is learned through practice and not in theory. I could say that my life as a feature film editor really started, or re-started, in 1971. The films which left a mark on me, which made me a different person – even if this may sound too strong – the films that helped me evolve as an editor were first of all my first two films. The first was called *'Tis mias drachmis ta yassemia'* (*'A Pennyworth of Jasmines'*) and the second was *'Oi yperifanoi'* (*'The Proud Ones'*), both directed by my uncle. That was my 'baptism of fire', violent and revealing as it was meant to be. After a ten-year break in 1971 I had total responsibility for editing a film produced by James Paris[3] and directed by Grigoris Grigoriou[4] called *'Oi teleftaioi tou Roupel'* (*'The Last Ones at Roupel'*).

A milestone in my career was a film directed by Pantelis Voulgaris[5] in 1979 called *'Eleftherios Venizelos'* (the name of a great Greek statesman of the first decades of the 20th century). It was a very big production, perhaps the biggest ever made in Greece, and established my reputation as an editor in Greek cinema. Apart from Voulgaris, other directors who influenced my work were Freda Liapa,[6] Michalis Cacoyannis,[7] and another director with an international profile, Nikos Koundouros.[8] Indeed all the directors I have worked with gave me something important and valuable. I wouldn't like to single out other films apart from one by Menalaos Karamagiolis[9] called *'Black-out'*. It was a very difficult job, which I remember for its particularities and the challenges it posed.

I've only cut one film for Theo Angelopoulos,[10] *'The Beekeeper'* in 1986, but it was an important experience in my life, with both positive and negative aspects. Angelopoulos is a great director, very widely known, who has a very personal way of making films. It was

'Eternity and a Day' by Theo Angelopoulos (Courtesy of Artificial Eye)

an honour for me to have worked with him. However I feel the same about all Greek directors I have worked with. It is a difficult job making films in Greece and whoever does it deserves to be praised for their endurance and perseverance.

* * * * * * * * * * * * *

It would be too much to say that editing is equal to directing but in my opinion it is the next most important job, because it is an overall re-evaluation of both the script and the directing. The editor has a decisive presence in the creation of a film. With his or her talent and experience the editor helps to give the film the right rhythm. He builds up the development of the story, which has already been set up in the script. Being aware of all intentions and having his hands in all the footage the editor can complement or re-evaluate the end product. Combining the original intentions and the fortunate or unfortunate moments that came up during the production of the film, the editor supports the intentions of the scriptwriter and the director regarding the dramaturgical development of the film. In the end he proposes a finished film, which unifies these elements and also takes into account the viewer, the ultimate judge of the film. Editing is the stage for vital decisions.

A scene in a film I cut that I remember for a special reason was a love scene in the film *'Black Out'* directed by Menalaos Karamagiolis.[11] Dramaturgically it was a violent scene, which had to render not only the nightmare of the protagonist, but also the Kafkaesque impasse of the story. I spent endless hours in the cutting room, moving the rushes back and forth until an idea occurred to me that I wouldn't be able to put into words. My hands implemented it as if of their own volition, following the thoughts that I couldn't express. It was very clear in my head what I wanted to achieve. It came from the way the two actors acted in that scene. The result was a violent cut with many rhythmic repetitions of the same movements. This I think helped to express what the director wanted to do in this particular scene to give it an autonomous and functional presence in the film. Since I believe that the particular sequencing of setups is part of the editing process this scene stays in my mind as a happy combination and an effective 'capriciousness'.

* * * * * * * * * * * * *

In my opinion the European cinema, the European director or scriptwriter gives great emphasis to people, to human relationships and everyday problems. On the contrary, Hollywood had focussed on action; most Hollywood films are based on action and sensationalism. With the development of digital effects we watch scenes we couldn't even imagine twenty years ago. Perhaps this is because profit is the principle aim of the American cinema. I don't criticise this; I know it's an industry that has to survive. In Europe where the industry is on a smaller scale, there is a scope for more freedom. In Europe a film can be made without the producer being worried whether it is going to make a lot of money.

While, as I've already said, European film-makers produce films that focus on people and their relationships, American films want to manipulate the viewers without allowing them to participate creatively. This is exactly the rhythm that one discerns in the editing of the film. That is one can say that dialectical narrative belongs to the European cinema. Fast editing, incredible action, that is cuts that come massively and successively – within seconds – only allow the viewer to appreciate the film by its rhythm; the characters disappear and emphasis is given to what will amaze the viewer rather than the substance of the story.

I believe that the demands of editing are different in an American film. When I worked as an assistant editor on both English and American films, with both English and American editors I noticed that directors usually say 'boom, boom, boom'; they give a tempo regardless of the dramaturgical requirements of the scene. The cuts have to change every sixty or eighty frames, perhaps even faster. This determines the way the director will tell the story; the way the atmosphere will work. In American productions – at least that is what I as an editor feel – rhythm is the most important aspect for the director; his concern is the harmony of the rhythm. He or she wants to make a film that rolls fast, whose rhythm is not uneven. By contrast the European director leaves silences in the film and creates plausible and realistic situations, aiming at the involvement of the audience and not at a cascading choreography of things that work only as entertainment. To the European mentality time and space are of primary importance and this attitude effects editing as well.

The silences that a European director leaves in a film allow the spectator to recognise things, which are not said or are not dramatised. However the need to have characters true to life, which give the full range of human feelings is definitely essential. Human reactions are unfortunately more complex than the one-dimensional and superficial behaviour presented in American films. In American films there is a more unified, a rather 'mass' perception of everything that concerns feelings, reactions and the psychological substance of things.

* * * * * * * * * * * * *

I have chosen this job because it offers unlimited freedom, which, however, has to be determined by strict, unwritten rules. I believe that technology helps but also exercises some influence. It may offer wonderful solutions and ways out, whilst also imposing severe restrictions. With Avid for example, so many things have to be taken into account for a cut to be made that they consume some of the creative thinking and participation in the narrative.

I believe that the ideal way of editing is to cut the picture on the Steenbeck and then fix the sound and music on Avid. If we were to talk about digital effects no one knows where all this is going to end. Two recent films, *'The Gladiator'* and *'The Lord of the Rings'* are two examples of what digital technology is capable of. I think that such technology may take away some of the magic of the cinema; it sets up characters and scenes that are not real, that are made by the computer, which, in my view, reduces instantly something of the astonishment we call cinema.

I do not believe that the Avid makes editing easier and simpler. Whenever I work on Avid I use an operator. The reason is that I don't want to be bothered with the operation of the machine I prefer to concentrate on the narrative rather than the technique. Over the years my approach transformed the practical process on the Steenbeck into part of the creative process. The automatic movements like cutting the film or stopping the Steenbeck at the right frame is like part of a choreography, necessary for me to be able to immerse completely in the specific requirements of each film. It is as if the material itself determined its own final cut, through a fundamental sense of the rhythm and the narrative process.

So the mechanical movements of the Steenbeck have served me well. The editor on the Steenbeck stops to make a mark and confirms the cut; then he takes two ends and joins them. At the same time his mind works on the specific cut. To do that on the Avid you have to press ten different buttons and press them in the right order; you have to concentrate hard because if you make a mistake, the result will be different from that intended. Computers have their own way of thinking and functioning; they remind me of a housewife obsessed with the rules, who, has a limited way of thinking and little inventiveness. Everything that creates trouble and takes attention away from editing is harmful to the film. When I cut a scene, I want to think only of that scene, so I always use an Avid operator.

* * * * * * * * * * * *

There is a classical Greek saying that 'everybody has the same chances and the future is unpredictable.' Of course, whoever said it, didn't refer to editing but to life itself. But isn't life a combination of things pursued and lived, and difficulties to overcome? Nobody knows the future. It is a fact that technological development is very fast, that invention and improvements to computers are tremendous. Let's hope that they will be used in the most creative way and that we won't abolish the most vital human assets: the breadth of the human mind, its inventiveness and ability to subvert.

Of course there is no way I would reject the Avid. I've already said that technology is indispensable. If used creatively it will definitely make the whole process of composing a film easier. I just don't think that technology should sweep everything away, and in particular it should not upset the unpredictable and amazing ability of the human mind to surprise. After all aren't all technological achievements creations of the human mind?

I can't say exactly what the future will be like. However I don't believe in artificial intelligence deprived of feeling. I don't know if there will be only hard discs and optical fibres. I believe that the editor will continue to be indispensable and that human beings will never be replaced by machinery. Improvisation and mistakes are all necessary, and can be realised only by the human mind. I believe that film editors will always be necessary, no matter what media for image or sound are to be invented. I don't think the director and editor should be the same person. In my opinion everything – be it a feature film, a documentary or even a commercial – requires what is called in Greek 'the third eye'.

At all stages film-making is based on collective work. A person more detached than the director is needed to judge the rushes objectively. Perhaps technology will reduce the editor's role as it stands today. At the moment Greek film editors who can't use the Avid are marginalised. Many directors will be satisfied using just an Avid 'operator' and this has nothing to do with proper editing, that is with synthesis. This is an example of how the role of the film editor is nowadays underestimated. This may get worse in the next two or three years, but even if this happens, when the first unavoidable excitement of digital film editing is over the needs of filming itself will re-impose the role of the creative editor.

* * * * * * * * * * * * *

Due to my genuine love for editing, this has become an essential part of my life. I feel happy at work. I am used to working many hours, as many as I can, with no limits or restrictions. I can't conceive that it is possible for anybody to edit well – something as fundamental as life itself, for it imitates life – following the timetable of a clerk. It is impossible for me to start editing knowing beforehand how long it will take, or to work at two projects at the same time. When an editor becomes involved in a scene, he is submerged and lost in its material. He enters the reality and psychology of the characters, and tries to re-create the situation in its totality. This can only be achieved if he or she spends hours in the company of the characters, as if cohabiting with them. Sometimes the characters themselves send the editor away, so that he may distance himself before coming back again, while at other times he has to sit back and wait. How then, can one finish when the eight-hour working day is over and leave a scene unfinished in the middle of the creative process?

There are perhaps some colleagues in Greece and abroad who can work like that, and I respect this. For me it is impossible to keep to such a schedule. I like to, sit in the editing room for as long as I want, maybe fifteen or twenty-four hours. My personal record is two-and-a half days of continuous work, but usually I work a fourteen-hour day. I don't have any particular rituals apart from coffee-making in the morning, during which I feel as if I am about to abandon outside life to concentrate exclusively on the editing process.

Being freelance there are times when there is no work, for say three or six months and times when one film follows another closely. When I'm not at work something really changes in my life rhythm; I feel insecure, something is missing, perhaps because my life is interwoven with what I do, and I look forward to the day I will start editing again. Being freelance I have to learn how to live my life when not editing.

I don't believe in good and bad editors. I believe in good and bad rushes. A very good editor may make a mediocre film because of the poor rushes. There are no editor – magicians; there are simply good rushes, which help in the making of good editing. For me the ideal editor is someone who loves his or her job and has a kind of love affair with it, who sees his job as if it were a lover. He should love it more than anything else, though this may be exaggerated, owing perhaps to the fact that I am not married and have no family.

The ideal editor is not someone who makes good cuts or edits a scene with great speed. The ideal or good editor is someone who gets into a scene and loves it, who composes with his heart, who gets involved passionately and actively. It is at this point that the actual sparks emerge and the creative differences of opinion with the director take place. The best editor is someone who lives the film as if it were his real life.

In my professional life of forty-five years I've worked with many directors. With some of them I've had a really good time, with others it was reasonable and with a couple of them it was awful. I think the relationship between director and editor can affect the final result in many ways. When the editor sits on his chair and cuts a scene he or she has to feel very comfortable. This can be achieved when the director who sits behind him is supportive, co-operative and easy to work with, communicative rather than over-critical. When the editor feels that the director is always critical, he starts wondering whether what he does is good or bad, and this creates a situation fraught with difficulties. When a good relationship develops this is visible in the film itself.

In the same way as there are good directors, good musicians or good writers there are also good editors. I don't believe people are born 'great' leaving apart geniuses, exceptional individuals, such as musicians who played great piano at the age of eight. We film editors ought to have a complex and creative relationship with things, to distance ourselves from our private life and environment, so that we may recognise the values of pauses, reactions and evocative rhythm. Undoubtedly the fact that editing is not only a creative process but a technical job as well, means that many things have to be taught and are learned while practising. Of course creativity, the ability to compose – because editing consists of composition and association – well this requires some talent, quite a lot of talent, but it also requires love for the task at hand, because if there is no love for the work, one cannot pay proper attention to it. In this case the editor does not develop and repeats himself. Thus it takes close attention and it takes effort.

However hard he or she may try an untalented individual who has no internal rhythm will never manage to create a film or even a scene with the right rhythm. Talent must be cultivated either by having a very good teacher mentor, sitting next to him or her, watching and learning or by going to a very good special school. Unfortunately, quality film studies are non-existent in Greece. I for one never went to film school and everything I know I learnt while working as an assistant, sitting for ten years behind Karydis' back. He was working editing a scene, while I was thinking how I would go about it if I were the editor. When the scene was finished I'd compare my thoughts to what my teacher had done. At times they were completely different, mine were entirely wrong, at other times they were almost identical. This was a great, often shocking lesson for me. I learned a lot from all those reversals and surprises.

* * * * * * * * * * * * *

Nowadays in Greece there are about 15–18 feature films shot each year and there is the risk of long periods of unemployment. Despite all that I could say I am very selective, or perhaps too fussy. I am very careful over who I am going to work with. In Greece we all know each other quite well. There are about two at most three hundred of us who have something to do with the cinema. When one knows the director one is aware of what kind of films he or she has done. Thus one can decide whether it would be best not to work with him but wait for something better to turn up. In Greece, as everywhere, there are many films of poor quality. Of course I try to avoid working on rubbish films, which I have succeeded in so far. I can't know in advance whether a film is going to be good or successful – nobody can tell that, but at least I try to work on films of decent quality, that can interest me in some way.

Having agreed to work on a film I take the script, read it two, or three times, and then leave it aside. I want to work and see the rushes without being influenced by the script because very often, at least here in Greece the rushes are very different from the script. This may be due to the problems of production or financial reasons or there may be special circumstances during the shooting. What the director shoots has often very little to do with the script. Thus the reality of the film is just the rushes and nothing else. I'll use the script when I have problems with understanding what the director wants to say with a scene. Then there is nothing to do but go back to the script, re-read the scene and the one immediately before and after it, so that I nay get the feeling of the action. I like to edit the film on the basis of the pictures and the way the actors play and not on the basis of the written word.

Every change that happens during the shooting can have a positive effect on the final result. Fortunately the rushes are live images of various situations whereas script pages are cold pieces of paper with black and white characters. In the rushes there are people who laugh and cry, who fall in love and who sometimes turn the substance of a film in a different direction. When one goes carefully through the rushes one gets the vital feeling which leads to an understanding of its specific significance and the successful editing of the scene.

When I edit a feature film I start from the beginning. I want to have the whole narrative line from the start – to have an assembly of all the shots in the right order. Then I start cutting as if I'm working on the final cut of the film. In my view editing first scene 15 and then scene 3 followed by the ending and then going back to scene 45 is pretty ineffective. In this way one can neither understand nor control the narrative and the rhythm of the film. The inner rhythm of the shots determines the final rhythm of the editing. When the director has given a slow inner rhythm to a film, in my view, it is wrong for the editor to try to speed it up. This will be disastrous, because there will be inconsistencies in individual scenes as much as in the film as a whole. In order to 'sniff', to understand, to get to know the rhythm of the film, the rhythm the director wishes to give, the editor has to work on the film from the beginning, as if he or she is to re-write the script after shooting, following of course the original. Only after half an hour of edited material can I start realising what kind of work is needed, what kind of rhythm the film should have. After the first fifteen or twenty minutes I am still searching for the director's rhythm.

Every time a cut is finished the editor has to watch it on the big screen. There is a great deal of difference between watching a film from a distance of 80cm in the editing room on an Avid, a TV monitor or a Steenbeck and seeing it on a proper screen. On the big screen it is easier to be aware of the rhythm and possible deficiencies. Monitors are like TV, not like cinema. After watching each cut I go back to it, to change and improve things, perhaps even changing its rhythm completely. Only after watching the film in one go can one feel the rhythm of it. Appreciate if it's too fast or too slow, if the plot evolves in the right way, if it has to be speeded up or slowed down. If the film needs to 'breathe' or if it needs what I call an 'American', that is a fast, cut.

* * * * * * * * * * * * *

If we assume that in theory there are three hundred rules of good editing there are also another three hundred rules that force on to disregard the first set. There has to be a certain freedom. The rules of editing come through the rushes and the scenes themselves. One should be ready to reverse the rules at any time, whenever they are inappropriate for the specific dramaturgical needs and the particular rhythm of a film. The editor may do jump cuts or put the same action twice, that is he or she should be free to exercise his or her own judgement and do things which are forbidden in theory but are nevertheless required by a particular scene.

Editing against the rules requires the right judgement and personality, and plenty of courage. This shouldn't be done to show off or as a display of power against the director and producer. It should express a fundamental need that springs from the editor's creative relationship with the film. This is because the editor offers a different point-of-view. The director may have something in mind – something which he may be taking for granted. It is the editor's responsibility to suggest two or three ways in which the scene can be cut that might work better than the director's original idea. Do you realise how vital it is for these two to co-operate and be well disposed to each other? That is why I think that this relationship resembles a game of table tennis, with both sides giving and taking all the time, until they get the finest results. Nothing is pre-determined, nothing can be taken for granted. Especially nowadays when, after a century of cinema, everything seems to have already been said and everything is being re-defined.

I believe that sound is as important as picture. I often tell my friends that the viewers, because it is they who should be our first pre-occupation, must first of all be able to hear clearly all the actors' lines. It is awful to go to a film and hear somebody in the audience wondering 'what did that actor say? I didn't hear it properly'. I say it as a joke, however complaints about the quality of sound are frequent, which means we must be very careful. I'm very interested in sound in relation to picture. I like working with it, because in Greece there are no specialist sound or music or dialogue editors, as is the case in America, England and the rest of Europe. In Greece the editor does everything on his own: He cuts the picture, creates the sound effects and atmospheres, lays the music to the picture and synchronises the foleys.[12]

Sound design doesn't exist in Greece. There are either no good enough reasons for dealing specifically with designing or creating sound or there is a shortage of money or time, and the outcome is that sound requirements for Greek films are kept to a minimum. This film, '*Black Out*', which I keep referring to because it was important to me, was the first film made in Greece which used the DTS[13] system in 1997, and it was a great experience. The subject of the film was particularly appropriate since it had warplanes, air battles and so on. Working on the sound was very interesting because we made sounds in the computer from scratch and it worked very well. I'm really proud of what we did for that film, given that it happened in a country in which sound techniques have neither a strong tradition nor trained specialists.

Music is very important, at times extremely important for a film. I believe music should be used wherever needed and be used for functional rather than decorative purposes. A film is not helped by music that is overtly forceful or at such a high level that constrains the spectator's feelings. I recently saw a film in which the music was out of context. Undoubtedly it was 'good' music, but it was the director's fault that he didn't communicate with the composer effectively and the latter came up with music that had nothing to do with the image and rhythm of the film. I've been known to experiment with various musical themes for hours at a time, overturning the relationship between music and picture, finding the right moments that hadn't been suggested for the particular music piece, but nevertheless work better than the original ones. Like everything else this needs experimenting and many rehearsals to achieve the necessary balance required by the script, the plot and the director's preferences.

I think that the film editor's personality influences his work. One's culture, sentiments, beliefs and general outlook all these affect one's work. With my cuts I manipulate and define the characters' psychology, the way each actor will say one line. Take for example a love scene, in which a young man confesses his love for a young woman. The scene can be presented through shots of just the man or just the woman, or the voice can overlap while concentrating on the reaction of the one who listens. This means that the editor uses his or her own personality, the way he or she experiences the human reactions. He may think that what is important in the particular scene is not the person who talks and edits accordingly. This has nothing to do with technique, it comes through the editor's own experiences of similar situations, his own beliefs and feelings, and the way he or she perceives the specific dramaturgical needs. It often happens that you watch a scene after a while and feel as if you have really lived through it.

I definitely prefer to cut a variety of films. I wouldn't like to limit myself to a specific genre. I'm not even sure whether there are genres in Greece. As I've already said, out of fifteen films per year an editor may have a share of one or two. So one doesn't have the luxury to choose genres and variety becomes a necessity. After all editing is a profession. Nowadays if one finishes a film one can't afford to wait for the next feature film, which might be the same genre, but has to do whatever job comes along to make a living. You can't abandon the job because it will abandon you in its turn. This means that the editor may have to work on a commercial, then go to a documentary about the Aegean sea, followed by a feature film on a totally different subject. So the variety of the films I edit is dictated by reality and the film demands in Greece, my country.

Notes

1. **Andreas Lambrinos** – director, writer, active in 1950s and 1960s.
2. **Aristidis Karydis-Fouks** – aside from his editing he has been a cinematographer, actor, set-decorator, writer and director.
3. **James Paris** – (1920–82), Producer.
4. **Grigoris Grigoriou** – born 1919, Athens, Director.
5. **Pantelis Voulgaris** – born in 1940. The film on the politician was made in 1980.
6. **Freda Liapa** – made *'The Years of the Big Heat'*, 1992.
7. **Michalis Cacoyannis** – born 1922 in Cyprus, came to prominence in 1950's with a series of films – *'Stella'*, 1955, *'Girl in Black'*, 1957, *'A Matter of*

Dignity' 1957. Work of cinematographer Walter Lassally in black and white was stunning. Greatest international success was *'Zorba the Greek',* 1964.

8. **Nikos Koundouros** – born 1926, made *'Young Aphrodites'* (1963), stunning imagery.
9. **Menalaos Karamagiolis** – director, born 1962.
10. **Theo Angelopoulos** – born 1935 in Athens, now the most prominent Greek director. ***The Beekeeper*** (1986), with Marcello Mastroainni. First major success *'The Travelling Players'* (1975) also *'Eternity and a Day'* (1998).
11. ***Black Out***, 1998, with Hanna Schygulla.
12. **Foleys** – replacement of sound effects named after a Tom Foley who invented the system.
13. **DTS** – digital sound system.

14 Peter Przygodda

I talked with Peter in his editing suite at the Bavarian Studios outside Munich. Peter worked with Wim Wenders from the latter's film school graduation film onwards. Before I could settle to the agenda he launched a scathing attack on the state of German Cinema.

PP: . . . and such a country with such a heritage of film making – doing only bullshit here – just to make more money.

RC: I think with some exceptions – its not just Germany.

PP: That's a whole European situation – I mean, but in Germany it's worse. The English Cinema, there are some people – it's not that way – in France too – you can have some hope. So many national cinemas with so many film languages – its such a richness. It will be destroyed by globalisation – everybody in Germany, students in Film School – they try to be like the Americans (shouting). But leave it to them, they're doing it perfectly, so there is a loss of identity!

I can only tell stories where I come from, what I know – that's totally missing.

I count myself as a tiny little part in a working machine.

RC: So let's go back to the beginning.

PP: I was born in Berlin on 26th October 1941 – just before the disaster of Stalingrad – that doesn't mean anything. My parents had some problems with the Nazis because of the name, Pryzgodda. We had to prove our racial purity. In East Prussia they found some people from the beginning of the 18th century. So we are German but my mother has a passport 'Eastern Baltic with a Nordic influence' – absurd!

So my parents were good Nazis or 'yes' sayers.

Father was a kind of engineer and then he went to the Reichsarbeitsdeinst – military formation – to build the autobahns. After that the war – wounded in 1942. Then after the war father and mother split-up. They divorced and I grew up with my grandparents.

I went to school and afterwards I wanted to study architecture, and then I gave up and stayed at the construction company. A lot of friends in Berlin – painters, artists – I was in that scene. I went to France – stayed there for a year. I painted and sold paintings at the Cannes Festival in the restaurants. 'Aux Bel Assise'[1] – there's one hanging there. It was 1967 and then I was a kind of cineaste, but I never had the idea of getting into the business. Until twenty-five years old I really didn't know what to do with my life, but I knew the French New Wave. I loved *'Last year in Marienbad'*[2] – the formality. In 1967 I went back to Berlin and I needed money. A friend of mine was a screenwriter. He said go to CCC Film Studios. You can earn 90 marks a week. I went there and worked the numbers. There was no machine – on the positive, on the rushes – and that was my start!

* * * * * * * * * * * * *

My first editing job was my own short film I made in 1969. It was not bad. I was an assistant at that time. It was a moment – The New Wave – the German New Wave. 'Grandfather Cinema is dead!' was the slogan, and that was the right time and the right location. I was in Munich, which was really the capital of German Cinema. Everybody knew everybody. One of the last I met was Wim Wenders.

I'd just edited three or four feature films and then he asked me, through somebody else, if I can help him with his last film at the Munich Film School. So I worked with him. Then he came out of Film School and made his first feature film *'The Goalkeepers Fear of the Penalty'*.[3] Then we became friends.

RC: What was his Film School film like?
PP: You don't know that film – *'Summer in the City'?*[4] He was learning more than me at this point. 'Oh it's so lovely, I like this shot'. 'Wim, okay that's enough, let's cut it there – it's too much – you have to think about the proportions'.

I think he was learning until the last films. Everybody needs everybody. Every film starts new. If somebody tells me he is a pro then I only can say forget it. You are learning continuously.

The young Peter Przygodda in Wim Wenders 'The *American Friend'* (Courtesy of Peter Przygodda)

If you are stopping to learn and you think you are ready, then stop totally – you are closed.

In Germany they started to have 'sound editors'. I think Germans don't like their language anymore. It's to show we are international. I was used to doing all the sound editing for ourselves and I am very proud of *'American Friend'*[5] and *'Paris Texas'*[6] in this respect. If you can't cut some bars out of music then you are not a picture editor!

RC: Were you musical when you were young?

PP: I played the banjo because we couldn't afford a piano. It was hard times. I played in a Dixieland combo. Musically I'm normal – doing the picture cut you have to love music anyway. If you are not musical I think it is very hard to cut picture. I have to work on two tracks from the beginning even to let the dialogue breathe.

The disadvantage of working on Avid is that the screen 'flatness' is deceiving. Not seeing on film is a mistake for features.

That fascination of the first years is the tension (I found it out later) to make a scene work like I haven't seen it before in a film, and that brought me to another idea; that my generation was just at the point when there was no new film. We just made it out of a deja-vu process, because every film was 'tort' at that time too. It was just to make it work like we have seen before. We are not the inventors of cinema and it fascinates me. I was trying and trying and later I worked out that I was just trying to make it work like in films I had seen before. That's a learning process how images can breathe – can tell a story – not imitation – a process of making it work in the same way, becomes deja-vu.

There's a feeling in your stomach that it works even if it is ridiculous. There's one example: in *'The Goalkeeper'* we had a problem with continuity. I said to Wim, no way, we can't cut out but it's boring. We have no way to put the two shots together. Then I had an idea. Wim – he's a good guy – he's shooting some inserts – out of his stomach – he doesn't know for what – an impulse. It was a closeup of an apple on a tree. I put that in between and it worked. It worked in that kind of deja-vu process, but with a different method, and you have to feel it.

You have to work on Avid completely linearly. For example if you think a cut is okay go back four cuts and look at the whole scene – how it's running. You can only judge it in the combination of four cuts.

My method is to first to do a rough cut according to the script but continuously real cuts, otherwise you have no idea what is working. Then fine cuts with manipulations, that is, structural changes.

* * * * * * * * * * * * *

The real crazy people are not working in the cinema anymore they are in the Internet video business. We have just opportunists. All their fantasy goes into their careers not their films. The surface is everything. It sometimes seems to me that the younger directors are older than me.

My advice to people who want to be editors is that the job of editing is to avoid cutting. You must first look and then cut as little as possible. The need of a cut belongs to the story. Go to a museum and stand in front of a painting, read into it. Now the process is making one image out of many – MTV.

Editing is about trains – toys – playing – back and forth. Study *'F for Fake'*[7] – there's everything in it. Playing makes it fun and enjoying it is essential.

I'm living partly in Brazil, which I have known since 1976 when I was on a lecture tour for the Goethe Institute. We have a house down there near Salvador. I have been married to a Brazilian for twenty-two years. My daughter has two nationalities and if there is no work in Germany or the world I am back in Brazil.

I made a documentary in 1979 – *'Born as a Diesel'* – two hours long. It was shown in the Edinburgh Festival at that time. I cut it myself – it was horrible. To fight with yourself is not the best situation. I also made a documentary on a woman taxi driver in Los Angeles.

Peter Przygodda at the Steenbeck and in front of a digital machine (Courtesy of Peter Przygodda)

'Nick's Film' (*'Lightning over Water'*[8]) – my version was too strong for Wim. Then he made his own version, which was much smoother with lots of changes and his own voice over.

RC: Yann Dedet believes that an editor has to be amoral to avoid taking an attitude to the film so that you only react to the material as it is.

PP: Completely right – you have to stay with the film to react to it. You have to change for every film. Someone is saying tell me about your special style. I am saying 'What?!' There is no style because I have to get the style that is already in the material. I have to purify it. If I had my own style I wouldn't be working anymore.

When I'm not editing, for years I have done my own visual notes. I also do photography and collages. I seldom go to the cinema, but I read – at the moment on the Renaissance. I write poems as a reaction to something. My language is a wonderful playground – it is my home.

Notes

1. **Aux Bel Assise (?)** – sadly no restaurant of this name can now be located in Cannes.
2. **Last year in Marienbad** (1961), Alain Resnais' elegant conundrum of a film, starring Delphine Seyrig.
3. **The Goalkeepers Fear of the Penalty** – Wim Wenders, 1972.
4. **Summer in the City** – Wenders, (1970). Peter worked with Wenders from this point. It is one of the most impressive collaborations between director and editor that I have ever come across. This director is very committed to European Cinema in particular. For instance he is President of the European Film Academy.
5. **American Friend** – Wenders, 1977.
6. **Paris Texas** – Wenders, 1984.
7. **F for Fake** – Orson Welles, 1976.
8. **Lightning over Water (Nick's Film)** – Wenders, 1980.

15 Juliane Lorenz

I talked to Juliane in the café of the Literatur Haus in Berlin. She was the editor for Rainer Werner Fassbinder during his highly productive last phase. Since his death she has combined running The Fassbinder Foundation with editing for a number of eminent directors including Werner Schroeter.

RC: So, to begin at the beginning – where you were born, what your parents did.

JL: I was not born into a really 'gutbürgerliche family situation'. But it would have been, if . . .! My father Wilhelm Waitzmann met my mother during his studies in Freiburg in Breisgau, a very interesting, although very catholic university city in the south-west of Germany, in the so-called Higher Black Forest. My mother, Frieda Ketterer, was an apprentice in fashion design. My mother told me I was the gift of her great love and so she treated me in my childhood like a treasure. As my parents didn't marry, I was born as Juliane Maria Ketterer. When I was two years old, my mother left her home village near Freiburg and went to Stuttgart, where she met her first husband Dieter Lorenz. He gave me his name, and as I felt he was my father, I would say that from then on there was nothing preventing me from feeling I had an ordinary family background. My stepfather and my mother had two children, so I have a seven years younger brother and a ten years younger sister.

    My stepfather was making little short films, which didn't really make money, so he was looking for a solid job to earn more. He then started to work as a projectionist and always took me to the cinemas he was working for. This is the reason I saw a lot of films from the age of five, sitting beside the projector and looking through the little viewing window into the screening room, like in *'Cinema Paradiso'*.[1] I would not say that I saw in those years highly sophisticated films – they were mostly German and American B-pictures of the 1960s, but I was taken from this time on into the experience of seeing movies. After some years in Stuttgart we moved to Wiesbaden, where my stepfather got a very good position at the FSK (Freiwillige Selbstkontrolle) a state institution which was founded after the war, and where all films shown in Germany had to pass through a commission to be approved for public screening. As I often visited my stepfather, in the castle of Wiesbaden-Biebrich where FSK, the Murnau Stiftung and other film institutions were located, and as he was now projecting for approval all the beautiful foreign films which were shown in Germany as well – films from the Nouvelle Vague and the New Italian Cinema – I learned from now on more about the art of cinema. Now I discovered film-makers: Luchino Visconti, who became my favourite alongside Renoir, Melville, Resnais and Pasolini.

I learned more from films than from any other medium. For example, when I saw *'Death in Venice'*[2] it made me to read the original novel, and then to read more books by Thomas Mann. When I was finding something in a novel, which really touched me and made me think, I looked for a film, which showed a similar story and this lead to other territories. These experiences inspired my whole early life; discovering literature, painting, music *and* cinema.

* * * * * * * * * * * * *

Then Hans-Wilhelm and Gertrud Lavies came into my life. They were friends of my family. Hans-Wilhelm Lavies was the founder of the first German Film Institute (Deutsches Filminstitut), which was also located at that time in Wiesbaden-Biebrich. He had donated his collection of early writings about silent films and film stills to the institution he founded and his wife was collecting art. When I was between the ages of ten and fifteen they took me under their wing, guided and trained me to see films, to see art, to learn and respond to these forms and to train my visual knowledge. And as I was often invited for weekends to their home near Wiesbaden, I also discovered their huge library. I was reading nearly all the books they had of Schiller, Goethe, Böll and Grass, just to mention the range in their collection. Some titles I never got to, others I really was absorbing into my brain and heart.

My mother divorced when I was fifteen, and we moved from Wiesbaden to a little spa village near Munich: Bad Wörishofen. There I had the first crisis of my life. I was no longer very good at school. The Bavarian school system was much stronger than the one I came from in Wiesbaden which belonged to the Federal District of Hessen. Suddenly I got sick, I got childhood diseases which I must have caught from my brother and sister, and I missed some months of school.

When I went back to school I quit after finishing the tenth class and went to Munich for six months to be an apprentice in a film laboratory, where I learned all about film materials, developing negatives, making rushes, negative cutting and the basic information about colour grading. I learned how a film negative gets from being exposed in the camera through processing on to the editing table. After six months I regained my self-confidence and went back to school. Now my mother started to develop herself. She was still young, forty years old, and wanted to learn something about synchronisation of foreign films and started to work as a dubbing editor.

In the next two years I finished school, while my mother was in Munich and visited us on her free weekends. This time, beginning of the 1970s, I remember as a very positive and fruitful period. It was a time of discovering the world and the experience of being totally free and self-determined and to be responsible for my family, as I cared for my brother and sister during the week. Then my mother decided we should move to Munich. I finished school and started to study political science in evening classes. Now I wanted to be really free, and not be financial supported by my mother. She suggested that I go to Bavaria Studios, and to the chief production manager and ask him if I could learn about making films and start as a director's assistant for example. At this time I was thinking of becoming a director or a scriptwriter. I wasn't that sure, to be honest, what I really wanted to be.

I ended up meeting him and he said if I want to be a director I have to go to a film school. But I thought: No, I want to learn to make films by working on them. He said: 'Well, our chief editor, needs a second assistant.' I had an interview with Margot von Schlieffen and she accepted me. At that time, Bavaria was a very interesting film production centre of Germany. They produced for example 'Fedora'[3] of Billy Wilder, and Bergman did 'The Serpent's Egg',[4] and the new German film was getting more and more known. After six months I decided I wanted to quickly become a film editor, but I couldn't get the position of a first assistant, which would have been the next step. There were long lines of second assistants waiting years until getting to be a first assistant, and to edit you needed to wait at least five or six years, maybe more. This was not my speed!

So I quit and Mrs von Schliefen was angry because I didn't dare tell her to her face. When she met the studio manager who told her I was leaving, she said: 'If you think you are ready, you will see!' (laughs) I mean, I didn't have any idea how to edit a film at that time. Sometimes I went behind the curtain, where Margot von Schliefen was sitting at her editing table, and then she asked me very quickly to leave. The curtain was closed! Sometimes I peeped again and she looked at me as if to say, 'Don't you have any work?' You see, it was very difficult to get on. So I left and worked briefly as a freelance first assistant.

* * * * * * * * * * * * *

Then my fate came and found me. I met an editor and he recommended me to the editor Ila von Hasperg.[5] She was going to edit a film Rainer backed, a film of Michael Fengler,[6] who used to be a co-producer of some early Fassbinder-films and belonged to the so-called Fassbinder group. But Ila and Michael Fengler didn't get along very well, so Ila quit after five weeks. I quit too, as I agreed with her decision, beside I was also very loyal. Then Ila said: 'By the way I'm going to do the next film of "Mary" – and I said: 'who's "Mary"? She said: 'Rainer Werner Fassbinder!'[7] I thought, Rainer Werner Fassbinder, how interesting. I had no idea about him, I had only heard people saying: 'He's crazy, he's a genius'. I'd only seen one of his films at that time: *'Ali, Fear Eats the Soul'*.[8]

The first film I was involved in was *'Chinese Roulette'*[9] and I was first assistant editor. Ila was starting to edit while the film was shot and Rainer came once to the editing room. I was very shy at that time, maybe one cannot imagine this today. And I adored and loved him from the first moment on. He was a person who came into a room, he didn't have to say anything, but he was really there. He was physically and mentally totally present. When the music score was prepared, he came again into the editing room when the recorded music was synched on to the film. He was really not often with us, I remember. Rainer was not a 'discusser' – he simply

Juliane Lorenz with Rainer Werner Fassbinder (© Rainer Werner Fassbinder Foundation, Berlin)

expressed his thoughts in a way we were able to follow. I would say that being an editor for Rainer Werner Fassbinder at that time (it was the summer of 1976, 'Chinese Roulette' was his twenty fifth film) was easy. He really created the films very precisely. Every shot was his shot – the cameraman Michael Ballhaus[10] followed his advice on the camera angles and framing, and Michael was concentrating on lightning and camera movement. I remember Rainer once said, referring to the editing: Even two frames more or less are very important for the rhythm of a scene. 'Chinese Roulette' was fully post-synchronized in the end, because they shot with a noisy Arriflex camera and I was more and more involved in the creation of the sound.

We finished editing in around six weeks, dialogue dubbing, effects and preparation for the mixing took four weeks, the film was ready by the end of August. Rainer was meanwhile preparing his next film, 'The Stationmaster's Wife',[11] a two part TV-production, produced by Bavaria Studios, after the novel 'The marriage of Mr. Bolwieser' of

Oskar-Maria Graf, a Bavarian writer who emigrated to the USA in 1938. At that time I still thought I would go back to my studies, but when Ila asked me if I was going to do the next film for Rainer, I agreed. We really were working wonderfully together, and I was getting more and more involved in the editing processes, into sound design. I loved *'Bolwieser'*, and when we finished the TV-version, at the end of November, Rainer asked me to work with him on a version from the TV-material for theatrical release. During this work I noticed how much he started to concentrate on me. He asked me about my studies, my life, my personal feelings about life, and we discussed cinema and art a lot, and about his life and feelings.

* * * * * * * * * * * * *

After we mixed the theatrical version of *'Bolwieser'*, Rainer started to prepare the shooting of *'Despair'*,[12] his first English language film, and the most expensive film at that time in Germany. Then Ila had decided to leave Germany for the USA, and Rainer was looking for a new editor. He chose Reginald Beck,[13] Joesph Losey's and Alain Resnais' editor. Rainer thought Reginald Beck would be the best editor, because he would love the main character, played by Dirk Bogarde. He thought Reginald Beck knows him as an actor very well from the films he edited with him. Rainer couldn't know at that time Reginald Beck didn't love Dirk Bogarde at all! However that was Rainer, the glorious, wonderful, sometimes also naïve person who also chose his team members from a very practical point of view. Then he asked me to be the first assistant of Reginald Beck, and a day later the production manager called me and said: 'Mr Fassbinder says you are the first assistant!' As I was getting more and more self-confident, I told Rainer that this was going to be my last assistant job. Rainer smiled and said: Mr Beck will teach us a lot.

> **RC:** Did Fassbinder admire film editors?
>
> **JL:** Rainer loved editors. He felt himself to be an editor. He used to say: 'I do my job on the set and you do yours in the editing room. You are a second director. You have to finish the film, it's your responsibility' He inflamed me with that idea and that's how I grew up.
>
>   Just to finish the story with Reginald Beck: He was a lovely person, but another generation and the way Rainer did his films was totally confusing for him. He didn't like it, he didn't

like it at all. Then I said: 'But you must know his films', and I took him to private screenings. I will never forget Mr Beck once looking at me and saying, 'You must love him, I don't think he's a great director!' (laughs).

I wasn't aware at that time about my passion and future dedication for Rainer's films, and my love and passion for him as well. I loved how we worked together, how we understood each other without talking too much. I learned from him to be well organised – like him – to be aware of the responsibilities as an editor, to be a co-creator. I was taken by his great intelligence and adored his respect for people who did their craft really well; editors, cameraman, sound engineers, costume designers and so one. During 'Despair' we learned from English sound engineers the art of original sound. At that time the qualities in this aspect were not on a high level in Germany. Dirk Bogarde, whom we loved and whom Rainer and I adored since Losey's *'The Servant'*[14] and Visconti's *'Death of Venice'* and *'The Damned'*,[15] was absolutely adorable.

RC: Why was *'Despair'* so important a film?

JL: *'Despair'* was a kind of 'step forward' in Rainers own development – he was always looking for more challenges to work with actors whom he didn't create from the very beginning. 'Despair' had a budget of around $2,000,000 which was a lot at that time and we had fifty-four shooting days, which also was a lot. I was very happy. Suddenly Rainer called me the youngest 'star editor' of Germany, and I was thinking: Well then I have to be good! When I recall the new experience of Rainer, the different way he directed, I remember mainly the way he shot: He shot more material than usual. Rainer was hoping Reginald Beck would really 'use' his material, and create something, which he couldn't even imagine would be possible. Unfortunately this kind of freedom Rainer hoped Reginald Beck would take, being creative with the material, was not the way Mr Beck was used to working I guess. Maybe Losey and Resnais were all the time in the editing room and said what they thought it should be. So, Reginald Beck's first version was about three hours. When Rainer came and saw it, he knew if he was going to show that long version it would have been thumbs down for him from the producers. At this time no commercial film in Germany was longer then two hours at the most.

RC: So would you say Reginald Beck was cutting in a different rhythm?

JL: No, he didn't create his own rhythm. When Rainer came to see this first version he said, we have to edit the film anew, and because Reginald Beck didn't want to be present for the screening of the cut, Rainer said to me after Reginald Beck had left: 'Now we really start to edit the film' My first thought was: am I allowed to do that? I'm the assistant of Mr Beck. And Rainer looked at me and said, 'but it's my film, and it's my future'.

So, in one night we re-edited the whole film. We had two editing tables – two Steenbecks. Rainer didn't talk, I didn't talk, all decisions we did in a way of silent understanding. I learned how to use material, how to propose new directions in the story-telling. After this night we had this magic connection, and we never lost it. I was very happy the following morning, an experience I never had in my life before. It's a kind of happiness, which comes from the power of creation. Mr Beck came at ten o'clock and saw the results. He was very sophisticated, gentleman, and said, 'Well, I suppose I have to go', and he left. When the producers saw our film version, they said: 'Wow! What a film.' Now they thought they had to look for another editor for Mr Fassbinder – I must add, I was just twenty-one years old – but Rainer said: 'Why? I have an editor. Juliane is going to do all my films from now on.' I thought he's just joking. That's the story of my beginning as an editor, and we finished six-and-a-half years later with our last film *'Querelle'*,[16] his forty third film, and my number 14 of the Fassbinder films.

RC: Is it possible to describe what was happening that night in terms of the mutual understanding of the way of editing?

JL: First of all you have the material, which you have in your head or not. You should know every take, every frame exactly. You should know the story. You try to rethink the story, when you feel something is not working well as you see the edited scenes on the editing table. We moved for example a scene from another part of the script to the beginning, we changed developments of scenes. Some scenes which were much longer in the first version were edited in another order, because we tried other connections of dialogue, of movement. I should show you now scene by scene what exactly happened – what was in the first Beck version and what we changed – but I remember more the results of our mutual understanding. If you are in connection with yourself – I am often deciding things in a more subconscious way, then in a so-called logical way – you do not remember creative actions very well. Rainer and I were working through these subconscious understandings permanently. And at the same time he was the 'guider', but not telling me exactly what really I should do. This was the way. I felt, he gave me strength because he trusted my courage plus this magic RWF touch and my response to this 'touch', and my talent I hope as well. All these components made it work.

Rainer was able to give you freedom and I had the luck to be the recipient of his desire to give freedom. Later sometimes I became afraid about this 'freedom' and was trembling and shaking during the editing periods and at the same time amazed, that I was doing it. Rainer never gave me the feeling that I am making mistakes and if he didn't like something, he just said: think about it again. And immediately I thought about it and knew what to do. The older I got, the more films we did together, and more confident I was.

* * * * * * * * * * * * *

Although I was a so-called 'star editor' in Germany, I noticed after Rainers death, German directors didn't really understand that I was a film editor who had the gift of creating a film. Maybe this is a very German story, or let's better say: it *was* a very German story. Thank God two years after Rainer died, in 1984, Werner Schroeter,[17] asked me to work with him, and I asked him if I can edit without him and offer him the result. He was totally open to this way and we did six films until today. It's totally different to work for Werner Schroeter, but in a way it's equal to Rainer. Werner has his own filmic language, and I am able to add something what he mostly calls: 'A new aspect has developed during the editing, and I like it'. Of course I need the opinion of the director, the 'yes' or 'no' for a direction I am following. Of course editors need the director, but I do not need an explanation of how to develop the story through editing. Werner Schroeter's films mostly do not have a concrete story-line and so I have the responsibility to create the story in a way the spectator can follow. When we first did 'The King of Roses' Werner said to me: 'No editor has ever made this proposal to me' and I said: 'Well, there is always a first time'.

RC: I wonder how significant the Reginald Beck experience is, because the English editors I have chosen to interview for the book, I have tried to choose those who have worked both with what I would call English/Hollywood films and with European films, but still most of the time I think the films that are made in England are more Hollywood than they are European.

JL: You are perfectly right.

RC: Losey is a very particular, intelligent – a real man of cinema. I wouldn't have called him your average Hollywood film-maker.

JL: No.

RC: So you would have thought that Reginald Beck could have adapted. What I don't know is the way that Losey shot. I suppose if he didn't like Fassbinder's style then he couldn't connect with it.

JL: Reginald Beck was a very sincere and a very polite person. Again: I think it is a question of generation. Also Rainer was a melodramatic, very passionate film-maker although he was an intellectual, sometimes you could say, a cool director. Maybe there was no connection to the stories Rainer was working on in his films, and to the themes Reginald Beck was interested in. I think this point of view is also important.

* * * * * * * * * * * * *

RC: So how did you adapt to working after Fassbinder died?

JL: My experiences from the time with Rainer, were still the standard I wished to work with. In Rainers time, I was involved from the very beginning that he started to prepare a film. When he wrote the script, sometimes I typed them or shared typing with his mother, I did researches in the archives, I shared discussions with Rainer and the script writers, I was really involved in all parts of the creating of his films. So, more out of this lack of fulfilment I started after Rainer died creating my own film projects. In 1983 I shot a little short film, in 1985 I was co-producer of *'The King of Roses'*[18] and I wrote documentary scripts. My last film *'Life, Love & Celluloid'*[19] was an old dream to make a film about the connections of the art of films of the early German film period, which influenced Hollywood. So I also had experiences of other disciplines of film-making.

RC: Going back to Fassbinder – did his approach evolve during the period you worked together?

JL: *'Berlin Alexanderplatz'*[20] for example: Rainer started to shoot only one take, so there were no takes to choose between any more. I edited, for example a scene, which was shot yesterday today, and presented it at the daily evening screenings.

Every evening the whole team saw the edited version of the scenes which were just shot two days before. This was a perfect production machine, going on for nine months during shooting, and after the last shooting day – we had altogether 152 shooting days – my final cut of the 15½ hours and fourteen parts were presented two weeks later. The way Rainer shot his films in the last years was to me the most acceptable way. So, this is a little bit also a reason I later tried to push directors I worked with in the way I was used to working with Rainer. Some directors were 'etouffe' (smothered) as the French say, they were trying to escape me, they didn't want to be the director I wanted to have! So, I had to learn to calm down and to say: 'Go your way, it's also a possibility. I will follow you, and make new experiences.'

Now I am very relaxed. Since 1992 I am not doing one film after the other, and when I did last year *'Deux'*[21] with Werner Schroeter, I got the feeling, I would like to start to edit a film on the new AVID-media. Oskar Roehler[22] has just offered me to do his film, on AVID, and I see this coming experience as a new challenge. I'm thankful that someone of the new New German Cinema period is asking me to do his film. The new younger directors are much more open, I have the feeling. Oskar Roehler doesn't have any problem with my proposal to edit the film without him, and then showing him a first draft. When we spoke about the way I would like to work, he said: I always wanted to make a film where I have nothing to do with the editing. I'm still a little bit afraid of the new technical experience, but I hope the fucking AVID machine doesn't fight against me!

* * * * * * * * * * * * *

RC: Are editors born or made? I personally don't think you can make an editor if it isn't in you.

JL: I think so too.

RC: You still have to be lucky – to have the opportunity. I think there are a lot of competent editors and not so many who have the opportunity to be brilliant.

JL: Rainer once said to me that there are editors who do good work and some are better. You have to find your own way and make it visible to the director and producers, that they trust you.

RC: The trust is so important that gives you the courage. At least one person has said to me that it's often the courage NOT to cut.

JL: That is an old wise sentence. Editing is sometimes also not doing a lot of cuts. Editing is to see the whole. I feel myself always like a writer, who sees a theme, who creates sentences and brings a whole story together at the end. With Werner Schroeter it's very funny. He likes to forget to give the spectator an idea of the subject, the theme of the film. So I usually start the editing by finding a scene for the beginning – for an intro- duction. And Rainer and I had this situation as well with the beginning of '*Querelle*'. I asked him: 'How does the film start?' He said: 'You're right!' And we put a scene at the beginning, which wasn't meant for the beginning, like a prologue.

I'm coming from the storyteller-idea background but I also ask, what does the film tell me, when I do documentaries. Like a film I did with Werner '*À la recherche du Soleil*' about the theatre of Arianne Mnouchkine.[23] It was a beautiful and fruitful experience, as I was searching for the story-telling line from the very beginning, during shooting. Werner offered me to be co-director, and this 'official' title is matching my co-director/co-script writer idea of an editor very much. When we did a film about the passion in opera music and singers '*Poussières d'amour*', I found myself again in this position.

* * * * * * * * * * * * *

RC: Going back to that night of '*Despair*'.
JL: Isn't it a beautiful line 'The Night of Despair'? It could be the beginning of a poem.
RC: I'm sure it could, with despair in every line!
   From that moment on do you feel you were learning your craft through his films?
JL: Yes.
RC: But were you to any extent stimulated to examine cinema itself in a different way or was it always through the films you did with Fassbinder?
JL: Not only through the films we did together. We saw films together, and his way of seeing taught me to see films from his point of view as well. But I always added my view, and we combined the results of seeing them. He also liked to have a partner with whom he could share experiences, and we learned by seeing films, but never in a way like: I am the mas- ter, and you are the student. I have to add: I didn't have too much time to see films alone as Mr Fassbinder was always making films, so there were no gaps between, but after

Rainer died I started to see films he had spoken about, and which I didn't see until then. I remember when we saw the German premiere of '*Apocalypse Now!*' or when we saw films in TV from the time we were living together, I always wanted to see them again, because I remember his opinion and my feelings when first seeing them with him. The result is: I don't know today what I learnt from him and what was my own experience. What I really can say he taught me was structuring my ideas, structuring a film story, combining the result of the ideas of myself and the film-maker's idea about his story.

* * * * * * * * * * * * *

What else can I say about my special way? I think I wouldn't be able to do a big Hollywood film. I met once Richard Marks,[24] when I was in Los Angeles, and he was so sweet and said: Oh, what an honour to meet the editor of '*Berlin Alexanderplatz*'. I was honoured, but I thought for a moment he is the 'bigger' editor, the more 'important' one, as he does films costing millions of dollars.

RC: One of the editors I've interviewed talks about a film which was a dreadful experience. He knew from the first rushes that it was going to be awful and he spent nearly eighteen months of his life on that film.

JL: I can say: All of the films I edited I stand behind them. One film I did with a very right wing German director, I would say I did it because I needed this experience – and the money! And I did it well. From a professional point of view I was very proud of the result at the end. The production and the director hired me because my name was giving the project more status. I remember the score was supposed to be by Michael Nyman[25] and he came and was clever enough not to do it, so they hired Elmer Bernstein,[26] and I was very thankful to meet him. He was very professional and I learned from him another way to use a music score. It reminded me again of Rainer who always asked us to do our profession, and referred to the idea that real artists have discipline, and do their profession with dignity.

An artist uses his craft, otherwise he loses it. Concerning this film I remember the director once said, 'Don't forget you do a big budget film and it's not the normal thing for you anymore – you don't have your Fassbinder behind you anymore'. I smiled and said: 'My dear friend, the budget for '*In a Year*

175

with Thirteen Moons'[27] was only 600,000DM, but it's a masterpiece'.

After Fassbinder's death there were directors in Germany who said to me you'll never do a film with him again, now you have to learn editing! I was sad about this kind of rudeness, but I always was very, very proud of the gift Rainer drew out of me, which obviously must have been hidden in me. I know today: The luck of having had a wonderful professional and personal experience can be short, but will fulfil your whole life.

RC: What do you think were the things in your background that made you available to be able to make that journey or if someone can't find a master what qualities do you think are valuable – aside from cinema in a way you talked about loving poetry and literature and so on – you didn't mention a lot about music.

JL: Oh, of course I have to add it.

RC: But you weren't a musician.

JL: No, I was a reader – I read, and I discovered music through the films of Rainer and later through Werner, beside my own experiences. When I saw *'Death in Venice'* of course I started to hear Mahler. Mahler from dawn to night – Mahler, Mahler, Mahler. I love very much Camille Saint-Saens, or Mendlesohn-Bartholdy, all these passionate people. Without loving and knowing something about music you can't be an editor – you have to have a musical ear.

Another basis of my education was and still is – beside reading – seeing and studying painting. I go a lot to museums. When I am standing in front of a painting or an old print, in front of Turner's early phase or of a painting of Rembrandt, or George De la Tour, or Caravaggio I am happy. I am studying again and again: How did he create shadows, light and expressions. You can transform these experiences and the inspiration your get out of it. Some painters are very simple, but Da Vinci wasn't! And I think you have to force yourself to be a great painter, or a great musician, or a great writer, or a good filmmaker or a good editor; by forcing yourself to go further on in your experiences of learning.

I have the great honour to be a friend of Susan Sontag as I know her since a long time, but never dared to talk to her directly, we just met recently in New York, and suddenly there was no 'way out', and I start now to learn from her. She adores Fassbinder films, she sees them again and again, and she knows a lot of other European films, she loves music, editors, film-makers, cameramen, painters and photographers. She writes poetry, she writes brilliant novels and essays. She knows such a lot of things and her spectrum of crafts is immensely wide. You see, this is, what I want to express: The craft of an editor is also a part of a wide spectrum. You can open more and more your spectrum, and learn more and more, and be a master in different aspects.

My only real problem is: I am sometimes too passionate and the films and their stories sometimes 'eat me up'. So I have to calm down after I finish a film, and try to do just normal things. And in these phases I rest and relax with literature, and studying paintings, I listen to music and I see new films or films again, and I go to theatre. Then I start again to create something new. This is a very healthy circle.

Notes

1. *Cinema Paradiso* – Guiseppi Tornatore, with Philippe Noiret, 1989.
2. *Death in Venice* – Luchino Visconti, with Dirk Bogarde, 1970.
3. *Fedora* **(1978)** – Billy Wilder, Viennese born director who made *'Sunset Boulevard'* in 1950.
4. **The Serpent's Egg** – Ingmar Bergman, 1977.
5. **Ila von Hasperg** – Editor, also actress.
6. **Michael Fengler** – Born 1940, writer, producer, director.
7. **Rainer Werner Fassbinder (1945–82)** – One of the main motors behind the resurgence of German cinema in the 1970s. Prolific and fascinating director of disturbing and thought provoking films.
8. *Ali, Fear Eats the Soul* – Fassbinder, 1973.
9. *Chinese Roulette* – Fassbinder, 1976.
10. **Michael Ballhaus** – Born 1935, multi-award winning cinematographer who shot many of Fassbinder's films and has established an exclusive working relationship with Martin Scorsese in recent years.
11. *The Stationmaster's Wife* (*Bolwieser*) Fassbinder, 1976.
12. *Despair* – Fassbinder, 1977.
13. **Reginald Beck** – Born 1902. Began his career as an editor in the 1940s, utting *'Henry V'* (1944) for Laurence Olivier. Became Joseph Losey's editor in the 60s and worked with him almost exclusively until the director's death.
14. *The Servant* – Losey, with Dirk Bogarde and Sarah Miles, 1963.
15. *The Damned* – Visconti, edited by Ruggero Mastroianni, 1969.
16. *Querelle* – Fassbinder, 1982.
17. **Werner Schroeter** – Born 1945, director, notably *'Malina'* (1991), with Isabelle Huppert.

18. ***The King of Roses*** (*Der Rosenkonig*), (1986), Schroeter.
19. ***Life, Love & Celluloid*** – Juliane Lorenz – a very personal tribute to the spirit of Fassbinder, 1998.
20. ***Berlin Alexanderplatz* (1979–80)** – Fassbinder's epic thirteen part series.
21. ***Deux*** – Schroeter, 2002.
22. **Oskar Roehler** – Born 1959, writer, director.
23. **Arianne Mnouchkine** – Born 1938, stage director and proponent of collaborative theatre – founded Theatre du Soleil in 1963.
24. **Richard Marks** – Born 1943, New York, editor who was one of those lucky enough to be a trainee with Dede Allen. First credit as editor was '*Little Big Man*' (1970), Arthur Penn.
25. **Michael Nyman** – Born 1944, pianist, composer, notably scores for the films of Peter Greenaway.
26. **Elmer Bernstein** – Born 1922, protégé of Aaron Copland. Prolific composer of film scores over 250 to date.
27. ***In a Year with Thirteen Moons*** – Fassbinder, 1978.

16 Sylvia Ingemarsson

The conversation with Sylvia Ingemarsson took place at her farm-house, where she lives with her husband and son, which is on the edge of a lake at Leksand, a town two-and-a-half hours by train at north of Stockholm. Sylvia has now worked with Ingmar Bergman on more than a dozen projects: TV dramas, documentaries and some of his greatest masterpieces, including 'Fanny and Alexander'.

I was born in Vase, Karlstad on 10th May 1949. My father was a road worker and my mother ran an open-air museum where we also lived for the first two years of my life. After that we moved a few times, finally settling down in Nordmark where life revolved around the mining business. Here my mother acquired responsibility for running the 'Peoples Restaurant', which for many of the miners who came from Sweden and around the world was like their home. Even weddings and funerals took place there. So me and my sister (I have an elder sister and a younger brother) had to learn early on to wait table and take part in everything. My father was absent and when I was eight years old my mother married again with my stepfather and six months later I gained a little sister.

My interests have always been horses, animals and nature – and going to the cinema. The village hall showed films on Sundays, and that's where I saw the Swedish 'Carry-on' films, all Jerry Lewis' films, '*The Glenn Miller Story*' and '*Psycho*' amongst others. I've always been good at drawing and wish I had learned about music, but there was nobody who could have led me in the right path when I was a child. I enjoyed acting and got to do that at school.

My school reports were good but after I finished lower secondary school I decided there was more to learn in life. My teachers were convinced I should continue but I didn't want to do that. My mother was very old fashioned – she was grown up when she was thirteen or fourteen and she thought that I was too. I think that she couldn't stand me in the house anymore and I wasn't interested in working in the kitchen or in the local factory.

So my mother managed, through a friend of a friend, to get me placed as a baby sitter with a family in Stockholm. 'My family', i.e. both parents worked in the film industry and it is because of them that I got involved. I moved to Stockholm when I was sixteen and by the time I was eighteen I was working as an editing assistant at Europa Film.

The more I learned the more I wanted to know about cinema, because I was competitive from a young age and so I always wanted to avoid being last or lagging behind. I did want to go to the theatre to learn to act – that was a dream but I didn't care about it after I started with film. I wasn't really at home with actors – I didn't want to be a person like that – I have never liked when people are anything else than they seem. I hate that – it's from my mother – I become insecure and uncomfortable, but I love theatre. Recently I've been on a course on how to express myself on a scene, just to find myself. It was wonderful!

I was an assistant at Europa Film for two years and I met Sidney Lumet who was recording '*The Seagull*'[1] and it was fantastic. I also worked on some other movies and a cartoon, '*Winnie the Pooh and the Blustery Day*'.[2] I woke up step by step – starting at Swedish Broadcasting. I felt for the first time a little bit off because I had no graduation from high school, but I was tough and I thought 'I will show you, I don't need your fine words and graduation – I don't care'.

At the beginning, when I was working with Sidney Lumet I was longing for the set – to be with the others where the action was. I was just sitting with my old Steenbeck, but the more I learned the more I loved it. So after a few years I had no longing for the set anymore.

I did feel insecure because nobody told me how to do it. There was a course at Swedish Television but it was more or less to be a news editor – it wasn't film editing – it wasn't enough for me. Although I felt frustrated many times I learnt from experience and by looking at other films.

* * * * * * * * * * * * *

I was working in broadcast until 1976 – I was free to do what I wanted and I had plans to go to the United States of America, but then I was employed by Bo Widerberg[3] and I decided to quit the TV job. Then Bergman's editor got sick. I knew Katinka Farago[4] who was Bergman's production controller. I knew her since I was a baby sitter. She was very glad that I had succeeded, more or less, with Bo Widerberg and the film, '*Man on the Roof*'[5] was a success. So Bergman accepted her advice and the first time I met him was at a meeting of the actors and crew – a read through for '*Autumn Sonata*'.[6]

It was a very hot day in May 1977. The only thing he said to me except for 'How are you – nice to see you' was 'Oh, are you also being affected by the heat?' I hate it when it is warm outside, because I was so er – the thing is I didn't sleep the night before – I was at a party. I didn't care – Bergman was just another man. So the day after I was sweating a lot – but I looked very nice in a white blouse. I did understand that it's very important to make a good impression.

I was employed from the first day of shooting in Norway, but he never wants to edit during the shoot. I collected the material and

Sylvia Ingemarsson cutting with Ingmar Bergman (Jacob Forssel (Photographer) Expressen, Swedish Newspaper. © PRESSENS/EMPICS)

did the synching up and put it in order. He only wanted to see the material on Saturdays, so we looked through the whole week's material then. Everything had to be in shooting order but also in script order. He would choose takes and I had to take care of all the tests on make-up, hair, costumes and lighting.

There was one occasion that he was furious at me in the screening room. We saw all the tests and there was one missing. The laboratory had put it at the end of some leaders I had ordered and it took five minutes for me to find it and give it to the projectionist. I went into the screening room again and I was smiling and he was yelling at me, 'That's nothing to laugh about – how can you stand and laugh about a thing like that?' I said I'm sorry, – but it's here and we can see it – I did my best to solve the problem. I was sitting behind him and he was yelling and barking like a dog. I repeated I'm sorry, I'm very sorry. He said, 'and you don't have anything else to do during the day than take care of this material!' His first impression of me was that I was not proper enough – not professional, but I was angry. He had no right to be so angry with me, so I disappointed him with no tears.

Sven Nykvist[7] said to me afterwards – I think you handled this very well, but even at the end of the day Ingmar came to me and said you will be angry at me many times – it was kind of an excuse.

At the end of the shoot we had to go back to Munich, because he was living there for six months of the year. I did understand that he was super-professional and he was expecting the same from me, so I decided that he would never have the opportunity to be angry with me again. So everything was in order and nothing could go wrong and it didn't, even though I had no assistant because he won't have anyone else in the cutting room.

He didn't stay in the cutting room all the time. He did everything basic to tell me how he wanted things to go. He didn't know exactly how to edit 'Autumn Sonata', because you know the film is based on closeups – so much talk. So we started at the beginning and the first time we went through the material we didn't use any closeups – we took all the long shots and the medium shots just to get the story in a very roughcut. Then we went back to the beginning again and edited the closeups with all the pauses behind and in front all the time – we couldn't decide where to put the overlaps at that time – and that was a very good school for me.

So we edited the film from November and then it was Christmas and we went home and we'd only just begun. I remember that Katinka Farago asked me when I went to the office in the days between Christmas and New Year's Eve, 'What have you done to Ingmar, he's so happy?' I hadn't done anything. 'He's so happy – he just loves to work with you'.

I felt relaxed although I wasn't at ease with the Germans – for the first time in life I felt like a foreigner – and I felt racism.

Ingmar was not satisfied with the film, he was angry with it, but I thought it was fantastic and I loved working on it. It's much better than the film he made immediately before, '*The Serpent's Egg*'[8] I didn't like that film at all – not after seeing '*Cabaret*'.[9] In my next life I will become a dancer with Bob Fosse[10] – I will be a dancer and a very good rider. I want to dance and do things with horses!

RC: These are both things which have very much to do with rhythm.

SI: Yes, and intuition.

RC: Yes a sensibility, but it's also a physical sensibility, isn't it?

SI: Yes it is. I just have to 'think' which way to go and the horse follows.

RC: It's not only the spirit but its also the way the body and the mind work together – and I suppose editing is trying to give that sensibility to material.

SI: Yes, and when you have been working many years together you don't have to explain, the signals are very small, you feel what your partner thinks.

RC: When you have the opportunity of course – sometimes you know you can't make it work.

SI: Mm that's terrible – because it's so easy to think maybe if I was a much more skilled editor – another editor could have made this much better than me and maybe it's so. But it's bullshit – I am as good as anyone else!

＊＊＊＊＊＊＊＊＊＊＊＊＊

RC: One of your other credits is '*Montenegro*'[11] with Dusan Makavejev[12] – clearly this is a man who works in a very different way.

SI: Very different – he's the opposite to Bergman. He was waiting for inspiration and it took time for him to get started with the editing and it was very frustrating for me. I couldn't at first understand what he wanted – which way to go.

There were scenes and shots missing because of his 'wait-ing' (*for inspiration*). There is a part in the bedroom with Erland Josephson,[13] the husband, and Susan Anspach,[14] the wife. She is very nervous and anxious and she tries to talk to Erland who is lying on the bed with his back to her and doesn't answer her. There were long shots and some medium shots on Susan but no closeups on Erland. So we had a lot of shots of apes from the beginning of the film and we decided to cut in the ape for 'shot missing' on Erland. She was asking him things and the ape was making faces – it was so wonderful.[15] I haven't seen the film since. It was difficult to adapt to his methodology – it took a lot of patience.

Bergman on the other hand is so methodical. He comes to the cutting room for two hours every day – eleven to one – and we go through the material from the beginning, reel by reel. Then he leaves and I do the editing, so I do everything that we have talked about – he gave me a lot of time because he knows so well what he wants. I never have to work late nights, maybe sometimes taking care of the trims and filing. I feel free to do what I want. If we have decided a cut and I think it will not be good of course I must make another cut – that's what he expects of me. At the beginning I was of course nervous – maybe I do it wrong – maybe he won't like it – but he's a very good teacher.

RC: So with '*Fanny and Alexander*'[16] – looking at the finished film – it looks as if he knew and therefore you knew what was the right shot at any given moment. For instance in the prologue when the boy is hiding under the table it could have been cut in a number of different ways, but it feels as if it had to be that way. Maybe it's just because you are a wonderful editor!

SI: (laughs) Yeah, of course. His view of the scene is in his head before it's shot, but there are still many different ways, but I understand what you mean – that's because of his thinking, his planning. The boy under the table was the only shot where a piece was lost. There were fifteen frames that he wanted to put back and I couldn't find them! I looked all over in every box, all over the room, and it was only him and me in the room (sighs). He said it doesn't matter, just order a new copy so I did but after two days I found the piece!

Even if you have worked in cinema for sixty years like Ingmar you can still be insecure. For instance, in the scene where Fanny and Alexander and the housewife are in the Bishop's garden and she tells the children the story of the chil-dren that once lived in the house she is looking at the screen right at Alexander and the problem was which direction should Alexander look. They had to take two shots because the script girl and Ingmar couldn't work it out.

I must tell you about the work. Many people ask me if I can decide on my own. Of course I can decide on my own but I can't make Sylvia Ingemarsson's version of the film. I must do the film that Ingmar likes. Of course if there is a sequence that he doesn't really care for and he feels that he can't do it then. For instance in '*Bildmakarna*' – the play '*The Imagemakers*'[17] – there was a sequence when the actors were dancing around and flirting and posing to music and he couldn't figure it out really. So he said to me 'do something' and then it's much easier for him to come and say you can take away that one or you can shorten that one a bit. It's always like that. The more we have worked together the more he trusts me.

I remember when we made the documentary about 'Faro'[18] in 1979. There was a sequence with a typical Gottland play and they play ball. He couldn't do it and I tried my best to edit it as good as I could and he was amazed. He said, 'It's wonderful – I couldn't do it better'. He's talking about that now and then because he thinks it was so exciting, but I was glad. I was very anxious to make it look good. So that's what I mean with competition – I have to compete – I am very serious about my things.

Bergman never lets intuition or chance rule. He must work with his reins very tight. I feel that we are dancing together when we work – it's not that I have to decide – today I have to decide something – its not like that. Its not a fight between each other – who's got it right – we do it together and his decision is not always the best – neither is mine, but we meet and we discuss and we do. When we have made the roughcut and we go through the film two or three times and when we come to the final cut then it happens he is there four hours a day, because then he is very excited. Then he thinks it's the best part – when we do the fine cut – and so do I of course. Ingmar is so critical about his own work. Sometimes he gets too hard with the scissors, so I have the feeling that he cuts away the things that give the story more life in his ambition to make it flow – not stop.

The sound editor takes care of the film after the editing is finished, and that's a pity many times because I have no control over that. With Bergman, when we are finished, the sound engineer comes to see the film with us and he has a tape recorder and he's noting all the things that we say about each effect and atmosphere – as you know Ingmar never uses much music.

It has happened with other directors that they have made a different editing after my work, just to suit the sound editor and that's not good. It's so frustrating when I meet other directors and they don't care – and I care a lot. I'm sitting prepared to do my thing the way I've learned it and they don't care if I come too late – oh, I must go to the dentist or manyana manyana – they don't care.

Since I started working as a teacher I have been very interested again. I feel the lust, the fascination of film-making and editing. I had a very good experience in Norway with Eric Gustafson. He made a little film based on one of Ibsen's not so famous books. It was very easy – every day he knew what to shoot and how to shoot it. I also had a picture manuscript – what do you call it – a storyboard for the first time – it was so comfortable. The material gets so easy to edit when there is thought – when I don't have to guess.

My best editing has always been a co-operation with a good director who knows the film language and also doesn't let chance decide through improvisation which is what inexperienced directors often do. They also usually listen to too many advisers and get the story muddled up and the consequence is that as an editor you have to wrestle with lots of problems and in the worst case get blamed for them as well. I have no opinion what is my best editing but the nicest is of course, '*Fanny and Alexander*'. In my opinion it is seldom you can tell who edited a film because it is a co-operation, but sometimes the director chooses his editor and it works well the first time and so it happens that they continue working together. It has a lot to do with the chemistry between people. It is important that an editor is patient, meticulous, has imagination and intuition. Therefore I believe that a good editor is both born and created through experience.

* * * * * * * * * * * * *

After I had visited Sylvia she went to work for Bergman again and I asked her to send me her thoughts about his latest project.

SARABAND

These last years, when Ingmar and I have met to edit one of his TV films he has said that this time is probably the last that we will work together. That, due to his age he wouldn't be making another film – that it drains your energy – the level of commitment required. We have therefore said goodbye and thanked each other for the good co-operation several times, and after '*Bildmakarna*' in 1999, which we edited on Faro I was certain that this was the last time.

In August 2001 the world was informed that Ingmar Bergman was 'pregnant with a script' and the news was given great space in the media accompanied by photos of Ingmar, Erland Josephson and Liv Ullmann who would be playing the leads and that it would be a sequel to '*Scenes from a Marriage*'.[19]

In January 2002 the phone rang and a production manager from Sveriges Television asked me if I would like to edit '*Saraband*'.[20] Usually I would get this call much earlier and often it would be from Ingmar himself, but times change. The film was planned to be recorded in a studio with four HD cameras but ended up being shot with only one because they were too noisy.

The editing would be done on Avid and this would be the first time Ingmar and I would work digitally. As I told you my experience of working on Avid was not particularly extensive but I thought to myself that it would have to work! I finally have to learn this (surely it can't be more difficult than getting an HGV driving license which I succeeded in doing three years ago) and I cannot pass on working with Ingmar. It would have been a betrayal as I know how important it is to him that I am editing the film. Adapting to a new editor after twenty-five years, I knew it would irritate him immensely. Despite this I was on the brink of calling him to decline several times as I became increasingly nervous the more the date closed in.

Luckily the college where I now work had bought new Avid Express 2D and I was able to take one home to practice for a couple of weeks. When I left for Stockholm to begin my work on the 17th November 2002 I felt pretty safe and I knew that I would have quite a lot of time to get to know the equipment since Ingmar nowadays only works every other day and since we always begin by watching all the material. It also turned out that Sveriges Television had bought editing suites similar to the one I had become accustomed to at home, so after a while it went pretty smoothly.

Of course I was very afraid of making mistakes and the biggest fear was of losing material but I had access to a good assistant editor who shared his knowledge and digitised everything, so I arrived to a 'set' table. He took care of everything outside of the editing itself, leaving me to take care of my business.

The editing room was small, miserable and disorganised as it usually gets when different people pass through it in various stages of stressful work and nobody has time to make it comfortable. Since I cannot work in disarray I tried to make the room nicer with the help of a couple of red chairs, a table and cloth and a framed poster from the silent screen. This really made a difference.

The editing work went very well and with the exception of my anxiety that something would go wrong (I'm sure Ingmar had anxiety as well, but for something different) we had a very nice time in the edit suite. The editing was not always easy. The shooting had a few difficulties which affected the material which made some of the cuts less than perfect but the story was not compromised and '*Saraband*' turned out to be a powerful experience.

As usual, each day we had a short break at three o'clock. We drank blackberry juice mixed with Imsdal (*mineral*) water and ate Brago crackers to top up our energy in order for us to be able to work until five o'clock. We talked about many different things but mostly about events from his long life. He is such a great storyteller and has such a wonderful memory despite his eighty-five years.

We would each light a candle and when the break was over we blew them out at the same time and would compete about whose smoke trail would last the longest. In the cold technical world we found ourselves in it wasn't allowed to light candles so we would wait for the fire alarm but to Ingmar's disappointment and my relief it never went off.

Now once again we have said goodbye. . . .

Notes

1. **Sidney Lumet and *The Seagull*** – 1968 starring James Mason, Vanessa Redgrave and Simone Signoret. Lumet's first major success was the court room drama '*Twelve Angry Men*' in 1957.
2. ***Winnie the Pooh and the Blustery Day*** – Disney animation, 1968.

3. **Bo Widerberg (1930–97)** – Most famous for the enchanting '*Elvira Madigan*', 1967.
4. **Katinka Farago** – Born Vienna, 1936. First worked with Bergman as script girl on '*The Seventh Seal*'. Subsequently as production manager and producer.
5. *Man on the Roof* – Bo Widerberg, 1976.
6. *Autumn Sonata* – Ingmar Bergman, with Ingrid Bergman, 1978.
7. **Sven Nykvist** – '*Sawdust and Tinsel*' in 1953 was his first credit as cinematographer for Bergman. He has since contributed his special skills to many international filmmakers.
8. *The Serpent's Egg* – Bergman, 1977.
9. *Cabaret* – Fosse, with Liza Minelli, 1972.
10. **Bob Fosse (1927–87)** – Choreographer, writer, director including '*All that Jazz*', 1979.
11. *Montenegro* – Makavejev, 1981.
12. **Dusan Makavejev** – Born 1932, Belgrade. Caused a stir with '*WR Mysteries of the Organism*', 1971 and has always been provocative and employed an eclectic style.
13. **Erland Josephson** – Internationally renowned actor, who first worked with Bergman in '*To Joy*', 1950.
14. **Susan Anspach** – Despite a part in Bob Rafelson's '*Five Easy Pieces*' in 1970 her acting career has never really blossomed.
15. **Apes** – They are still a wonderful surprise, which even Bunuel might have been proud of.
16. *Fanny and Alexander* – Bergman, perhaps his most effective masterpiece, 1982.
17. *The Imagemakers* – Bergman, 2000.
18. **Faro** – The island where Bergman has his home.
19. *Scenes from a Marriage* – Bergman, 1973.
20. *Saraband* – Bergman, 2003.

17 Michal Leszczylowski

I talked with Michal over a leisurely lunch at an old established restaurant, Ulriksdals Vardhus, which is set in a royal estate over-looking an inlet on the outskirts of Stockholm. I was eager to learn how this man from Poland had ended up in Sweden cutting Tarkovsky's last film, 'The Sacrifice'. Since then he has become the editor of choice for the new Swedish generation that includes Lukas Moodysson.

I was born in Poland in 1950, on a Sunday afternoon. 'Lazy guy', they said he is going to be, which I still try to prove to be false. My parents were both chemists and of course they wanted me to be a pharmacist too, which I did not want.

One of the main things which formed me professionally almost from the time I was born is that I had a brother three years older than me who was supposed to be a pianist – at least since he was five. So from when I was two, he practised piano at home for at least five hours a day – so this is the way I got the music. Then they tried to make me a pianist but I wanted to play football! So I got some education in music for three years and then I said thank you very much while my brother continued to the age of nineteen at which point he closed the piano at home and said never again and became a mathematician. That's how I got music in my veins, in my blood, in everything. Basically what I do in films is to deal with the musical part of it as far as feelings are concerned.

I studied at the University in Poland. I was born in a town called Lodz,[1] which is the second biggest city in Poland. I studied economics for three years. Then I came to Sweden and stayed here.

RC: So you were in Lodz but you didn't go to the Film School.

ML: No, no, no! I was at a couple of parties in the late sixties. That was my only contact with the Film School. Then I came to Sweden and tried to continue with economics – then I said no way. I was twenty-one years when I emigrated.

RC: Apart from music had you developed a love of other culture including cinema or theatre?

ML: Yes, yes of course – it was a part of our middle class life to consider the existence of the arts – not as a guide in moral or emotional life but it was present there. So I've seen theatre and read books like all middle class children do – for what reason though was hidden from me.[2] They were the things you did but nobody told you about the reasons.

One of my closest friend's mother was a film editor. I was a little interested in what the film business was and she said, 'I will never do anything to help you get your foot in the production company – it's a place where all the alcoholics and all the prostitutes are gathering'. So that was the only thing I knew about the film business, alcoholics and prostitutes, which I now understand what she meant, though I don't agree.

RC: But did you think of cinema as serious?

ML: No, no, never although I was a member of the film club when I was small I never understood that there was something behind it – that you made them – that was out of the range of my understanding.

So I came to Sweden at twenty-one years and I met some guys in Film School who always wanted someone to carry their things. So I started with that and then I started taking sound. I was very young – I had no idea and then by chance I started editing and said wow, this is something!

RC: Somebody wanted something edited?

ML: No, no – first of all I went for a reportage for TV and this had to be edited on the spot. So the cameraman said I'll do that so I was sitting watching him and I understood that I could do it five times as good. He didn't know what he was doing really, and I said maybe I'll try it and since then I am editing.

I went to the Film School in Stockholm in the sound department as there was no editing department at all – with an aim to edit so I edited everything during those two years I was in the School – everything that was made I edited.[3]

RC: So when you were in Film School and began to do things did you feel differently a bout cinema?

ML: Oh yes, very much so.

RC: You convinced yourself it was a serious occupation?

ML: Exactly, but something I was not conscious about was that I could dive into the emotions and stay in there in them for a long time – I have a patience in that respect that is independent of me. I was very allergic as a kid so I had some very severe skin problems. What developed in me was the patience because it was itching and the pleasure when I could scratch. Those two things are also fundamental with what I do as an editor: I have a patience to get into the emotions and to stay there and work with them.

RC: And the pleasure comes from this?

ML: I wouldn't say that it's conscious – that I consciously use those elements of my life, but now I see that it's not accidental – I really took what I had and used it.

RC: So was Tarkovsky a turning point?

ML: Oh yes, very much so in several different ways. One of the things I did in my youth was to watch movies, especially the movies I did not understand – and Tarkovsky was on top of that list among others. So I could see his movies several times 5–6–8–10 times and each time I found something new in them.

RC: What were other examples of films or film-makers?

ML: Bergman, Kurosawa and Fellini – those are the ones I think of immediately when you ask – and Wajda,[4] but later. I loved all the films they made because they show *their* reality. Not one of them is fully presenting the inner world. I at least met two of them – that's fantastic!

So Tarkovsky was a turning point in several ways. I will tell you a little anecdote about how we met. I met the producer of ' *The Sacrifice*' two years before the shooting started. At that time I was thirty-four and I felt I was ready to edit big movies but I hadn't made it yet. I met her at a party and she was kind of 'happily tensed' by something and I felt that. I said 'what is it?' and she said 'I am going to produce Tarkovsky's next movie!' and I said 'And I am going to edit it' and she laughed and said 'Oh, the queue for that job is very long'. I said, 'Don't worry'.

Half a year later I started a conversation course in Russian. I had a good education in Russian, partly because under the occupation the Soviet Union demanded education in Russian, although most Poles didn't want to speak it. On the other hand I also had private lessons in Russian so I spoke it more than most Poles. So I started the conversation course because I had never used Russian since I left Poland – it had been thirteen years.

Michal Leszczylowski working with Andrei Tarkovsky (Courtesy of Michal Leszczylowski)

In the end Tarkovsky refused all the editors and said I am going to edit the film myself, so I need an assistant and I was the only assistant who could speak Russian, so we could communicate without a translator.

I remember meeting Tarkovsky for the first time. He sat alone in the cinema watching dailies. It was dark and I only saw the silhouette of the great master. The takes were silent. He made some comments by saying 'Oh no!' and other unprintable expressions. The takes were long but few. I did not know at that time that the film would only consist of one hundred and forty images.[5] After thirty minutes or so the lights were turned on and we shook hands and he asked when I was able to start working. Almost two years of waiting for that meeting were over.

We started working the next day. We spent eight hours with one cut which we did not succeed in making. It resulted in shooting extra picture to put in between the two images. I noticed how extremely accurate he was in analysing the images and making the final decisions. That was the first lesson. I went home that evening with a clear feeling of having seen something very important – the accuracy.

The next day Sven Nykvist[6] came to me and congratulated me. Tarkovsky liked me and accepted me for the job. I was not nervous for the job itself, I knew that a great master knows all there is to know about film-making. I was nervous because I did not know whether I knew enough how to serve the film. I was really happy now, in front of me I had a year of flying on the highest possible level in films. I enjoyed every minute of it. Those endless analyses of the images, the light, acting, contrast, camera movements. And the motto of our first day in the editing room: 'If it is not good enough, re-shoot'.

That was perhaps the biggest lesson – you write, you shoot, you edit and then you evaluate it as a ready piece of the movie. If it is not good then you have to consider what can be done. Tarkovsky was always in doubt whether what was done was good enough. Now I know that only debutantes do not doubt – they know. The great directors I worked with have in common the ability to doubt and so to adjust, re-shoot, re-write and in the tense atmosphere monitor their own feelings of what is right or wrong, not forgetting the audience, the true receiver of our efforts.

Tarkovsky had in me an eager and hungry listener. As we got close in the working process much of our common time was spent talking about life, philosophy, perception, religion, politics (that was a social background we shared as members of the Eastern European middle class) and on that base the art is being built. Editing is merely to choose the pieces of a recorded reality.

I was talking about what constitutes the real differences between film-makers. I realised that it's partly the sense of time, the feeling for rhythm, and more importantly what kind of memory a person has. Tarkovsky had a very good memory for atmospheres for 'feelings around' – not that kind of mathematical memory – the numbers of the cars or the houses or what happened in what order – but the aura of feelings around the people, and he was talking only about that. While Bergman has an extreme memory for relations between people and it's only that, which is not very little. They both were very true to their memories. They did not elaborate more or change them.

RC: Do you think it's also honesty about that?

ML: Very – as artists – and it's a big difference to be honest as an artist from honesty as a person. As people they were normal, perhaps Bergman is more 'normal' than Tarkovsky was. Tarkovsky was not 'negotiable' while Bergman is more realistic and has a big knowledge about people, which is very funny, because he once said 'I nowadays don't think that I know that much about people – I only know things about actors'.

Which is exactly the same phrase as Kazan[7] told me, 'Oh you know people are complicated, but the actors, I know something about the actors'. That was very funny – only Kazan and Bergman could say this.

RC: You met Elia Kazan?

ML: Yes I met Kazan because he was supposed to make a film in France and I was suggested to him by the producer. I left with a job after forty or fifty minutes of talk – he was in a very good mood. Later I met him again in Stockholm after he had had a stroke and he did not remember – he didn't recognise me. He was an ageing giant trapped in a weak body and it was so painful to see. The film was called '*Beyond the Aegean*' and was never shot as the French Minister of Culture did not support this kind of American production.

* * * * * * * * * * * * *

But the memories, these different artists have; it's like for a painter – the way of seeing things – I don't think we see exactly the same things – we are different people. The artists like Tarkovsky and Bergman they tend to remember different things than we do. So it was amazing to get into the universe of Tarkovsky and see those memories and emotions.

They were very documentary the films he made. I mean that everyone is making documentary film in one way or another – on the emotional level – but not on a practical and concrete level – but on an emotional level all productions are documentary, that's why Bergman was making the films he was making.

RC: Do you think working with someone like that demands something different from the editor, or is it just more intense – is it possible to describe a difference?

ML: I would say it is less demanding working with someone who is dealing with factual life than with someone who is trying to execute fantasies. It's much more convenient and for me much more understandable to approach a director like Tarkovsky. I've never worked with Bergman except that I was working with a script he had written and I met him several times. The film was directed by Liv Ullmann and we were re-editing the film for six weeks and he was partially present in the process as the scriptwriter, because we made major changes.

I always approach even what you call conventional movies in the way that I am looking for true emotions. Without true emotions there is no way to make a movie at all. So even if the 'young guns' are sometimes making very 'wild' feel good movies it's still the question about real emotions.

'The Sacrifice' had a contract for two hours and ten minutes and we ended up with a film that was two hours thirty minutes. I was called by the French co-producer, Anatole Dauman,[8] who is not amongst us anymore unfortunately. He said I want you to come to Paris to have dinner with me. At that time Tarkovsky was sick. I said I really don't have time because we are finishing the sound, but he insisted. So I went for an evening and the question came, 'Can we shorten the film down to two hours and ten minutes?' I told him it is always possible to shorten a film, but if we cut down this film to two hours and ten minutes it will not be a Tarkovsky film. You will end up with a film, which is not Tarkovsky's universe. The films are always built on an emotional basis. The rhythm is built into the script and it's transferred into acting with the same emotional ear and eye of the director and in the editing you have to take care not to kill it.

I never understood the meaning of the word pause, in relation to film rhythm, because for me things are happening all the time, so hopefully I never violated this life nerve of the film. It is exactly what is in common between music and film. It is feelings developed in time. If you try to speed things up they will not be the same. Probably you lose both the timing and the feelings.

There are things that I have learned during all these years. For instance you really have to cry yourself and then to see the audience cry to see how long you can stay in a universe like that. Before starting to edit a film, I read the script and, watching the rhythm of the acting and the pace of the dialogue I decide how long the film should be and then execute it and not the opposite. It's not that I am stupid that I would try to fit the film into the form that I have prepared. I am certain that sometimes I am wrong, but for the last six years I can judge the film within a minute. It's not that I take out the things that are bad. It has to do with approaching the world of an artist – I ask how long do I want to be in this environment.

RC: That reminds me of the story of Kurosawa cutting a sequence with a particular piece of music in mind and finding when he had cut it that it fitted to the frame.

ML: That happened to me several times – it will fit because the emotions are developed in time. For instance, in the last movie of Lukas Moodysson[9] I used a Vivaldi adagio in a very slow recording. I listened to twelve recordings and only one worked on a musical level. It fits to the frame with pauses, with everything. So now I know it's a rule that if I make my emotional decisions right then it will always match someone else's work who made his decisions right. We have very common feelings – some of us are more tense and some more relaxed – but within a certain range we are the same.

RC: Do you have routines? I remember not being able to cut because my rhythm had been disturbed. Do you have a kind of mental aerobics?

ML: Oh yes, yes sometimes I don't feel like making this scene today. I'll make it tomorrow because of some personal private reasons, or through reasons that I'm not really conscious about. So I really live out all the emotions because I know this is the only guideline we have.

RC: Sure, because I know musicians who, when they are honest will say, almost know that they will not perform well tonight. Whatever they do, they know they are not in the right state of mind to do the work justice and they can't necessarily control that.

ML: In music it's a very good example – I would like to convince once in my life the producers that there is a very good film to be made when the music is born. What is the difference between the guy who is reading the notes and the guy who is reading the notes and making the music, because technically you can play all the notes and it will not be music and these cue the emotions. Unfortunately the producers do not understand my point. The musicians do – all musicians know exactly at once what I am talking about. The same with the film – when is it that those 'notes' in the script and 'notes' during the shooting start to live their own life in the editing room – it's when somebody puts his or her emotions into it.

On the other hand I try to cut the acting as little as possible, because the audience are not watching the splices they are watching what is in between. So the more perfect the performance we can deliver the better it is. Sometimes it's perfect and we can say like Buñuel 'We take away the clappers and that's it',[10] which happened to me a couple of times only with Liv Ullmann[11] as director. She knows what acting is and she doesn't think, maybe we take a little cutaway here and there. No she is really fighting until it is done and sometimes those performances are six, seven minutes long in a closeup. Tarkovsky burning the house (*In 'The Sacrifice'*) was eight minutes and I put one cut in that scene – which is not noticeable – to make it even better. But it really is 'to take away the clappers'.

If you take a film like those of Bob Fosse,[12] as he was a choreographer he knows how important the performance is. You can't cut the dancing – you have to dance and that's very interesting to see how he uses it – not only in the dance numbers, but with acting. So he is a very good example of what pace is, what rhythm is. I never met him but he was very like his films and Tarkovsky is something else.

* * * * * * * * * * * * *

RC: Whenever possible do you remain involved right to the mix? Do you work on the sound and the music?

ML: Right now I'm doing it because the whole film is in Russian[13] so I have to be available for dialogue editing. The music is part of me that has to be ready when leaving the editing room. But I am more involved with script work with Lukas now from draft two to draft eight, because I know to edit a film well you have to guard yourself very heavily in the script. Not with the pictures, but you have to trace the feelings to where they start, and it's very difficult to judge the script, how strong the feelings should be and how clear – how clearly told it should be.

So I am more involved with the script than the sound side, because with the sound the main parts I make in the editing. But there are many things you can only work on one to one. You can only judge when it's done. You cannot judge by assumption that this probably will work – no you have to do it. So I do all the major things – music – all the dialogue which is a kind of music for me too – and the major sound effects.

You have to expose yourself to them in time so it always goes back to time. What editors, myself included, do is that we think the more we work the better things will be, while we have to rest to expose ourselves to other parts of life than the editing room. It's very easy to dive into the film and get out of the room four months later.

RC: Do you mean that the film is always with you or that life itself has to be contiguous with the film?

ML: It's both – like '*Together*'[14] – I laughed through that film and it had an effect on my life. I laughed through that film all the weeks except the last – when we realised we had major problems.

RC: And you stopped laughing?

ML: Stopped laughing and started working.

RC: You were enjoying it too much perhaps.

ML: In this movie there are twelve major characters and that is the problem. Each one of the scenes was very good but put all together they kind of killed each other. So the last two weeks was a fight for us to get it right. I said don't worry we have good scenes and if they are not good put together they are put in the wrong order.

RC: So it was a structural thing.

ML: Yeah and sometimes you can do something about it and sometimes not. It's always about time and emotions and what sequence emotions come in and how fast: will I be disturbed by watching the next scene, in the feeling I have, or will it boost the feeling I already have.

RC: Or do I need to be disturbed.

ML: Well it's a very 'ephemeral' thing, editing – you cannot really grasp what the core is except for these feelings in time – that's the only thing that's important I think.

* * * * * * * * * * * * *

RC: You said that when you grew up that you learnt about culture but you didn't know how it was supposed to connect with life – which I understand totally – and of course our culture, our society for many centuries now has not in that sense been integrated.

ML: It's more integrated in the West than in the East of Europe.

RC: That's an interesting statement. For me almost the soul of Russia is represented not only in Tarkovsky, but also in some other Russian cinema. There is a sense that what I am seeing is not just a story but something that is part of a culture. So the New Wave in Czechoslovakia somehow spoke to me about living in that society, even through metaphor perhaps, so I felt it was saying something beyond telling me a story in a way I could relate to emotionally and deeply.

ML: It's that Western Culture, with all the 'good things', is putting the individual at the centre of the Universe, whilst in the Eastern European culture or even more in Asia you are part of time, of society, of culture and then you are like a medium yourself. While in the West you are a human being with a right to talk, in Central Europe and the East you are at most allowed to be a medium for cultural movements, time movements – all the wars, all the accidents – you can use your sensitivity to talk about it.

Tarkovsky was a supreme example of that. He was like a medium. He was not always aware of why things came to him and how they came. Whereas these young guys I work with now kind of feel what's going on in their country – on an emotional basis. They don't make action stories just to be directors – they really are sensitive. So I think there is a big difference between storytelling that is a western approach to art and developing your sensitivity for the time environment you are in.

Between my home in Lodz and Warsaw – it's only one hundred and thirty kilometres – and I often went to Warsaw to visit relatives – on the way there is the place where Chopin was born and I remember it from my childhood. Whenever I am in Poland I always go to Zelazowa Wola where Chopin was born and raised.[15] In my childhood – I'm not certain about it today because it is so changed – but in my childhood I had a very strong feeling that no other music was possible to write there. With the light, with the nature, with the trees, with a small river, now polluted, and so forth – he was like a medium for the environment. Sometimes I go to places where people were active. I visited the place where Freud was active. I don't think he could come with any other theory in this building, in this architecture, with this light. People are mediums for something else. You can disturb it and try to be somebody else or see things in other ways but that's in vain really. Just as I don't believe you can educate people. As a teacher the most important thing is whom you allow in the School. You can help release what is already inside. Creativity is the struggle to be effective.

RC: Was it true that Tarkovsky also admired Bresson?

ML: Yes, very much, very much. Bresson's 'Notes on Cinematography'[16] I pump into the heads of my students.

Tarkovsky and Bergman never met, but once, at Film Huset in Stockholm they saw each other and turned and ran away. Bergman said: 'Tarkovsky freely moved in the room, where I succeeded only to open the door a little to look in'.

* * * * * * * * * * * * *

RC: You mentioned Kazan but he's not a typical Hollywood film-maker. Do you think it's false to try to distinguish between the typical Hollywood film and the best of European cinema?

ML: I understand the distinction and I totally agree that there is a very big difference between the film as entertainment, which is typical of Hollywood, while the European cinema has it's roots in other forms of culture which is not entertaining first of all. I think it's a very great distinction and very necessary. I had a very big disagreement with my young students four years ago when I told them that they are beginning their careers at the worst possible moment of the culture or of the history of art. They said what do you mean. I said I am raised on film-makers who, have their roots in other arts – painting, theatre, literature, music. While you are raised by people who are raised on the films only. Only your position is even worse because you are raised, educated, by people who are raised on TV.

My hope is that film-makers will try to get nourished by other arts to make the films richer. Otherwise we are going to be – I don't know the word in English, when you grow crops on one piece of land, the same crop. Then you drain the earth – you have to cultivate not only the crops but also the earth.

RC: Otherwise it becomes sterile.

ML: And that's what's happening in the States.

I think there are people like me with similar abilities and dis-abilities, because editors are disabled on the social level. It's not normal to be alone in a room with people who look alive but are not. It's a kind of dysfunctional element that editors have, that they can relate to people who are not really people. So I know there are a lot of people who are formed in that way too.[17]

Ready movies and the false appetite for making them. Holly-wood makes movies that only create appetites for another of the same kind. 'Hamburger films' – consumerist film-making – out of one cinema and into another.

Notes

1. **Lodz** – Home of the famous Polish Film School, which has produced gen-erations of special filmmakers – directors and cinematographers. It has no editing specialisation.
2. **Middle classes and culture** – A depressing thought but sadly true that bourgeois life treats everything as something to acquire – including cul-ture – thus negating its significance.

3. **Swedish Film School** – Has no editing specialisation either!
4. **Andrej Wajda** – Father figure of post-war Polish cinema. Established his reputation with the war trilogy in the fifties: '*A Generation*', '*Kanal*' and '*Ashes and Diamonds*'.
5. *The Sacrifice*, Tarkovsky – 1986. The average number of shots in a feature film is in excess of 500.
6. **Sven Nykvist** – Bergmans cameraman for many years – since 1953.
7. **Elia Kazan (1909–2003)** – Theatre and film director, who usually got the best performances of their careers out of actors.
8. **Anatole Dauman (1924–98)** – Producer for Bresson, Resnais, Godard, Marker, Oshima, Wenders, etc.
9. **Lukas Moodysson** – Born 1969, the next Bergman, according to Bergman.
10. **Luis Buñuel** – Was remarkably economic when shooting and would often stop at one take, even if there might be technical imperfections.
11. **Liv Ullmann** – Born in Tokyo, 1939. Her first appearance with Bergman was in '*Persona*', 1966. Her first feature as director, '*Sophie*' in 1992.
12. **Bob Fosse (1927–87)** – Dancing and rhythm is one reason why some editors think you should stand up to cut.
13. *Lilya-4-ever* – Lukas Moodysson, 2002.
14. *Together* – Lukas Moodysson, 2000.
15. **Chopin's Birthplace** is about 50 kilometres west of Warsaw. I respect Michal's belief in place as a specific inspiration and influence.
16. **Bresson's *Notes on Cinematography*** is in print (Sun and Moon Press) and the most relevant text for filmmakers that exists, along with Bazin's '*What is Cinema*'.
17. **Editors as Dysfunctional Beings** – And yet they mostly seem rather well adjusted to me.

18 Andrei Tarkovsky from Sculpting in Time

(Copyright 1987 by Andrei Tarkovsky, used by permission of Alfred A. Knopf, a division of Random House, Inc.)

Contrary to the theories developed during the classic period of early Soviet Cinema, Tarkovsky did not believe that editing or montage created the meaning of a film. For him it was more that editing has to bring out the meaning implicit in the material that has been filmed. It was not that editing was unimportant to him but that it was an integral part of the whole process as this extract from his book underlines.

No one component of a film can have any meaning in isolation: *it is the film that is the work of art.* And we can only talk about its components rather arbitrarily, dividing it up artificially for the sake of theoretical discussion.

Nor can I accept that editing is the main formative element of a film, as the protagonists of 'montage cinema', following Kuleshov and Eisenstein,[1] maintained in the 1920s, as if a film was made on the editing table.

It has often been pointed out, quite rightly, that every art form involves editing, in the sense of selection and collation, adjusting parts and pieces. The cinema image comes into being during shooting and exists *within* the frame. During shooting therefore, I concentrate on the course of time in the frame, in order to reproduce it and record it. Editing brings together shots which are already filled with time, and organises the unified living structure inherent in the film; and the time that pulsates through the blood vessels of the film, making it alive, is of varying rhythmic pressure.

The idea of 'montage cinema' – that editing brings together two concepts and thus engenders a new, third one – again seems to me to be incompatible with the nature of cinema. Art can never have the interplay of concepts as its ultimate goal. The image is tied to the concrete and the material, yet reaches out along mysterious paths to regions beyond the spirit – perhaps that is what Pushkin meant when he said that 'Poetry has to be a little bit stupid'.

The poetics of cinema, a mixture of the basest material substances such as we tread every day, is resistant to symbolism. A single frame is enough to show, from his choice and recording of matter, whether a director is talented, whether he is endowed with cinematic vision.

Editing is ultimately no more than the ideal variant of the assembly of the shots, necessarily contained within the material that has been put on to the roll of film.

A still from '*Mirror*' by Andrei Tarkovsky (Zerkalo [Mirror] (1974). Courtesy of Artificial Eye Film Company Ltd.)

. . . To refer again to my own experience, I must say that a prodigious amount of work went into editing '*Mirror*'.[2] There were some twenty or more variants. I don't just mean changes in the order of certain shots, but major alterations in the actual structure, in the sequence of the episodes. At moments it looked as if the film could not be edited, which would have meant that inadmissible lapses had occurred during shooting. The film didn't hold together, it wouldn't stand up, it fell apart as one watched, it had no unity, no necessary inner connection, no logic. And then, one fine day, when we somehow managed to devise one last desperate rearrangement – there was the film. The material came to life; the parts started to function reciprocally, as if linked by a bloodstream; and as that last, despairing attempt was projected on to the screen, the film was born before our very eyes. For a long time I still couldn't believe the miracle – the film held together.

. . . There are about two hundred shots in '*Mirror*', very few when a film of that length usually has about five hundred: the small number is due to their length.

Although the assembly of the shots is responsible for the structure of the film, it does not, as is generally assumed, create the rhythm.

The distinctive time running through the shots makes the rhythm of the picture; and rhythm is determined not by the length of the edited pieces, but by the pressure of the time that runs through them. Editing cannot determine rhythm (in this respect it can only be a function of style); indeed time courses through the picture despite editing rather than because of it. The course of time recorded in the frame, is what the director has to catch in the pieces laid out on the editing table.

Notes

1. To be fair to Eisenstein, when he was teaching at the Moscow Film School in the 1930s his main concern was to develop in his students a proper understanding of dramatic form and staging for the camera. Far from being obsessed with meaning established through montage he concentrated on how the dramatic action must dictate the mise-en-scène. Indeed to be

clear he coined the phrase mise-en-**shot** to show how the essential skill is to emphasise all significant moments by the way the action is presented to the camera, rather than being necessarily achieved in the editing. I believe Tarkovsky would have been in tune with this approach by Eisenstein. Those interested can read further in 'Lessons with Eisenstein' by Vladimir Nizhny.

2. ***Mirror*** – Andrei Tarkovsky, 1975.

19 Lidia Zonn

Lidia has spent a distinguished career, editing mostly documentaries. In Poland the documentary is a refined, carefully constructed and often poetic form. Amongst her collaborations was that with Krzysztof Kieslowski for whom she cut more than a dozen films – mostly before he made the transition to dramatic feature film.

Lidia Zonn (Courtesy of Lidia Zonn)

I was born in Vilnius in 1934. In 1938, a year before Second World War my parents moved to Warsaw. My father was an astronomer. My mother graduated in history. After marrying she did not work professionally, but stayed at home and looked after me and the home. I was an only child. My father came from a German parentage, settled in Russia until the revolution and totally russianised, but traditional family. My mother came from a Jewish family totally russianised. I did not know her family as my grandparents were already dead when I was born.

I was brought up in an atmosphere of Russian culture, my parents even read western children's literature to me translated into Russian. This atmosphere and my mother's personality made a large impact, maybe even a decisive impact on my attitude to life, and in some way to the choice of my career. Even more so when during the Second World War, because my mother was Jewish, she had to go with me into hiding (my father was a German prisoner of war). I could not go to school and only my mother taught me all subjects.

After the war, from the moment I started a normal school I wanted to become a physicist. All my interests centred around, primarily the sciences. I went of course to the cinema to see the most interesting films. I also went to the theatre and the Philharmonia (concert hall). These were however interests of no greater intensity than the average intelligent person. I had no talents in the arts, or a greater awareness of my own surroundings.

When I was in middle school, an inter-school Olympics (competition) in Warsaw in Physics was organised. It was then that I realised that my talents in this direction were limited (even though I had received good marks at school), and to teach in this subject or any other I was not well suited. During this time, in growing doubts as to what direction to go in to choose a career, I happened upon a report on the production of one of René Clair's[1] films, the title of which now escapes me. The report spoke of the work, in the team, that is of the group of people co-working with the director, thus having – as I understood – their own artistic input in the film being made. This was something for me – my own, larger or smaller part, in a large creative project.

I submitted my application to the Lodz Film School and I passed the entry exam. From the start of my studies I accepted the fact that I would never be an independent director, although my concept of the particular responsibilities of the director within the team – being myself the assistant to the second director/film editor – were very vague.

The decision to become an editor became more clear in the third year of my studies, I had to independently edit my school exercises and then I understood how important editing can be in the process of creating a film. At this time Jaroslaw Brzozowski, a documentary maker, came to the school. Now he has almost totally been forgotten. For the younger years he organised something in the form of an editing workshop, and he engaged me as his assistant. Even then his workshop seemed to me to be outdated: the staging of scenes/situations, the tireless and painfully precise composition of the team, the 'artistry' in lighting. I reassured myself however that editing, especially in a documentary film, has a huge impact in the building of the piece and requires much invention.

After completing my studies in 1959 I worked as an assistant to editors at the Documentary Film Studios (Wytwornia Filmsiv Dokumentalnych) in Warsaw. I arrived at a very fortunate time. Just in these years a young group of editors/directors from our Lodz film school and from the VGIK in Moscow began a 'new wave' in making documentaries. They discarded scenery, commentary, and excessive music, which always so easily dramatised any scene. They decided to base their films on authentic observations and authentic sound. For some years, already in the United States of America, England and France there existed new research in documentaries. Now these new trends reached Poland.

I was fortunate that two director/editors in this group – Wladyslaw Slesicki and Kazimierz Karabasz,[2] who then worked together, were left without an editor. They offered me the opportunity, as their younger colleague from school, to collaborate with them. Of course I agreed. In the mornings I worked as assistant to an editor and in the afternoons I worked as an independent editor for their films.

All that I learned in my career I thank and owe to the directors I worked with. Those from my generation (Slesicki, Karabasz) and younger, mainly Krzysztof Kieslowski.[3] All the time they searched for something new, in the subjects they undertook and in the form of those films. And so the editing of their subsequent films was an exploration and search for something new. I am sure I learnt much from foreign films, but this only included specific thoughts/ideas, or fragmentary solutions, which today I do not remember. I do not remember any specific film which introduced any change or new solution to the basic method or ideas in my work. Maybe this is linked with the character of Polish documentaries, which formed their own style, own way of telling stories, differing from such trends as *cinema verite* i.e. *cinema direct*. Only now, working in my chosen career, I sometimes watch films made with a digital camera, edited with long lasting shots (sometimes linked with collage sequences or video clips). I see totally new subject areas and self-explanatory documentaries, but I could never edit in this sort of fashion.

I paid great attention to the detail of form. I considered that documentary should be no different from fiction in the care taken in planning each sequence or scene, in the precision of putting together shots or clarity of construction. Although this formal approach in fiction is already involved in the writing of the script and the realisation of the images – editing is only its continuation. Whilst in documentary the editor can only have a limited control of the character of the pictures. The shape and form of his film the editor builds in the editing suite. These decisions I undertook with the directors. Karabasz, Kieslowski and Halladin[4] with whom I worked most frequently, had a similar feel for the material as I did, similar requirements of the form – we worked on the same wavelength.

On the question of construction the editor, especially in documentary, can have a great influence, both in individual scenes and in structuring the whole film. I am thinking of the ball scene in '*Roku Franka W*'.[5] I received a very considerable amount of material shot during this event over which the director had little control. Predicting the action or even setting up scenes had virtually no influence in the end on what was shot. But the event unfolds, interesting situations appear, interesting reactions of participants, thus one has to record them. During this ball which lasted many hours the director only instigated two scenes/situations. In the first, he asked Franek to go up to a girl and ask her to dance. In the second, after registering a number of scenes of Franek and his friend, whilst they observe the hall and exchange comments amongst themselves, he took a number of shots of a girl sitting alone, assuming that the two situations would become linked. The rest of the material was a collection of mixed observations of the tables, the dancing, and the orchestra. It was only in the edit suite that we created a scene from these images, creating a continuity, the stages of the ball and a dramatic evolution. The shape of such scenes is as much the work of the editor as the director; both heads and pairs of eyes are necessary.

Between European and American films I see basic differences. American films, with very few exceptions, are characterised by a systemised traditional industry method, keeping to defined and tested rules. This is based, on the one hand on a rapid tempo of narration and its dynamic and, on the other, on a defined approach to size of shot and editorial changes and an appropriate use of screen space. So the viewer does not lose his place in the action or any changing situation.

The European tradition is based on the individuality of the director. These are films with individual character: Fellini, Godard, Anderson, Bergman, Wenders. Each director creates his own style and approach to his craft/creative method. Working with such a director the editor must be able to identify the director's vision, his way of treating space and time (very often including the manipulation of different time frames), with his method of recounting a story, his rhythm, his style.

The term 'poetic narration' (as is well known), we associate most of all with a lyrical form, is based on moods feelings and reflections. This form consigns to the background the action with its events and active and dynamic needs of its heroes. In Poland, in documentary film, we have given this form of narrative a name – 'stan rzeczy' (state of things). This term has been borrowed from a speech by the Czech director, Ivan Passer, the creator of the unforgettable film '*Intymne oswrietlenie*' (*Intimate Lighting*).[6] Passer said, 'We are not interested in little stories, we are interested in the state of things'.

However, irrespective of the genre and film form, the viewer looks for some kind of development of the story or dramaturgy. If this development does not clearly arise peripatetically or from turning points in the story, then one needs to establish it by other means. The material we use in this poetic form is mood (of the place and situation), expression (I have in mind the example of Fellini's visions) and dialogues expressing the heroes feelings, reflections and, to a minimal degree conflicts that move the story forward.

In the presence of such material the way to develop a story is by applying these moods, expressions and dialogues in the correct measures and intensity. Another important element is the successive introduction of new 'plots', such as the appearance of the woman neighbour in 'The Whales of September'.[7] One may treat such introductions as specific turning points on the condition that they don't change anything in the current situation and that they do not move the subject material onto a new track, but only enrich it.

For this kind of storytelling I would not be able to define any principles or rules. The degree of mood intensity and expression in individual sequences one must simply feel or sense. Fiction films usually have synopses or at least outlines of construction, which contain the basic development of the subject matter. However, only the editing process reveals how much the assumptions of the director are correct. Only in the cutting room can you eliminate that which disturbs the proper gradation, change the order of sequences or, what is enormously important, give the whole film its proper pace. It is my deeply held belief that with such materials the work of the editor requires the highest competence which goes unnoticed by the critics – unlike the thickly cut chase scenes and flashy effect of a James Bond film.

Is the 'workshop' of European films easier or more difficult than the 'workshop' of American films, worked on over many years, passed on from master to master and each time improved upon? In my opinion both 'workshops' are equally hard. Hollywood editing is rather conservative, but so much is required of the editor there. Not only precise control in the 'grading of planes' and the clarity of dialogue and fluency of narrative, but also the consequence and legibility of storytelling, keeping the true character of the protagonist and the reality of characters who are in and out of the story. In European films, of which it is written that they 'describe and examine problems rather than supply dramatic solutions', the evolution of the drama and its crises, very often, does not take into account generally accepted rules. The most detailed basic rules of editing are often broken. To be able to suit the editing to the vision and style of a given director one has first to know the basic rules, because only then can you avoid them or break them, when you understand their purpose. As with the grammar of language, to break the rules or change the meaning of words you have to know the language and feel it, otherwise you create elemental faults and not literature.

Secondly, you not only have to understand but also feel the directors vision. Otherwise the editor becomes a mechanical manufacturer of his wishes. I often ask myself in relation to the changes in modern films the following question: Are there any editorial rules which exist regardless of either the particular directors style or the evolution of language and the changing tastes of film-makers and audiences? In my experience the most important thing is construction. Regardless of the individuality of the director the film and its specific scenes have to have some point of entry, development and exit. This point of exit, supported by the editing, must be clear so that the audience has no doubts, that in the case of each scene, its 'Theme' and 'Temperature'[8] are suitably complete so that you can go on to the next. In respect of the whole film that it is indeed the end: there must never be two or three endings.

The next question is the ability in film to work with and control the perception of distance/space, especially if you want the audience to be able to imagine it. I have in mind the way the action unfolds and the positive accentuating of distance/space, even as we are moving elsewhere. To precis this – it may not interest us, e.g. to know the location where the young hero of '*Les Quatre-Cents Coups*'[9] opens his heart to the psychologist/lawyer/prosecutor but the audience must become aware at once that the next scene takes place elsewhere. One other problem of distance is distance between characters. They stand close together, far apart, in the same location or different locations (e.g. a conversation between kitchen and living room), on the same side of the road, across the road, facing one another or with their backs to each other.

The third challenge is the ability to link all the connections. Some directors prefer a greater continuity between shots, others like sharp breaks. Some prefer voices to run across cuts, others observe pauses and silence to achieve a change of thought.

Notwithstanding individual tastes and temperaments only a great experience and feeling allows for successful integration of material that represents action in space, controlling the risks inherent in the collapsing of time often found in modern forms of narrative. After cutting one can clearly see the difference between an amateur and professional.

I see rather dramatic differences between film editing and editing on computer in that on film one cuts by feel, both sound and picture, thus more subtly and freely than on the computer where each operation has to be calculated.

If film-making survives as an art form, the role of the editor will remain. No director can be without an editor. Not in the sense of technical help, but as a 'censor' of materials that have been realised, for which the editor is indispensable. Milos Forman[10] writes in his memoirs that you would give your soul to the devil in return for the eyes of an editor.

I had no particular habits or rituals or a set daily routine. In recent years I have spent more time on didactics and more rarely on editing. So the organisation of my school activities, editing time and free time looks very different now, therefore I must refer to times past. The editing of a documentary film requires different organisational skills to the editing of a fiction film. In fiction the editing material arrives daily and each day must be made ready for screening – that is the first stage of editing. In the second stage begins the precise editing of the proposed sequence.

In documentary making it is different – each film requires, depending on the subject, a different timescale for the shoot and assessment of the editing schedule in relation to the shoot. '*Szpital*' (*Hospital*[11] by Krzysztof Kieslowski) was realised during two severe/busy rounds of duty in the orthopaedic department. 'The Year of Frank W', as I already mentioned took a year, most other films a number of months all with breaks waiting for a specific shooting situation, e.g. army enrolment, the hero's birthday, the last firing of raw material in a steel works about to close. Therefore the editing of documentaries such as the ones I dealt with would often happen at the same time and the work would be very stressful and time consuming with long hours including Saturdays and Sundays. Interspersed with snatched free time to catch up on private and family matters. Therefore the life style was totally dictated by work although the intensity of work varied.

I am convinced that to carry out this kind of work one must have a vocation. I have in mind three important qualities: firstly – imagination, which reflects the imagination of a chess player, which allows the mind to place things in order and perceives what those things will be in relation to one another and in relation to the whole. You edit a film in your head. Work on the table purely confirms in reality your thoughts.

Secondly, feeling the rhythm of sequences and scenes of the whole story. I cannot define what this rhythm depends upon, but a good editor has no problem in recognising a good rhythm from a bad one. This does not depend on the length of thought/ideas. Some images can last a few minutes in length – some longer – but it is their worth, length of feeling, expression, the moment has a finite length. It is the relationship of this moment to other pieces, sections of film. They do not have to have a specific time limit but they have to correlate.

Thirdly, the ability to undertake so called 'masculine' decisions. You can improve a scene countless times, sometimes slight variations, but at some point you have to say stop, either because it is good or that it can be no better. The editor like the director cannot constantly waiver. To lose ones own opinion does not help the director but rather hinders him.

Regarding how I choose which film to work on, amongst the Warsaw Documentary Film makers there was an un-written agreement between directors and editors. Sometimes one had to part for various reasons – conflict, illness – but then a director could not just go up to any other editor. The current editor would have to confirm to his colleague that indeed the work had been stopped. The habit of normal working practice was that each editor works with a specific director and therefore worked on whatever project the director had.

It is difficult to talk about the 'script' in relation to documentary, where the material is the source of the structure. As a rule I would get to know the script before and during the filming. Sometimes I was able to suggest some helpful ideas or sequences. In a number of films I was on the location to get to know the characters and their situation. Thereafter I would try to work with the given material as if I knew nothing more than what was in front of me, using that as my guide.

Throughout the thirty years of my professional life I had the same room and cutting table – not just the type of table but the same one. It was a Polish table constructed on the same principles as the German Kostareff table. With one track for picture and one for sound – a horizontal table with pedals. In the seventies in Poland there appeared far more modern tables: KEM and Steenbeck originals, but constructed to their design by Polish engineers. I preferred my old table (today it is no more!) for three reasons. It held synchronisation very accurately; it stopped exactly where I wanted it to and it had a very faithful sound reproduction. I could establish the precise difference in the silences between words.

Until the invention of 'Scotch' (*tape joins*) I used a lot of blank frames (*filler*?), sticking it between ideas. Dede Allen speaks of this same method. The 'blank' enables you to place a number of variants of each scene without the loss of any frames. I have to stress that each time you redo a cement splice you lose two frames.

Most of the time in documentaries is spent on notes, describing ideas, writing down dialogue and from them establishing a correct sequence. However one does not have to edit a lot of material each day. The tempo increases however once decisions have been made regarding construction of scenes and the overall shape of the film. Therefore the editing is not rushed. Speed does not count for as much as in fiction.

Each documentary film requires a different approach to the material. Sometimes there are very few good ideas, then the choice is stark. Then one has the problem of how to create a good scene. More often there is far too much good material. Then one has to choose very carefully, stage by stage, to be sure one has chosen the best. The construction of the scenes as well as the film is not fully decided upon until the editing is finished. So the whole time one has to be aware of the excluded material.

I am convinced that in documentary films (more so than in fiction) sound plays an important role. It can strengthen a particular scene but it can also destroy a scene, especially if it is incorrectly used. That is why I insisted on applying the sound and background music myself to all films that I edited, even if it is specially composed for the film. On the whole I decide with the director the type of music and in which places it should be used.

In any profession, not only the film world, there are few brilliant personalities. Editing does not seem to be a specific profession. If it differs in any way from the skills of an artistic operator, it is that the operator can show his particular skills in a particular film, and his vision even if the editing skills are weak and badly set. On the other hand the editor is tightly controlled by the material he is given to work with. This includes fictional film as well as documentary. Only if the editor is given good interesting material can he expand and develop his own mark. There are few brilliant editors, even fewer brilliant films, because not every film of a brilliant director is a success. That is why I feel there are so few good editors. Some do not have the opportunity to show their skills. Another important factor is that film critics and theorists do not understand the role of the film editor. They cannot see him on the screen and therefore cannot establish his input in their critique. (But that is a subject outside the framework of this interview.)

Notes

1. **René Clair (1898–1981)** – Most renowned for his films of the 1920s and 1930s – e.g. '*The Italian Straw Hat*', 1927, and '*À Nous la liberté*' (1931).
2. **Wladyslaw Slesicki and Kazimierz Karabasz** The forma made 'In Desert and Wilderness', 1973. The latter was born in 1930 and has become a renowned documentary maker and teacher.
3. **Krzysztof Kieslowski** – As far as I can tell Lidia worked with him fifteen times over a period of twelve years starting with '*From the City of Lodz*' (1968) up until '*Railway Station*', 1980.
4. **Halladin** – Director of the same generation as Kieslowski.
5. *Roku Franka W* – Karabasz, 1968.
6. *Intimate Lighting* – Ivan Passer, 1966.
7. *'The Whales of September'* – I am sure Lidia means '*The Whales of August*', (1987), Lindsay Anderson, where Ann Sothern as 'Trisha' disturbs the equilibrium of the central characters played by Bette Davis and Lillian Gish.
8. **Temperature** – Emotion?
9. *Les Quatre-Cents Coups* – François Truffaut, 1959.
10. **Milos Forman's memoirs** – 'Turnaround – a memoir', written with Jan Novak, 1993.
11. *Hospital* – Kieslowski, 1976.

20 Milenia Fiedler

There is, in this response to my questions, an intense feeling of dis-illusionment. The wonderful heritage of Polish cinema seems to have been obliterated by the changes that have resulted from the break up of the Soviet hegemony since the fall of the Berlin Wall. On my last visit to Lodz, where Milenia was born, the largest cinema with five screens had four Hollywood films and one Turkish – not one Polish. However we should not forget the incredible amount of visionary work that has come out of Poland, especially since the Second World War. It is unacceptable to imagine that a renaissance will never happen in this country for which cinema seems such a natural medium. For there is cause for optimism in the work of the current film-makers in Poland. In her relatively short career, Milenia has worked several times with Wojciech Marczewski and Witold Adamek two of the brightest directing talents currently working in her country.

Milenia Fiedler (Courtesy of Milenia Fiedler)

I was born in Lodz, Poland and both my parents were teachers. Literature has always been my love. I used to read everything as a child, then I started to choose more carefully, but I still get satisfaction reading Stephen King or Borges[1] (different kind of satisfaction, but satisfaction). Theatre has never been a space which I could sink into – I usually watch a theatre performance as a kind of ritual that belongs to a strange religion – I can be impressed but not involved. However four or five times in my life I watched performances that were just pure magic (once it was ballet, the other times puppet or mime performances). Music is what I love although I don't understand it (and I don't want to understand it).

I started to go to movies when I was ten or eleven. The reason was that my brother damaged the TV set at home. I used to go to the cinema even three times a day. In those days (the 1980s) there were over forty cinemas in Lodz with an interesting repertoire – film was considered an Art in Communist countries, so I learned film from Bergman, Losey, Kurosawa, Tarkovsky, etc.

At the age of eighteen, I wanted to be a film director – so I went to the Lodz Film School and passed the exams but not well enough to be accepted for the course of directing. But they proposed me for a scholarship to FAMU.[2] I knew nothing about what film-making really was in those days. After a few months in Prague I learnt that I would never want to be a director, and I fell in love with editing.

I learnt at school – from my teachers, especially Professor Valusiak[3] who never told us how to edit but taught me how to read the hidden universes from the pieces of film in the editing room. Maybe I can't express myself clearly enough – watching the rushes is like standing in front of the entrances to many possible worlds – you must compose them, but they are not your creation, because they were always there. It's like following the rabbit in the woods, when neither the rabbit nor the woods exist unless you pursue them. That's why editing is the greatest adventure I know.

Some examples of the work I have done, which show the value of editing, are 'The Gateway to Europe' by Jerzy Wojcik, 'Weiser' by Wojciech Marczewski and 'Monday' by Witold Adamek.[4] Only the last one is a good film. The first two films are just a promise of something interesting and original but they contain great scenes created during editing. I love director's mistakes – they encourage me in my work.

'Hollywood' film-makers deal with the audience, European film-makers deal with reality. In the first case the goal is to tell a story – people have always loved to hear stories because story is a structure that helps us to understand reality, it gives sense to a stream of events experienced by a human being. When you present a film you always say, 'Hey, look, life is like this'. And you can give an explanation to the phenomena of life recovering the chain of reasons and results, recognising a man by his actions – simply, telling the story. But that doesn't explain everything. So instead you can focus on what's beyond the story. And that is what non-Hollywood film-makers do. It makes editing much more difficult. There are no ready solutions, there are no schemes and there is nothing except your own mind to direct you.

I love digital technology. I think it gives an editor freedom to experiment, to test any possibility that comes to his or her mind. Film in the process of creation is virtual so the digital environment is natural for it.

I guess I have no routine that is necessary for me – I can work in any place and under any circumstances. People are what are essential for me – people that I can discuss with – the more the better.

Empathy, curiosity and a vivid imagination – these are the qualities that are essential for this job. Then you must use intuition or analytic skills. And you have to be patient and optimistic to believe you will eventually find the way to fit all the parts of your puzzle together.

There are no rules of editing – there are only examples of solutions that have worked. When you learn them and follow them you are competent, but when you have the courage to follow your own path then you have a chance to be a genius. And the courage is something you are born with.

Seventy per cent of the time I work on projects that come along otherwise I couldn't pay my bills. But when I have a comfort to choose, I choose the director. I never read scripts unless I am asked to discuss it before shooting.

I don't like to know the script. It's not because I'm afraid it will narrow my imagination or influence my judgement (I can free myself from any influences) but because it is a pleasure not to know what will happen next.

I prefer the Avid Film Composer – it's the most comfortable of the non-linear systems I have tried. The only thing important for me is to place monitors about seventy centimetres in front of my eyes and a bigger display about two metres from my head to the right, and no reflections from any sources of light on the screen.

I can't perform a rough-cut. I always work till I feel I have a fine cut of a scene. After I assemble the scenes I can see what is wrong – I start to rebuild the scenes, to cut them again, to test alternatives till it's done.

Picture without sound and the same picture with a sound effect are not the same pictures – they have different meanings. When you cut a closeup of a man with his POV (a parked car, let's say) that means he sees the car. When you add the effect of the engine, your character would see the approaching car. Sorry for this primitive and obvious example, but I try to explain why I can't edit without designing the sound. I usually just think about sound effects that should be used, but quite often I edit sound effects together with picture just to make sure that the scene has the shape and meaning that I planned for it. That doesn't mean a real sound design – often after finishing my job I remove all the effects I used and wait for a sound designer to do his job. He is another person who can enrich the film.

I try to avoid using music during editing. The rhythm of cuts starts to be musical, the mood and emotions are forced by music instead of picture. It doesn't help me. I am usually able to influence the way music is used in my films. In most cases I am invited to discuss it with the director and the composer. As regards my particular feelings about music in film – nothing original – music is very important because of the reasons described thousands of times by persons much more experienced in this field than me.

I always want to have an assistant who is capable of taking care of all logistic and technological problems concerning the project, to communicate with others involved in post-production (laboratory, sound, graphics, etc.). But good ones are very rare these days.

I cut on film during my school. As a professional I started with analogue linear systems (which was hell) and then used non-linear digital technologies. Only once in my professional career I had to cut on film and had to change my methods from non-linear to traditional. I found it less convenient. But I don't think that technology can determine the final result.

I am convinced that personality affects ones work. My personality determines my attitude to the film's characters, to the idea of the film. But I can't describe either my cutting style (perhaps I have one, but it's beyond my control – each of the films I've done seems to be completely different for me) or my personality. I think that I change when I work in the way actors change when they perform. I feel I am different when I work on an action movie or when I edit a film that examines the complicated relations between people. Perhaps it is just an illusion, but I feel so.

I can't predict anything. When I observe the way film changes in Poland (or should I say dies in Poland) I could only say that the best thing is to quit. The quality of TV production, which is what we do here for the most of time, is so low that it doesn't matter who edits it. It requires just basic skills and no personality at all. I am afraid that this routine kills creative potential forever.

Notes

1. **Stephen King** – Born in US in 1947. Writer of thrillers often dealing with the supernatural and **Jorge Luis Borges (1899–1986)** – Argentinean writer noted for his dense but moving prose and poetry in which he expresses the deep conundrums of human existence.
2. **FAMU** – The Czech Film School in Prague. The Polish School in Lodz does not offer editing as a specialism.
3. **Josef Valusiak** – See interview in this book.
4. **Films: *The Gateway to Europe*** – Wojcik, 1999.
   Weiser – Marczewski, 2001.
   Monday – Adamek, 2002.

21 Anna Kornis

Anna's first editing assignment 'Family Nest', was also the first feature film to be directed by Béla Tarr, whose own thoughts about the medium are included in this book. As you will read the strongest influence on Anna was that of Gábor Bódy who only made three feature films before his early death. His particular passion for the medium of cinema clearly left a deep impression on Anna.

I was born in Budapest. My father was a director of shorts and educational films and my mother was the financial executive of a film studio. When I was a kid we had no TV (or video like nowadays). The visual culture consisted of father telling a tale every evening with a special slide strip-film. It was very popular in Hungary. Each strip had fifteen to twenty frames illustrating well-known tales or novels. I read books all the time and everywhere – most often history and fiction. My love and understanding of literature have certainly helped me as an editor, if not in a direct way, certainly in the background. It is as much a part of education as music and art, and all this together adds up to what forms the taste of somebody.

I had no special skill in the arts, but I had a very good teacher of art history. She showed us how to 'see' paintings and sculpture, and how to benefit from visiting museums. It became very important in time. Later cinema became part of my cultural interest like literature. In secondary school I had season tickets for different series and I saw many films which are essential in film culture, old silent movies, American films from the 1950s, English films from the 1960s and many others. I remember when I was fifteen- or sixteen-year old, going with my father to see '*Blow-Up*'.[1] I wore big sunglasses because I was afraid I wouldn't be let in as I was under eighteen.

Afterwards my father asked me whether I liked it or not. I liked it very much and my father asked why. I couldn't tell, but I felt it was something for adults – a new way to express things which we want to know or explain.

Editing wasn't my first choice as a career. I came upon it through both accidental and obvious reasons. Due to the Hungarian higher educational system – I failed my university entrance exam in Hungarian and English – I had to work for a year before I could try again. It was obvious to work at my father's place as an assistant editor – and it was love at first sight. Then I spent three years from 1981 to 1984 in the School of Drama and Cinema in Budapest on the film-editing course and received the diploma.

I learnt editing in the beginning from every man who moved in the editing room. I followed with attention what the director, editor, cameraman and everyone else said, and why and what would be the consequence of all this for the film. It was very edifying. But the great and real lesson was when I made the first steps alone. The greatest part of learning editing was the practice for me.

I recall something which made a special impression on me. In the late 1970s I worked on films by István Dárday and Györgyi Szalay.[2] They worked together, their speciality was a feature film in documentary style. They didn't use actors, they wrote the story and then hunted for the right person for the role. When they found the right persons, they didn't give them lines, they only outlined the situation for them and it was an improvisation and very lifelike. I like these films very much, because they were very close to me and the world in which I live. My favourite was a very long film (three hours and a half) entitled '*A Film Novel – Three Sisters*', but I could mention their other movie '*The Prize Trip*'.[3] Béla Tarr also started his career in this vein. I don't know whether this style is still viable, but I like it very much.

The first big experience was the first film of Béla Tarr. '*Family Nest*'[4] was the very first for both of us. As regards myself I didn't know much about how to edit or cut film. I wanted to prove that I was able to do this thing. Both of us tried to persuade the other, but in the end we asked somebody with more experience. What I did wad impulsive – not conscious – even now it is important to me to 'feel' the film and not have an ideological approach.

In the first scenes of the film Iren, the main character is going to work early in the morning and she is moving away from us becoming smaller and smaller (Tarr said this was the kind of film beginning others used for an ending). This is similar to what we can see in his later films.

As I see it his way of film-making is very logical from the documentary style with some improvised elements added to the precisely composed images, where every movement, step or dialogue has a special meaning. One has a close connection with the other, that is the reason you feel he is denying the function of the cut. As I see it he wants to make his films in one sequence, therefore he tries not to separate two things with a cut but to combine them. Whereas in Jancsó's[5] films the long scenes were more formal than functional.

My greatest lesson (and the greatest absence) till now was Gábor Bódy.[6] He was a man with special talents, with great curiosity about new things and he was a 'naughty boy'. He gave me tasks but many things he did alone at the editing table: good ideas came to him when he touched the film. When we made '*Narcissus and Psyche*'[7] I was in one editing room and he was in another. I cut the traditional scenes and he cut the experimental ones. Then we put the whole thing together. He was a very autonomous man in his films and in his work methods too. We worked several times at night or at weekends when good ideas came to him, but he was very open to suggestion in spite of all this.

I learnt another point of view about the world. It was especially interesting on '*The Dog's Night Song*'.[8] Before the shooting I asked what kind of film it would be. He answered that it would be a 'Dárday' film in 'Bódy' style. Dárday worked with documentary elements and described a piece of Hungarian reality. Bódy also showed us Hungarian realities but with a special point of view. This sentence, Dárday film in Bódy style, was a cue for me to understand what he wanted. I started to learn the 'Bódy language' and this lesson is not finished. This is the reason and his particular personality why I, and others, miss him.

In my opinion Hungarian cinema is not a reaction to Hollywood, rather it is a result of the specific social, cultural and historical background of our country. Money is also a big problem. Hungarian directors also have ideas, which involve many extras, nice costumes, big sets or want to use the new technologies, but the possibilities are very limited and this is constricting. For such a little country like Hungary, in my opinion, the only course must be not to imitate American cinema but to continue the old traditions and values.

In my opinion the editor has a very special place in film-making. He or she is inside and outside at the same time. I mean we get the scenario, we can give ideas but it isn't our story. We have a view of the film but it is a little bit different. The editor's work is to support the director's ideas. I can't show examples because every film is different, every film requires a proper style, which is not mine, but I try to follow that and this is the core of my work. It is important to try many ideas, including those that seem at first to be bad, because who knows what will help the final structure in the end.

Non-linear digital technology made many things different in the process of editing, which is good and bad at the same time. Everything is quicker we can try more things but it isn't always good. There is no time to think after the influence of many ideas and it is easy to lose the way among the experiments. It is very important to see the film on the big screen because it can be very different from what we see on the monitor. But the computer is not absolutely bad and this is the new way for editing. For me it is not easy because I learnt the traditional method and my system works well in that way. My hands know the task on the traditional editing table and my brain is ready for the film itself. The computer uses a big part of my brain and the film gets less.

Every film and every director demands another system and 'humour'. The editing room is a very special place – we spend so much time together there and can develop something which can be a ritual. We often quote words, sentences or actions from the film and this is part of editing. When I'm not working my life changes radically. At first it is not easy to switch to another rhythm. Editing is a very intensive thing, which needs much energy and power. When it stops from one day to another it leaves a big void. Often I can't use my time well, but I need this inactivity.

The editor must have patience, diligence and submission to the profession – a good character and personality. It is important to learn many things: literature, music, arts and needs good taste. Much depends on luck – the right people in the right place at the right time. I mean who you meet – can you understand each other – are you free at that time. Who is a great editor? The film needs good specialists who like the film and not the career.

I don't choose the film, the film, namely the director chooses me. There are some directors who are my old customers, with whom I have worked together for a long time. And sometimes others come. The Hungarian film industry is not too big – we know each other more or less.

If I get a script I read it but I don't annotate it. I await the rushes with curiosity, because there are always different from my pre-conception. My imagination starts working after seeing the rushes.

Every attempt at a cut is meant to be a commitment, but ten minutes later it can be clear that it wasn't a good idea and we start from the beginning again and again – changing the choice of shot, cut out, put back – as long as it doesn't look good. This is the way of editing for me, but it varies from film to film. Sound is an internal part of the film and I consider it of equal importance to picture. Sometimes the image is more important, sometimes the sound (e.g. sound effects). The image and the sound together make the film complete – only their proportion can be different.

Music is a very important part of the film. The music and the image together can give something that can't be expressed in words. But it can be very dangerous when the two don't meet: the result can be ridiculous or boring. The film has a proper style which includes the music, but sometimes it is worth making experiments with something else, because we can get very interesting results.

I miss my good 'old' assistant. I could leave many things to her. She knew my taste; she could follow my ideas. With the computer I have become acquainted with others who are doing the digitising. Generally young people who are very enthusiastic and they help me very much with the new technology.

I can't change my attitudes. I started with film and this determined my editing system. However sometimes the computer needs something else and the new technology can have its effects on my methods. This is the time for me to learn something else, but I want to keep the old method as far as possible.

Why do I like being an editor – because it is a mode of expression for me. I never wanted to be a director (I was asked about this many times), but at the editing table watching the reels my imagination starts to work and I feel that I am creating something. Not many people are given the opportunity to earn money by doing something they actually like to do so I count myself fortunate.

Notes

1. *Blow-Up* – Michelangelo Antonioni, 1966.
2. **István Dárday and Györgi Szalay** – Have made six films together including the intriguing: '*East from the West or the Discreet Charm of the Media*' and most recently '*Reflections*',1998.
3. *A Film Novel – Three Sisters* **(1974)** and *The Prize Trip* **(1974)** – Dárday and Szalay.
4. *Family Nest* – Béla Tarr, 1979.
5. **Miklós Jancsó** – Director born in 1921. Co-incidentally Béla Tarr's partner and editor, Ágnes Hranitsky, was assistant editor on Jancsó's film '*The Round-up*', 1965. See also Roberto Perpignani interview.
6. **Gábor Bódy (1946–85)** – Committed suicide – he had made three major films each of which won prizes – yet another special film-maker who is hardly known outside of his country.
7. *'Narcissus and Psyche'* – Bódy, 1980.
8. *'The Dog's Night Song'* – Bódy, 1983.

22 Béla Tarr Interviewed by Jonathan Romney, National Film Theatre, London, 15.3.01

With kind permission of Béla Tarr and Jonathan Romney. The simultaneous translation was by László Hackenast.

The Hungarian director, Béla Tarr, has created a radical cinema which subverts conventional narrative and amongst other things ignores continuity as an editing device. His partner, Ágnes Hranitzky, is also his editor and co-filmmaker. Their films are built on long takes usually involving considerable camera movement, which at one level are reminiscent of that other Hungarian radical Miklós Jancsó. Yet there is something more disturbingly everyday about the milieu conveyed by their work. Their relationship with the composer is particularly unusual – more akin to the way animators work in the fact that the music is written before the film is shot.

'It's very difficult to talk about what we really think to be a film. The question really is what is film for? It's a long time since we came to the conclusion that film is not about telling a story. It's function is really something very different, something else. So that we can get closer to people, somehow we can understand everyday life. And that somehow we can understand human nature, why we are like we are'.

'We believe that apart from the main protagonists in the film there are other protagonists: scenery, the weather, time and locations

'*Werckmeister Harmonies*' a film by Béla Tarr (Courtesy Artificial Eye Film Company Ltd)

have their faces and they are important, they play an important role in the story'.

'From the very beginning the way we handled time was probably different from other films. First of all because we cut and edited the film differently, most films are edited in the way pieces of information are edited, we didn't do it that way. We are paying more attention to the internal psychological processes. And we concentrate on the personal existence and the personal presence of the actors and actresses. That is why meta-communication is that important, indeed is more important than verbal communication. And from here it is only a short step to put it in time and space'.

'. . . there is a huge difference between literature and film. They use two different languages. Writers have much wider opportunities in terms of writing hundreds of sentences and they can invoke feelings in a much more varied way. Film in itself is quite a primitive language. It's made simpler by it's definiteness, by it's being so concrete and that's why it's so exciting. It's always a challenge to do something with this limited language. The writer Krasznahorkai always says 'How can you do anything with such limited options, with such limited tools?' He is exasperated by the fact that we, as he sees it, deal with such cheap things. Film is a cheap show in the marketplace and it's a great thing that we can develop that into something valuable'.

JR: 'The other person that you worked with really closely right from the beginning is your partner and editor Ágnes Hranitzky. And she has really been more than an editor, because she is very close to the whole conception of the film'.

BT: 'Well she is present all through the making of the film and she is co-author and no decisions are made without her. Not only because she really knows and understands things, because we do work together, we make the films together. There is an everyday process of making these films with the preparations, the shooting and the editing.

There is another very important member of the family and that's Vig Mihály, the composer with whom we have worked together for the past fifteen years. And without the composer the films wouldn't be what they are. He goes into the studio a month before the actual shooting takes place, composes the music, gives it to us and then we use the music during the shoot. So the music plays an equal role to the actors or the scenes or the story. And we trust him so much that we don't go there into the studio. He composes the music and brings the music to us. It's a very close and very profound, very friendly relationship which has been shaped over the last fifteen years and it's a relationship where we don't need to talk about anything serious. We never talk about art, we never talk about philosophy, we don't discuss aesthetics. We always talk about very concrete, very practical issues'.

23 Éva Palotai

This modest contribution from Éva Palotai belies her perceptive perspective on Hungarian cinema. She has cut several times for György Molnár during her editing career.

I was born in Deggendorf in Bavaria. My father was a sculptor and my mother a civil servant with lots of skills. I was always very fond of reading and I loved literature. In my teenage years I read Hungarian and foreign novels and poetry. Hungarian translators are excellent and books in Hungary at that time were very cheap. As my father was a sculptor, from an early age I lived in the world of arts and artists.

In the early 1960s I spent a month in Ireland, when the film '*West Side Story*'[1] was released. It had a tremendous effect on me, as at that time Hungary was still an 'Iron Curtain' country and 'such bourgeois shit' was banned. Later our country began to open up to Western culture. I remember that around 1964 there was a British Film Week held in Budapest, and young people fought for tickets to see '*Becket*'[2] with Burton and O'Toole, '*Hard Days' Night*'[3] and so forth.

In my parents' time – Hungary after the war – cinema didn't play a big role in entertainment. They (and of course me as a child) preferred to go to exhibitions, opera, concerts but very seldom to the cinema because – at least that's what I think now – they showed mainly Russian (Soviet) films. It was a type of passive resistance in the 1950s and early 1960s. I first encountered film as an art form in Grammar school when it was obligatory to see Soviet films. Some of them were excellent, e.g. '*Ballad of a Soldier*'[4] by Grigori Chukhraj and '*The Cranes are Flying*'[5] by Mikheil Kalatozishvili. Later, at the end of the 1960s I think it was mainly the French 'nouvelle vague' that developed my interest in cinema – and I became hooked.

Editing was not my first choice as a career. I wanted to work as a graphic artist, but I wasn't admitted to the Academy of Fine Arts. I worked for five years – believe it or not – before the decision to be a film editor came to me as 'an inspiration from heaven', without any knowledge of the work itself. At that time I met someone who was an assistant editor at Hungarian Television (MTV) and as she was expecting a baby I got her job.

I was lucky, at Hungarian Television I worked for the Dramatic Group, which produced TV features – about fifty single films and plays a year. From the editor for whom I worked I was able to learn all the technical skills, which were needed for cutting on 16mm and 35mm film as well as dubbing. While I was working at MTV I studied two days a week at the Academy for Film and Theatre. So our company, MTV, supported our studies. The aim of our training was to get a general education including music, arts, film history, dramaturgy, philosophy, etc. We had practical sessions in the cutting room trying the possibilities with material together with discussions. Beyond the lessons we edited all the films shot by director and camera students at the Academy. Our editor teacher at film school was very important as she taught us a lot about the attitude towards the directors one worked with. For me the directors who were important then were Károly Makk[6] as a professor and Miklós Jancsó[7] for whom I edited a 'subjective documentary' film.

I was also strongly affected by some particular films amongst which were Károly Makk's '*Szerelem*' (*Love*), Miklós Jancsó's '*Szegénylegények*' (*The Round Up*) and István Szabó's '*Álmodozások kora*' (*The Age of Day-Dreaming*). Internationally '*Á Bout de Souffle*', '*Jules et Jim*', '*Blow-Up*', '*La Strada*', '*Eight-and-a-half*', '*Easy Riders*', '*Cabaret*', '*All That Jazz*' and nowadays the Mike Leigh films.[8]

I'm not sure that any of the films I have cut can demonstrate what editors contribute to cinema. Several of them were important in my life, but one never knows, watching a film, what is the editor's part in it. Here, and I think everywhere in Europe, where film-making is not of the Hollywood type the editor is good if his/her contribution remains hidden.

Most European 'art' films are films of the director. In Europe the editor is a discussion partner for the director – of course also an expert (maybe the best) in editing. The main demand is to be a partner in every sense of the word, not just someone who moves around bits of film in a film factory. Of course I can only speak for myself.

I love digital non-linear. No lost frames, no long rewinds. The 'undos'! I think this technology only differs from film editing in its quickness and effortlessness, and has given back the freedom of editing after years of analogue technology. You can retry and keep all the versions you've ever made and it presents no problem if the director decides after twelve different attempts that after all the second was the really good one. The possibility of having all the effects at hand and not waiting for the lab, to see a transition or a motion effect for the first time frightened me, but now I feel liberated and I can use my creativity for the sake of the movie.

I think each type of editing has its reasons for existence. The Hollywood type movie needs the expert. The European film needs a partner, but the editor is becoming redundant for those who make their films with only the editors technical help and not with an intellectual partner, but this is the director's loss. Joking apart I believe that in non-fictional and low-budget independent filmmaking the demand for an editor is decreasing.

I am sure that a proud and vain person has difficulties being an editor. If you cannot push your egoism and vanity to the background, if you want to be praised and appreciated all the time you may be a good editor but you will be an unhappy person. I think many qualities which are useful for an editor are the so-called feminine qualities – being like a good mother or a gardener, who is tolerant and loving, but on occasion can be strong-minded and forceful for the 'child's' good. I might be mistaken but in Hungary at least, all the editors who are/were 'masculine types', whether by gender or temperament, have become directors.

I don't even know who is a good editor. I really mean this. I don't know whom we can call a great editor. Coming out from the cinema, you can hardly tell whether the editor of a film was really good or not. You can judge the film but not the editor. Maybe this sounds disappointing from an editor, but this is how I feel. You can never stand in the spotlight if you are an editor, except if you – or your film – wins an Oscar.

Notes

1. *West Side Story* – Directed by Robert Wise, 1961.
2. *Becket* – Directed by Peter Glenville with Richard Burton and Peter O'Toole, 1964.
3. *Hard Day's Night* – Richard Lester, script by Alun Owen, 1964.
4. *Ballad of a Soldier* – Directed by Chukhraj, 1959.
5. *The Cranes are Flying* – Kalatozishvili, 1957.
6. **Károly Makk** – Director born 1925, e.g. '*Another Way*', 1982.
7. **Miklós Jancsó** – Director born 1921, e.g. '*Red Psalm*' (1971), Best Director at Cannes.
8. **Films and filmmakers:**
   Love – Károly Makk, Jury prize Cannes, 1971.
   The Round Up – Miklós Jancsó. A revelation at the time because of Jancsó' daring choreography of movement in shots sometimes as long as seven or eight minutes. A style he sustained through many films, 1965.
   The Age of Day-Dreaming – István Szabó, 1964.
   Breathless – Jean-Luc Godard, 1960.
   Jules et Jim – François Truffaut, 1962.
   Blow-Up – Michelangelo Antonioni, 1966.
   La Strada – Federico Fellini, 1954.
   Eight-and-a-half – Fellini, 1963.
   Easy Riders – Dennis Hopper (with Peter Fonda), 1969.
   Cabaret – Bob Fosse, 1972.
   All That Jazz – Bob Fosse, 1979.
   Mike Leigh – e.g. *Secrets and Lies*, 1996.

24 Josef Valusiak

Professor Valusiak became a film editor at the time of the Czech New Wave in the 1960s and he edited all the films of one of its leading lights, Jaromil Jires. At the same time he began to develop as a teacher at FAMU, a role he still fulfils with distinction. His erudition and passion are a potent combination.

I was born in a working-class family on 16 December 1934. From childhood I lived in a small town called Jilemnice, which is north of Prague in the Krkonose Mountains, where I graduated from High school. I was interested in reading imaginative and historical literature and in theatre and sports too. I played violin and accordion, but not very successfully. I also acted in some plays with a non-professional theatre group.

After an unsuccessful application to the Theatre Academy I started to study at the electro-technical faculty in Prague. Since I had come to the capital city with its many cinemas I became a frequent film-goer – sometimes I saw three movies a day. But I still didn't quit my theatre group.

Later I specialised in the radio, film and TV at the electro-technical faculty and completed my Masters examination in 1958. In the same year at the world technological exhibition: Expo 58 in Brussels the two Czechoslovakian inventions carried off the award – these were the Polyecran and the Laterna Magica.[1] After my graduation I worked as an engineer in Polyecran and later as a scenic technician at the Laterna Magica Theatre. But I still aspired to creative work and I started to study in the direction department at FAMU in 1961.

As I was mostly interested in fiction films and felt that I wouldn't be the best director, I decided to change departments and in the third year I started to study editing which department had recently been developed by the director and editor, Jan Kucera,[2] who became my biggest influence. Also the director Elmar Klos (Academy Award winner in 1965 for *'The Shop on Main Street'*[3]) was my teacher and I edited his last film *'Touha zvaná Anada'*[4] some time later. Very important for me was also the co-operation with Jaromil Jires,[5] one of the directors of the Czech New Wave, whose 13 features and many of his TV films I edited. Of the many world film-makers who affected me one I must mention is Andrei Tarkovsky.

In 1965 I worked as an assistant editor and from 1966 as an editor at the Barrandov Studios in Prague. In 1972 Doctor Kucera asked me to lecture at the editing department in FAMU where I continue to teach to this day. I was also influenced by many talented people – the variety of genres, experimental forms and subject matter were the sources of experiences that influenced my mind and work. At that time I started to publish many reflections and essays in professional magazines.

Editing is the basic principle of film-making and we could talk for a long time about the creative force function of the shot by shot shooting. Sometimes the director edits his film by himself and I know of some good ones made in this way. But the educated editor brings new, fresh eyes to the film process, he is not influenced by the stress of the shooting or by the plans and purposes as the director is. Basically the editor can see what really is in the material, not what was supposed to be there, so that he can find new variants and possibilities that the director who is fixed in his imaginings cannot see. Also the editor comes with his specific experiences, skills, talent, sensibility for image and sound expression, for the rhythm and tempo, combination and association thinking, etc. And when the director and editor are close in their intellectual, creative and also personal side, and they are also close to the subject matter of the film then their participation in the result is not just added but multiplied.

I don't know enough films to categorically judge the differences between the European and Hollywood styles. In recent years it is rare that I have the opportunity to watch European films but I have the feeling that many of them copy Hollywood. The objective of the Hollywood film is profit, that means the highest number of viewers.

The subject matter, genres, stars, merchandising all address this agenda, and these criteria become important in my country too.

The European film also addresses the viewer, wants to make him laugh or touched. But it doesn't use the dreamt-up banality, it tries to show the living characters, everyday situations, it shows social problems and existential problems, from the most ordinary and the most practical situations to the most spiritual ones. Typical of the European film is the expression 'authors film'. The subject matter, the co-operation on the screenplay writing – this is all connected to one person who presents through the film his own reflections, doubts, thoughts that he has to share with other people, to commit himself. He feels he definitely HAS to make the film. And the best directors bring to the film their unique quality like Anderson, Antonioni, Bergman, Fellini, Tarkovsky. . . .

The difference is that you don't go to the cinema to watch *'The Seventh Seal'*[6] but to watch Bergman, whereas you don't go to watch Ridley Scott but to watch *'The Alien'*.[7]

I can only judge the work of Hollywood editors from the results of their work, by the films I have seen. Talking about their craft skills they are really good. Their work is more complicated because they have many variants in the number of shots taken for each scene, often by more than one camera. On the other hand this means that there are always alternatives to cut to and the real limitation is the causality of the story. The decisive point of his work is achieving the right rhythm and tempo (accent, psychological pause, gradation, etc.). With respect to the demands of films which appeal to the audience the tempo is getting faster and faster to avoid boring the spectator, not to let him think, and not to let him see the shallowness and weakness of the subject matter, but to overwhelm him with new action and situations. If we remember the tempo of films from ten or twenty years ago, it is unbelievable how much is now fitted in. And when the acceleration is not enough the film-makers bring a new interesting idea: the infraction of the story chronology. (In the cult film *'Pulp Fiction'*[8] by Tarantino – which is not that good in my opinion – the infraction of the chronology is the main and only attraction.)

The European film is not just about the story, but about the subject matter, its message, the presentation of the relationships, causes and effects, introspection of the life and the soul, which is different from Hollywood films. The European film-makers also use the editing 'inventions' of the Russian avant-garde sometimes – by connecting the shots, their content is not only added to each other but multiplied, elevated so that a new consequence, hidden meanings or associations grow. The magic of the 'area between the shots' where the unspoken, magical and transcendent communication is born and where the attributes necessary for a work of art appear. The tempo of the storytelling does not depend on the frequency of the actions and attractions but on the control of timing where the emotion, philosophy and beauty are born.

The future of editing depends, of course, on the future of culture and on the future of mankind. The truth is that man has suicidal tendencies (the nuclear wars or ecological illiteracy, for example). Also the tendency to want to change culture for the entertainment industry and to forget about art is becoming powerful. In this respect I am not an optimist but I still hope the human soul will live on. Even if the worst happens, where film continues to exist – and I think it is in less danger than literature – editing will continue to exist because it is the basic element of film language. And this was not even changed by Jancsó and his film *'Beloved Electra'*,[9] which was in fourteen shots or Sokurov's film *'The Russian Ark'*[10] in one shot. On the other hand experiments with form and other developments in film language (release of conventions) can bring new ways and variations in film editing. Because of this the film editor will always be indispensable.

With reference to work habits I am not a flexible man. I am not particular about any special rituals but in the editing room I prefer routine systematic procedure and order. Since the dissolution of the Barrandov Film Studios I have continued as a professor at FAMU and I have edited films very rarely. It is a gradual transition into retirement rather than a radical change. But of course, when I left the editing room after twenty-five years of working there, I felt sadness and regret. On the other hand every year I have the opportunity to meet new students, adepts in film, with different characters, opinions and temperaments.

To be an editor one needs to have specific abilities, of course, as any other artist. But how to define it? At FAMU we try to find the applicant's general scope and sense of the film language (picture composition, sense for the music, rhythm, co-ordinated skills) during the application examinations. Patience and the ability to concentrate for a long time is very important for this work too. As long as the art is polymorphic, the artist is as well. There definitely does not exist a prototype of the ideal editor. I know many editors who are great in their profession but they are all different characters. And something, which is very important is that, the editor must be able to co-operate with many different directors on many different kinds of film.

If I refuse to believe in destiny, I do not believe that one can be born as an editor. I definitely do not know a person, including myself, who as a child, wanted to become an editor. Thanks to TV there are many kids who want to be 'a part of film-making', but they usually mean directing or camera work, and mostly acting. Also the truth is that editing is a specific and unknown profession for most viewers, something they can't even imagine and which is not the main subject for film magazines. The editor completes the work of all other contributors to film-making starting with the scriptwriter and the film crew – he knows about all the processes of film-making. He knows what was done well and what could have been done better. That is why editors, sooner or later become directors. That might be one reason why there are not many good editors. The other reason might be the anonymity of the editor's work. The editor is dependent on the material that he works on. He cannot make an ingenious film with an ordinary screenplay and with uninspiring material. A magnificent editor is able to save many catastrophic scenes and can make a watchable film from below standard material. Neither the viewer nor the film professional watching this film knows the original material and therefore is unable to appreciate the ingenious editor's efforts. So besides the question of why there are few really good editors, the editor could ask why there are just a few great films (including the Academy Award winners).

How do I choose which films to work on? The situation in my country is different, the director chooses the editor. I can only accept or refuse. Several that I had to refuse were mostly because of a weak screenplay. Unfortunately, I've had to refuse about twenty films in which the screenplay and director were good but the postproduction plans overlapped. I quite like working on average films with nice directors, but I also worked on interesting films with less pleasant directors. The optimum was to work with friends whose name guaranteed more or less-quality films. The opposite combination was a disaster.

I prefer to read the script in advance and to be surprised by the shot material after some time. But I also worked with some directors who wanted to consult over dramaturgy and co-operate on the storyboard. The way of editing depends on the director and on how the shooting is organised. In the Barrandov Film Studio some directors wanted me to edit the scenes during the shooting so they could check whether their intentions were right or they should re-shoot. In other cases – and it is common nowadays – when the shooting is finished the director comes to the cutting room. Then we mostly do the rough cuts, set up the dramaturgy (order of scenes, flashbacks, etc.) and finally we correct the rhythm and finish the final cut.

The concept of sound design ('vertical montage' by S.M. Eisenstein)[11] originates in the final stages of editing. I am disillusioned by the new tendencies of editors who edit the film only with the sound recorded during the shoot and the rest of the sound is up to the sound designer. During the editing I consider the dramatic sound that gives the character a deeper meaning; or an intense atmosphere, which needs a couple more frames as an afterglow. When the sound is a couple of frames wrong or it absolutely misses then it makes the final cut bad or poor at least.

The silent movie illustrates that the picture is more important than the sound. But nowadays movies are audio – visual work, and although the sound cannot totally compensate for the picture – although some less adept directors try to say everything of importance with the dialogue – the film should be improved, aesthetically and significantly by the sound design. We sometimes designed the sound as a trio in Barrandov Film Studios – the director, editor and sound designer so the latter already knew what sounds he would need to record during the shoot.

The same group of people, plus the music composer met again in the editing room when the final cut was almost done. The definitive final cut was done after the music was composed and precisely placed. In this situation I could influence the way music was used. I had even more influence when we used archive music, where the use and positioning were decided between the director and myself. Usually it is the editor who has control over the rhythm of the film – often by adjusting the timing of dialogue – but in special cases like with playback or in musical films – the music takes control of the editor. It is not necessary to be a music specialist but the editor should have a musical sensitivity and especially for its reference to picture. I suffer when I watch a film I edited and, especially in documentaries, music has been added which I did not know about. I can feel the picture and the music flow independently from each other and in some places accidental fusions come up causing wrong and disturbing combinations.

My opinion regarding digital technology, thanks to my age and experience, is very conservative: I miss the subjective contact with the film material, I miss holding it, physically cutting in between specific marked frames, making a rough cut shot-by-shot. The pictures appear on the computer monitor, the variants and the combinations change and I react like I am playing some kind of computer game – and the result is not a roll of film but some virtual scheme of signals that can disappear by some lapse forever in a moment. It may seem ridiculous but I think it is like a designer creating a vase by vectors and lines on a monitor compared to a potter who makes it from clay on a wheel.

But lets forget the sentiment; I realise the two most important differences. Originally the editor had to work with the material that was shot by the cameraman. The tricks and the double exposures, the fade ins and outs were made much later as opticals in the laboratory and the editor had to believe his experiences or just his imagination, and often he saw these things in the final print without having the chance to change them. In digital editing the editor can manipulate the material considerably. In my experience he can change the size of the picture, the colours of the whole shot or a part, can remove unwanted parts of the image, prolong it by freeze frame or slowing it down, change the rhythm by adjusting the speed of all or part of a scene or shot. The second difference is in the organisation of the work. In the classical way the film was born in a couple of months – sometimes with breaks. In the digital editing room you can achieve the work in a couple of weeks. It is technically possible to make the film in this time but not with the meaning that comes from a process of creative maturation. It is difficult for me to accept this way.

This leads me to a thought about my own character. That is my 'personal inner rhythm'. I think I have a meditative character. I like to deeply analyse the thoughts and situations, the metaphoric, inner and transcendental purpose. And I would appreciate the same interest from the audience but in general they don't care. But I still like to give them the opportunity to meditate by themselves. This means that I prefer a slower tempo and do not like to needlessly edit shots just for the sake of a fast rhythm. I prefer to keep with a shot in order to achieve a psychological and symbolical effect, to enjoy its aesthetic quality. But I am not surprised when directors want me to speed up the rhythm at the final stage of editing.

For my taste and as witness to my nature I can add other names and films: Delvaux, Olmi, Sindo, Wenders and from England, Leigh (*'Secrets and Lies'*) and Rickman (*'The Winter Guest'*). Also many Russian directors – Abuladze, Ioseliani, Konchalovsky, Lopushansky, Michailkov, etc. Finally films of the Czech directors – Passer, Gedeon, Slama.[12]

There are films, which, rightly or wrongly, I call spiritual films which show the human soul in the deepest way and also contain providential and existential dimensions. And these are the films that I would like to edit. But there aren't a lot of films like this in the world, especially in my country and they are rapidly decreasing. But we cannot have everything that we want and I can put up with the new films that bring something new and interesting and allow me to look for new solutions. I am grateful for the hundreds of feature and TV films and many documentaries, particularly the musical ones I have worked on.

I am glad I was an editor.

Notes

1. **Polyecran and Laterna Magica** – theatrical techniques for incorporating imagery on film allied to live actors.
2. **Jan Kucera** – teacher, actor, director.
3. **Elmar Klos (1910–93)** – director *'The Shop on Main Street,'* 1965.
4. ***Touha zvaná Anada*** – Jan Kadar and Elmar Klos, 1969.
5. **Jaromil Jires (1935–2001)** – director, e.g. *'Valerie and her Week of Wonders,'* 1970.

6. ***The Seventh Seal*** – Ingmar Bergman, 1957.
7. ***The Alien*** – Ridley Scott, 1979.
8. ***Pulp Fiction*** – Quentin Tarantino, 1994.
9. ***Beloved Electra*** – Miklós Jancsó, 1974.
10. ***The Russian Ark*** – Alesandr Sokurov, 2002.
11. **Vertical Montage** – **Sergei Eisenstein** – See his book *'Towards a Theory of Montage'.*
12. **List of Directors** with an outstanding credit:
    André Delvaux (1926–2002) – *'Woman between Wolf and Dog' 1979.*
    Ermanno Olmi – Born 1931, *'Tree of Wooden Clogs'* 1978.
    Wim Wenders – Born 1945, *'Goalkeepers Fear of the Penalty'* (1972) *'Paris Texas,'* 1984.
    Mike Leigh's ***Secrets and Lies*** 1996.
    Alan Rickman's ***The Winter Guest*** – and actor, 1997.
    Tengiz Abuladze (1924–94) – *'Repentance,'* 1987.
    Otar Ioseliani – Born 1934, *'The Butterfly Hunt,'* 1992.
    Andrei Konchalovsky – Born 1937, *'Maria's Lovers,'* 1984.
    Konstantin Lopushansky – Born 1947, *'Letters from a Dead Man,'* 1986.
    Nikita Michailkov – Born 1945, *'Burnt By the Sun,'* 1994.
    Ivan Passer – Born 1933, *'Intimate Lighting'* 1969.
    Sasa Gedeon – Born 1970, *'Indian Summer,'* 1995.
    Bohdan Slama – Born 1967, *'The Wild Bees,'* 2001.

25 Alois Fisárek

Alois Fisárek is another witness to and participant in the flowering of the Czech New Wave of the 1960s and 1970s. For instance he was the editor on three of Vera Chytilová's important features. More recently he has worked a number of times with Jan Sverák. The decay of the State Cinema Industry in the Czech Republic has created an artistic vacuum which leaves Alois sceptical about the future.

I was born on January 7th 1943 at Opočno which is in Eastern Bohemia (Czech Republic). My Father was an academic painter

Alois Fisárek (Courtesy of Alois Fisárek)

and a professor at the Artistic-Industrial University in Prague and the Academy of Fine Arts in Prague. His creative period was between the 1930s and 1970s. My Mother was a literary agent and publisher.

In 1960 I graduated from the gymnasium (academic secondary school), and in 1968 I completed my studies at FAMU (Film and Television Faculty of the Academy of Performing Arts in Prague) having specialised in film editing under senior lecturer, Jan Kucera.

In my youth I was interested in sports, literature, art music and film, but I have no special skills. With regard to cinema, in the 1950s at the Cas Cinema there was a regular programme of films about nature, popular educational films about various disciplines and mainly comedies – Chaplin, Frigo, Laurel and Hardy, Harold Lloyd.[1] It was comedy that initiated my deeper interest in film.

In 1961 I started studying at FAMU under Professor Karel Kachyna without any detailed knowledge of film editing. In view of the fact that a director needs an ability for criticism in order to accomplish his work and because I do not possess this ability, I began studying film editing in my third year at FAMU.

After graduation, I began to work at Armadni film (the army film studio) and during studying I assisted the prominent editor Pavlicek at Kratky film (the short film). He taught me all the basic things (including the mentality of the editor). The first outstanding directors that I encountered were Elo Havetta and Ivan Balad'a (who became my close friends), as well as Juraj Jakubisko. Of interest is the fact that all three are Slovaks.[2]

Although Eisenstein, Griffith, Clair, Fellini, Antonioni and Buñuel, etc. influenced me from the past, when I started studying at FAMU there was a huge revolution sweeping across cinema. In France the New Wave emerged under the leadership of François Truffaut, Jean-Luc Godard, Alain Resnais and others.

In Czechoslovakia a New Wave emerged with Vera Chytilova, Evald Schorm, Jan Nemec, Jirí Menzel and Jaromil Jires.[3] They were my older fellow students at FAMU. They were giving life to the whole school, and I worked with all of them, except Menzel. I worked with Vera Chytilova on three of her very important feature films as well as a one-hour documentary. I worked with Schorm at the Laterna

Magica and with others. All of this had an effect on my opinions and influenced my subsequent professional life.

In my career I have worked with every kind of film – documentaries, educational films, television films, feature films, Laterna Magica and multi-projectional advertising. The film editor is the partner of the director in discussions about the concrete editing of the film. His collaboration in the evaluation of the ideas of the film is crucial – ideas which could be poorly scripted or even more poorly realised and which should therefore be softened in the editing or even completely cut out. Independent decision making about the component ideas is extremely complicated. I therefore see the component ideas as new ones without an understanding of the entire final assembly and cut of the film. For these reasons I think the discussion between the director (or producer) and the film editor are fundamental to the quality of the resulting film. Obviously, I prefer discussion in my work.

If I compare European cinema and that of Hollywood, I believe that European film is searching for a thematic place in the person and for the person on earth, whereas American film is searching for a place for the nation. For example the films of Antonioni and Bergman are very different but in their searching they are very similar. At the same time I believe that European film is just as dramatic as American.

The application of non-linear technology has resulted in the elimination of a great deal of the physical work in editing. The search for clips (trims) and single frames has been greatly sped up and simplified. But the work of the editor has been sped up only in the mechanical sense: there is no way of speeding up thinking. Unfortunately a problem has arisen. Everyone who has learned how to use a computer believes he or she has become a film editor.

At the same time the opinion has arisen among producers (and for this reason among other members of the film crew) that for financial reasons it is not necessary to see the film on a screen in the course of the film editing – at least in my industry. As I see it, the main problem lies in the fact that everything gets done very easily on a digital computer and for this reason nothing is done with due consideration and concentration. This is also how bad mistakes are accepted as if they were entirely well edited sequences. At this time however I consider digital technology to be an accomplished fact from which it is no longer possible to back away.

Looking back, in the 1960s there were very few film editors. Today, because of the new technologies, anybody who wants to can make recordings of pictures and sounds, but then it is necessary to process the recorded material further. Here is where the growing need for experienced and educated film editors is seen. That is why I think that there will always be a need for editing and demands on editors will steadily increase. In the course of my pedagogical work at FAMU, it has been possible to observe the growth in the number of candidates for studies in the Department of Film Editing. I also believe that the technological development will bring about an expansion in thinking about editing.

I work in the cutting room (when I have work) roughly from 9:00 a.m. to 7:00 p.m. with a break of about an hour around noon. In the main, I am able to work with all kinds of directors, because I place work and the discussion connected with it, ahead of all surrounding influences. I try not to pay attention to side issues – e.g. a talkative, aggressive, dictatorial director. Otherwise I have no special habits, and I am even able to free myself during work from any sort of external influences, even from outside of the cutting room. The only time I lose my certainty is when a producer wants me to work with what is for me a new computer system. In this situation I have to think about how the computer works in addition to my own editing. For me even the script is not as important as the recorded material and the results of the rough cut projected on the screen.

I have worked a great deal all my life (I am now sixty years). I used to work from nine o' clock in the morning until midnight, including Saturdays and Sundays. There were years in which I was not able to take a vacation, but for a long time now I have not had enough work. This has come about with the development of technology. There has also been an increase in the number of young and gifted editors. Many of the directors with whom I worked all my life have died or now devote themselves to something completely different.

The lack of work in my country can even be traced to the total disappearance of state cinema, which was not all negative. It had a functioning script editing and dramaturgy. 'Customary rights' were observed – beginners worked as assistants for older and mainly more experienced colleagues. State cinema had certain financial resources with which it financed films and in this way set up a small film market in our Republic.

Today, the law of the jungle rules in the world of film, and new ways and alternative habits are searched for very slowly, which may improve the situation not only for film editors but for the whole of cinema. Today in the Czech Republic we live in a time of great searching not only in financing films and film-making but in creative searching in general.

The ideal editor is a person who, besides having a cultural and general education, can remember all the picture material including camera movements, lighting actors performances, etc., and all sound material including its quality and its breadth. He has to know how to improvise professionally with this material. He has to know about film genres. He has to know how to work the timing of the material in such a way that there is nothing unnecessary and at the same time nothing missing – which is often a very difficult decision. To be able to make such decisions without mistakes requires a definite talent, or it even requires that a person has an instinctive feeling for it. However the editor must let go of his decision, if the director or producer wants something different. So an editor has to be a patient and communicative person, who can feel collectively.

In terms of choosing projects for the most part I don't read scripts, instead I follow the director whom I trust. The same is true when I start to cut – I am not interested in the script – I am interested in the rushes or recorded material.

Formerly in the days of classical film editing, I had my own cutting room and my own permanent better quality cutting tables. The last classical table was a three screen KEM, which had its own facility for video. Today I usually work with an Avid or Lightworks, and I work where the producer wants me to.

When I start to cut I always try right from the beginning to produce the final version, but in the final cut I always realise that the material has been cut very roughly at the start. This happens because in the beginning I know very little about the material and I have to make decisions in unfamiliar circumstances. Sometimes I do the final refinement of the cut several times.

Sound is just as important as picture. Today space has to be made for sound because five- or six-track sound recordings are being made. I always have to pay attention because this can be quite tricky. When I was editing a film of the Second World War about Czech pilots in Britain '*Dark Blue World*', directed by Jan Sverak,[4] which was using a six-track sound recording, I had to have a very precise space for the sound (e.g. the flight of one plane from the right rear corner to the front left corner of the screening room). For the most part, though, I can tell how many frames are needed.

I feel that my cutting has a huge effect on viewers, but that they are unaware that it is done by editing. I find this very pleasing. I am doing work about which no one knows the kind of effectiveness and influence it has. I probably like comedies most of all, even though I am not a particularly humorous person. I have the feeling that it is possible to communicate serious things even more in comedies.

Notes

1. **Comedies** – Chaplin/Lloyd. Why is it that people who mention Chaplin ignore Keaton and vice-versa?
2. **Elo Havetta (1938–75)** – '*Field of Lilies*', 1972.
   Ivan Balad'a – Born 1936.
   Juraj Jakubisko – Born 1938, e.g. '*The Deserter and the Nomads*', 1968.
3. **Vera Chytilova** – Born 1929, e.g. '*Daisies*' 1967.
   Evald Schorm (1931–88) – '*The Joke*', 1969.
   Jan Nemec – Born 1936, '*The Party and the Guests*', 1966.
   Jirí Menzel – Born 1938, '*Closely Observed Trains*', 1966.
   Jaromil Jires (1935–2001) – *Valerie and Her Week of Wonders*', 1970.
4. **Jan Sverak** – Born 1965, '*Dark Blue World*' (2001). Also '*Kolya*' (1996).

26   Tony Lawson

Tony talked to me one day at Beaconsfield Studios. His work with Nic Roeg and Neil Jordan is envied and admired, but in his distinguished career he has also worked with some other mavericks from Sam Peckinpah to Dusan Makaveyev and the unique Stanley Kubrick.

I was born in Paddington, London. My mother was a nurse, my father was a film cameraman, and my grandfather, whom I never knew, was Charlie Chaplin's press agent. So there's a sort of history of the film business in the family.

As a child I didn't have any ambitions in that direction, except that I went to the cinema quite a bit and loved westerns. My grandmother took me – it was an enormous local Odeon with a restaurant and a giant auditorium. I can't say that I ever had a great love of movies, but enjoyed going to see them.

I went to King Alfred's School in North London, but I didn't do very well academically. I decided I wanted to be an engineer, I don't know why, except that the overriding feeling was not to follow my father, who by then was a Film Operations Manager at the BBC working at Ealing Studios.[1]

So I rebelliously said I want nothing to do with my Dad, but unfortunately I didn't get the grades that would have allowed me to get into the kind of engineering I was interested in. So I was stuck at home at the age of sixteen, with my father and mother getting really fed up with me.

My father's job brought him into contact with independent documentary film companies, that the BBC contracted to make television programmes. One of these companies offered to take me on for a summer job. So I went to a small documentary company in St. John's Wood run by Marcus Cooper. I became the Tea Boy and Cable Monkey for the sound department, which was one man plus me!

The companies main business was making government documentaries and I think that was my downfall. They were secret and because I was young and because my father had been a paid-up member of the communist party, I wasn't given security clearance. I had to leave, but by then I think I was bitten.

While I was there I used to hang around the cutting room.

It was run by a very friendly and welcoming woman called Dot, or Dorothy. I suppose, if I think about it now, what made me attracted to editing was the fact that there was this warm person who, when not busy, was quite willing to talk about what she was doing. Her assistant was easy going. It seemed like a nice place to be.

Anyway I had to leave, and I went to work for Athos films, for something like four years. They gave me the opportunity to go through an entire film from beginning to end (driver, camera assistant, spark and assistant editor), which looking back now was invaluable. Even though I enjoyed it I wasn't committed yet. I didn't have any great passion.

While I had been working at Athos films, one of the editors, Teddy Darvas[2] was offered a Boulting Brothers film called '*Rotten to the Core*',[3] he knew I wanted to move on, and he introduced me to his sound editor, John Poyner.[4] I became an assistant sound editor. I stayed with John when he later did the sound for a film directed by Charles Crichton.[5] I remember Charlie sitting down at the Moviola and cutting a sequence himself, and it was probably the first time I realised what an editor *could* do, certainly in a dramatic sense anyway. You could see how he made it an enjoyable emotional experience for an audience. A smile came to your face when you saw the sequence. Essentially he made it up out of 'documentary' footage.

After that I carried on being an assistant sound editor on several features, but I didn't really feel that sound, as an end in itself was particularly interesting to me. Also at that time sound wasn't considered to be that important.

* * * * * * * * * * * * *

Probably the first time I became interested in film editing was when I worked on a film with Ann Chegwidden,[6] called '*Daleks Invade the Earth*'.[7] Ann was wonderful in that she let me sit behind her on a high chair, watch and ask her why she did things. She didn't say Oh, shut up leave me alone, she was very open about it and almost pleased to be asked. I was probably rather arrogant in those days and I really didn't think there was anything unusual in my prompting or prodding her. I started to become aware of technique.

By now I was an avid Paris Pullman[8] devotee. From my days at Athos my cinema going was developing and by now I was seeking out the more interesting movies. I remember the seasons of Bergman at the Everyman.[9] I used to be depressed for weeks after that! I am still haunted by 'Summer with Monica'. That's not to say that I was particularly critical. I still loved westerns. Even now I feel it's one of the saddest passing of genres. I used to love going to westerns on a Sunday afternoon.

After having worked with Ann I started to think 'this is really what I want to do'. The next important phase was when I met up with Norman Savage.[10] He had cut '*Doctor Zhivago*',[11] and typical of those times when someone is nominated for an Oscar, nobody then offers you a job. It seems to go hand-in-hand. People obviously thought he was too expensive so they didn't call him. As a fill-in he was going to do sound editing on '*Reflections in a Golden Eye*'[12] which Russell Lloyd[13] was cutting. Les Hogdson[14] was the main sound editor and Norman was going to do spot effects, and took me on as his assistant.

Meeting Russ Lloyd and seeing how he worked was a real eye-opener. I would arrive early in the morning but Russ would already be there working away with the film, and John Huston[15] wasn't around. He would do a cut – smoke his pipe – look at it again – think about it and put it back together. I realised he was building a film. It sort of dawned on me that an editor could work on his own, can actually do things unprompted by a director, without outside influence. Of course, I knew editors worked on their own a lot of the time but there was something in the way that Russ worked that was more to do with him putting something of himself in to the film. His style was very imaginative.

The other thing I learnt on that film was how you could build a sound track. I don't know whether you remember, but there is a sequence when Marlon Brando and Elizabeth Taylor are riding horses through a forest. Les Hogdson had gone out with a portable recorder and actually recorded horses galloping through forests, hitting bushes, over different surfaces all for real and then fitted each individual hoof beat. It gave the sequence an incredible vitality that coconuts and leaves on a Foley stage just wouldn't have achieved. It was like the difference between a polished piece of work and something which just had sound. From that point on I began to understand how sound could be an equal to the pictures.

After that I moved on to do three or four films with Norman Savage, of which '*The Prime of Miss Jean Brodie*'[16] was one of those defining moments I think for me. I remember we were working in a cutting room with Ronnie Neame[17] and there's a scene in the film where Jean Brodie is talking to her students and telling them about Florence. She's standing by the projector and showing them some slides. The idea was that whilst she was telling them about the place, she was really going in to her head. Every time we cut away from Maggie Smith it broke the mood. I said to Norman and Ronnie, why don't we just jump-cut or dissolve from one shot of her to the next instead of cutting away to the class to change angles. They liked the idea and it stayed that way in the film. It made me realise again that the purpose of editing is to create a mood, an emotion. I remember at the time I was doing what assistants normally do, rewinding film or putting trims away and Ronnie turned round to me and said 'Oh, shut up and concentrate on what we're doing!' In a sense I think he was asking for help really, and not necessarily complaining, but asking me to join in.

The second one of those defining moments was when we were cutting '*Ryan's Daughter*'[18] with David Lean. There was a scene near the beginning of the film when Rosie, played by Sarah Miles, is running off down the beach, to meet the school-teacher's role played by Robert Mitchum. She's wearing this rather drab old mans cardigan and in order to look more beautiful she discards it to show off her pretty blouse underneath. She hides the old cardigan in a shipwreck that is lying on the beach. There were two shots. The first was a big establishing shot of the beach and this wreck, with the little figure of Rosie walking along the sands and disappearing into the wreck. Then there's a closer shot with overlapping action where she comes into the wreck hides her cardigan and walks out, in this lovely blouse to meet Robert. David wanted a continuity cut of her arriving at the wreck and cutting as she enters it. I said why don't you let her disappear into the wreck in the long shot so there's a mystery about what she's doing, and it's a surprise when she comes out in just the blouse. He wouldn't have it. He insisted on doing the continuity cut. The difference is one creates a mystery and one just shows what happens. It pointed up again this worm in my head saying you can do two things here and one does one thing and the other does something else.

They never went back to that scene. David was quite pig-headed and I think even if he thought it was a good idea, he probably wouldn't have done it, because I'd said it. He was a little bit precious about his own ideas. He claimed that he used to listen to the fireman, the doorman and the projectionist, but I don't think he ever did.

* * * * * * * * * * * * *

The real crunch came when I met Nic Roeg. The editor of 'Don't Look Now'[19] was Graeme Clifford.[20] He had worked for Robert Altman on a film called 'Images'.[21] He was looking for an assistant and we met and I got the job. Nic was very much a free spirit. There were no rules. He was totally open to suggestions from any quarter. He would embrace things where other people would run screaming in the opposite direction. A perfect example from 'Don't Look Now' is a scene where Donald Sutherland thinks he sees his dead daughter, but it's really the little beastie in the red mac. He just had to walk through a little palazzo and cross a bridge. They arrived on the location and Nic noticed that there was a doll, floating along the canal and there was a little child's glove on a windowsill. He made those two things the central point of the scene, which of course it was – the loss of the child. That was pure chance. He would never close the door to anything that might help him.

To me coming from someone like David Lean who would not shoot unless it was in the script this was extraordinary.

You probably remember the controversy over the love scene in 'Don't Look Now'. Julie Christie was very worried about it when she saw the film before it was released and at that time she was very close to Warren Beatty, and he must have seen it as well. He advised her, I think, that she should put pressure on Nic to change it, because it was too revealing, and would damage her career. So Nic agreed to her request that he look at the sequence again. By that time Graeme had already gone off back home to America, so Nic asked me to look at it and go through the material to see whether I felt that I could do anything. I worked on it for about two or three days and it seemed like a pack of cards. You'd take one thing out and it just knocks everything else to pieces. I struggled with it for a while and it very plainly wasn't going to be what it should be in the film. Another problem was that the mix to the scored music meant that I was trying to change it but keep the same length. So we showed it to Julie and she acknowledged that it wasn't like it should be so it ended up being the way it was intended, but I think that was what cemented my relationship with Nic.

* * * * * * * * * * * * *

Working for Kubrick was an entirely different experience. I was very much a pair of hands. There's no point in trying to pretend otherwise. I don't know what it was like for those who worked with him prior to my being hired for 'Barry Lyndon'[22] but I suspect it was much the same. Having said that I was there and did contribute. I don't think Stanley was the perfectionist he is made out to be – a perfectionist sets out with an image of what he wants. Stanley didn't know what he wanted – his search was for knowledge. He covered himself by the number of takes or the length of time he took to edit a scene. He finds out what he wants by eliminating what he doesn't want. I don't really believe that's perfection. That's not to say it isn't a valid way of making films. In fact it patently is. It was just his way of approaching the thorny question of creativity.

He was fascinating in that he was tenacious. For instance, the duel scene in 'Barry Lyndon' towards the end of the film took six-and-a-half weeks of cutting and re-cutting before we stopped. Six days a week, long days, we cut it and cut it and cut it and cut it. The interesting thing was, and I don't know whether it's true of the other films, that we never ran the film as a whole. We'd work on a reel and run that reel, but we'd never run the whole film. His method of working was quite strange, and now as an editor of some experience, I just don't understand how he maintained a clear view.

After the film was released and received appalling reviews and box office Stanley rang me up with a proposition. All the way through the editing we had joked about telling the story backwards. When things started to get tense one of us would say why don't we just tell the story in flashback. He really rang up about six months and wanted to experiment with telling the story in flashback like we joked about. So I said I'm sorry but I'm busy! (laughs).

* * * * * * * * * * * * *

Then there was Peckinpah. I got a call from Sam to work on '*Cross of Iron*'.[23] I'd already worked with him as an assistant on '*Straw Dogs*'[24] and during the post-production became the third or fourth editor. Early on in the shooting period of '*Straw Dogs*' the original editor, Norman Savage, left the film without having cut a frame. He and Sam were like oil and water, they just weren't able to mix. Which left Sam in a very awkward situation as far as the backers were concerned because for an editor of such high profile to walk off sent them the wrong signal. So Sam was persuaded that he had to show the backers that the film was alright. It wasn't enough to just send them some dailies; we had to cut a sequence. So I had to cut a sequence very early on in the shooting. Sam had got a cold and he came into the cutting room one weekend, eating raw onions! We worked literally through the night cutting a sequence to ship off to ABC the backers. It was the first pub scene when Dustin meets all the strange locals. From that point on I couldn't do any wrong really. I didn't continue editing, at that stage anyway. Another editor came on and he subsequently left also! Then at the stage that we were shooting on location in Cornwall and doing the interiors at Twickenham Studios it was obvious that the amount of footage coming in was too much for one editor. So I also cut sequences – fairly uncomplicated sequences but I used to cut things just to keep ahead of the dailies. I think we got on quite well Sam and I. He was quite appreciative and obviously I was loving it. Cutting a Sam Peckinpah film, even if it was only short sequences, it was great!

So '*Cross of Iron*' came up. Sam called me out of the blue, and said I'm doing this film in Yugoslavia and I want you to be the editor. You can imagine, I just ran. I said yes please! In fact it gave me a way out of working with Stanley, because once the film was finished with Stanley it didn't mean the work was finished. It just went on and on, checking prints for China or Japan or wherever. Or he would send you out to check out the theatre that was going to run his film. Quite instructive actually, because then cinemas were appalling places technically speaking. I went to check out the ABC in Fulham Road and they had a third of the light on the screen that they should have had. One speaker was dead, just appalling. When I pointed it out to the chief technician he said well, so what!

Peckinpah was another huge leap. It taught me a lot about how to, organise a cutting room, because of the sheer amount of material. It taught me the importance of writing notes and also planning the editing. You can imagine a battle sequence; five cameras, several takes over two or three days, inserts and pick-up shots, second unit shots. You had to have a very good idea of what you are aiming at. Otherwise you could set off on a path and reach a stonewall and have to start again. Desperately depressing, when you've started to cut a sequence and realise it's taken completely the wrong direction. So working with Sam made me realise how important it is to know what it is you are trying to achieve, before you start. I found that if you take too long to get your first edit of a scene together you'll lose it. You can't look at multiple choices every time you want to make an edit. I found it best to crash a sequence together as quickly as I could, just so that I had a rough idea of what I was getting, and that the direction that I had decided on was the right one.

Sam's thing was that film is a montage. I mean the whole film is a montage. I think you kind of gather the point of view as one goes on rather than through a character in a particular scene, it's more by osmosis. As far as '*Cross of Iron*' it's more the character played by James Mason or David Warner, rather than James Coburn,[25] that gives the point of view of the film. Sam loves details – shooting multi-cameras there is always a camera on somebody's hand or something seemingly insignificant. The same is true of Nic. That's what makes it difficult to determine the point of view. Sam had learnt to place a lot of trust in the editing process, he would cover a scene with a loose idea of how it should look, but not a fixed idea. The editor would have to search the material – find a way through and Sam would either say yes that's great or keep trying. Once a scene was together in a rough cut Sam would know exactly what to do. He was very astute and bright in that respect. He was a very good editor in terms of editing as storytelling.

We had all seen '*The Wild Bunch*'[26] and been completely bowled over by it. If an editor walked away from '*The Wild Bunch*' and thought he knew everything, he should just start again. It was just startling the effect of that film. I had never cut normal speed cameras and slow-motion cameras together, certainly in the way Sam required. I found that when mixing various speeds you often needed something to kick off that change of speed. So if you take something which is quick or sharp or fast violent action and lead into slow-motion from it, it gives it a launch. It launches it off and makes it appear even slower in a sense. It makes it more obvious rather than slipping into it unannounced, and being only aware that it is slow motion after a moment or two. So the impact of the cut became stronger just by virtue of the fact that you are going from something violent to something much slower.

Cutting the battle scenes made me aware of sound and how it's very necessary to work with the full knowledge of the effect of sound. Of course, you cut with the imagined sounds in your head but it's amazing how incorrect you can be. In your imagination you say 'bang', its quick but the sound of an explosion is actually quite long. As soon as I started to apply sound tracks to the battle sequences, however rudimentary they might be, I immediately realised that I was making things too short, particularly explosions.

It was quite interesting because I hadn't cut extended battle scenes before, and I always remember the German producer who called me Mister Lawson, saying 'Mister Lawson, have you ever cut a vaw film bevore?' (laughs).

The battle scenes also point up another aspect of editing in the wider sense, the linking of actions. You can combine similar actions together by never allowing the action to be completed. By using a visual link you can extend and emphasise. The battle scenes becoming flowing, one action leading naturally to the next. A kind of continuity of action making a satisfying visual experience. In the wider sense it is something you should be looking for within the structure of the story – to link the ideas and themes. To think about how you move from one scene to another, at what point in a scene you enter or leave. Would a change in the order explain the story more directly, by eliminating would you be bringing ideas closer together? Look for the links. If you don't you are working with your eyes closed.

It was also one of the times where I used music a lot. It wasn't always music for the film but music for the head, as an aid to concentration and engagement. If Sam heard loud music coming out of my room, at that time it was probably 'Pink Floyd', he would say 'well if Tony's working we can leave him alone!' (much laughter). Anyway it was great fun working with Sam. Definitely a formative experience.

* * * * * * * * * * * * *

To say that Nic Roeg and Sam Peckinpah are similar would be totally wrong, but in many ways they are quite alike. The style, their attitude to film-making. I had stayed in touch with Nic Roeg and he came to one of the screenings of '*Cross of Iron*', afterwards he was very generous, he said: 'My God did you do that?' So '*Bad Timing*'[27] came up and luckily his delayed start date meant that I could cut the film. I think if I could have a film on my gravestone that would be the one. It was an editor's film, definitely, even if I look at it now I think, did I really do that?

Nic Roeg directing Art Garfunkel and Theresa Russell in '*Bad Timing*' (Reproduced with courtesy of itv pic (Granada Int'l)/Lfi))

At that time I was very arrogant you know I believed the editor could do anything. It didn't matter what problems there were in the script, what problems came up in the shooting, the editor could fix it, no problem. So I breezed into it. I'm sure I thought this is going to be great! Although it doesn't bare any relation to the shooting script, nevertheless the finished film is very much in the same spirit. It was always meant to be hoppity skip all over the place. That was a given, but nevertheless an enormous amount of structural work went into the final film, that is not represented in the script. If there's any lesson, and there certainly was for me, it's to be absolutely fearless in throwing the film up in the air and reconstructing it in another way, if you feel that's necessary.

Again, the need to be organised became very important. We used to have long discussions about structure. We used what would now be a computer but in those days was a kind of 'scandex'. It was literally a one line description of each scene, and we used to move them about. They were on little sticks and you could pull it out of its position and put it somewhere else. We used to spend lots of time just moving bits of paper essentially, around before we tried editing. In those days to structure an edit on film was very time consuming and if you set off in the wrong direction, there was a lot of wasted time.

Nic would terrify me by inviting all kinds of people to early screenings and I remember a rough-cut screening which was quite long, must have been over two hours, and we had a full theatre. You can imagine, my first film for a director; his agent was there, Theresa[28] was there. I thought my God this is mad; we're going to end up with egg on our faces and it's going to be my fault. But he loved getting people to talk about the film. I don't think it quite prepared us for the adverse reaction when the film came out. Now of course everyone says did you work on that fantastic film?

He taught me how to use the other side of my brain. To look at something and say, yeah that's alright but supposing we did something completely outrageous, going with a wing and a prayer and just trying something. I can't stress too much how important that experience and that film were.

* * * * * * * * * * * * *

The next thing, which was important from a technical point of view, was a film called 'Dragonslayer',[29] which introduced me to the problems of working on a special effects film. It wasn't digital but the effect would be the same. There were lots of shots where you had to imagine what was happening. That's one of the hardest things for an editor. In an effects film you have to imagine the action and still construct a scene without it. One of the lessons I learned on 'Cross of Iron' was if you don't have all the elements for a scene don't cut it. In a special effects film you don't have all the elements and you still have to cut it. Seeing films like 'The Matrix' its obvious that people have managed to surmount the problems. Certainly I was aware that if I cut a sequence with blue screen imagining what was going on it would end up slow and boring. Crudely animated drawings were used to indicate the action and 'plot' the scenes. I cut a sequence with these 'animatics' that would stretch anyone's power of imagination, just so that we could work out what was necessary. In those days they reckoned each shot cost $20,000 to do the optical work. I found it a nightmare. Digital technology has made it easier but just as costly.

Then Nic again with 'Eureka',[30] which was a clash between independent cinema and Hollywood – not entirely a happy marriage. Amazing material, fantastic scenes, and very enjoyable, but the final film was a kind of compromise. We had a version, which was about ten minutes longer that was a much better film. Given the nature of the film, ten more minutes was not going to turn people away but made a big difference to the story and the way it played out. One of the things that always bothers me is that if somebody employs somebody like Nic Roeg they must have seen his body of work. Then to expect him to turn in a polished Hollywood type film is just ridiculous. Why not just let him get on with it. Nic's got a very particular way of seeing.

'Manifesto',[31] with Dusan Makaveyev[32] would be the next one worth talking about. He's very undisciplined as a director. I don't mean that in a bad sense, because he just allows things to happen in front of him. He has a very loose attitude to the script and he enjoys improvisation and getting into the process of the actor–director relationship and working through things. A very intuitive director, and in the editing he showed me that you sometimes don't know what you do until you've done it. Then you look at it and look for the patterns and the tendencies and then you polish them, bring them out. That's what he did. When we were editing he'd take a cassette of the film away at night – he was a terribly bad sleeper – so in the middle of the night he would run the film. In the morning he'd come in and point out things that he'd noticed about the film that made him realise what he was trying to achieve, without knowing.

He also came out with some very strange things that you couldn't really use. For instance, one day he came in and he told me that he had counted the number of animals in the film; so many dogs, so many cats, so many horses, so many chickens. So I said 'well what can we do with that?' and he said 'oh, nothing I just thought it was interesting!'

On a more serious note, he would come in, in the morning and say did I realise that a character was such and such, and perhaps we should look at the performance and shift it to make it more interesting, to take advantage of it. He allowed actors to take liberties with the script and wasn't overprotective towards it then later saw that it was playing into his hands and that he could use it.

It's the same sort of thing that Nic does, where he'll arrive on the set or location, see something and take advantage of it. Dusan would do that in a rather more introspective way, but he had no problem with ignoring the script. Simon Callow[33] who was in the film, wrote a book after the experience called 'Shooting the Actor'.[34] Dusan's approach rubbed up against Simon's view that the script is the bible, whereas Dusan believed the script is the notes.

* * * * * * * * * * * * *

'*Two Deaths*'[35] is the next film I want to touch on. It was made for BBC films from a novel. It was shot on 16 mm, which I hadn't touched for years. As you know 16 mm film equipment is miserable. I couldn't use a Moviola because it destroys the film physically, so I ended up with a Pic-sync, which is a Heath Robinson contraption which should be thrown away and a Steenbeck, which is really only a viewing machine. Bumping up against this alien technology made me question every editorial decision I made. Because it's so fucking difficult to make an edit I was saying to myself why do I want to cut here? It made me go right back to the basics; why do you edit, what is the point, things that I had forgotten in a sense. It made me totally re-examine the process and ask myself why am I doing this? I enjoyed it because of that getting back to the basics. It happened again when we converted to electronics.

After that came 'Michael Collins',[36] which I came on to after the film had been cut and they had had some previews. I had a phone call from first Stephen Woolley,[37] and then Neil[38] called me. He wasn't convinced he had got the best out of the film and didn't know how to proceed. He didn't feel confident that the editor he was working with could help, so he asked me if I would go and have a look at it. One of the hardest things as an editor is to see what you've done and alter it when you believe that it's not correct.

We persuaded Neil to shoot some extra scenes, and we did quite a bit of restructuring and happily the preview figures were greatly increased and everybody was very happy. It's really the editor's nightmare in a sense; how to retain your objective point of view. In the final stages of a film you get lots of voices coming at you, outside pressures to conform to some preconceived idea of what the film should be and it's really hard to retain your objectivity.

* * * * * * * * * * * * *

There are three or four critical moments for an editor. The first one is obviously when you see the dailies for the first time. It is the only time you see them with fresh eyes. You set up a lot of thoughts and feelings about the material at that stage and you have to hang on to them. I make quite a lot of notes, either at the rushes screening or immediately after and again when I look at the material immediately prior to editing.

The second critical moment, and it's critical in two ways, is the first cut screening. It's critical because you have to remain totally open to your emotions and feelings about the film, because you are never going to be in that position again. It's also critical because it's the moment of greatest danger, from a political point of view for an editor because this is what you have been working on all by yourself for the last several weeks. If it doesn't look good or the producer or director doesn't like it you are in a very difficult and dangerous situation. You've got to be able to think clearly and make constructive criticism.

The next one is when you reach a fine cut. That's the time when it's too late to say this could be shorter, we should take out this scene, or turn the whole thing into flashback. That's a critical time when you've locked the film down and you're saying that's the film! It's all to do with that thing of trying to retain an overview. It's really hard.

There's a period at around about the director's cut, like ten weeks after the shooting, when you've become familiar with the film. A time when I must stop looking at the edits and start looking at the film. So you've got rid of the technology in your head, and you're looking at story. I find that I have to get through the boredom factor. I have to become bored with the film in order to be able to forget the film, to be able to see it with fresher eyes. I look at my watch and say Oh god we've got another hour of this, I can't sit here. Then once I've done that I can then see it again. I re-engage with it, but it means I've forgotten how much it took me to get to that stage.

The editor's conundrum, I think this is the key to editing. The dilemma, the paradox for an editor is that you've got to constantly surprise people with the construction of the editing, and yet you've got to satisfy their desire to be obvious. So you've got to give them what they want and you've got to surprise them. That's the key to almost all aspects of editing, to make it look surprising and yet obvious.

I remember when I first started editing I'd worry a cut. I'd spend a whole morning on one edit. By the end of the day I'd moved on fifty feet (*thirty seconds*) or less and completely lost any sense of what the scene should be doing, I was so tied up with finding the right frame. That's what you've got to forget about. The editor shouldn't worry about frames. You've got to worry about the story and the emotional feel of the scene. You mustn't worry about continuity in any shape or form. It's a red herring.

There's a lovely story that Dusan told me about his film '*The Coca-Cola Kid*'.[39] There's a scene where one of the actors has a cigarette, which just keeps going from one hand to the other, because of the rest of the continuity and of course nobody ever notices. If you cut the scene in the correct emotional way and tell the story properly nobody's going to give a damn, whether the cigarette is here or there. On '*Insignificance*',[40] which I cut for Nic, there is a scene where Michael O'Neil is undressing and he takes off three socks!

(Both dissolve into guffaws of laughter)

Notes

1. **Ealing Studios** – Formerly the home of Ealing Films, Michael Balcon's company which produced a whole generation of top British filmmakers and movies after the Second World war.
2. **Teddy Darvas** – Editor active in 1960s and 1970s.
3. *Rotten to the Core* – Directed by John Boulting. One of Charlotte Rampling's early films (1965).
4. **John Poyner** – Sound editor – Oscar for sound effects on *'The Dirty Dozen'* (1967), Robert Aldrich.
5. **Charles Crichton (1910–99)** – Editor then director, from *'Lavender Hill Mob'* (1951) to *'A Fish Called Wanda'* (1988).
6. **Ann Chegwidden** – Editor, cut *'The Masque of the Red Death'* (1964), for Roger **Corman**.
7. *Daleks Invade the Earth* – 1966.
8. **Paris Pullman** – Former art house cinema in London's Kensington.
9. **Everyman** – Repertory cinema in Hampstead, London.
10. **Norman Savage** – Editor short but distinguished career between 1963 and 1972.
11. *Doctor Zhivago* – David Lean, from Boris Pasternak's novel (1965).
12. *Reflections in a Golden Eye* – John Huston. Based on Novel by Carson McCullers, 1967.
13. **Russell Lloyd** – Editor, worked several times with Huston.
14. **Les Hogdson** – Sound editor from early fifties.
15. **John Huston (1906–87)** – Writer, actor, director – Oscar 1949 for *'The Treasure of the Sierra Madre'*.
16. *The Prime of Miss Jean Brodie* – Ronnie Neame, starring Maggie Smith, 1969.
17. **Ronnie Neame** – Distinguished cameraman who became a director.
18. *Ryan's Daughter* – David Lean, 1970.
19. *Don't Look Now* – Nicolas Roeg, from the story by Daphne du Maurier, 1973.
20. **Graeme Clifford** – Australian born editor who became a director.
21. *Images* – Robert Altman, with Susannah York, 1972.
22. *Barry Lyndon* – Stanley Kubrick, based on novel by Thackeray, 1975.
23. *Cross of Iron* – Sam Peckinpah, 1977.
24. *Straw Dogs* – Sam Peckinpah, 1971.
25. **James Mason, David Warner and James Coburn** – The kind of disparate collection of talents that Peckinpah seemed to thrive on.
26. *The Wild Bunch* – Sam Peckinpah, 1969.
27. *Bad Timing* – Nicolas Roeg, 1980.
28. **Theresa Russell** – Born 1957, starred for Nicolas Roeg several times after *'Bad Timing'*.
29. *Dragonslayer* – Matthew Robbins, 1981.
30. *Eureka* – Nicolas Roeg, with Gene Hackman, 1986.

31. ***Manifesto*** – Dusan Makaveyev, 1988.
32. **Dusan Makaveyev** – Born 1932, Belgrade, director of many anarchic/comic films with dark undertones.
33. **Simon Callow** – Prolific stage and film actor.
34. ***Shooting the Actor*** – Still available as a Picador original.
35. ***Two Deaths*** – Nicolas Roeg, 1995.
36. ***Michael Collins*** – Neil Jordan, 1996.
37. **Stephen Woolley** – Born 1956, producer, well known for his successful partnership with Nik Powell.
38. **Neil Jordan** – Born 1950, director/writer, won Oscar for original screenplay for '*The Crying Game*' (1992).
39. ***The Coca-Cola Kid*** – Dusan Makaveyev, 1985.
40. ***Insignificance*** – Nicolas Roeg, 1985.

27 Jonathan Morris

The conversation with Jonathan took place in his home in a north-ern suburb of London on a quiet Sunday morning, before three gen-erations of his family gathered for lunch. Much of his distinguished career has been dedicated to a sustained and fruitful collaboration as the editor for that very special film-maker, Ken Loach.

I was born on 6th of March 1949 at home in Hendon. Parents con-sidered themselves to be middle class – were probably working class; Jewish. My father was a tailor and shopkeeper – mother was a housewife and occasional helper in the children's wear shop. Elder brother, by six years, Anthony, who now works with me as my assistant, and a brother ten years younger, so quite a span.

First desires and inspiration would have been Fred Astaire, I'm afraid, and I did dance a bit like Billy Elliot – tap dance – and was at the age of twelve in '*Oliver*' [1] with Ron Moody, Georgia Brown and the rest of the crowd on stage. By co-incidence years later I discov-ered that Ken Loach, who I work with, was actually understudying Lance Percival in the theatre next door in St Martin's Lane, which is an amazing co-incidence, in a review show called '*One over the Eight*',[2] which you might remember, which starred Sheila Hancock and Kenneth Williams, which funnily enough I had seen at the Hippodrome, Golders Green a bit before that, because my mother used to arouse my interest in film and theatre particularly – she loved all that and we'd go and see shows.

At eleven I passed, the eleven plus, went to a very good grammar school which I didn't like at all – called Christ's College – by co-incidence one of the boys in the year above me is now the Chief Rabbi, but that's another story. They weren't very happy with me doing professional acting – and I came out of '*Oliver*' after three months, to my annoyance. They said either carry on with your acting and leave the School – I had a snotty headmaster – or stay at the school and come out of '*Oliver*'. So I was due to go to the States with the show – so I didn't do that, and I did one film after that as an actor – I was in Judy Garland's last film. Judy Garland and Dirk Bogarde directed by Ronald Neame – a film called '*I Could Go on Singing*'[3] – her last film – not a very good film I'm afraid, but that wasn't really down to me, but my eight guineas a day for ten days was fantastic. Then a lot of acting at school and played football as well of course.

I went into the lower sixth and after one year, my brother, who at this time was now working on '*The Saint*'[4] TV series at Elstree Studios said there's a trainee job in the summer if you're interested. So I did that, I absolutely loved it and didn't go back to school – took the trainees job – the business was so busy they could give me the job on a contract basis so within weeks I was the second assistant trainee on something called '*The Baron*',[5] and kind of went on from there – I enjoyed it so much. I didn't have the courage to become an actor basically – I really would – I still do – I tell Ken come on sort something out for me, but I don't think I'd be brave enough to be an actor – I've got a lot of respect for actors and anyone who lays their emotions on the line as they do. I don't think people realise sometimes how much they expose of themselves – not physically – emotionally really. So I've got a lot of time for actors.

RC: So you were straight into the cutting rooms.

JM: Yes – I think I was in the union by October having started in July, which was like unheard of.

RC: Did you immediately feel comfortable in the cutting rooms?

JM: I loved it – I absolutely loved it. I still think that was one of my most enjoyable times in the business. It was quite regimented. I like things to be structured – rushes, sound pick em up 8:30 – picture arrive from the laboratories at about a quarter to ten – rushes viewing in the theatre with the producer, who I was petrified of – just because I was a young kid – at eleven o'clock. So you had a real structured day. After that was numbering the rushes, logging the rushes and breaking down the rushes for the editor. Then at 5:30 you'd be done – I quite enjoyed it. I wanted to be in show biz and that's where I was.

Editing really suited me as opposed to any other aspect of film-making in that I quite value family life. I quite value being able to go to the school concert and not being on location. I valued being able to read the kids a story at seven o'clock when you got home. Almost any other grade in film-making you can't rely on that. The only time you're home is when you're out of work. Pathetic though that might be it is one of the reasons I stayed in editing.

RC: When did you begin to feel that you were learning from somebody?

JM: Straight away. The first person – the guy that taught me when I was a second assistant trainee on '*The Baron*' was the fellow I was replacing, and his name was Richard Hymns, who is now an Academy Award winner[6] several times – he ended up in San Francisco, married an American girl, sound editor – I haven't seen him for over thirty years – works with Spielberg regularly. He was the first person who taught me anything and it was basically the shiny side of the mag up – dull side down[7] and this took me several weeks to master (laughs). Rewinding a roll of film – do you remember?

RC: Absolutely – getting a flat tight rewind.

JM: Absolutely the little things that have to be done.

RC: But this was Moviola days.

JM: Yes, well actually Ciniola.[8] I'll tell you a funny story about Moviolas – when I was working on this corridor at Elstree one of the editors was a chap called Ted Hunter. Known often on credits as Inman Hunter[9] and as it turned out very influential in my career. The nicest man – bit of an Alistair Sim look-alike. He was working on a Ciniola on '*The Saint*' – you remember the Ciniola – silver – with a minute screen – tiny. One day he gets in on a Monday morning and his Ciniola had been replaced by a Hollywood Moviola – fantastic with that terrific brake – green – square picture – much bigger – twice the size probably and a bit quieter. He got in touch with the producer and said what's this, and they said well marvellous we've given you a new machine – terrific. He said no, I don't want that – I want my Ciniola back. They said oh really, okay and they gave him his Ciniola back. Then he confided in a few of us – we said why on earth. He said no Johnny boy, once you get one of those machines in the room you'll have the director in there all the time! I don't know how he would have coped with a Steenbeck or Avid.

This guy was very influential. I assisted him in about 1970–71. We were working on documentaries on 16mm which

I hadn't touched before – frightened the life out of me – bootlaces as we called it, as you remember. We were coming to the end and I didn't have much going – it was quiet in the early 1970s – the Americans withdrew a lot, and he said look Johnny boy – on the old Union Job Sheet – there's a job here ATV,[10] assistant editor, why don't you apply for that. I said I don't want to work in TV and be on this 16mm all the time, no – he said go on – so I said alright, so to keep him quiet I applied – I got an interview, which I was very relaxed at, because I didn't want the job – then I got a phone call the next day when I was first week on a feature as first assistant – it was a TV spin-off with Irene Handl and Wilfred Pickles – '*For the Love of Ada*'[11] – so it was hardly big time, but it was five months work – quite good money. But ATV were saying you've got the job – can you start next Monday and I said what – I'm not even sure I want the job. I said can you give me some time to think about it. They said we'll give you twenty four hours. At this time I was just about to get engaged. It was half the money I was earning. I spoke to my father he said no, don't bother with that, but my future father-in-law said take it because he was happy with me getting a staff job. So I did and that was the best decision I ever made. Not only was I there eleven years – I would have been there now if the franchises hadn't changed – but within four years I was editing and within seven or eight years I was working with people like Ken Loach, David Munro, John Pilger, Adrian Cowell, Anthony Thomas – Charles Denton[12] was my mentor and it was actually my University – ATV was when I became, I was going to say politicised, its a bit strong, but compared to what I was its true. It was my University – brilliant, brilliant – terrific place. Very, very lucky to make that decision.

I was all of a sudden working on documentaries and I was put in with a good editor – good in every sense – called Mike Nunn.[13] He was the kind of editor who after he got to know me a while said 'do you want to cut this sequence?' the kind of thing you would never have got on a feature or a TV series because there wasn't the time and the editors were busy doing their job, they hadn't got time to bring people along – to nurture them like they would in a staff job.

* * * * * * * * * * * * *

That's how I got to know Ken Loach – and I got to work for him because Roger James[14] said I would be the best man for the job and Ken, for once, didn't know where to start.

RC: So what was he doing at that time?

JM: It wasn't at his best of times – it was the late 1970s. He'd had a really tough time in the early 1970s on a personal level. He did a drama for ATV called '*Gamekeeper*'[15] and he'd been allocated what was their number one editor in the corridor at Elstree Studios, Roger James, and he got on very well with Roger who then got promoted to be assistant to the Head of Documentaries, and eventually became the Head of Central Documentaries and is a mate of mine to this day. After Roger had been promoted he couldn't do any more editing even though Ken tried to get Roger to come back to do it – he wasn't allowed by the Union so he was then allocated another editor and after a week or two Ken wasn't happy and then he comes to me. Great, you know – I've got this famous awe-inspiring director who ends up with me and it's a documentary called '*Auditions*'.[16] Just a little film following three dancers looking for work.

Ken's usually around all the time while you are editing, whether he's looking out the window or not, he's in there, but on this particular one because he was living in Bath and we were editing in Elstree it was a nightmare for him travelling up every day by train – three to four hours each way so he wasn't as involved with the editing as he has been I suspect on almost everything else he's ever done. So I didn't get to create a great relationship. That was the first thing I did for him.

RC: Did you feel comfortable – immediately?

JM: No, no not at all.

RC: But you had done some cutting before then.

JM: Yes for three or four years. I was comfortable with most other directors I'd worked with. No, it was Ken – it was Ken Loach. Its difficult for me to remember back because we are good mates now in all sorts of things and we have a terrific time – a great laugh. But at that time I was just thirty. Ken was this man with a reputation. I thought he was quite severe and wasn't sure if he had a sense of humour. Wasn't aware of his sporting interests which we both share – cricket and football and because he's someone you don't get to know quickly and I suspect I'm not particularly either it was not that easy, and it took a year or two. Obviously he wasn't too unhappy with me because we kept on working together. But Ken brings a lot of baggage with him which is none of his fault which is his serious – everyone thinks he's very serious – people think his films are very serious those who don't see them. Anyone who sees '*Riff-Raff*'[17] or '*My Name is Joe*'[18] or '*Sweet Sixteen*'[19] there's lots of comedy and lots of laughs and Ken is as interested in music hall comedians as he is in Trotsky.

But at that time it was difficult to discover his interests partly because we didn't spend a lot of time together and also because I knew I was like third or fourth choice in the line up – it doesn't help does it?

RC: No. So was it more documentaries after that for Ken?

JM: Yeah, all documentaries – after '*Auditions*' we did '*Questions of Leadership*' four programmes – banned by Channel 4, never shown. Then I did a film called '*The Red and the Blue*' also for Channel 4 which was shown. A documentary called '*Which Side are You On?*',[20] for The South Bank Show during the miners strike.

RC: What was '*The Red and the Blue*' about?

JM: The party conferences – good actually – the Labour and Tory conferences of 1982. But '*Which Side are You On?*' was commissioned by Melvyn Bragg[21] and he was very shocked when he discovered how partisan it was! Don't know why. He said basically we can't show this on the South Bank Show and we sneaked it to a festival in Italy where it won a big award. Then London Weekend Television were getting press releases about a programme they hadn't shown so they sold it to Channel 4 who felt, rather like BBC 2 being the minority channels, they could show rather more opinionated programming.

Ken still ended up on '*The Right to Reply*'[22] programme where a police commissioner had questioned the validity of the sound effects of truncheons hitting heads and accused Ken of adding sound effects. Ken was very good and this guy was hoist by his own petard, basically because he eventually said that's not the sound of truncheons hitting heads and ken said you obviously know the sound better than I do. So it was quite hilarious really.

Then there was a film about Northern Ireland for BBC 2, about getting the troops out and there were two films one for and one against that opinion and obviously Ken was doing troops out of Ireland. The first feature I did was '*Fatherland*'[23] which was about 1985–6. Of course, I was desperate to do a drama with Ken so I did that one and all of them since, except a couple of documentaries.

RC: You've said that you eventually found out about Ken's interest in sport, did you begin to have conversations with him about the political slant of things?

JM: I'm not that political an animal but whenever I've worked on a documentary I've always thought it helps to get to know something about the subject. I did a film by Rex Bloomstein[24] on American Jewish humour and I thought wow this is right up my street, fantastic – there's no effort to get into the subject. With '*Questions of Leadership*' it was about the trade unions and very heavy subjects really. Now if you know you are going to be working on a series of four films for about nine months you'd better get interested in the subject otherwise its going to be a nightmare. I read the papers – you follow the stories and you maintain an interest in it. Now I've kind of tended to do that whatever I've been working on really.

It wasn't just Ken who got me interested – it was John Pilger. Many of the film-makers – Alan Bell, John Ingram there were a lot of good guys there – it changed my outlook on a lot of things. On so many things – David Munro – these guys were passionate about all sorts of different things and you got interested in them. My father was like Ken's father funnily enough – Ken's father was a lower manager in a factory in Coventry and was right wing as was my father and a royalist and I'd been brought up to follow my parents line. As soon as I went to ATV and meeting these people brains you admire – whose intellect you admire – and you see they're thinking something completely different – I'd better examine why they'd come to those conclusions. Over a period of time that's what you do naturally enough. You think they're bright guys – they're people you admire – what's there beliefs – um there's something to this Socialism.

I'm not a great political animal but I certainly changed my beliefs from my early twenties to my late twenties because of the people I was meeting the same as people do at University a bit younger or can do and although I wasn't living away from home I was working seven days a week, many hours a day with intellectuals. I don't quite agree with John Pilger on everything but I can see where he's coming from.

RC: The same thing happened to me. Although my father was a shoe repairer he still voted Tory.

JM: Exactly the same – its what they were aspiring to wasn't it really. My father thought Ted Heath and Willie Whitelaw[25] were marvellous – they admired these people – you know, my father always thought unless you had the right accent how could you govern, which is a strange thing to think really.

RC: But is it possible to describe how you felt about the relationship of putting shots together and making material work and understanding the subject – it was always very important to me. I'll just give you one example when I was a trainee assistant I noticed the next thing on the schedule was a documentary on Kierkegaard the philosopher and I brought a book on this guy into the cutting room.

JM: Yeah, very good.

RC: I thought it would be good to read up a bit, even though I wasn't cutting it, I was the trainee. And the editor I was working with said, 'I don't mind you reading that but don't have it around when the director comes in – he'll think we are interested in the subject of the film'. I couldn't believe it.

JM: How strange. On the other hand there is always this quite good aspect – if an editor knows nothing about the film, him being the kind of first viewer, whether it be a drama or a documentary, he's sitting there first of all saying to the director what's this all about – actually its one of the few trades where a little learning is quite good. If you knew too much about Kierkegaard then you might presume the audience knew where he was born and this happened or whatever, but you have to be very aware of what the audience might know – it's a delicate balance.

When I was an assistant at ATV I was aware that editors jobs came up very rarely. There were only six editors at that time so it was dead men's shoes – the department wasn't expanding. I started there when I was twenty-three and I had been an assistant for six years already and I wanted to be an editor within another four years maximum – that would be ten years. So I thought there would be few jobs coming up I'd better be damn sure I get it when it does. So I went to International Affairs and Relations classes at the Burnt Oak Co-operative not far from here. I went with a friend of mine every Monday evening – it was a discussion class – brilliant – all sorts – there were char ladies there, there were doctors – fifteen of us with a chap we really liked called Guy Arnold who encouraged you to talk out about things which was very good because at that time I was a little bit shy, a little bit uncertain. It gave me a little bit of confidence, knowing a bit about International Affairs. So when I sat at the back of the viewing room with Charles Denton the Head of Documentary and John Pilger and John Ingram the producer, and the editor Mike Nunn and the PA Julie Stoner and then there was me, the assistant editor at the back of the room sat on a bench and Pilger's doing a rough commentary to picture and he comes out with the line 'Here in Bangladesh one-twelfth of the world's population is doing . . . ' and I'm sitting there at the back thinking 'one-twelfth of the world's population – I don't think so'. Now because I'd been to International Affairs classes I had a bit of confidence in myself so I said, 'Excuse me everybody', all the heads turn round, 'I don't think one-twelfth' getting very nervous as I'm saying that, 'of the worlds population is in Bangladesh'. John says, 'Oh carry on, carry on'. Meanwhile the producer sent the PA, Julie, out to check. She comes back and says, 'I'm sorry John was right, Its nowhere near that'. So John Pilger, who's a mate of mine, he turns round and says, 'Christ Jonathan, I've been using that fact in the Daily Mirror for years!' (much laughter).

So International Affairs classes gave me the confidence and when boards came up for a job I didn't know – there's about six assistants going for it all mates, all colleagues and people applying from outside – this was in June 1976 – and erm I went for my board. One of the assistants was a lovely woman called Hazel Sansom and she worked for the supervising editor, George Clark,[26] and they were quite close, and he obviously was going to go for her. Anyway, I got the news in a week or so, and its fantastic and I wandered down the corridor and I bumped into Richard Marquand, who directed the third Star Wars film,[27] he was working with Pilger, lovely man. I said 'Richard, I got the job!' he said 'Of course you got the job, everyone knew you'd get the job'. So I went into George Clark, because I thought I should thank him, even though I think maybe he hadn't gone for me. He said, 'Don't thank me, I didn't go for you, bloody Charles Denton' and I left the room. As it turned out Hazel was my assistant on '*Which Side are You On*', the miners film, with Ken, years later.

RC: But its not just to do with helping you to get on in your career but taking an interest in the subject of the film affects your attitude to the work.

JM: Of course, '*Land and Freedom*'[28] for instance, I went and read '*Homage to Catalonia*',[29] I mean I'd be silly not to wouldn't I to just get a bit in my head about what's going on. I don't suspect it added anything to the film at all, but it did for me. So its for your own benefit.

RC: Is it possible to know what the relationship with Ken was built on – I mean clearly you became relaxed with each other and then it worked.

JM: It did work. I don't know – I was lucky. I had to leave ATV when it became Central rather than go to the Midlands and Roger James offered me the series '*Questions of Leadership*' and '*The Red and the Blue*' with Ken. I said are you sure Ken will want me to do it, and Roger said don't worry, Ken will want you to do it. It was a freelance series – he could have had anyone he wanted. So I left Central for that work with Ken. He was still travelling up from Bath and he would get in at 10:00, 10:15 and we would have a cappuccino and we got into a routine and we got to know each other and the relationship built from there really.

In the last ten or twelve years I've built my career around being available for Ken's films. It had happened that people have said to me at Cannes or wherever do you do any other dramas at all and I've had to say until recently, years ago I did but no – that's why I did '*The Other Boleyn Girl*'[30] for Phillipa Lowthorpe because I thought it was about time – there was a bit of a gap between Ken's last one and this one and I knew I could fit it in. But I like to be available for Ken because first of all I know I'm going to have a good time and secondly, I know I'm going to be working on class with people who know what they're doing. It's not only Ken its Rebecca O'Brien[31] now, the producer, who's great, we have a terrific time, really nice person to work for. We do the music with George Fenton[32] – it almost sounds too comfortable, but there's nothing wrong with that – the films are edgy enough without anything else being edgy. So we have a good time, we don't have anything of the executive producer crap that you do tend to have to put up with – I don't know whether the guys like Jon Gregory[33] and Mick Audsley[34] have to put up with that on the kind of films they do.

* * * * * * * * * * * * *

On '*The Other Boleyn Girl*' which was very good – it was a great challenge for me; it was a four-week shoot, it was shot on DV, I was cutting on Avid, I hadn't worked with the director before, she's very talented, but hadn't done a lot of drama before, there was no script – it was totally improvised – I was getting three hours of rushes a day – which my assistant would digitise in the evening and I would have in front of me the next day and I had it assembled within three days of them finishing filming – I was very proud of myself!

RC: Three hours a day – were they shooting multi-camera or what?

JM: Sometimes two cameras, but it was DV – there were fifteen-minute takes – no script so once they were going she let 'em go – quite right, but I had to pick the scene out of it – I don't know how I did it! It was a terrific challenge but a very good end product, but we had viewings – six, seven people in the room all charming all terrific all trying to be helpful, but nevertheless when you've got six people – what have you got – you've got six opinions – you've got a committee – and there wasn't a huge amount of time, and at the end of it all one of the people is in charge, David Thompson,[35] very nice, helpful man and even then you think he's satisfied with what you've got now, and they say you've got to send it off to Jane Tranter[36] now. This is yet more. Not only that but we'd finish our viewing at five o'clock and they'd all get their diaries out – so when are we coming to look at it again – two days time – so you've got these pages of notes – we could always do the changes, but there was never any time to consider what they wanted. Strangely enough, for us there was no time to look at the film – there was no time to think okay this morning we'll look at the film – we were too busy doing things.

In the last ten years since Ken went to Parallax with Sally Hibbin[37] as well, they've now got it sussed. They've got about six investors from various countries, and nobody's got a fortune riding on it and they come and have a look and we do have suggestions – from the writer as well, Paul Laverty[38] – all suggestions considered. Invariably time is allowed for it. We have Roger Smith[39] the writer he comes in and has a look, and they are people who's opinion we value, but nobody says do this – nobody says that to Ken, and he's very fortunate, and it's brilliant.

I've been for interviews where I've said to the producer I'm actually a directors editor and I've known that they won't like that, but I've thought I've got to tell them and I think I'm not going to get this. I've always considered myself as working for the director. I suppose its part of the ATV training really. I had six-and-a-half years of freelance editing before ATV when I learnt the technical stuff of films and cutting room procedure but not much else, between the ages of seventeen and twenty-three, but at ATV I learnt the rest of it really.

* * * * * * * * * * * * *

RC: During that period when you first got into the cutting rooms were you beginning to be aware of cinema more than just as audience?

JM: I always loved the cinema. My parents being shopkeepers, Thursday was half-day and they used to pick me up from school and we used to go to a matinee at Temple Fortune Odeon. So films were part of my life. I have to remember the 1960s when I use to watch '*Play for Today*' and '*Kes*'[40] was one of my first dates with my wife – I remember where it was – ABC Golders Green. As a young person in the film industry working on what was disposable, rubbishy films I always dreamt of working on films like '*Kes*' like Ken's '*The Price of Coal*',[41] like all of Mike Leigh's[42] TV stuff, actually – loved those things. Then I saw '*The Conformist*', Bertolucci,[43] which blew me away and '*Z*', Costa-Gavras.[44]

I was always very partisan, its part of my nature. Its like football, Arsenal is everything. I've always been very partisan and although I'm saying some of the films I worked on at Pinewood[45] in the 1970s were rubbish I'm sure I didn't think they were then, but they were I'm afraid.

RC: Well there is this thing isn't there, that all of us are proud of our craft and when you are involved in a film in a sense you suspend absolute judgement – you do a good job on whatever it is.

JM: Yes, well I was still young then and I was always horrified when you took the reels up to the projectionist and he said, 'what heap of rubbish is this then?' And I would think oh, charming – this is my film, and that is the other thing that I've always considered, and I've always thought it was very important for anybody on a film, whether it's the boom swinger, the gaffer or whatever, is that they should think its their film, and I've always thought whatever I'm working on its my film. Ken always says films are collaborative and I think you put a lot more effort into things if you think its yours.

* * * * * * * * * * * * *

I did work on one good film in the 1960s. It was the first film I was a dubbing assistant on. It was a nightmare job – it was like ninety-nine per cent post-sync and that was '*Witchfinder General*', Michael Reeves,[46] and I didn't get a credit, because as a dubbing assistant I joined after the roller was made.

RC: Now out on DVD and looking beautiful!

JM: Is it really – well its ninety-nine per cent post-sync that film and I was making the loops – what a job that was and they bought cheap spacing, I remember, which we were told you could use either way up and when they got to the dubb they discovered you couldn't and the emulsion was coming off on the head, and we had to switch it all round, which wasn't that simple because they were diagonal joins, a nightmare job, dubbing at Warwick with Hugh Strain,[47] but a good film and I met Hilary Dwyer[48] a year or two back on the plane to Cannes. I spoke to her about it – she looked really good. Of course, Mike Reeves died soon after.

That was made by Tigon[49] where I worked on a number of films and one of the executive producers used to ring me up when I was synching up rushes and the question would be 'Any tits today?' and the answer would be yes or no; if there were he'd come to see rushes – so I've worked at all ends of the film business you know!

It was three brothers, Gerry Levy, Howard Lanning and Denis Lanning and their little company in D'Arblay Street[50] and it was wonderful training. It was two rooms. First one in, which was supposed to be me, would sweep the floor and I thought, I was nineteen I'd been an assistant for two years, what's this – sweep the floor, and one morning I got in after the Managing Director, Gerry Levy, and he was sweeping the floor and I thought, well, if he can do it I can do it. It was good training.

RC: You mentioned being a dubbing assistant there – as you developed in your career did you develop an attitude to the value of sound?

JM: Yes, of course. You probably laid all your tracks at the BBC, well we track-laid at ATV and I used to enjoy that very much. First of all it gave you a week or two away from the director, didn't it, so it was really enjoyable. The first thing I cut as an editor was a comedy series for Ned Sherrin[51] called '*The Rather Reassuring Programme*' – six-and-a-half hours went out on a Saturday evening – this is me – first job – network series Saturday evenings at 9:30, which is amazing to get that really and it was very good fun, but the sound was very important. It was all drama. Lots of actors who became famous like Tom Conti, Nigel Hawthorne, Bill Fraser, John Le Mesurier, Ronald Lacey.

I had recorded sound effects for '*Witchfinder General*' which were censored. There was lots going on in that.

Someone was sick – the splash – it was censored – we had to tone it down. All sorts of things. John Trevelyan[52] used to come into the cutting a lot there. I was a first assistant on a film called '*What's Good for the Goose*' – Norman Wisdom,[53] sex comedy – those phrases don't go together do they?

RC: No, not really.

JM: But that's what it was a Norman Wisdom sex comedy for Tigon with Sally Geeson.[54] It wasn't unsuccessful – the director was Menahem Golan[55] and I was the first assistant and John Trevelyan came into the cutting room to discuss a few things. One of them he wasn't very happy about. Sally Geeson saying to Norman Wisdom 'Do you Frugg?' So I'm in there – we're showing it to him on the Moviola – we didn't have Steenbecks – and he says 'What's this Frugg? You can't say that, do you Frugg – we all know what she means'. Denis the editor said, 'It's a dance John'. He looks at me, John Trevelyan, because I was nineteen or twenty, 'What is this dance the Frugg – do you know it?' I said, 'Yes it's a dance' He said 'Is it – could you do it for me?' I sad, 'No sorry I can't'. I mean, honestly.

RC: I thought you might have risen to the occasion, Fred Astaire and all that!

JM: But it was a dance, The Frugg, and it got through. Funnily enough I was at an awards do in February – The South Bank Show awards and '*Sweet Sixteen*' was nominated and I sat next to Norman Wisdom. I said to him 'You won't remember me', but I was the first assistant editor on '*What's Good for the Goose*'. He said, 'No, I've got no trouble remembering you – I've got trouble remembering what happened yesterday though!' But it was funny after all those years to be sat next to him again.

* * * * * * * * * * * *

RC: I remember going to the cinema at the French Institute when Ken Loach – they did a series called Carte Blanche when famous people could choose to show their favourite films and he chose . . .

JM: The Czech film '*Fireman's Ball*'.[56]

RC: No, actually he chose '*Mouchette*' by Robert Bresson[57] and I remember his introduction because he was quite apologetic saying I haven't seen this film for fifteen, maybe twenty years I hope it stands up, and I was interested in what he connected to. In a way looking at Ken's work and your work with him its very difficult to imagine such a particular view of the world finding a place elsewhere, especially in Hollywood, although of course the Europeans admire his work tremendously. His films are never simply entertainment – they are always about something in a way that so much of cinema isn't. With Ken there is always a deeper agenda.

JM: No I know, well he's famously quoted – strangely I didn't expect this to come from Vadim Jean, who made '*Leon the Pig Farmer*'[58] – being enormously impressed by Ken saying at some do or other, 'Its not how can we make a film, its why are we making this film', which is terrific but its not what most would think. Its got to have something more to it than just making an entertainment. Although he can do all that stuff really well. I mean they are the easiest scenes that I have to cut, when there's a punch up in a bar. In '*Joe*' there's a big punch up and one of the young critics said Loach does the fight scene better than John Woo and they are a piece of cake for him he shoots them in no time at all – it's the easy stuff for him, but he could do a Hollywood action movie no problem but he wouldn't because his heart and soul wouldn't be in it. We'd all love to, everybody else. Ken could have done '*A Chorus Line*',[59] he loves all that – loves shows and that kind of theatricality.

RC: I can understand that now you've told me that he was in a West End review.

JM: Yes well, Lesley, Ken's wife, says he was the kind of actor that he would never employ – you see I think he became politicised at the BBC – not at University particularly – but at the BBC there was a whole group with Tony Garnett[60] and Roger Smith and I'm sure others.

* * * * * * * * * * * * *

RC: You mentioned some of the writers and what's always fascinated me, and it must mean particular things for you as the editor, is the relationship between the writing and the material you get to cut, because clearly Ken's worked with some splendid writers, not just radical but special writers like Jim Allen[61] and more recently Paul Laverty, and yet the material you get is often the result of intense – not improvisation in the sense of Mike Leigh – but of translating what's on the page in a way that's still alive because the actors are given a certain kind of freedom, which means that what you get is such that the structure has to be brought back to it.

JM: Funnily enough more often than not the script is kept to. Often what does happen though, because they are relatively free, the actors, some of whom may not have done a lot, most of whom are actors, in one way or another – once you are doing it you are an actor – sometimes it is all in a different order and that can be problematical – there is a pace they are at and it is very tricky. There are other times – like the scene we are cutting at the moment. I've read the script twice but not when we are cutting I just see what's there, but the other day I did and the scene reads very well of course, and then we are looking at it and it's the same lines but it doesn't sound, well, as Ken would say, it sounds written – sort of corny and not natural so actually we won't use it – I know we won't. Ken hates sentimentality you see.

RC: Because I remember you talking very interestingly about the collectivisation discussion scene in '*Land and Freedom*' as being particularly interesting to work on.

JM: That scene will be with me forever. Its fascinating from many points of view. It comes halfway through the movie. Its basically what the film is all about. In the script I think it was about three pages – in the finished film I think its round about fourteen minutes. In the first cut it was about twenty-three minutes. They shot for two days with two cameras a group of people most of whom were re-enacting what their relatives or parents went through sixty years earlier and it is the crux of the film. For my taste I have to say its a long scene, and its slightly buttock twitching in the middle of a movie. When I bumped into people when the film was on in the cinema one said that scene is absolutely fantastic, absolutely brilliant. I bumped into another fellow I know, a writer, who said that scene in the middle of '*Land and Freedom*', oh, how terrible, it went on and on and on. For those who understand the subject of the film they realise that's what the movie was made for – it would not have been made without them feeling as they felt for that scene. Its what Jim and Ken were making the film about – it's the political heart of the movie.

First of all, '*Land and Freedom*' is my most favourite of all the films I've ever done. If I could take one with me it would be that one. I still think I should have cut that scene down a bit more.

RC: Do you remember what it felt like when you got the rushes.

Landowner's house: The large room

Next morning Salas and a dozen leading people of the village are gathered to discuss the setting up of a collective.

Lawrence, Bernard and some members of the section are also there, sitting away from the main meeting.

'How do we divide up the land?'

'Do we collectivise
everything? What happens to
the family that owns two pigs?'

'Each family should be allowed
their own plot to grow food
and to keep livestock for
their own consumption.'

'But if one man has a yard
more land than his neighbour
there will be arguments.'

SALAS
From each according to his
ability, to each according to
his need.

'Let us leave politics out of it.'

SALAS
How can you?

'Let us collectivise politics
so that we are all of the same mind.'

'Politics does not make the grass grow.'

SALAS
The land will not go away. It
will be here when we are gone.
What is important is who owns
it. Land and freedom go
together but we need a plan
and a destination or the
bosses will be back.

'But how many among us are
educated enough?'

'Learning is a weapon and we
must arm ourselves.'

'How?'

Script page from 'Land and Freedom' by Ken Loach (Courtesy of Parallax Pictures)

Still from the above scene in '*Land and Freedom*' (Courtesy of Parallax Pictures)

JM: We were surrounded by cans of film. It was generally two cameras, which was of course terrific, but it was kind of how you imagine painting the Firth of Forth Bridge – by the time you got to the end you'd forgotten what was going on at the front, because it took at least two days just to view the material and most of it's in Spanish. Its like the nightmare scenario isn't it really. Though actually that turned out to be great because the leading actress came to sit with us – she happened to be in London – and she was lovely – and it was great to get to know her.

RC: This is Blanca in the film.

JM: Yeah – Rosana Pastor[62] and it was marvellous to have her around, for me anyway, because she's attractive, lovely, vivacious and exciting!

In those situations the only thing you can do is an assembly which I suspect was longer than any twenty-three minutes – more like an hour.

RC: Were the two cameras complementary or did you treat them as separate entities entirely.

JM: No, they were complementary – so we usually had some-where to go, but you're an editor you know when you've got two cameras they always miss the moment don't they. It took about two weeks to cut, and I had to talk it through with Ken. I had to lean on him a little bit to cut it down as short as I could get it, because I knew that for many people it would feel long, and its sort of documentary in the middle of an action film. But many people loved it. John Ingram rang me from France where he has retired to and he managed to find me and he said 'Rossellini is alive and well!' Now I'm not a great Rossellini expert so I wasn't sure quite what he meant but I knew it was a major compliment, and obviously I told Ken about that.

RC: I suppose in a sense it comes as a surprise because the action that leads up to it is so effective and affecting. In a nor-mal conventional movie there would be a moments pause before we move on to the next action. In that sense it's a shock – we have just had the death of Blanca's lover, and the attack on the village is beautifully done.

JM: You see that's a piece of cake for Ken – we cut that so quickly and it all goes together – that's why I say to you – he could do a western – Ken could do a western.

RC: But the choreography is so good.

JM: Listen he's sixty-seven now and he is a technical master – he's an expert at everything he needs to do.

In that collectivisation scene, near the beginning there's a French guy who gets his English wrong, and they all have a laugh at him, which of course is just the actor getting his English wrong, which I found – well Ken loved it – then an edi-tor friend of mine, Tony Sloman,[63] said it was terrible when that actor fluffed his lines. He didn't actually fluff his lines, but that's what it looks like, and I felt a bit vulnerable there.

RC: He's also quite emotional, that actor, he may be having trou-ble with his lines but there is an undercurrent there.

JM: I always felt a bit defensive about leaving it in, but as I say, as an editor, I've always been a directors editor. There are plenty of excellent editors around who consider what goes in is very much them. I've always considered that the man to satisfy is not me – it's the director. Which is strange from where I started from on TV series, where the director was lucky to even see a cut. It was TV as factory – it was a conveyor belt – very successful and it still happens.

* * * * * * * * * * * * *

RC: When did the switch to non-linear happen for you and how was it?

JM: The first funny story is that Rebecca O'Brien was teaching at the National Film School in 1990 and they got me along to speak to the students and they asked me about this non-linear thing and I said no, no, no, its not going to catch on. Within five years I had my own Avid – I think it was wishful thinking, I was really frightened of it, because the technique is so different. I was fortunate. I did three jobs on Lightworks, kinda got to grips with that. First was 1995, I did a documentary on Maradona so that helped and then I did a couple of others. Then a mate of mine, Mike Rossiter, who I have worked with a lot, said we've got a job – lovely – thirty-three-week edit – one two-hour documentary. I said great, but he said we've got to do it on Avid. I said what, I've just got to grips with Lightworks. He said, no, they're doing the rest of the series in Boston on Avid and they want us to work on Avid. But what we can do he said is you can buy one on the strength of them hiring it from you, so I thought well that's something.

So we bought one and then there was a young lad who I had met as an assistant editor who said I want to sit with you and learn Avid, I know a little bit about computers and I'll be able to help you. So we both went on a course still baffled and it was alright – just. Went away at Christmas – we had a week or two off and the whole of Christmas I'm thinking god I can't even remember how to switch that machine on, let alone use it. Came back in January and it had all clicked into place. I was really surprised, and for the first time I was comfortable.

It is a brilliant machine, in a way its too good. Everyone thinks you can do anything and they all want VHS's of the cut. Its just not great for the atmosphere you used to have of the editing team. The editor the two assistants, the sound editor and the guys all together. My mag would be what we would dubb from. My track that would be that – there would be no doubt in the dubbing theatre. We always run the mag when I'm dubbing with Ken to check it against the Audiofile[64] to see that everything is as I've done it, especially with Ken we use so many bits from other takes, but it was your mag that was actually there. Nevertheless the non-linear is brilliant you want music here a dissolve there you want to speed up. It used to be you had to order an optical and you didn't know it would work and then the quality would be rubbish – it would look like a dupe and it would take two weeks to come back, now in two minutes you've got it and the quality is great.

However, funnily enough at Goldcrest,[65] where I'm working now, there is more cutting on film than in the last three years that I've worked there, including Tony Sloman, and Barrie Vince, so there's a few people resorting back to it, and when you are working on something that doesn't have a lot of special effects and the director knows what he's doing and you've got a good couple of assistants I think people are finding out economically its better. The first reason for Avid was economy – not printing rushes, you know. But I don't think that's worked out because everybody wants to conform – so you have to print at least selected takes then you still end up with an assistant and a Steenbeck and a comp-editor, matching what the editors done, if they can. But it is a wonderful tool nevertheless.

* * * * * * * * * * * * *

RC: Do you think there are personality traits that make you potentially a better editor?

JM: I don't think everyone can be an editor. You need to have an aptitude for it. Rhythm. I always think if you can dance you can probably edit. Its about rhythm, pacing, sensitivity but I actually think first and foremost to be able to get on with people. You need to be able to communicate with the director. There are sound editors who have tried to become picture editors and not succeeded. You don't really know until you try. If you are lucky enough to work as an assistant with an editor who gives you a chance. I found that the hardest thing – I found I was editing for the editor and the director. When I became an editor it was so much easier than when I was an assistant editing.

Now after many years of experience I realise that the first film I do with someone is the hardest because you don't actually know the mind of the person you are working with. There are occasions when the first film you do with someone is fine because they are very positive – they know exactly what they want and they tell you very clearly and then there are other directors who can't communicate what they want and its difficult to get inside their head. When I did '*The Other Boleyn Girl*' for Phillippa Lowthorpe, who is terrific, I'd never cut for her. I had these rushes arriving every day – hours and hours worth – no script and I was assembling it. After about ten days no one had been in touch with me – I thought they might want to see something I'd done from their point of view. I should be pleased about this but I just felt I was in a little bit of a vacuum, and I wanted someone to say yeah that's just what we want or not. So after about ten days I rang up Phillippa at home and said look I've got half-an-hour of stuff I can put on a VHS will you look at it for me. She said okay yeah fine. I sent it down to Bristol, where they were filming – I didn't hear for days – were now half way through filming. So I rang her again and asked her if she had seen it and she said she hadn't had the chance. Then she did over the next weekend and she rang me and said, oh lovely, thank you very much – that's all she said. That's all I wanted to know that I was on the right track – I felt so much better.

RC: With Ken do you talk when he's shooting?

JM: A bit – less on this one than ever. I always go up there for a day or two – they like me up there – don't know why, I'm really spare, but they treat me quite royally now I know a lot of the crew, but I have nothing to do. On some films Ken will ring up and say what's it looking like?

RC: But for instance on '*Land and Freedom*' and '*Carla's Song*'. . . 66

JM: He was away you mean – well he doesn't worry about it you know or if he does he worries about the next days filming not the last.

RC: That must be because he's so comfortable with you.

JM: I also used to think that Ken had more of a plan than he does. He's not like Hitchcock knowing which shot goes next to which. He does look at his notes from time to time when we are cutting but we tend to not look at anything than the film. But I'm not cutting it whilst he's shooting either – no one could cut one of Ken's films while he's shooting – you couldn't do it – I could do if I was on Avid maybe, but not on film, because he prints all the takes – but there will invariably be, on the big scenes, six or seven takes and five or six angles and you don't know which take he is going to go for, so it's a waste of time.

Basically when he's filming I look at the rushes and I select takes for us to put on tape to send to Ken wherever he is. Whether he looks at it or not – that's up to him, so often I'll give him the first and the last but I'll look at the continuity sheets as well and sometimes just give him one. On this one that he's just shot I don't think he rang me – or he might have done to find out about what's going on in the football. It's a very cushy number for me when he's shooting – I'm not on full pay – I'm on half pay. I go in and view rushes maybe three days out of the five and then they are short days.

****

RC: So looking back, since we started with Fred Astaire, would you have liked to have cut a couple of musicals?

JM: Oh, love to, well '*Auditions*', the first one I did for Ken was actually the best job I did for him. I hardly had any contact with him. A huge amount of it was music and it was all cut to music – it was a challenge to cut – didn't know the director – wasn't sure about what he wanted, it was the best job I've done for him – no love to do a musical. I was green with envy over '*Chicago*', which I'd seen in the theatre. I thought they did a good job of the film and Martin Walsh[67] cut it – bugger – he's a contemporary of mine – don't know him particularly and he cut that – how annoying is that – then he won the Academy Award I think – fantastic. We're always trying to talk Ken into doing something – he loves the old music hall and the old music hall comedians. I'd love him to do something like that. I bought him a book about George Robey[68] eighteen months ago when he was ill. If there was the right vehicle he would do it. But I don't suppose he will – it's the why again isn't it, why and the why to entertain is not enough unfortunately.

You see the current one we are doing is perhaps the least political – it's a love story. A love story between an Asian Scottish boy and an Irish catholic girl who's a teacher and the problems they have with their relationship, because of her catholic school and because of his Pakistani Muslim family. That's it. Basically its anti all religious hypocrisy of any kind.[69]

Its an irony really, considering my original interest was in show business and I ended up with all those heavies in documentary at ATV, as far from show business as you could get but that's what I really like – I've been to Cannes six times now and I love the show bizz stuff!

Notes

1. ***Oliver*** – Stage show before it was filmed in 1968, directed by Carol Reed.
2. ***One Over the Eight*** – Stage revue. Lance Percival is a comedy actor and Chelsea supporter.

3. *I Could Go on Singing* – Directed by Ronald Neame, editor, John Shirley, 1963.
4. *The Saint* **(1962–9)** – TV series with Roger Moore.
5. *The Baron* – TV series, 1966.
6. **Richard Hymns** – Sound editor, three time Oscar winner – '*Indiana Jones*' (1989), '*Jurassic Park*' (1993), '*Saving Private Ryan*' (1998).
7. **Mag** – Magnetic sound track which must have the oxide side against the sound head.
8. **Ciniola** – Was probably inferior to the Moviola in every way, but editors like the machine they are familiar with.
9. **Inman Hunter** – Born 1914, editor, cut '*The Overlanders*' starring Chips Rafferty for Harry Watt in 1946.
10. **ATV** – Associated Television, held the commercial TV franchise in the English midlands for many years.
11. *For the Love of Ada* – Directed by Ronnie Baxter, editor Anthony Palk, 1972.
12. **Ken Loach et al.** – A unique collection of serious and seriously talented British documentary film-makers, all of whom later distinguished themselves in particular ways. **John Pilger** is still making films that cause discomfort amongst governments and institutions wherever he investigates corruption and crimes against humanity. **Adrian Cowell** made *The Opium Warlords* and *The Tribe that Hides from Man*. **Anthony Thomas** investigated South Africa under apartheid and **Charles Denton** has produced both documentary strands for TV and fiction films.
13. **Mike Nunn** – Was post-production supervisor on the 1995 film of '*Richard III*'.
14. **Roger James** – Editor who became eminent documentary producer.
15. *Gamekeeper* – Ken Loach, 1980.
16. *Auditions* – Ken Loach, 1980.
17. *Riff-Raff* – Ken Loach, 1990.
18. *My Name is Joe* – Ken Loach, 1998.
19. *Sweet Sixteen* – Ken Loach, 2002.
20. **Ken Loach documentaries** – '*Questions of Leadership*' (1981), '*The Red and the Blue*' (1983), '*Which Side are you on?*' (1984).
21. **Melvyn Bragg** – Now Lord Bragg, novelist and screenwriter also TV producer notably '*The South Bank Show*' a review of the arts.
22. *The Right to Reply* – TV show which allows film-makers, their subjects and the public to debate issues contained in programmes.
23. *Fatherland* – Ken Loach, 1986.
24. **Rex Bloomstein** – Director, e.g. '*The History of Anti-Semitism*', 1993.
25. **Ted Heath and William Whitelaw** – Tory politicians.
26. **George Clark** – TV film editor.
27. **Richard Marquand (1938–87)** – Director '*Return of the Jedi*' (1983) and '*Jagged Edge*' (1985). A special talent who died too young.
28. *Land and Freedom* – Ken Loach, 1995.

29. ***Homage to Catalonia*** – George Orwell's chronicle of his time in the Spanish Civil War.
30. ***The Other Boleyn Girl*** – Philippa Lowthorpe, based on historical novel by Philippa Gregory, 2003.
31. **Rebecca O'Brien** – Producer for Ken Loach since '*Hidden Agenda*' in 1990.
32. **George Fenton** – Film composer who emerged through TV in 1970s and 1980s.
33. **Jon Gregory** – Editor, several of Mike Leigh's films and '*Four Weddings and a Funeral*', 1994.
34. **Mick Audsley** – Editor, see interview in this book.
35. **David M Thompson** – Executive producer, BBC Films.
36. **Jane Tranter** – BBC executive.
37. **Sally Hibbin** – Parallax Pictures, executive producer on many Ken Loach films.
38. **Paul Laverty** – Screenwriter for Ken Loach since '*Carla's Song*', 1996.
39. **Roger Smith** – Screenwriter and valued collaborator on many radical projects since '*Up the Junction*', 1968.
40. ***Kes*** – The seminal film that established Ken Loach's reputation in the Cinema, 1969.
41. ***The Price of Coal*** – Ken Loach, 1977.
42. **Mike Leigh's TV work** – Was hugely important and influential, e.g. '*Abigail's Party*' (1977), starring Alison Steadman.
43. ***The Conformist*** – Bernardo Bertolucci, 1970.
44. ***Z*** – Costa-Gavras, 1969.
45. **Pinewood Film Studios** – Britain's pre-eminent studio.
46. ***Witchfinder General*** – Directed by Michael Reeves who died soon after thus cutting short a promising career at its inception, 1968.
47. **Hugh Strain** – Highly regarded dubbing/sound mixer.
48. **Hilary Dwyer** – Liverpool born actress who became, and still is, an executive producer.
49. **Tigon Pictures** – **Gerry Levy** (producer), **Howard Lanning** (also an editor), **Dennis Lanning** (credits as sound recordist).
50. **D'Arblay Street** – Part of London's Soho.
51. **Ned Sherrin** – TV producer notably '*That was the Week that was*' (1963) and other satirical shows. Later films.
52. **John Trevelyan** – Was President of the British Board of Film Censors.
53. ***What's Good for the Goose*** – With **Norman Wisdom**, stage, TV and film comedy actor, 1969.
54. **Sally Geeson** – Actress sister of more successful sister, Judy.
55. **Menahem Golan** – Prolific writer, producer, director.
56. ***Fireman's Ball*** – Milos Forman, 1967.
57. ***Mouchette*** – Robert Bresson, 1967.
58. ***Leon the Pig Farmer*** – Vadim Jean and Gary Sinyor, 1992.
59. ***A Chorus Line*** – Richard Attenborough, 1985.

60. **Tony Garnett** – Producer, born 1936, an exemplary career committed to social drama.
61. **Jim Allen (1926–99)** – Screenwriter, TV then film culminating in '*Land and Freedom*'.
62. **Rosana Pastor** – Splendid Spanish actress in films since 1987.
63. **Tony Sloman** – Editor and post-production supervisor.
64. **Audiofile** – Digital post-production sound track laying platform.
65. **Goldcrest** – British production company with own editing suites.
66. *Carla's Song* – Ken Loach, 1996.
67. **Martin Walsh** – Editor, also cut '*Bridget Jones*' *Diary*', 2001.
68. **George Robey (1869–1954)** – Legendary music hall star, who was billed as 'The Prime Minister of Mirth' also in films including as Falstaff in Olivier's '*Henry V*', 1944.
69. *Ae Fond Kiss* – Ken Loach, 2004.

28 Mike Ellis

The conversation with Mike took place in his edit suite as he was finishing off a film with Mark Herman, with whom he has collaborated several times. Mike has edited for a whole host of distinguished directors from Lindsay Anderson to Bill Forsyth, and including a prophetic thriller directed by Bertrand Tavernier set in Glasgow!

I was brought up in a flat at Notting Hill Gate in London by my mother and my granny. My father was an RAF pilot but he was killed a few months before I was born. My mother worked at the Ministry of Defence – I never managed to discover much about what she

Mike Ellis in his edit suite (Courtesy of Mike Ellis)

really did, but knew that her knowledge of the main European lan-guages (having been born and educated in Switzerland) was quite a significant aspect. She sent me away to a school near Bath that had been recommended by a colleague at the office. There I developed interests in various activities – for instance I started a magazine and later formed a jazz band.

Apparently my father had been pretty musical; he was a good banjo player and sang – so perhaps that's where I got it from, although my grandmother was also very musical and used to play the piano at home. I had regular piano lessons from the age of about eight or nine and that carried on through school until I was eighteen. I was quite good in the classical area but I lost interest, which I regret now because I would like to be able to sit and play something by sight – something I have never learned properly. I can do it but only very slowly. You go to a music session on a film and see these musicians who haven't prepared in any way and they play perfectly the first time – they're fantastic. But a lot of them can't improvise at all, which is what I was able to do quite early on. There was one session we had on '*Brassed Off*'[1] when we wanted some bum notes and they just couldn't do bum notes to save their lives. We ended up using what I had done in a synthesiser.

When I was eleven or twelve, I bought some sheet music of a piece I'd heard on the radio called '*The Black and White Rag*' by a popular ragtime pianist of the time – Winifred Attwell – and I learnt it by heart in the holidays and went back to school and astounded everyone, not least the music teachers. One of them, who taught saxophone and clarinet, and was also a bit of a 'jazzer' off school limits got me some more sheet music and taught me quite a few things about playing with a band.

I recently found all my school reports and nearly every year the headmaster had written things like 'if you applied yourself to (such and such) the way you do to jazz you'd get on a lot better'. The school prided itself on its music, with wonderful facilities for prac-tice and performance. I used to have to get permits from the head of music for the band to be able to rehearse. So it was half-frowned upon, but it became a great success; we managed to pack the school hall whenever we gave a concert, usually to rapturous applause and by the end of my time there I think we were rather cherished, even by the music staff.

I did think for about two years that I would go into jazz professionally, but I got interested in so many other things – I started doing a lot of photography and making my own prints in the kitchen at home and in the school darkrooms. At the same time I was becoming very interested in writing and literature and I wrote short stories, a play, even a novel! I continued through university with a trio, and some well-heeled student actually paid for a record to be made of us, but as soon as I started working in films I realised that the frequent late nights demanded of you meant that it was hard to commit yourself to engagements far in advance, so eventually music became very much a hobby, as it remains.

* * * * * * * * * * * * *

When I was wanting to get into the film business originally, I wrote letters to all sorts of people, and I received a very nice letter back from Richard Lester.[2] I happened to have a Pentax S1A which was what he used, and he saw other similarities between my interests and the ones he had when starting out, including the jazz, so it was very encouraging even if it didn't lead to a job. But I remember it being instrumental in pushing me on – I wasn't sure whether I wanted to devote myself exclusively to music or photography or writing, so it was almost an intellectual decision to settle on film-making which encompassed all of those other things, and his letter put a seal of approval on my thoughts. Apart from anything, I had grown to love movies by the time I was finishing university, being a regular at the art cinemas of Oxford and London. So Dick Lester helped to set me off on course.

RC: Were you aware of cinema in a serious way at school?

ME: They did run films on occasional Saturday evenings for the whole school – they set up a 16mm projector in the gym – and I use to enjoy that. I also vividly remember going to the cinema with my grandmother or mother in London. I particularly remember '*Gulliver's Travels*'[3] at what was the Classic Cinema in Notting Hill Gate because the film broke down; the projector stopped, the frame froze and then the screen slowly appeared to burn up, quite spectacularly, until the projectionist realised what was happening. This was the first time I, a ten-year old, was aware that someone or some people, actually made films, it wasn't just a sort of theatre that happened only in that building. Today people are used to slamming a VHS in a machine, rewinding, pausing, fast-forwarding and so on – in those days the cinema was the only place to see what celluloid could do.

RC: What did you study at university?

ME: I did a degree in ancient history, which I took up because I was interested in the subject – without any notion of teaching or doing anything practical with it and I saw a lot of films whilst at college. It was the time of the New Wave movement and I loved Antonioni, Godard, Chabrol, Truffaut, Fellini and so on. We would wait avidly for their next offering – rather as now one might look out for the next Woody Allen or the Coen Brothers, I suppose, but I do think it was a rich time, from all points of view – film music, literature, photography – everyone was experimenting and there was a sense of excitement.

I had a friend in London who went straight into documentaries, which he thought was an important medium and I used to visit him occasionally in my holidays and I saw film hanging up in bins and I remember thinking how exciting that was. I just thought 'that was film-making', and I realised the importance of editing.

* * * * * * * * * * * * *

I came out of university determined to work in the film business and as one had to do, I walked around Soho and visited the studios. In those days you needed a union card for a job and a job for a union card. After about six months I was on the point of giving up and I started looking into the world of publishing, and I was actually offered a job in a publishing company, where they wanted to do a whole series of classics for children, shortened versions, rather dubious I suppose, and in the same week I got an interview with somebody in Rediffusion Television as it was then, and he had seen that I was a jazz enthusiast and he was too, and he ran the film library and he needed a trainee. So we had an interview in a jazz pub in Putney, The Bull's Head, and that was it. I got that job and that automatically got you the union ticket, so I left after four months, as soon as I got my ticket.

So I got a variety of jobs, often just for a day. Then the opportunity arose to work with a director who was also going to edit his own film – a chap called Stephen Cross.[4] We did a couple of films where I was assistant director and assistant editor. At that point we were at Document Films when David Gladwell[5] was looking for an assistant and they seemed to think I would be alright so I got a job on '*If*'.[6]

RC: Had you already decided that the cutting room was where you wanted to be?

ME: Yes I had. I wanted to direct, like a lot of people, but I did feel that the cutting room was the place where films get made, but I didn't lose my enthusiasm for directing, so that was like my ultimate goal. I've always enjoyed creating things. At home I had a puppet theatre and I used to write stories for these puppets and I used to bring my family in at sixpence a time, and then we did commercials as well!

RC: So with David Gladwell and '*If*' were you aware of Lindsay Anderson[7] before that?

ME: I had seen '*This Sporting Life*'.[8] I may even have seen one of his plays that he'd directed at the Royal Court. It was just very new and very exciting. I can almost smell it now the feeling of the cutting room and having to go to the set one day. There I was synching up rushes for the first time.

David was putting it together while Lindsay filmed, but then when he came back he was in the room all the time. We were all in one room – looking back I realise how unusual that was – I guess it was a low-budget film: there was the editor and the first assistant and me, the second assistant, all in the same room and then Lindsay as well.

I was sitting at the numbering machine at one end trying not to go over each slate! So it was very good being so intimate, especially when Lindsay came because everyone had to look at things. From time to time he would say what do you think of this and you had to respond.

I remember we used to have lunch in the pub every day. Lindsay was such an ordinary man really. He was never pompous or pretentious. If any one came everyone was always part of it. Michael Medwin – Albert Finney – of course it was his company, Memorial Enterprises.[9] I remember once in the pub I asked the most incredibly naïve question, I said, 'Did John Ford direct anything else besides westerns?' I got the royal look from Lindsay, the eyes to heaven – 'My dear boy!' But he was never nasty.

He could really rip people off. I heard him on the phone to mainly production people. He would just have them in ribbons, in shreds. His language was so meticulous – so exact – it just poured out – he was so articulate – brilliant to hear. I was terribly fortunate to be in this milieu.

Eventually we got the sound editing and I became an assistant to Alan Bell,[10] and I was booked on to do the footsteps or Foley as it's called now. The guy who recorded the Foley was this gypsy called Johnny Lee,[11] who had quite a reputation at the time. He was a lovely guy to be around but he would nip off to place bets, go to the pub, he'd play cards. Eventually he was fired by Lindsay who found him during the dubbing, upstairs playing cards for money. He saw a good thing in me – he shot the footsteps and showed me how to fit them in an hour and I fitted all the footsteps. I was very happy to do so, but I'm sure this was frowned upon by the others who were not getting the benefit of a hardened professional – this was my first time.

As a result of that my next job was with Alan Bell. I then worked for about four years in the sound side. I acquired that experience which I was very grateful for in retrospect. I suddenly realised four years had gone by and I don't want to be in the sound side anymore, but I'd done some wonderful things. I'd worked in the dialogue area, the effects area and on music.

One of the things that Alan Bell used to do, for fun really, when he had a spare ten minutes, he used to make up loops. It was just putting together sounds in a certain way, usually to make something comic. It was like a wonderful use of sound, if you can imagine a thirty- or forty-five-second loop of things going on, and crazy things – putting in dialogue. It's that sort of playing which I thought was very creative actually. How it relates to picture editing – I think it's to do with the rhythm and pacing. There's all sorts of ways that the sound experience was useful. For a start you know what can be done and what can't be done. I did subsequently work for some editors who had no idea and they would do a cut from one scene to another and you'd think this is going to be a problem for the sound editor to make that smooth. Sometimes I know you've just got to sort the sound out and the picture has to take second place. I think working with a good effects editor as Alan was, you learn the importance of good sound effects and how sometimes it's good to hold something for a period of time where you can afford to listen to something and feel a mood.

It's a bit like music. You place a piece of music and you can feel that you need more time to make a mood out of it. I did a stint on 'Fiddler on the Roof' with the music editor. That was fascinating, because it was recording two musical numbers before it was shot, and that was just the technical business of recording the orchestra recording the vocalist and watching it all being cut together by this American music editor who had worked on '*Some Like It Hot*'[12] and things like that. He had made Marilyn Monroe sing in tune, which he claimed would be an impossibility without certain tricks. It was great to see this expertise, making it into what would be used for playback later on. I thought afterwards, my God, they are paying me for this – I would pay to have this fun.

* * * * * * * * * * * * *

I was working on the sound side of '*Galileo*' which Joseph Losey[13] directed for the American Film Theater, but I was realising that I wanted to move back to the picture side. So I made this known to the editor on 'Galileo', a chap called Reggie Beck,[14] and he took me on as the first assistant on the next picture which was called '*The Romantic Englishwoman*'.[15] It was just very pleasant from that moment on. Reggie had decided I would be good editor material – he was seventy then – but incredibly fast – but he wanted his trims handed to him, while he sat there like an oracle – it meant that you were looking over his shoulder all the time. So I would see exactly how he cut and how he would have a cut and move it in relation to the sound. He would move the picture a frame, two frames until he felt that the cut was in the right place. Then he'd cut it in sync as it were. You could see how he tested for the perfect place for that cut, rather than actually lacerating the film with splices. So in other words I learnt the importance of the cut – not simply going from A to B but actually when that moment occurs in relation to the sound, which is vital really. You can have two very easy images to cut between if you're cutting on the first syllable of the word or the last, or even many words earlier.

RC: Was Losey with you all the time?
ME: Losey hardly ever came to the cutting room. I remember him there once maybe. For an emergency actually. There was one occasion when Reggie couldn't see a way to do something at

the beginning of a scene which Joe had wanted. I had privately thought well you could you know if you did this. . .

I must have said this to Reggie and he said you try it then. So I did it and then Reggie said well okay let's get Joe. So he called Joe into the cutting room to look at it and Joe thought it was fine. That was the only time I remember Joe coming to the cutting room.

One would have a day. There was a theatre in Audley Square he liked to go to. You'd run the film in the morning then you'd stop for lunch in the pub round the corner – everybody – I worked on '*The Go-between*'[16] subsequently and I remember Pinter[17] came and we all sat around having beers. In the afternoon we would rock-and-roll, and maybe we went to that theatre because it was one of the first where you could rock-and-roll and you just had three buttons in front of you and you could just go back over things if you had to. Joe would be there commenting and I would be next to Reggie making notes, which is exactly what would eventually happen on a Steenbeck. Lindsay was totally different and liked to be there all the time. He was obviously a great exponent of editing and very interested and that was a vital part of the whole procedure for him. Whereas Joe was an old Hollywood director who never stopped working really. At least once we went from one film to another. Literally you finished dubbing one film on a Friday and started shooting the next on the following Monday.

RC: Somewhere in here was '*My Ain Folk*' with Bill Douglas.[18]

ME: Yes, I was the sound editor, at the British Film Institute (BFI) in Waterloo. One day I chased Bill Douglas through the street market – he had run off with his film under his arm – he had six reels, and he was probably pleased to be relieved of some of them and I made sure I got all the picture. He just wanted to make a gesture I suppose. It wasn't because of something I did – he had been on the phone and was clearly disturbed. He was given to volatility – I didn't see much of that but you hear stories.

There was something that I did which Mamoun[19] used to talk about to other people as being so brilliant and I thought it was a temporary solution. At some point when the boy is taken away in a van, Bill wanted the sound to be as if from his point of view – sort of muffled, although we were on the outside of the van. I did something that I'd learned in Hollywood, amongst other little tricks with magnetic sound, I just turned it over so that the sound bled through the base.

One of the tricks one did was to scratch the magnetic off the film with a razor blade so if you had something which was too harsh and sharp leading up to a cut you would scrape off a little bit to give it a fade out basically.

* * * * * * * * * * * * *

RC: You said just now that you learnt things in Hollywood – when were you there?

ME: I was in Hollywood on '*Straw Dogs*'[20] in 1971. I went as the assistant sound editor and then I became the dialogue editor. The reason it moved from Twickenham was that Peckinpah was doing another film in the States called '*Junior Bonner*'[21] with Steve MacQueen and he was setting that up. So lucky me had to go for four months.

RC: So when you said you 'learnt that in Hollywood' it was clearly a learning opportunity.

ME: Yes, there were sound editors, old hands, that we worked with and they would teach you these little tricks. To begin with it seemed such sacrilege – you turn the film over – what! – but its just so delightfully simple and a very organic solution to a problem. Later in the dubbing theatre I said well I've done this but I will give you the track and you can do it properly, but they could never actually duplicate the effect, so that particular sound is what we went with.

During the mixing of '*Straw Dogs*' Sam wanted to make a trailer and it was decided that I should cut it, being the most expendable having finished my work on the dialogue. I had three days to cut a trailer which Sam remembered and was very complimentary – they didn't use it in the end but they used some of the ideas in it: Dustin Hoffman had this little toy thing on his desk with these balls that bang against each other and I used that as the basis for the trailer, as a sort of time machine, ticking, and that's what they used and Sam remembered that and subsequently I got the job on '*Cross of Iron*'[22] with Tony Lawson, as one of the editors.

RC: So was '*Cross of Iron*' the real breakthrough for you into picture editing?

ME: That was my first proper credit, yes. At the height of the editing I think we probably had two cricket teams[23] working on it, including all the sound and music editors. So it was quite an atmosphere and this was at Elstree Studios and on the lawn right outside the cutting room block was a caravan where Sam lived. Sometimes he'd take the weekend off and go into town and live it up, but basically he lived in this caravan on the lot all the time. He had two assistants who, together with him, would stoke up a barbecue every night, so we'd have very good food and a very good salad and wine, he provided. We'd be there until eleven o'clock, twelve o'clock every night – it was living the film. If you think of the way he directs, what he does is set up a situation and shoot it like a documentary. So his films are to do with setting up the event – its not make believe – he really makes it happen and I feel that was how he liked to be – the editing was a bit like that. He wanted to forget we were in London, it was like we were in our own little universe doing this great film. We were his group like the '*The Wild Bunch*'[24] actually.

He used to go from cutting room to cutting room – we had Steenbecks – and sometimes he would run scenes in the screening room upstairs and one of us would come out and shout 'Next!' Just like going to the dentist – you would go and run your scene and if he was in a bad mood you would come out with a toothache rather than going in with one. It was all very good humoured, obviously competitive between us editors, but everyone was totally committed and loyal – no sort of back-stabbing.

RC: What Tony Lawson said was working with Sam Peckinpah taught him to be organised because of the amount of material and it was suicide if you got lost amongst it.

ME: Yes, the first scene I was given to do had forty thousand feet of rushes (seven hours). I mean that's a lot of film. I was sort of prepared for this – I had spoken I think to Kevin Brownlow[25] and I had a plan of how I was going to do this. I devised a scheme of how to deal with this vast amount of footage, which involved going through every piece and cutting out good bits. I divided the scenes into a, b, c, d, e, f, g and I'd have pegs in the bin and I'd put the good bits on to these pegs accordingly. So having gone through everything I had a bunch of bins in a rough order.

It happened to be very well received, the scene I did, and I wasn't there when they ran it one evening, but he was so impressed with it they ran it three times and it was only on the third screening that he or someone else spotted a cameraman in blue jeans. This is a whole bunch of the platoon when there's a birthday party and one of the soldiers goes a bit nuts – he's had enough of the killing and goes mad and they all end up singing, and in the middle of this – I hadn't spotted – there was a cameraman – right in the middle. So they hadn't seen him until the third running so I could be excused that!

Peckinpah's watchword was 'Go for the moments!' He did set it up in very much a documentary style. With three cameras and often slow motion, which he used so well, which explains a lot about the amount of footage. Working on a film like that is like working on three other films, you know, you cut it so much. People might well say that Peckinpah's films got over cut, which is possibly true in some cases, but despite that one did get to work the material so much. He would always be pushing for something better – it was never completely forgetting what he'd said before – like some directors will say well why didn't you do that and forget that you were going down a certain path – he always remembered the path he was on, and he'd never come up with new things that didn't fit with that. He knew how to manipulate the material – he was a very good editor I think.

Mad times – I remember he went off the wagon – he started drinking again and to celebrate he gave us all a bottle of brandy, a very nice Dellerman brandy, one of the finest which I have enjoyed ever since, which was his way of justifying it for himself that everyone would have some, so we'd all be in the same boat.

* * * * * * * * * * * * *

RC: How did you get involved with Bertrand Tavernier on '*Deathwatch*'?[26]

ME: I had cut a little film called '*The Godsend*'.[27] It was a small horror film – a sort of '*Omen*', with a little girl who had evil powers and this was for a women called Gabrielle Beaumont.[28] A very nice woman who subsequently went to Hollywood. Any way she knew Bob (Robert) Parrish, writer and director, and ex-editor indeed, who was a great friend of Bertrand Tavernier, and so I think that's how I got that job.

RC: I caught up with it recently at Canterbury – he came over and it was his print and I very much enjoyed it.

ME: It was slightly odd one in that I worked on the film from the beginning up in Glasgow, where it was shot and when I finished I had cut the whole film and then it went back to Paris and another editor took it on from that point, but I went over for the mixing and actually they hadn't changed it much at all. I got on very well with Bertrand – it turned out that we had very similar jazz record collections and that was a big connection and I worked very hard – I really loved it – it was a beautiful film to cut, but subsequently I would have wanted to trim it down a bit. I thought it was a little bit indulgent, which a lot of films are. It was bit mournful, a bit melancholy, that maybe was part of its character. Some wonderful performers: Max von Sydow and Harvey Keitel. Harvey was there with his girl friend, whose father was a fire chief in New York, and I was the only person who he invited to his hotel for dinner. I realised that it was really that he wanted more closeups. He used to come into the cutting room and look over my shoulder and say, 'Wouldn't that be good if we had a closeup of me there?' I'd say, 'Yes, Harvey, that's an interesting idea, I shall think about that'.

RC: So you would have enjoyed cutting Tavernier's jazz film, '*Round Midnight*'.[29]

ME: Oh, very much so – I wish I had so much. In fact I keep in touch with Bertrand and he has a plan for a film about Billy Strayhorn, who wrote for Duke Ellington – I've certainly put in my word to be on that if it happens.

* * * * * * * * * * * * *

RC: Then there was '*Britannia Hospital*'[30] after '*Take It or Leave It*'.[31]

ME: That was a film about the pop group '*Madness*' – how they started and eventually achieved success. I had cut some promos between features including some for that group so Dave Robinson, the head of Stiff Records, who directed and produced the film asked me to cut it. The script consisted of five half pages and it was all improvised and great fun to cut because we were inventing much of the film in the cutting room. It was shot with two 16mm cameras and blown up to 35mm, and is still available on video!

RC: Then back to Lindsay Anderson.

ME: Yes, I think the producers, Clive Parsons and Davina Belling, knew I was cutting by now and I had seen Lindsay from time to time since '*O, Lucky Man!*'[32] anyway it was a very good experience. I had an assistant at that time called Denis Mactaggart, a very, very good assistant, but he was so amazed by the force of Lindsay's personality that it took him several weeks to get used to it, he was a very strong charac-ter – someone who was never relaxing. A lot of directors would at some time just want to sit down, have a cup of tea and be quiet, but Lindsay was never like that; always mentally on top form – he never coasted, and that's quite impressive to come across when you are not used to it.

On '*O, Lucky Man*' he hadn't wanted David (Gladwell) to be cutting whilst he was shooting and eventually that was taken over by Tom Priestley,[33] but on this film we discussed it a bit and I thought it was useful for me to be cutting without the constraints of a director saying this is how it should be. So I did cut it during the shooting and it was fine. Afterwards he came in and did a full days work with everyone. Lindsay was of that school – if you're doing a film this is what you are occupied with and you don't do anything else.

There's one cut right in the title sequence that I still don't like. It's a terrible continuity thing, where a nurse is walking along and she throws a cloak over her shoulder and then you cut and she's doing the same thing again, and it was purely to accommodate titles or music or both. Lindsay's attitude was oh, it doesn't matter, of course it doesn't matter!

* * * * * * * * * * * *

Then I did '*The Lords of Discipline*' with Franc Roddam,[34] for Paramount, probably his best film, I would say. The one he did before it was quite famous – '*Quadrophenia*'.[35] He picked me because he liked the '*Madness*' film – he probably liked the slight roughness of that. It was all set in a military academy in America, but shot in England, except ten days on location over there. We did a lot of previews on that – I think I had five trips – to and from California, all first class and a Concorde trip to New York at one point.

The person in charge of Paramount at the time was Jeffrey Katzenberg, who subsequently started Dreamworks with Spielberg and Gethin.[36] He used to just sit down and make notes – go through the film one, two, three and in one case I remember he had forty-two points all neatly written. Frank would get so mad about this. It was one of those films – set in the deep south, Frank envisaged it as slow paced, lazy Mississippi feeling with occasional bursts of violence and this didn't work really. His images just weren't Kubrick images that you could look at for ages – you know – they didn't have whatever it takes for a Kubrick image to be something you want to watch for five minutes. You have to have that intensity and drama within the frame and it ended up being quite a pacey film, very well regarded in that sort of way, instead of a lazy three-hour Mississippi epic.

> **RC:** Was that hard work, actually getting it down or did the material allow you to?
>
> **ME:** The material seemed to be more comfortable at that pace. I never quite got this slowness thing – the images weren't there. It was probably the first major experience I had with the problems of endings. We ended up with a freeze frame.
>
> Then it was '*Comfort and Joy*' with Bill Forsyth,[37] for which I had an interview with him and Clive Parsons and Davina Belling. Having done '*Britannia Hospital*' they thought I might be good with Bill. I remember he hardly ever looked at me and I thought he's not going to like me, but he did and I got the job and went up to Glasgow for two months.
>
> Bill loved to come to the cutting room to see what I'd done – often at the end of the day. The shooting process is not his favourite thing so he always enjoyed being in the cutting room and he could be very creative in a unique Bill way, as he is in the writing.
>
> **RC:** Then '*The Bride*'.[38]
>
> **ME:** Yes, Franc Roddam again. Jennifer Beals and Sting. It was a strange film really – Franc wasn't concentrating, partly because he was concentrating on a certain person. Columbia again – the American circus, the previews – one learns things politically as you go along the executives especially. Frank didn't want to hear what they had to say, and if I could see there was some sense in some of the suggestions then I had to try and express this without appearing to be on the other side. It's silly not to try good ideas, just because of the person who said them. That's a frequent conundrum really.

* * * * * * * * * * * * *

> **RC:** I suppose you get used to it, but since I've never experienced it I always think if you think you've done your best with the cut, and then someone or several people come along and say no this isn't the finishing line you've got to do another lap and then another – it can be tough I'm sure.
>
> **ME:** It's very tough and it's happened on this film really. You get executives coming and not wanting to leave it alone. Thinking it can still be better and you can do this and that and sometimes they are not altogether bad ideas – sometimes they are – sometimes

they are stupid and you think how could you imagine that, but sometimes there are things which are worth implementing. It seems to happen quite frequently now and whether this is the result of the famous Robert McKee[39] – all executives going to script writing classes – I don't know what this is, but everyone seems to think that – there's a sort of language isn't there – the third act and redemption and all that sort of thing that people talk about and they think they have something to say. A lot of the time it maybe justified but you think well, it's not their position to say – it's certain people's position to say things, but part of the reason we're in the job is to make a contribution and you have a say – so this is a political thing in itself. In the olden days you get one strong executive who would be a film enthusiast too, which nowadays nobody is – they're business people really and that's a little bit sad. I mean we were given locked picture last week, but there was no sense of happiness amongst the executives, it was just sort of oh well that's another job done. Even the dreadful or dreaded Harvey Weinstein is an enthusiast – he's one of the last moguls who you know loves film. He may be pretty brutal in many ways, but for better or worse he really does enjoy – he can be a child in the cinema, which the grey executives can't, and they'll never make a decision.

* * * * * * * * * * * * *

RC: Then there was '*Jewel of the Nile*'.[40]
ME: I met Michael Douglas when I was on '*The Bride*' in Los Angeles. I think there had been a recommendation from another editor to see me. The director came over here five months later and I was on the list and got the job – as though it had been set up. Michael was the producer as well as the star. It was a very good experience. There was one unfortunate aspect – they were shooting in Morocco and France, and so on and I used to go out and take them scenes. One time I was supposed to go with a very important part of the film where an aircraft gets taken over by mistake and Michael Douglas can't fly it and he ends up driving down the main street of this town with all the donkeys and animals, and it was quite a big set piece. I had planned to have it mixed – to have all the sound effects put on, so it would make it work, but they advanced my trip by about five days. I went without it being dubbed, which was a mistake. So they started to worry, probably about me. Until they came back at the end of shooting – they saw the

whole film and it was great – it was all rough mixed – but I had sensed disquiet – it needed to have sound – I could see it mute and know it was working, but they just saw it as a series of rushes. It's like making a scene out of, as I did once with Laurence Olivier, when he could only remember one line at a time, and I had to cut this together, so all his lines eventually flowed beautifully and he could actually read the legendary telephone book and make it sound like a piece of Shakespeare. When you string things together that's what you are doing – you're sort of taking little tiny sections and knitting it together, but if you are the producer and director, and you've only seen the bits – it takes a little bit of eyewash – something to make them see it as something different.

Anyway it all finished happily and for a time I kept in touch with Michael – sending him the occasional script and so on – he was always good at getting back in contact.

RC: So you've kept doing literary things.

ME: Yes I kept knocking off the odd script.

RC: Scripts rather than any other writing.

ME: Yes, film scripts, well it's a great way if you are not working – we all of us have a period of months – we have our retirement spread out over our working life – that's a great time to make films without it costing a penny – sitting at your table and writing.

RC: And are these original scripts?

ME: Yes, although I wrote one based on a novel, which I tried to get – this was my push for directing – in fact it was Bill Forsyth – he suggested I show it to his agent, and he suggested I should go to Australia which was where the script was set and he put me in touch with an agent there who was William Morris in Sydney, and I spent six weeks there setting it up and when I left somebody had said that they would make it and it was in a go position. Then it collapsed – it was a shame really! It was a Colin Wilson novel called '*All Day Saturday*' – a love affair between young people set in the sheep farms of Australia. I suppose it was written in the 1930s. So that was my main attempt to direct a movie, but I don't feel any great regrets at not having done so – especially seeing the nonsense that some directors have to go through – every day they have to put up with idiot executives – and I really enjoy playing with the toys, and now that we have Avids there's so much more possibilities because you can now play with the sound in a way one never did.

RC: When did you make the transition to non-linear from cutting on film?

ME: It was '*Samson and Delilah*', which Nicolas Roeg[41] directed. That was made for – it was part of a long biblical series – co-financed from Italy and America. I worked on '*The Man Who Fell to Earth*'[42] as a sound editor and Nicolas remembered me from that. He was going to be shooting in Morocco for eight weeks and I thought that would give me the opportunity to learn the machine. The producer paid for me to go on a two-day course at Lightworks and I took to it like a duck to water, because I'd already done a lot of computer music at home – I'd been doing this for a decade or more and I just loved it. I wouldn't go back to film now – by comparison it is so slow and cumbersome.

RC: Do you however create your own thinking time – rather than do another version of a scene?

ME: Oh yes, but I don't do alternative versions and, touch wood, I haven't worked with a director who says lets do another version – I've heard about this – but its never happened. Once on this film we went back to the cut I did originally of a scene and its quite good for the ego – 'Why don't we try?' – 'That's how I did it first' – and out it comes. It's a funny thing – a bit like the first impression on meeting someone – your first impression is something that lasts forever – and I'm sure its true of a film in a way – if you see a certain version it often sticks in your brain and you realise you are spending quite a lot of effort trying to recover that and there it is, now, in the Avid at the click of a button.

* * * * * * * * * * * * *

RC: So would you say its been a 'normal' career – a combination of serendipity, accidents, fate and going back to people you have worked with before?

ME: Well, its good working with people that you know, and you know that there is mutual trust, but its also good to work with new people – actually its funny how many of them were first time film-makers, but Mark's[43] the only one who has gone on to make five – it's a tough world really. It is very organic you realise its all people – you never benefit immediately from a film it takes four or five years usually.

RC: If someone wants to be an editor now do you think that the route that life took you – was a good way to develop?

ME: Oh, very good, oh yes – I think the sound background has been invaluable especially now with computers. On several films I've done previews in a cinema from the sound that I create here in the Avid. I've got a permanent eight tracks up – two or four of them devoted to music and the others with dialogue and effects. You just know how to deal with it. Also you can do EQ here, I can change the pitch, I can change the length. It's just a wonderful toy to play with. So I think that sound career was very useful for me.

RC: And watching Reggie Beck have that flexibility.

ME: Absolutely.

RC: Looking back, have there been films or types of films you would have liked to cut?

ME: I would have liked to cut a musical. What's that film with Michelle Pfeiffer where she sings 'Making Whoopee' draped across the piano?

RC: Oh, '*The Fabulous Baker Boys*'.[44]

ME: I would have loved to have cut that film – all sorts of aspects to it: the comedy, the music, the story – it was just something I would have liked to have done. I would have liked to have snuck in one or two big films. I did enjoy '*The Jewel of the Nile*' very much – a sort of adult romp. The day-to-day work on one of those big Hollywood films is quite pleasurable and you have a great support system. The studio post-production department is there at your call to help you, and its fantastic. I enjoy the pressure – just delivering on time – I'd have liked one or two more opportunities like that.

RC: Looking at another aspect – did the Tavernier experience – would you have liked to have done any more European films?

ME: Um – yes – yes I would absolutely. Funnily enough last year I had a meeting with a Portuguese director – he'd made one award winning film. I really tried to make it happen. It was a really good story too, so that I would have liked to have done. European films are not quite the same as they were, you know. One of the other sound jobs I did was I worked for Antonioni in Rome on '*The Passenger*'.[45] Not for long – only about six weeks, but I went out to do the automated dialogue replacement (ADR) for the English actors in it. He asked me to bring some sound effects and Antonioni had cut three frames out of about twenty or thirty shots and they were mostly desert and some city shots and he asked me to find sound effects for these shots, based on these frames. It was the most extraordinary thing I've ever had to do. I tried to put my imagination to work – I wasn't sent a script, apart from the scenes I was going to ADR. So I went out there with all the sound effects and it was interesting except I never got to see the film.

There was one screening and the windows all around the projection area were covered in newspaper and there was a tiny little thing for the projectionist to focus. I sort of assumed that I would be going to the screening because it was just him and his editor. We were in the bar having very pleasant discussions about this, that and the other and then he went off and shook my hand and said goodbye. He was very protective of his movies even though you were working on the film. Interesting and sad – I mean it was quite a good film.

RC: No, I like that film a lot. I've been reading Wim Wenders diary of working as Antonioni's amanuensis on *'Beyond the Clouds'*[46] – a very sad book really – not being able to communicate properly – having to find a way of conveying his desires. Maybe it's partly his personality even before he became ill.

ME: Probably a combination, but one of his films would be in my top ten if not two. *'L'Avventura'*[47] I just thought was superb. It was so impressive to see these films coming out at the time. A great visual sense – a great intellectual sense too. One looks to America for films like that now, I feel. Films like *'Being John Malkovich'*[48] are the sort of films you might have expected from Italy thirty years ago. It's that sort of film you know – Spike Jonze and those sort of people.

RC: Yes, there's a 'European' feel to the Coen Brothers.

ME: Well I think that America borrowed from Europe a lot. You think of *'Bonnie and Clyde'*[49] and they actually wanted Godard to direct that on the basis of his film, *'Breathless'*.[50] I think there's a whole bunch of other films too, like the Taviani Brothers in Italy who have influenced – and it obviously takes decades before people can do this with a sense of authority.

Notes

1. ***Brassed Off*** – Mark Herman, 1996.
2. **Richard (Dick) Lester** – Director particularly anarchic comedy, e.g. the Beatles in *'A Hard Days Night'*, 1964.
3. ***Gulliver's Travels*** – Jack Sher, 1960?
4. **Stephen Cross** – Editor, film-maker.
5. **David Gladwell** – Editor, director – *'Memoirs of a Survivor'*, 1981.
6. ***If*** – Lindsay Anderson, 1968.

7. **Lindsay Anderson (1923–94)** – Stage and film director. Passionate leader of 'Free Cinema' movement in Britain in the 1960s.
8. *This Sporting Life* – Lindsay Anderson, 1963.
9. **Memorial Enterprises** – Michael Medwin and Albert Finney's film company.
10. **Alan Bell** – Sound editor, highly regarded by peers.
11. **Johnny Lee** – His true identity remains a mystery.
12. *Some Like It Hot* – Billy Wilder (1959) – certainly Monroe sounds convincing.
13. *Galileo* **(1975)** – Joseph Losey (1909–84) who came to Britain to escape the witch-hunts of the Macarthy era and whose films were never less than interesting.
14. **Reggie Beck** – Editor for Joseph Losey from '*Eva*' (1962) to '*Steaming*' in 1985.
15. *The Romantic Englishwoman* – Joseph Losey, 1975.
16. *The Go-between* – Joseph Losey, 1970.
17. **Harold Pinter** – Very distinctive writer for stage, TV and cinema. Also actor.
18. *My Ain Folk* **(1973), Bill Douglas (1937–91)** – The middle part of his auto-biographical trilogy. His was a great talent that left us too few films.
19. **Mamoun Hassan** – Editor, producer ('*No Surrender*' – 1985) formerly Head of BFI Production Board and passionate supporter of radical talents like Bill Douglas.
20. *Straw Dogs* – Sam Peckinpah, 1971.
21. *Junior Bonner* – Sam Peckinpah, 1972.
22. *Cross of Iron* – Sam Pekinpah, 1977.
23. *Two cricket teams* – At least 22 editing staff.
24. *The Wild Bunch* – Sam Peckinpah, 1969.
25. **Kevin Brownlow** – Editor and champion of 'silent' cinema for whom we have to thank for some remarkable restoration of gems like '*Napoleon*' (1926), Abel Gance. His books make wonderful reading especially 'The Parades Gone By'.
26. *Deathwatch* **(***La Mort en Direct***)** – Bertrand Tavernier, 1980.
27. *The Godsend* – 1980.
28. **Gabrielle Beaumont** – Director, most recently, '*Diana, the People's Princess*', 1998.
29. *Round Midnight* – Bertrand Tavernier's tribute to jazz, 1986.
30. *Britannia Hospital* – Lindsay Anderson, 1981.
31. *Take It or leave It* – Dave Robinson, 1981.
32. *O, Lucky Man!* – Lindsay Anderson, 1973.
33. **Tom Priestley** – Editor, including '*Deliverance*' (1972) and '*Tess*' (1979).
34. *The Lords of Discipline* – Franc Roddam, 1983.
35. *Quadrophenia* – Franc Roddam, 1979.
36. **Jeffrey Katzenberg,** *Dreamworks,* **Spielberg and Gethin** – The company formed to create a different kind of 'Studio' in Hollywood.
37. *Comfort and Joy* – Bill Forsyth, 1984.

38. ***The Bride*** – Franc Roddam, 1985.
39. **Robert McKee** – Script guru.
40. ***Jewel of the Nile*** – Michael Douglas, 1985.
41. ***Samson and Delilah*** – Nicolas Roeg, 1996.
42. ***The Man Who Fell to Earth*** – Nicolas Roeg, 1976.
43. **Mark Herman** – Talented writer/director, most recently '*Hope Springs*', 2003.
44. ***The Fabulous Baker Boys*** – Steve Kloves, writer of the Harry Potter screenplays, 1989.
45. ***The Passenger*** – Michelangelo Antonioni, 1975.
46. ***Beyond the Clouds*** – Antonioni with the collaboration of Wim Wenders, 1995.
47. ***L'Avventura*** – Antonioni, 1960.
48. ***Being John Malkovich*** – Spike Jonze, 1999.
49. ***Bonnie and Clyde*** – Arthur Penn, 1967.
50. ***Breathless (À bout de souffle)*** – Jean-Luc Godard, 1960.

29   Mick Audsley

I met with Mick in his edit suite in London's Soho where he was cutting a film directed by Mike Newell, whom he first worked with on 'Dancing with a Stranger'. Mick has also worked with Stephen Frears many times, starting with 'Walter' and 'My Beautiful Laundrette' up to the recent 'Dirty Pretty Things'.

I was born in Rochester in Kent, and brought up from the age of four in Sevenoaks, where my parents still live. I was educated there and my father was at that time and still is a wonderful furniture

Mick Audsley in his edit suite (© Lightwork, Courtesy of Mick Audsley)

signer and maker. At that time he ran a small furniture manufacturing business. As soon as we were old enough my mum pitched in as well, rolled up her sleeves and did a lot of the business side. I'm the youngest of three – an elder sister and an elder brother neither of whom have had anything to do with film-making.

There's one strand near all this which is that my grandmother on my father's side was a notable photographer – having a shed down the garden and making plates and doing all that stuff. She did a lot of interesting photographic work, as my father has done also – he's always been very interested in photography. So we used to convert the bathroom into a darkroom and process stills. Very early on I can remember looking at these things coming up in the orange light, thinking this is wonderful – this is magic!

My aunt on my father's side is a painter – so visual arts and craft work was very strong on my father's side of the family. I never went near a piece of wood because he's so damn good at it! So I sort of fell into the artsy side of things very early on, because I wasn't academic at school either in primary or secondary school, and realised that I could hide behind being an arts student. I drew a lot from early on and was interested in music. My father is also a very good amateur flute player. So there were musical interests and visual arts interests in the house.

I veered towards animation originally. At school I thought oh, that sounds interesting and I started doing flick books. Then I realised how labour intensive it was.

RC: Was that based on seeing Disney films?
MA: Yeah, I think I must have seen Disney films but I was more interested in those weird European short films – more painterly things – do you remember George Dunning[1] and people like that? I saw a Norman Mclaren[2] film very early on.
RC: Are we talking about during your adolescence?
MA: From about the age of twelve to fifteen, sixteen.
RC: Was any of that encouraged at school?
MA: Very much so – in fact I had a wonderful arts education at Sevenoaks. Three people in particular who were very key figures: the music teacher, my art teacher and my English teacher.

We did film-making and photography at school. We did little projects like there'd be a jazz concert – lets make a projected image to go behind one of the pieces and we were able to use 16mm cameras and do that. It wasn't formal – it had a sort of crossover with painting – you know that era – this was late 1960s obviously – moving slides and visual things like that – also re-photographing stills and a certain amount of drawn animation.

About that time the school had a relationship with the Paris Pullman cinema. I think there was a student whose father was running it. They asked us sixth formers to make posters for the films that were on. So we would get to rent the films which were shown at a film society. The one that really had a huge impact on me, which was where I suddenly thought, oh, cinema is a lot more than Hollywood was '*Vivre sa Vie*'.[3] So I got completely intoxicated with Godard, and fell in love with Anna Karina, and once you hopped on to Godard you found yourself in Truffaut and either the cast would take you there or the people who shot the films. I would come up to London to go to either the Paris Pullman or the Everyman in Hampstead.

RC: Was that a solitary activity or did you have friends who you came with?

MA: No pretty much – I had a few mates but generally I used to come up on own, and that was encouraged, and I thought I want to be near film-making. I was also introduced to a gentleman called Peter Arnold,[4] who again was the father of a fellow student. They lived nearby in Sevenoaks and he had produced '*Morgan, a Suitable Case for Treatment*'.[5] I went to see him to say I don't know what I want to do but I'm interested in getting into film-making proper. He arranged for me to visit animators up here in Soho, which was an eye-opening experience because I realised how labour intensive it was. Those were the days of cell animation, and I just didn't see myself entering into a world drawing chocolate wrappers undoing and all that stuff, which was generally the bulk of the work that people did to keep alive. Feature animation films seemed unattainable.

* * * * * * * * * * * * *

So I then had this love affair with Godard films and the French cinema and also the Czech films – Menzel, Forman and all those guys – '*The Fireman's Ball*',[6] '*Closely Observed Trains*',[7] and the Japanese films, Kurosawa. Due to this connection with the Paris Pullman and of course the Academy in Oxford Street we were encouraged to do that, but Peter Arnold said if you want to make a good living don't go into the film business. Which thankfully spurred me on, but I didn't quite know how to go about it.

It came about that our School at that time had such an advanced progressive art department that I was able to be a sixth former and do A levels, Art, English and so on, but also do what was really a foundation course at Art School. So I went from school, straight on to a diploma at Hornsey which at that time was regarded as being the cool place to go for graphics which was the department I went into. I thought I ought to keep my other draughtsmanship skills alive in case the film thing goes down the toilet. Ironically one of the people who helped me most was a drawing teacher who was absolutely crazy about cinema and he would encourage us to see films and have discussion groups.

So I went up that road thinking I want to get near movie making proper and I started to let go of the animation, although I made a three-minute animation to apply for the Royal College of Art Film School. When I got there I had an inclination that I wanted to do something in the cutting room but I never achieved that at that school, which was very frustrating.

The best education I got there was from fellow students: Michael White, Peter Harvey, all those people. As I was interested in music and had musical activities as a hobby, and was involved in making records at that time, I just got lumped into the sound department and would go out on shoots recording. By the time I got to thinking I've got to earn a living now, having gone through the film school, I started to do sound recording jobs. The Union situation was so strong then, I could only work on BFI (British Film Institute) films, Arts Council drama films those sorts of things. I sort of fell in with Mamoun[8] at the BFI. We would do these little 'pilots', two- or three-minute films which people were doing who were applying for Production Board grants. I would shoot sound on those and I started to cut sound to dubb them. It was a great place to step out from because Kevin Brownlow was there making '*Winstanley*',[9] and Charles Rees, and Andrew Mollo and I remember Bruce Beresford was there at some stage. Peter Smith was there making films. They in a way became much more of an education for me after leaving the Royal College of Art Film School, or maybe I was just more focussed.[10]

It was a lovely time because people would invite you in and you would look at a scene. People were very sharing – Bill Douglas too of course. I remember watching '*My Childhood*'[11] in a little back room and it was quite the most powerful film I had ever seen. I felt like a nail had just been driven through my forehead.

So all of were fantastically helpful because I found them speaking a language I could understand and it was in an area of cinema that I could completely relate to. I'd had no real interest in American cinema. I really only got interested in American cinema that came out of the late 1960s – that sort of hey day – all Dede's (*Allen*) stuff – '*Bonnie and Clyde*', '*The Last Detail*',[12] when suddenly it had gone back to the independents.

****

It was by a fluke at the BFI Production Board that Peter Harvey and I were asked to shoot a pilot for a version of '*King Lear*'. We went off to Wales and shot a test. It was really a filmed piece of theatre. We got back and Peter phoned me a few days later and said there's nobody to cut this thing together why don't you have a go. It was something I was really interested in and had been unable to do at Film School, because people wouldn't trust you. I almost got a student film to cut but the girl that was directing it walked in after I had done all the preparation work and said I'd like to do it myself! I felt there was nobody there to educate you and help ease you into that. It was like you've got to go into a cutting room and deliver a film – pull it off from scratch.

So the time I'd spent sound editing I'd managed to learn enough from Charles (Rees) and watching Kevin (Brownlow) who was always so gracious and enthusiastic and vocal, and just a wonderful source of energy and passion as was Mamoun (Hassan). I was desperate for a week's wages so I accepted and the minute I started I thought ah, this is what I want to do. Anyway I did that and the director never knew I'd never cut a frame in my life – I got through it – it passed and they got the whole film. The conditions were that we did the same trick and that I would cut it.

Once I started editing Charles Rees taught me a lot about the visual side of it. Ways of looking at things, because he's got such a heightened particular personal view of cinema. You could either go with Charles or you could react against it. Then I was being shown cuts of films that were being made and people were so much more generous than they are now. So you could get involved in editorial debates which slowly I started to feel that I had a voice to participate in, which I had absolutely not had before.

I worked on a lot of things, which were extremely mediocre, but it was around then that I thought I really want to edit so I taught myself how to use the Moviola. I got hold of some old 35mm commercials and I just chopped them up to learn how to use the machine, because everyone was so terrified of Moviolas, they were always available. So I taught myself to use the gear, and I thought I'd better teach myself about structural issues. I bought everything I could find about screenplay writing, because I was looking at films I'd done thinking they are put together well in one way but it doesn't work in another.

The contact I had with Bill (Douglas), even prior to getting involved in making any of his films – because he was so passionate about a visual, non-dialogue orientated storytelling and an editorial purity – language of sizes, progressions of rhythms – I got very interested in that through him. It was ringing a lot of bells in my head.

I did another little film for the Arts Council – they were the only things I could do because I wasn't legitimate. They were those funny days when you would be working in a cutting room and people would jump into trim bins to hide because they'd say the ACTT (Union) guys are coming round.

I did sound recording jobs to get work, and horrible pop-promos, films about biscuits and a whole series of news reports for Italian Television. Where this rather wonderful man called Paternostra would stand in Parliament Square and say 'here I am in Liverpool', because he couldn't be bothered to get on the train to report some story up north. They offered me a permanent job doing news stuff that came in at mid-day and you had to work the reversal film all afternoon. Then a guy would rip it off the Steenbeck at five o'clock take it to Broadcasting House where it would be beamed to Rome and it would be on the news, on RAI by the time you got home. It was actually wonderful because it really loosened you up and you couldn't be precious about it. All the time I was waiting to do proper cinema films.

* * * * * * * * * * * * *

I think it helped through all these to know that was where I wanted to go. Mike Ellis[13] who was also a mentor gave me very good advice which was don't go up the wrong ladder – work at a lower level in the area you want to be. If you want to work in movies stay there, don't go into TV, and I think Mike was right. The BFI was my springboard in that respect because at least I was dealing with people who wanted to make films, and there was this lovely discussional, open atmosphere.

Then I had that wonderful day at Beaconsfield with Sandy Mackendrick[14] when I asked him to look at Terence Davies' film. There was that wonderful remark which you must have heard. He had seen Terry's film '*Madonna and Child*',[15] which was the one I did. Somebody said 'Oh, that's the gay one' and Sandy said, 'It isn't at the moment', because it was a very heavy lugubrious film.

I had one of the most illuminating days ever in film-making for me, sitting in that little corner cutting room in Beaconsfield with the blinds down because the film was so dark. Sandy broke down the story and analysed it, and talked about the writing and the shapes of that particular film, and the intentions. He said something which I'd never heard anybody say which was 'this issue which you are trying to compensate for is a writing issue, do not even attempt to go there – this is an editorial issue which you can address if you have these sorts of pieces'.

This was like a light coming on in my head to differentiate and to have somebody whose overview of a film was so analytical but was also so astute. It was absolutely wonderful. In fact I think I spent two days with him and by coincidence later on through Stephen (Frears) we used to go and visit Sandy in California. He saw several cuts of films we had done. Staggeringly, Gladys his wife said how wonderful it was that we came. I just thought it was the most privileged position to be able to sit and have an hour over a drink and talk to this man. So often you have people responding to work in progress and being unable to talk in a certain language. Maybe it's cynicism on my part but I find more and more that people are unable to express the real issues of what's going on with films when they are in their evolutionary stages. To meet somebody of that calibre who understood it inside out and could guide you was absolutely wonderful. There have been only two or three people like that: Sandy was one and the lovely Dede (Allen) as well. There are not many people who can talk about film in that analytical way and constructively and without bringing all their interests which are not the same as ours as film-makers.

* * * * * * * * * * * * *

I can't quite remember the order of things but it was through sound recording that I became involved with '*My Way Home*',[16] because again I needed a job so I went off to Egypt. Through sound recording there and Bill's difficulties in finishing the film I ended up taking that over. That really was the first complete feature film that I edited. That was a springboard to several other things. First Richard Woolley's '*Brothers and Sisters*'[17] and then Chris Petit's '*Unsuitable Job for a Woman*'[18] which was through Michael Relph[19] who very kindly helped get me onboard because I had helped out with Bill's situation.

RC: Thinking back to those early experiences are you conscious how you developed as an editor and in your relationship with directors?

MA: Absolutely, particularly the whole Bill, Mamoun and Kevin, ethos of film language. In a way I still feel I hear their voices in the back of my head: the repetition of sizes, how to forward stories visually. I think that was an enormous grounding to do with the relationships of how you help make a film with somebody or sit in a room and thrash it out. I really don't know what the rules are for that, because I never worked as an assistant to other editors, certainly not on feature films. I did a bit of assisting to get by with the wonderful Jonathan Gili[20] when he was cutting BBC documentaries, but we just used to sit in the cutting room and talk about movies and music, and then realise we'd better throw something together!

I didn't know how that hierarchy worked. In fact it was very embarrassing on '*An Unsuitable Job for a Woman*' which was the first time I'd had a proper crew, because I'd previously done all the work myself. I had two assistants and I didn't know what I was supposed to do and what they were meant to do. So when I offered to sync up a roll of rushes on the second day of shooting they thought I was mad and they gave me a very hard time about it, because I was much younger than them. I was miserable because they really made me feel inexperienced and I did a lot of sitting in the toilet weeping. Until they made one very big mistake and then everything flipped over, but I learnt a lot from them as well. They were very surly and from the 'proper' film business. I'd just come from the backwoods of the BFI which was considered very lowly, so it was a very tough time.

RC: Interesting that your early experience almost reflects the way editors will have to develop now – without being real assistants.

MA: Of course, with the whole digital thing.

RC: In retrospect would you have liked to have worked for a couple of special editors?

MA: I think it was a huge help that I didn't because I was arrogant enough to walk in and say I know how to do this, which you can do when you are twenty-five, with absolute blind ignorance and then swim your way out of it. Whereas if I'd watched other people and the pressures they are put under, diplomatically and politically in the vortex of making films I think I probably would have felt I don't know how to do that.

RC: I suppose being around minds like Kevin Brownlow and Charles Rees and Mamoun Hassan was an ample substitute in a way, because you could have a dialogue, certainly about how to put something together.

MA: The wonderful thing was that it had no connection to commercial film-making at all. There was never an incentive to make money from the movies. It was just about cinema proper. It soon dawned on me that I wasn't going to be able to live in that world for very long because it's just not possible. No, I think they were absolutely an enormous influence because it was an open plan set-up there in Lower Marsh[21] and they would be tearing their hair out and wanting to share it. Saying, 'I can't see my way out of this can you have a look at it, what's wrong'. I think that was a terrific privilege because it's not easy to do that now. I haven't experienced that since.

323

RC: Also I suppose it was a privilege to work in an environment where, okay there wasn't much money, but almost all of it was on the screen. It wasn't that other kind of industrial infrastructure.

MA: We did make conscious decisions to live in such a way to get by with low overheads so you could wait to get another film. I mean I did driving taxis and the whole thing. They were all very supportive and it was good fun but it was hard and not sustainable indefinitely.

* * * * * * * * * * * * *

RC: So was the Chris Petit film a breakthrough?

MA: It was a huge breakthrough and again one of those incredible flukes – when that film finished my dubbing editor Rodney Holland went to a Christmas party and bumped into Stephen Frears who was looking for a new editor and Rodney said he'd like to meet you for a job. I didn't know Stephen personally but I'd seen '*Gumshoe*'[22] and all his TV films. So we met up and I had a very amusing interview for '*Walter*',[23] which ended up being the first FilmFour for Channel Four. I remember walking out on to Oxford Street after we'd finished the film and seeing a poster which said 'Handicapped film – shock horror – opens Channel Four' or something! It was a wonderful film.

RC: When you started with Stephen Frears, did you feel you were changing gear?

MA: I was terrified from our brief interview, because I admired his work so much. I was very frightened and nervous and lacking in confidence, but I think because I'd had a grounding and we had a lot in common, with Bill and the whole BFI thing, I remember that's what we talked about when we met. I talked about ways of doing things. The one thing I'll never forget he said, 'Well, in the end it either works or it doesn't'. Anyway it was beautifully shot and I have to say the work had all been done for me. Chris Menges[24] and Stephen had shot it beautifully. It wasn't incredibly montagey at all. I benefited from all the work they had done in the design of it, and it was very, very emotional material – the wonderful Ian Mackellan[25] and genuinely handicapped patients who were integrated.

RC: I vaguely remember that each scene was very moving but sometimes the structural difficulty was moving from scene to scene.

MA: Getting from a to b yeah, I don't think I really got, I didn't understand that and also in terms of working with somebody new – having to work out what my position was and what's okay to say. Still, to this day, I'm not sure how much Stephen enjoys being in the cutting room or not – he's busy not being in it quite a lot of the time, but we would talk all the time. We would talk on the phone at the end of every day's shooting and we immediately had a very good rap in that way. Or he made me feel very free with the film that I could participate and do what I wanted with it. There was no sense of this is mine. He was extremely generous and always has been about letting you muck about and have a go.

I developed an ease of talking with Stephen because of his generosity and willingness to hear what you have to say so it allowed him to trust me and to be a pair of eyes and respond to the material. So with '*The Hit*'[26] because it was a road movie and there was no real base, I was just in London looking at the rushes at the laboratory at five in the morning and we'd speak on the phone before he went shooting about the previous days work. They were relying on me how each scene was reading. So we developed a very efficient loop about the film as it was being shot. It was a lovely film with John Hurt.

RC: Very sharp, very brittle, harsh – again another change of style.

MA: Beautifully written by Peter Prince.[27] I remember being frightened most of the time making that film because Jeremy Thomas walked in and said as the producer, remember I've been an editor for a long time as well. I thought oh God, I'm going to be cooked here, but we had a lovely time. I thoroughly enjoyed that film. Those films were all made in about twenty, twenty-one weeks top to bottom which now seems amazing but in a way editorially that's a quick turn over. They were such fun to do because, you were in and out of them pretty quickly and so it felt very fresh and lively. We made them for ourselves – we didn't preview them. We'd show them to friends but it very much felt like we were given this toy to play with. I don't know whether Stephen would corroborate this. Very supportive producers, Margaret Matheson,[28] Jeremy Thomas,[29] all those people we adored, still do, and they created a wonderful nest for you to work in full of trust, and I loved every minute of it.

RC: Having done everything on the BFI stuff, did you then carry on doing picture and sound editing?

MA: No I had to drop sound editing pretty quickly.

RC: But did you develop a way of offering a template for how the sound should be to compliment the picture?

MA: I did feel very strongly about it and often I found it a difficult stage for me because I'd often think oh, I wouldn't have done that, so I still find that quite tough. I think in terms of sound right from the word go. Of course the digital technology allows you to cut immediately with multi-track.

In those days of one bit of film and the cutting copy and the music banging in and out and the overlaps not there – I think in a way that grounding, which you had as well – seeing films naked like that without any of the frills and atmospheres and things which smooth them out forced you to confront the real bones of the editorial process. I still prefer to see films as stripped down as I possibly can, because if it plays like that it's only going to get better. You can't hide behind bits of music and so on.

* * * * * * * * * * * * *

RC: So going back to the progression – after '*The Hit*' it was the first time with Mike Newell.

MA: Yes, '*Dance with a Stranger*'.[30] Stephen introduced me to Mike and we hopped straight on to that after a few weeks – it was a wonderful film. It just seemed a privilege at the time: the pleasure of a Shelagh Delaney[31] script. I remember Miranda Richardson's first day's rushes so well – my jaw dropped – I just couldn't believe where this woman had come from! Richard Hartley[32] did a wonderful score for that. I found it such an upsetting film I haven't been able to watch it since – strong stuff, but again a very happy experience.

RC: Is working with Mike in any way a contrast with Stephen?

MA: Everybody has their different methods. I think it's difficult because I've made fifteen or sixteen films for Stephen now over twenty years the short hand that that allows you because we know each other so well and the trust. You can streamline the process.

RC: My memory of having you both teach at Beaconsfield around this time was the sense that you both had a very good lack of respect for the material, that, as Truffaut said, you have to be prepared to violate the film.

MA: I think that's true and again I remember that being perpetrated by Stephen, but I remember very early on when he looked at the first cut of '*Walter*' saying, 'well, you've been far to respectful to the actors'. I remember it because I used to have Ian Mackellan sitting in my cutting room because my room was warm, it had a little electric fire. It was a pretty dodgy place and he used to come and sit, and because I was relatively inexperienced I used to feel the weight of this giant of the stage and screen behind me.

Until at one point I said to Ian, who is the most delightful man, 'look erm, I'm feeling a little uncomfortable' and he said, 'no, no don't be intimidated by me but do tell me what's going on in your head, while you do this'. So I said this is what I'm thinking I'm making this choice because of that. I remember also being impressed by the fact that he got pleasure from seeing what to me – somebody of his calibre – he'd look at it and say 'Ghosh, I really look as if I've been asleep!' when he was waking up in bed. I thought, he still worries about that stuff, this is Ian Mackellan for Christ's sake!

I then said, 'well the process of cutting a film is in a way ripping it apart'. Stephen would often say don't worry about which take you put in, just pick the first one – they're all good, and in a way they were. I was thinking all these choices, and he'd say we'll worry about that later, because he has a remarkable memory of what he's shot, not by looking at it, because he seldom looks at the rushes. He doesn't work in that traditional way at all, he wants somebody to respond and see if they are picking up what he intended it to have, which is the sort of technique, which we developed over these years. I think he would agree with that. That's why we talk every day – how are you getting on with that – we've got a very tight loop, beat by beat. If I was worried about something I'd say that's not reading quite right and he'd say no I understand, I'm ahead of you. His understanding or memory of what he's shot and what it's going to do is so acute that he didn't need to look at the rushes. He'd say this is what I was trying to get and if you follow-up the takes you will see it going that way. Editorially one of the biggest things you have to help you in the lonely part of assembling a film is trying to work out why they've done another take. I sit here constantly puzzling over what that process is and what might have been said and why.

I think that lack of respect for the material in order to move it around and let the film's montage start to speak and let it be inflected is really what its all about, and of course it's a plastic medium which now, with digital, is even more so. You can always go back, so for example this scene I've got now – three hours of material for a five-page scene – huge amount of cover but very consistent performances. The agony of choice is huge except once you know the story you want to tell and the progression of ideas and the climate that the scene exists in when you start the first frame of that scene, which gets easier as the film gets built. I now just say I will do something – so I've got something to respond to. I'll come back tomorrow and usually I'm horrified at how bad it is, and how it doesn't seem to express things, which I felt when I saw the rushes, but I've started and I just have to wade my way through it. After these twenty years I think it should get easier but it doesn't, because you feel this enormous responsibility of realising this thing and you don't want to look foolish. It is your perception and response to things which people are hiring you for, because loads of us can cut the films together but it's what you choose and the way you choose to see it.

* * * * * * * * * * * * *

RC: Are you still very nervous when you start a new movie?

MA: I am actually. I feel sort of apprehensive because I don't know how to make that film. I've only ever made the last one and I think somebody's going to find out I'm a fake. I genuinely think that. I sit in front of the rushes and none of it seems to be how I imagined it would be. I do as much work as I can on the screenplay beforehand, and I've been lucky enough to always have friends to talk with and that's a terrific help, because it means I can mug-up the issues early on. You think do I want to live with this thing for six months or a year or more of my life, which is a big question everyday. Seeing the writing develop or being able to say I'm worried about this – to be a part of that conversation is an enormous help.

So people who I've worked with more regularly have been kind enough to let me in on that process before we make the film. As was the case with '*Dirty Pretty Things*'[33] or '*My Beautiful Laundrette*'[34] we talked a lot about issues when this thing was so raw and disorganised and wonderful. How time scales needed to be rationalised because they were going to stop you enjoying the flow of the story, for instance. On the other hand something like '*Dangerous Liaisons*'[35] was just a perfect script by the time I read it and we never touched it.

The film was that – we made one tiny change at the end after a preview – moved one scene – but what Christopher Hampton[36] had written was what it was.

RC: In keeping that process going through the cut of not being respectful or being willing to rip it apart is it in the working relationship that when one of you thinks we have done our best with that sequence the other might say I don't know . . .

MA: . . . I think there's a bit more to come. Yeah, I think that just happens. I'm absolutely reliant on screening these things. I'm reliant on screening rushes. I sit there in that blur overwhelmed by the volume of stuff because I find, Roger, after thirty minutes I can't take in the detail.

RC: In those screenings do you take notes?

MA: Never take notes. The traditional thing of people whispering in your ear in the dark 'I'd like you to use that and that' has never happened to me – ever. It's happened in as much that if there is one take that is definitely the one, but because you're dealing with fragments the whole issue of the good take doesn't exist. I do get feelings about things and I try to memorise. I can remember angles very easily. Memorising the performances takes longer and I get feelings about what I've left out. I know when I've cut something I haven't expressed this idea and I know its there so where is it. That's what I mean about this thing of having to commit to a cut for the first time and look at it and say is this the film, is this going to fit in when its all in place?

I think if people trust you to make a fool of yourself which is what I'm very grateful for to all these guys to let me do – to say I've had a go I don't know but we will discover it. Then when I screen the film I start having strong feelings about it, but I have to see the film in the cinema and I have to have a memory of the rushes. If I haven't I'm at sea. I do get apprehensive, I constantly feel when I'm assembling a film that I'm in a mess, I'm not doing it right, until you see the whole film.

Sometimes you think that is the film. '*The Snapper*'[37] was a bit like that, it was so beautifully written and done and Stephen had realised it so brilliantly. It was just complete and balanced. This wonderful occasion when literally a day or two days after we'd shot the film in Ireland, I banged the last bits in because I'd managed to keep up. I said go out and get a bottle of champagne and we sat with our feet up on the Steenbeck and laughed our way through the film. I thought its fine and it didn't really change – that was it.

Others you spend months trying to configure what it is you haven't got right. I think that trust of I don't know, I'm not sure but this is what I feel, and the ability to listen and filter the enormous weight of criticism and dialogue that comes at you which at best can be helpful and at worst thoroughly confusing and demoralising. Listening to other people's opinions is a skill in its own right.

I've always wanted the cutting room to be like a safe haven during shooting. The place where you can say look it was a complete mess, everything went wrong today, all the usual film-making problems, but that we are in it together and those failings are what the cutting room's about. As well as the failings I'm going to have of not seeing things because your perception of the film changes.

RC: When you say you must see it in the cinema does that mean you take it to a big screen as frequently as you can?

MA: Yeah, we do. I mean now with the digital thing you have to plan the conforming, but they are sort of blocked out, but its that experience of sitting there that I'm entirely reliant on to do the next bout of work. Or it fuels what I call bedroom ceiling editing, which is when I'm lying in bed thinking why does the film collapse in the middle, all that sort of thing.

RC: So have you always had the luck or the privilege of having a print that you can conform, because some people are so frustrated at having to watch a play out from the Avid which you can't judge on the big screen?

MA: Yes, we have. It's something we insist on and I'm working with that age group who are used to seeing film during editing. I don't know how else you can judge it. When we have all these previews and someone like Dede will come along and debrief afterwards as a supervising editor, and she'll say I thought it was getting a bit sticky here and you say I felt that too, what can we do about it? She's lived through the experience in the cinema, and its to do with sitting in the dark for two hours trying to read what five hundred people are going through as the thing unravels, but I don't know how else to do it. I think I was taught that by Bill, definitely Stephen and Mamoun – its an old fashioned school.

We all had trouble reading the film off tele's, because we were so used to Moviolas, and whinged about that for a while. There was a lot of moaning about looking at tele's saying I've got to see the actual stuff.

* * * * * * * * * * * * *

RC: Having said an hour ago that in those early days you didn't really engage with Hollywood cinema, where do you think that most of the cinema that you have been party to making fits?

MA: I don't know. I've always thought of them, even the American ones, as being European films.

RC: Interestingly Stephen said to me, after the cast and crew screening of '*Dirty Pretty Things*', 'I think I've made a European film'. For him to say that now after so many films, implying that he's not done that before, seems rather strange.

MA: It's funny because I think they are European films. '*Dangerous Liaisons*' is an odd one because it is a film made in Europe with people speaking American for French, or Scottish if you are one of the lower mortals in the hierarchy that the film presents, but I suppose that was an American film. Although to me it reads like a European film although it's got American stars. Aren't we talking about films that assume a level of intelligence and sophistication and ideas that are largely to do with character, rather than more mundane storytelling and lesser issues perhaps. Isn't it to do with the density of the material and the issues of humanity that they represent?

In a way we tried to make an American film with '*Accidental Hero*'.[38] I loved the screenplay but I feel that maybe it didn't do well, because some people took against a star like Dustin Hoffman. Looking under the bonnet of the way media represents events and our desire to have personalities in the media, and newspapers and TV is something America couldn't laugh at or take a satirical view of and that in my view was why the film didn't do well. To me it has a European core to it.

I guess '*Dirty Pretty Things*' is naturally European because its based here and is about people trying to get to America or trying to climb up the ladder of the social scale or get legitimacy. It's a bit too soon on that one.

* * * * * * * * * * * * *

RC: We must go back to your last experience with Bill Douglas on '*Comrades*'.[39] How was that?

MA: I was very fond of Bill and he had taught me an enormous amount and I owed him a great deal, as difficult and volatile and exciting and terrifying as he was to be with. I loved the whole '*Comrades*' concept and what we were trying to achieve and this huge tapestry of the film. At the time I felt very sorry that he didn't want to cut the film and compress it and condense it more. In a way he'd written himself into a corner with very, very intricate ellipses in the film which all needed to be seeded and paid off, and yet just the scale of the piece meant that it needed cutting down. He became quite reticent and unwilling to do that and it was my job to support him although in my heart at the time I felt I would love to have a go with more freedom to make a more concise film and one that moved a bit quicker. I felt that it would have become more accessible. There were also some things that hadn't come off and they needed in my view to come out, and he would have had to give up some of the elliptical elements that he felt bound them into the movie.

RC: My memory is that the first half is more successful than the second.

MA: Yeah, it has one of the best openings of any film I know. The first five minutes are absolutely staggering. If somebody asked me now to do another cut of the film to make it more accessible to a wider audience I'd love to do it. I suppose you'd feel that Bill isn't here to argue his side of the case – it would feel like a sacrilegious thing.

RC: There is a process isn't there in the diplomacy between editor and director where trying to go further than they want to go, however strong the relationship and the trust between you, there really is no way. At a certain point, how-ever you broach the idea of changes, their antennae are already – even before you open your mouth – they know you are going to suggest – and whatever strategy you try they will resist.

MA: I think I have been lucky in ending up working with people who have very much not been like that and have been very open and very free. Stephen for example or perhaps Mike the same, although working with Terry Gilliam on '*Twelve Monkeys*'[40] was an absolute joy too. Although everyone made me feel that he was going to be terribly protective he gave me wonderful freedom and was supportive and flexible.

RC: I remember you saying how good that experience was.

MA: It was. I adored the script. It was a huge editorial challenge that film and I just had a great time making it. It was very hard work. Terry was so stimulating and supportive of what you were trying to do and the problems we had. It was a happy experience. I've had a sheltered life really!

* * * * * * * * * * * * *

RC: Now I know, because you've told me, that a couple of more recent experiences have not been the greatest. Without libelling anybody are there things you can say about what an editor needs to do to achieve good work or how you cope with serious problems?

MA: In the case of '*The Avengers*'[41] it was a unique set of experiences. Things were going off the rails in that case within three or four weeks of the start of shooting. Not only in my mind and also with my friends who were other HOD's, Stuart Craig and Roger Pratt (designer and cinematographer, respectively). When you put up your hands and say look I think we are getting into very deep water here, when a film is coming at you in little bits all out of order with special effects, and the reply is we're happy, what can you say? You carry on and stay as supportive as you can.

RC: Did it read okay on the page?

MA: Yeah, but they didn't shoot what was on the page, and there were fundamental story issues which weren't addressed as they went along. Daily I would look and see what was on the page and it didn't match what they came home with. It was a more formal relationship with those guys and there was a culture gap but we absolutely waved the flag.

It was Dede (Allen) who saved me from throwing myself off Hungerford Bridge. At one stage in total despair after we'd had the worst previews ever, I went to Dede and said, 'I don't think I can finish this film'. I remember her wagging her finger like this and saying, 'It's not done to leave', and because I respect her entirely I never entertained the idea again. She said 'you'll get through' and I did.

RC: Changing the subject – we haven't talked about '*The Grifters*'.[42]

MA: '*Grifters*' was heavenly really. A really intimate group of people – cast and crew. Martin Scorsese as executive producer – a bit like Sandy Mackendrick – there are so few people who can talk about film with that level of understanding. He used to see cuts for which I have never been more nervous in my life. Thelma[43] was involved as well and was incredibly supportive. One day Stephen suggested we go through the reels with them in the cutting room, which I thought would be fantastic. We got to about reel three and Marty said, 'Look I'm making another film next door, I'm only going to be imposing all my rhythms and stuff that I've got going there on you – what you're doing is great – just carry on'. We never did get to the end of the film.

RC: Interesting thing to say – 'imposing my rhythms'.

MA: Yeah, well he was making '*Goodfellas*' at the time and sort of snapping his fingers. He said your rhythms are yours they're fine. We had some issues with the placement of Elmer Bernstein's music and we jiggled around with it a bit, but by and large it was a very smooth birth. I just remember the excitement of standing in the studio in Dublin and hearing Elmer's fantastic score for the first time. It was just wonderful – a big brass section playing. It's often used as a 'temp' for other people's films and I relive that moment – it was very, very exciting.

* * * * * * * * * * * * *

RC: Going back to discovering cinema – how have your taste and enthusiasms evolved since?

MA: I feel that the thing of being taken by a film happens less and less. That is a sorrow because you think why am I a plumber always looking for a leak – why can't I just sit back and go with it and accept. When a film is great the pleasure you have in seeing it is immense. Plus the fact of knowing that all films are such hard earned items to make. Bad films are as hard to make as good ones as they say. You can appreciate all these incredible skills but feel disappointed that perhaps the germs of the ideas are dull or uninteresting. I only judge films by whether I have been taken out of myself.

You have this memory of films that had an enormous impact on you earlier in life, Bergman or those touching warm funny and sad Czech films or Kurosawa, and you end up wanting to look out for something that will hit you in that way or elevate you.

Talking about being nervous on a film I do frequently sit in the cutting room thinking I am not qualified to do this. These are very expensive movie stars and I am making very radical decisions about what they've given us, which often people don't go back on once you commit and I really haven't had any formal training in this at all.

I didn't watch somebody else – I didn't stand and watch somebody make a whole film – I got it in bits and pieces. So I sit here and do think I'm a fake – somebody is going to find out soon. I don't know how I'm qualified to do this, even now, but in the end you just try and make a film for yourself. I literally sit there and say would I want to see this in a film, does this represent the person well. You can only go so far to accommodate others. I have made performance changes and been close to tears watching the film veer off in another direction and think that's fine but it's not the film I thought we were going to make.

I think a quality that is absolutely necessary to do this job as I understand it, from the perspective I've had, is to *listen* to other people. Take it onboard, mull it over, chew it over, digest it, and try and filter it and in the end what is true to you will stick. Don't take it at face value and learn to interpret what they are really saying. They often talk, as I call it, with forked tongue and they will be saying do this, do that, but they are actually trying to tell you that there is a problem. Don't listen to what their solution is because you will probably have a better idea because you have built the thing shot by shot, frame by frame from the very first day and bolted the damn thing together! I want to hear about problems not solutions.

One of Stephens many directions to me, having seen the first cut of '*The Hit*' was, well you've made the film about Willy Parker now I want you to make the film about Mr Braddock! I thought oh right, okay, I was looking at the oppressed not the oppressor, and of course that's what we did. One needs to have those sorts of perspectives planted in your mind, but you can only make those judgements if you've got well constructed and strong material, shot in a way that allows you to make such choices and editorially swing the balance this way or that. If you work with someone a lot then that's going to happen much, much quicker and earlier on in the process.

RC: Do you think you have a natural sense of rhythm?

MA: I hope so after all these films! It's such a weird commodity in films. In some ways I can look at something and say that's not been done rhythmically and yet in relation to film it's quite an abstract idea to get your head round. If somebody says to me that's not rhythmical I'd probably understand in my terms but I'm not sure I know in their terms. It's a strange word attached to editing. I can look at my own work and say I haven't got the rhythm of the scene right, but I'm not sure I can vocalise exactly with that scene what it is that makes that happen.

Yet seeing student editors some of them you can look at something and it's beautifully realised and seems effortless. Other times you know you are never going to get them to cut in a certain way, because that sense of rhythm is not inherently there. All I know for myself is that when a film is working and is rhythmically correct to me I can watch it and be detached. It is telling me what I need to know and nothing is jarring or if it is jarring it is doing so in a way I've designed.

To judge this I find myself constantly going back literally to half-way through previous scenes before I run into the next one because I'm so concerned about the shift of ideas or the accumulated knowledge thing. To a ludicrous extent now that I think God I'm probably spending hours every day running the same thing, but I'm trying to get my bearings on where I am to make a decision which I can't see in the isolated climate of the scene itself.

What is interesting now is that because of the digital technology you've got the chance to actually, let's use the word, 'rhythm' something and sophisticate it very early on, because you've got the time to do it. Before I'd have to construct a scene and it would take me all day, now I can do that in half-a-day and I've got the rest of the day to integrate it into the film or make adjustments or try alternative takes or another version. It works very differently. Before you were just grateful if you got something that big (*gestures with his hands at a 1000-feet roll of 35mm film*) at the end of the day that you felt remotely happy with and then the process of 'rhythming' it would come later. Now people seem to demand things, which are much more sophisticated earlier. I don't show stuff unless I think it is rhythmically pretty sophisticated, because I feel embarrassed.

Even a first cut I think should be a very articulated version of what was shot in relation to the script. Then when you start reinventing the film for cinematic reasons rather than literary, you've got a record of it as written. I feel that the assembly process is so misquoted in film-making jargon. Literally today on the end of the shoot of this film I got a phone call from the DoP saying ha ha, I guess you are going to start work now! The assembly process to me is the most crucial stage of making the film, of building it and responding and hopefully being able to guide and shape alterations into the shooting. It's the biggest jump the film makes because I think generally people find rushes very difficult to watch and don't really understand the editorial process. They don't know what to look for. It's a very sophisticated job. People get sent tapes and I have conversations where I know they haven't seen the material. There's a lot of grey areas in the process of rushes, but the whole thing of calling a cut an assembly or an editors cut or a first cut is something I would so like to clear up publicly so the terminology used when dealing with us guys in the cutting room was clearer.

'Oh, just do a rough cut of that scene' what does that mean? I'm going to do a version of that scene which I think is the best thing since sliced bread until I know better. It's not going to be rough its going to be sophisticated. What may be rough is the writing or lots of other things, but it's not going to be a rough cut. I prefer to do it by numbers. There's a first cut, which is like a draft – and generally this is verbatim: 'exterior house cut to interior' – okay there it is. Boring, we'll get rid of that next time round. The first cut is going to present the material as designed in its first incarnation in the director's head. He may well want to cut a whole lot out but he feels he has to shoot it and then we'll dump it later.

RC: One of the things I found very early on when I was dealing with performances which were pretty good in a movie was that if I followed the rhythm of the performances it usually felt alright. I then remember getting a film where the actual style and rhythm of the performances of the two leads was so different that it was a real bugger. Especially inter-cutting and going from wide shot to closeup, it would be a totally different emphasis and weight. I suddenly realised that editing is more than following or respecting or supporting the rhythm of the performances – you have to intervene.

MA: I think it is also true that good directors understand and control that instinctively. For instance you know that a brief hesitation can kill you and you don't want to put a cut in. So the cranking of those rhythms in the directors job is so crucial to the way the film then gets cut. So I need one simple statement here or one gesture – I don't need five and I don't need it to last thirty seconds I need it to be 'click' like that. Having somebody that understands that and is presenting the opportunities to allow you to either get at that or even better not get at it is great. Where you do have to intervene on a big scale I always feel guilty. I don't want to have to cut there because I'm interfering but I need the next line to be there and not there, and it could be literally a foot later and it's weird. That's maybe what we were talking about earlier; that is an understanding of instinctive rhythm or the rhythm of the way humans' interact, and how quick it can go. The shock you always have is how fast people pick up information. The perception of visual information is hugely sophisticated. I sit there in a preview thinking is this going fast enough? They're soaking this up pretty fast and its going a bit slowly for me.

* * * * * * * * * * * * *

RC: Finally, the transition to digital – how was it for you?

MA: I was very ready for it. I found it very gruelling hanging film up in bins and the terrible 'bench neck' as I used to call it. It was frightening. I didn't ever see myself as sitting operating a computer, because that wasn't my idea of what film editors did. But the minute I started I thought, oh this is absolutely fantastic; the speed at which you could manipulate images. You could almost make things as quickly as you could think them, whereas before your thinking was always way ahead of the time it took you physically. The feeling that what people were asking you to do was not undoing hours and hours of work, which could be terribly upsetting to pull something apart, which we physically used to do as you know. It makes you much more versatile, flexible and conversational. Investigating ideas just feels much safer because you haven't got to rip something to bits and you can make comparisons. So I found it absolutely liberating in every way.

RC: But do you have techniques for rather than doing another version having thinking time?

MA: I still follow the same routines. The only thing that's different is that if you've come to work without an idea in your head of what is the first beat of the scene to start you can sort of get away with it, because you can follow a route and think I've done it wrong, I'm going to have to go back and start again. Whereas before on the way to work on the bus I would sit there thinking I've got to work out where I'm going to start this scene, because by the time you've made all those selections and bound them together half the day had gone. Then you think I've made a mistake, hell, I've got to undo it all. Having come up through the discipline of film I think I have been very lucky to have been part of both of those worlds. I still think of it as film right down to cutting out little men and putting then at the bottom of the computer screen to imagine that that's the cinema – these are all little people watching.

Notes

1. **George Dunning (1920–79)** – Canadian animator who directed '*Yellow Submarine*' (1968) and is credited with 'saving' the polyvision sequences of Abel Gance's '*Napoléon*' (1926).
2. **Norman Mclaren (1914–87)** – Scottish experimental film-maker and animator – '*Neighbours*' (1952). Did most of his important work at the Canadian Film Board.
3. *Vivre sa Vie-Film en Douze Tableau* – Jean-Luc Godard, with Anna Karina, 1962.
4. **Peter Arnold** – The producer credit on 'Morgan . . .' is Leon Clore.
5. *Morgan, a Suitable Case for Treatment* – Directed by Karel Reisz, with David Warner, 1966.
6. *The Fireman's Ball* – Milos Forman, 1967.
7. *Closely Observed Trains* – Jiri Menzel, 1966.
8. **Mamoun Hassan** – Originally an editor who became an important figure at the BFI and later at the NFFC for his passionate championing of new talent. Intelligent analyser of films and film-making.
9. *Winstanley* – Kevin Brownlow with Andrew Mollo, 1975.
10. **The British Film Institute Production Board** – Late lamented source of support for independent film-making in Britain, which, in the 1970s encouraged a number of special talents. Apart from Kevin Brownlow, champion of silent film classics, Charles Rees is an editor and passionate cineaste with a particular obsession for Robert Bresson, Andrew Mollo is a production designer who is a specialist in military history, Peter Smith became a director ('*No Surrender*', 1985). Bruce Beresford is an Australian director who ran the Board between 1966 and 1971.
11. *My Childhood* **(1972)** – First part of the trilogy by **Bill Douglas** (1937–91), a remarkable talent.
12. **Dede Allen** – For some of us the greatest editor ever. Born in 1925 and still cutting; '*The Final Cut*' (2004). *Bonnie and Clyde* (1967) was her first major success.
13. **Mike Ellis** – See interview in this book.
14. **Alexander (Sandy) Mackendrick (1912–93)** – Scottish director. First film '*Whisky Galore*' (1949), and after several other splendid Ealing Comedies made his seminal film, '*Sweet Smell of Success*' (1957) starring Burt Lancaster and Tony Curtis. Inspirational teacher at California Institute for the Arts also at National Film School in Britain. It was a privilege to be his colleague.
15. **Terence Davies** – Director, made *Madonna and Child* in 1980 whilst at National Film School. Most recent success, '*House of Mirth*' (2000).
16. *My Way Home* – Bill Douglas, 1978. Final part of his autobiographical trilogy.
17. *Brothers and Sisters* – **Richard Woolley**, who subsequently became a film teacher, 1980.

18. ***Unsuitable Job for a Woman*** – Chris Petit, 1982.
19. **Michael Relph** – Producer, born 1915, Dorset. Enthusiastic and loyal supporter of young talent.
20. **Jonathan Gili** – Documentary film-maker whose brilliant work concentrates on 'real stories about real people'. Originally an editor.
21. **Lower Marsh** – Then the location of the British Film Institute production facilities, south of London's Waterloo Bridge.
22. ***Gumshoe*** – Stephen Frears cinema debut film with Albert Finney, 1971. Script by Neville Smith.
23. ***Walter*** – Stephen Frears, 1982.
24. **Chris Menges** – Eminent cinematographer – Oscars for '*The Mission*' (1987) and '*The Killing Fields*' (1985). Has also directed.
25. **Ian Mackellan** – Superb actor, stage and screen, both TV and cinema – most recently '*The Lord of the Rings*'.
26. ***The Hit*** – Stephen Frears, 1984.
27. **Peter Prince** – Writer. Later adapted '*Waterland*' (1992) for the screen.
28. **Margaret Matheson** – Highly regarded producer for TV and cinema.
29. **Jeremy Thomas** – Courageous producer, including many films by Nicolas Roeg and Bernardo Bertolucci. Former editor.
30. ***Dance with a Stranger*** – Mike Newell, 1985. The Ruth Ellis story – riveting performance by Miranda Richardson.
31. **Shelagh Delaney** – Writer including '*A Taste of Honey*' (1961).
32. **Richard Hartley** – Composer, film and TV.
33. ***Dirty Pretty Things*** – Stephen Frears, with Audrey Tatou, 2002.
34. ***My Beautiful Laundrette*** – Stephen Frears, with Daniel Day-Lewis, 1985.
35. ***Dangerous Liaisons*** – Stephen Frears, with Glenn Close, John Malkovich and Michelle Pfeifer, 1988.
36. **Christopher Hampton** – Writer for stage and screen. Also director, e.g. '*Carrington*' (1995).
37. ***The Snapper*** – Stephen Frears. Based on the Roddy Doyle novel, 1993.
38. ***Accidental Hero*** – Stephen Frears, 1992.
39. ***Comrades*** – Bill Douglas – his final film; the story of the Tolpuddle Martyrs, 1987.
40. ***Twelve Monkeys*** – Terry Gilliam, 1995. Futuristic nightmare film inspired by Chris Marker's '*La Jetée*' (1962).
41. ***The Avengers*** – Jeremiah S. Chechik, based on British TV series, 1998.
42. ***The Grifters*** – Stephen Frears, with Anjelica Huston, 1990.
43. **Thelma Schoonmaker** – Self-effacing but brilliant editor for Martin Scorsese on a regular basis since '*Raging Bull*' (1980). Was wife of the late, great Michael Powell.

30 Pia Di Ciaula

I talked to Pia when she was editing 'The Escapist' for Gillies Mackinnon, with whom she has now worked six times, including 'Regeneration', 'Hideous Kinky' and 'Pure'. Their latest collaboration is on 'Gunpowder, Treason and Plot'. We met in her edit suite at De Lane Lea in London's Soho.

I was born in Toronto to Italian parents. My father was a dental technician and my mother raised five girls. She stayed home until we were all off at school. My mother loves entertainment, theatre

Regeneration (Courtesy of Artificial Eye)

opera and dance, and she always played music at home. She is very vivacious and loves ballroom dancing and salsa.

She was sixteen years when she emigrated to Toronto and my Dad was twenty-one. They had known each other in Italy, but they got together and started dating in Canada. They came from Bari on the south-east coast of Italy. My father's brothers and uncles were/are all dentists or dental technicians. My mother's mother stayed at home and raised six children and my mother's father worked as an electrician, but was also an impresario. He would bring over acts from Italy, mainly singers, and entertainers to Toronto, where there was a large Italian community.

During High School I wasn't sure what I wanted to do so I applied to George Brown University for dentistry but it was not my first choice. I applied to the University of Toronto for languages as a back up, but I also applied to Ryerson for a photography course and I was shocked when I was admitted. I created a portfolio of portraits, animals, action shots and sports. It was really just thrown together for the interview, but I had no idea that I would be accepted.

During the first year we had to study film-making as well as still photography, so we had thirteen hundred-feet exercises to shoot and they were amazing. One exercise would deal with depth of field and depth of focus; another with lighting; another motion and so on, and it was really eye opening. A hundred foot Bell and Howell 16mm, so two-and-a-half minutes for each exercise. There was very little editing.

Up until the end of the summer after the first year I still thought I was going to major in stills. Then I thought no I want to work with people, I like the collaborative effort. Even though I'm in the cutting room now I still go to set, and I still want to deal with the crew members.

Towards the end of the second year or beginning of the third year we all shot one scene and we all got the same rushes. It was just then that I knew what I wanted to do. I created something that really wasn't part of the scene. I was using images before the slate and after cut and just giving it a different look. I just discovered it myself, with no tutoring.

I remember starting the scene on a poster with one line played over and then I cut straight to singles, and no master, unconventional

I suppose. From then on all my friends asked me to cut their films, because they were just too lazy to do it! (laughs). I just was having fun and fell into it.

We did study the history of film. We studied different genres; I took a Western course, which really opened my eyes to that genre. My favourite course was music in film, which was a two-year course. The professor was Madame Sevigny, and she really knew her stuff. She had a musical background and she knew how it applied to film so she really enlightened us.

We also had another exercise putting different audio, music, sound effects, voice over against the same visuals and that was very interesting. So I was able to be experimental and play with images and sound. It was a good time. I chose to work on others films rather than make my own in the fourth year, I just edited.

Years later I realised that from the age of about ten years I used to walk down the street and what I would do was like editing. For instance a car would whip by and I would cut. I would look somewhere else, at a person and wait until they did something interesting then I would look away. I would do that on the subway and buses. I realised that I was putting together these images and just editing, either by looking away or in my mind.

* * * * * * * * * * * * *

When we graduated we were told not to go into the business, that none of us would get jobs. We were wasting our time. In my own case I had been a camera assistant at college on many films and they were the only jobs I could get for the first year. I've always loved cameras so it was fine but I was really wanting to get into the cutting room. Then 'Sunrise Films' was doing a 'Movie of the Week' and I asked if I could be the assistant editor. The director/producer, who is a good friend of mine now, Paul Saltzman,[1] suggested that if I agreed to be their camera assistant then I could follow the film into the cutting room. So I was offered two jobs in one interview! So that was the beginning of my cutting room experience.

The editor really wanted to be a producer, so he cut that film and then became post-producer on a long running series, *'Danger Bay'*, that ran for six seasons, which I worked on too. I started off as an assistant sound effects editor. The next season I became a dialogue assistant, and then the third year picture assistant. The following year there was an episode that nobody wanted to cut, because it was really bad and it was on the shelf all season. Finally they asked me if I wanted to do it and of course I jumped at the chance. So the next season I was on as a fully fledged editor. The background in sound was very valuable. It really helped cutting picture, under-standing what sound would bring to it.

Although there was a variety in the series in terms of style and con-tent, which gave me great experience, it was really hard to break out of TV series. People felt that you could only cut a half-an-hour and not a sixty-minute or full-length movie. The next step was to do a one-hour series, and whilst I was doing that we got to work with the directors more and so I met a director who was doing a movie of the week right after and he asked me to do it.

From then I did a lot of TV movies, and unfortunately that was the bulk of Toronto's work.

The natural step would have been to move to Los Angeles, because all these movies were co-produced with the States, but I just couldn't. I don't like the whole business there. So after thirteen or fourteen movies of the week I finally got a low-budget feature, '*Intimate Relations*'[2] but it still didn't lead anywhere, and I cut several more movies of the week.

* * * * * * * * * * * * *

It was only when Gillies[3] came to the Toronto Festival that the chance occurred. He had '*Small Faces*'[4] in the festival and I had '*Intimate Relations*'. He was interviewing for '*Regeneration*'[5] which was a co-production so he had to hire a Canadian Director of Photo-graphy (DoP), composer and editor. So I went to meet him and luckily I got the job, because it was the best script I had ever read. I was just so thrilled I couldn't believe it.

So that allowed me to come over here, because I had wanted to move to London for a while. I came here in 1988 and fell in love with it. I just knew it was a place that I wanted to be for a while. So when I went back to Toronto I got my Italian passport and kept it in a very safe place. I knew it was a matter of timing, which comes in handy with editing!

Gillies said he knows instantly whether he can work with someone or not. He looked at a film I brought which was a beautiful film. He said it was between me and another editor, but I was more enthusiastic. You really don't know how a person is going to cut your footage. Also you don't know what material they had when you are looking at somebody's demo reel. So it is a gamble.

When I was doing those movies for the American networks I'd have to, for instance, get reactions from every character in a scene. I'd have to go around the table, show what everyone was doing at that moment. It was always a matter of faster, louder, bigger, and then I did '*Regeneration*'. So I had to slow myself down and I had to really breathe it in and take in a whole major change, and it meant something. It wasn't a matter of cutting to somebody for the sake of including them in the scene, for a production value or to make it faster, so it was really important and I think it's great for an editor to have those opportunities. To cut something and aim it for a certain market and then do something completely different for someone else's sensibilities.

When I did '*Regeneration*' I had come off movies of the week, back to back, so my rhythm my timing was a little 'speeded up'. So I assembled the first few days and Gillies saw it at the end of the week and he just felt that it had to slow down. He said to me to let the material speak to me about the pace of the film. So I did that. I just found a slower rhythm. It helped to imagine him there because obviously you try to take in that rhythm of his sensibilities at the time.

I hate to say this but I think I am self-taught. I didn't have any heroes or influences. Though I love a diverse range of films and directors, from Antonioni and Fellini to Scorsese and Coppola. Also Truffaut, Hitchcock and Billy Wilder and De Sica too. But if there is any influence on my editing it is by osmosis rather than consciously. I haven't analysed a film and tried to emulate what they've done.

* * * * * * * * * * * * *

As much as I love all the aspects of editing, assembling scenes is the least enjoyable. I get a sense of accomplishment when a scene is completed but I really love fine cutting. I feel this is where the art is, this is where the editor can truly show what they're made of. The transformation that a film goes through between the assembly and a fine-cut is astonishing. You get to re-direct the film in the cutting room. You can accentuate the poignant moments. You can improve the timing of an actor's performance. You try to mask all the problems and blemishes that are present in every film. You get to retell the story in a more concise and visual way. You get to try various styles and techniques. You get to create the pace and rhythm that the individual scenes require and that the film deserves.

That's the beauty of editing, you can always change cuts, replace shots, change the emphasis, sculpt, finesse and create. Just when you think you've done everything you can to a certain scene, you'll get another idea that sends you off on another tangent. I really love the craft. There are many ways a scene can be cut but once you've explored every way possible and you keep returning to a certain cut, you know its right.

Talking technology, I started on film using the Moviola. Then I worked on a 3/4-inch system, then I moved up to the Grass Valley, which was a little more sophisticated. Then I used the D-vision, which was non-linear hell. It was the first one in the country. No one knew how to run it. I'm not a computer nerd so my assistant and I had to teach ourselves how to run it. So it wasn't ideal. Then I used Lightworks and Avid and I was hooked.[6]

Non-linear systems have revolutionised the way we look at images. We can mould them into whatever our imaginations can create. One great thing about working with Gillies is that we both see every frame as non-linear entities that can be placed wherever we want to serve the story I really enjoy these moments when you think of something you had discarded for some reason but it works brilliantly out of context.

I was forced to cut film again three years ago. I didn't want to. The director and the DoP thought it was a great idea. It felt like going backwards, because I knew what you could achieve on a non-linear system, sound wise and picture wise. It was very frustrating for me because I didn't have the time – it was just not ideal. I loved cutting film and I had a great system which was well organised, but once you know what a non-linear system can do it is difficult going back.

It's a little overwhelming when you think about all the footage you get for a major scene but it's a matter of organisation. When I have a large scene I like to create a selected clip in the Avid, which has the best bits from my preferred takes. This clip will be the foundation from which the scene will be cut and I can always refer to it months from now instead of watching every take again. If my instinct tells me to drop a shot or a few shots I do. It gives me great pleasure to tell the director that I didn't need something. The opposite usually happens; you end up asking for pick-up shots. I start compiling a pick-up shot list as soon as possible so that I have a better chance of getting what I need. Some of them were originally planned but they ran out of time on the day. Some of them are abstract images that I think could be useful down the road when we start layering and being more creative. I also compile a list of wild tracks that help with the mood and timing of the film. Some of them are specific sound effects or ambiences of certain locations and others are actors' lines and voice over.

For the first time in a long time I think editors are in the limelight to a certain extent because of films like 'Erin Brockovich'[7] and 'Traffic'.[8] I choose those because of all the deliberate jump-cuts – mismatched action which was completely intentional, and the fact of same director – two different editors. I watched both films and there are court scenes in both films and they are cut exactly the same way. If you watch them both there is a word that precedes the cut for the dialogue in the court scenes in both films. So you just wonder did Soderbergh[9] steal from Anne Coates[10] and then take it on to 'Traffic' or was it his vision?

I think there is more freedom in editing and we are not really confined to the rules and laws that exist that I don't believe in anyway. It means you can try things and if they work for the scene and the film then fine, like the way we are using freeze frames in 'The Escapist'.[11]

* * * * * * * * * * * * *

I think Gillies or my assistant would say that I am a little weird in my habits. For instance I can't stand working with my back to the door, so the Avid isn't necessarily in the best position. Feng shui perhaps! I like candles, I like to have a peaceful atmosphere. What's weird about me, which I think many editors would understand, is that I get really involved with the screen. So if someone is smiling I might smile back!

I think an editor has to be calm. You have to play psychologist some times between the director and producer. You have to be diplomatic. I think patience is important, because sometimes things don't happen quickly, and you have to work on a scene for weeks before you get it to a stage where you might like it. I think you have to explore all different avenues. Sometimes you have to be ruthless. There are lots of traits that come in handy.

The editor has to pursue ideas, they have to solve problems, they have to love putting the puzzle together. I really enjoy the job, and I think that's a big part of it too because if you are miserable and if you hated the whole idea of it, it wouldn't work.

The first assistant director on '*The Escapist*' said 'We all read the same script, but we all see a different film'. It takes a lot of restraint to make things simple. You have to be organised, focussed not afraid of trying things. I say this because there is a tendency to second guess what the director wants so you try to load the film up with everything that was shot. This is the beauty of working with someone you know and trust, you tend to try anything and sometimes you go against what the director wants in order to show a different point-of-view.

I was a camera assistant when I first finished film school and although I loved it, I prefer the control of the cutting room. Oops, that 'control' word slipped out. I guess you have to be controlling to a certain extent. You have to control the material otherwise it can overwhelm you and you have to control what enters and exits the cutting room. You have to protect the space and department from politics, you have to be diplomatic and you must play psychologist because you're always in between the director and producer.

The approach to sound is very important so I tend to build it into the way I cut. I don't think the sound editors like it because it doesn't give them a lot of leeway. I'm not saying that my effects are great. They are just guides, but if I do want something pre-lapped it is built in. If I want a certain kind of sound, for instance if I want to accentuate something I will put an explosion on it, even though it is a plane landing or a wave crashing or just anything like that. I just try to use sounds to help me portray the feeling of it. I'll just steal anything and make use of it.

I love using sounds out of context. I find it interesting to test what audiences accept as true sound effects. One example of this is that I used a sound effect of a lighter for a lamp being turned off. On this film I have used explosions when Ricky drives through the gates. I used bellows effects during the hospital scenes because it's surreal and sounds like unnatural breaths.

This is minor compared with what David Evans[12] has proposed for the track. He suggested using only mechanical sounds at Sullen Voe so that nothing is natural. Sullen Voe is surrounded by the sea and David is going to use explosions when the waves crash against the rocks. He is going to make the sea an evil breathing force. He is going to slow down sirens and use them for seagulls. He is going to use a roller-coaster in the coal yard so that we are surrounded by conveyor belts and we feel trapped. David is going to make Sullen Voe a medieval setting with pulsing steam, only male voices and distant foghorns. He will play with reality and then switch to surreal sounds. I was very pleased because the film will get the added dimension that it needs to darken it and enhance the world we are trying to reveal.

I have a close relation with the sound editors. I give them detailed notes and Gillies is pretty detailed about sound as well. On 'Regeneration' he handed me a whole script with sound effects ideas throughout the whole film, and I thought that was brilliant. It was the first time I ever received anything like that. I do give them detailed notes of what I want in every scene.

With composers I like it when they don't just support the emotion of the scene. A good composer will dive into the subtext and they try to tie in themes and ideas from other scenes and they try to connect various characters together with melodies. On the other hand I really hate it when you've got an emotional scene and the music precedes the emotional line. It just takes away from the performance and the film if you are spoon-feeding or telling the audience how to feel before they have had a chance to discover it for themselves.

Its funny because in this film we had a little opening sequence and we had music that really belonged at the end because it was reflective. I felt that we had to foreshadow some of the action or mystery or thrill of the story, but we don't have anything in there now. I think we have to hint at it, but to give it away would be a mistake too, because you have to introduce the film and characters which is not the mood that you are going to find ten or fifteen minutes later. So it's a fine line and I think a clever composer can achieve this.

I feel it is important for the editor to follow the film through to the end of the mix. No one knows the film better than the editor, how the sound was designed, what the opticals should look like, what performance was selected, if automated dialogue replacement (ADR)[13] is actually better or worse than the original, etc. I do love the music recording. I also like the final mix because you finally hear the full stereo sound, which is what you've been imagining for months.

In the end the most important thing is the film and you have to work at every stage towards enhancing that.

Notes

1. **Paul Saltzman** – Producer, e.g. '*Map of the Human Heart*', Vincent Ward, 1993.
2. *Intimate Relations* – Philip Goodhew, with Julie Walters, 1996.
3. **Gillies Mackinnon** – Director, born Glasgow, 1948.
4. *Small Faces* – Gillies Mackinnon, from his script, 1996.
5. *Regeneration* – Gillies Mackinnon, based on the novel by Pat Barker, 1997.
6. **Technology** – Pia's journey through from the Moviola to the Avid is quite typical of the generation of editors who started on film before so-called non-linear came in.
7. *Erin Brockovich* – Steven Soderbergh with Julia Roberts, editor Anne Coates, 2000.
8. *Traffic* – Soderbergh – not as good as Simon Moore's original TV series, 2000.
9. **Steven Soderbergh** – Director, sprang to fame with '*Sex, Lies and Videotape*', with Andie MacDowell, 1989.
10. **Anne V. Coates** – Eminent and still active editor, born Reigate 1925, who went to Hollywood after establishing successful career in Britain gaining Oscar for '*Lawrence of Arabia*' in 1962.
11. *The Escapist* – Gillies Mackinnon, script by Nick Perry. An excellent thriller, sadly not released, 2001.
12. **David Evans** – Experienced sound editor, recently did sound effects editing on '*Die Another Day*', 2002.
13. **ADR** – Automated Dialogue Replacement.

31 Lucia Zucchetti

The conversation with Lucia took place in her flat in Notting Hill, not long after she had edited 'The Deal' for Stephen Frears and just before she was off to Luxembourg to start on Michael Radford's film of 'The Merchant of Venice'. I had first met Lucia when she was a student at the same time as Lynne Ramsay, with whom she has established a close working relationship as her editor, including on 'Ratcatcher' and 'Morvern Caller'.

Lucia Zuchetti (Courtesy of Lucia Zuchetti)

I was born in Monza near Milan where I spent my childhood and my teens to then move to London when I was nineteen. From a big family – so the youngest one of four, which I would say is something that has affected the way I am – massively, being the last one in a big family. From parents who were not involved in the arts: my father is a doctor and my mother is a teacher of teachers – what we in Italian call a pedagogist – a specialist in teaching methodologies. She worked when she was younger and then she gave up to raise the family and then went back to work when we were teenagers.

I had a fantastic childhood, I don't know if I have ever told you this actually – with parents who were not quite hippies, I guess because in 1968 when there was a student movement, they already had a family and were a bit too grown up to get involved in all that . . . but, had they been born a little later . . . They came from quite a working class background so they were completely – my father definitely made his own path – going to college in the context of family where no one had ever studied so I think they were very in touch with their roots and they wanted us all to learn that. We spent our childhood travelling with them in a little camper van, discovering the world.

From the age of six my mother and father drove us every year around Europe – even to the Soviet Union when I was seven – during the time of Brezhnev – they were keen socialists and they wanted to see for themselves what was there – and part of Africa and places like that, so quite extraordinary travels which have really stayed with me in my growing up. Their philosophy has always been to encourage us to discover and follow whatever we were interested in. So I spent my childhood and teens doing all sorts of artistic things, because I knew their support was driving me – moving from music to painting to dance and physical theatre and as much as they could help me and encourage me to explore they would.

RC: Was this alongside a conventional education or didn't that happen?

LZ: (laughs) No that happened too but – no, a conventional education in an Italian sense is Italian comprehensive school which is pretty much the norm for us – because there isn't the division between public and private education in Italy as there is here. So after my basic primary and secondary school up to age fourteen, I chose to go tan 'alternative' state funded high school, a mad place that was the result of a 1970s experiment of alternative education: full-time studying, unconventional teaching methods and the opportunity to explore – learn – subjects connected to the visual arts like photography, film and graphic design, all backed up by more classical studies. I guess it was all part of that exploration that had been ongoing from the age of seven when I used to think I would be a painter, or when I was ten and was writing little plays and performing in them as well, or when I was thirteen and composed little piano pieces . . . I didn't know what I wanted to do – I was just trying everything out.

RC: Was this School in Milan?

LZ: Yes, in Milan. I actually met a film director, contemporary of mine, not long ago: Anna Negri,[1] who, you may know because she worked over here for a while after studying at the RCA, and she also went to this School. When she discovered I was there too she said, 'Oh my God, Lucia, whenever I meet someone who went there who has ever achieved anything I am always amazed'. So that's just to give you an idea of what kind of place it was. A school where freedom and individuality were encouraged, but where people got lost in it.

So I think I had quite an extraordinary growing-up – part of a big family doing quite a lot of learning in an alternative kind of way.

RC: and was cinema. . . .

LZ: Well, I was trying to recollect and cinema was just part of that – there wasn't a special attention to cinema. I think I discovered it quite late. I was trying to remember the very first film I ever went to see – and maybe, apart from the Disney films I saw as a child, my mother and father – and this probably says it all – took the whole family to see Kurosawa's '*Dersu Usala*'.[2] This is the first memory I have of going to the movies as a big event, grandparents and all, and that film was made in 1975, and that means I was probably six or seven. I think it was part of my parents thinking of this as an amazing story on a human level and they were just very keen for all us kids to see it, and I still remember it quite vividly.

So quite a lot of cultural stimuli, but within the possibilities and limitations of a family which had quite a few children to nurture. My parents would say: 'If that's what you want to explore right now we'll let you explore that'. Equally if I wanted to give it up, I felt free to do that. We were never pushed into anything. I actually feel a bit angry that I was never pushed to, e.g. stay in music more, because I studied piano for a few years. My mother used to play the piano as a young girl. The piano that her father gave her as a big present when she was a young girl, that still sits in their home now, was the piano that all of us kids learnt on. Then when I got to my teens I got bored and never pursued it and it is the one thing that I say to my mother I wish that someone had told me you'd better stick to that – and I never did, and I've got quite a lot of regrets.

RC: I have the same regrets.

LZ: My awareness of cinema started becoming more and more apparent in my teens. I started studying photography and taking pictures and then watching films and thinking about cinema at school.

A film that hit me when I was in my teens was '*The Icicle Thieves*' by Maurizio Nichetti,[3] an Italian film-maker who is not very well known over here but who I used to look at with interest, because he comes from Milan and has a background in physical theatre and mime, something that has always interested me. '*The Icicle Thieves*' is a sort of post-modern parody of '*The Bicycle Thieves*',[4] and is a social commentary on the state of Italian Television and culture.

I've seen it again and wondered why it hit mew so much but I guess it made an impact on me because it was the time I was starting to have an interest in how films were made. It was probably then that I was becoming aware of what editing could be about. Although that took a while to develop, if I have to be completely honest.

RC: So it wasn't necessarily only the editing that interested you.

LZ: No I think it was more to do with what you can say with films. I think that was the first thing that made me start to be passionate about it – working out what one person could say in choosing what kind of film to make.

Then I would say it was my luck to come to this country, which happened almost by chance, in the sense that it wasn't part of a big plan or anything. I wanted to study film and in Milan there was no place to do it. I would have had to leave home and possibly go to Rome. I had a sister who was in the UK studying, and I thought well I might as well go and investigate. That was in 1988 and I came to investigate and I have been here ever since. I'm still investigating! (laughs).

RC: You stayed – you didn't come and then go back.

LZ: No, I came and I thought, oh well, I'll learn English and I'll find out what's on offer. I guess my dilemma was that I knew that in Italy my choice would be either a really academic one or a very practical one and I knew that I wanted to read more books and study a little bit more, especially because the school I had come from I felt that it had taught me to think but had not given me a lot of academic knowledge. I wasn't ready to give up on that, so when I arrived here and discovered I could do a course that combined the two I got really excited. I spent my first year in the UK studying English and applying to different degree courses. Then I was offered a place on the course I really favoured and I was very happy about that. It was a degree in Film, Video and Photographic Arts at the Polytechnic of Central London.[5]

I remember, and this is really funny now, that although I wouldn't admit it to myself, my ambition was already to get to the National Film and Television School. I thought that saying it out loud would bring me bad luck, but I remember going to the interview at the Poly and wondering whether it would be the place that would lead me to a more vocational course like the NFTS.[6]

RC: But at this point you hadn't decided on editing?

LZ: No, it was in those three years at PCL where I discovered editing really, and almost by chance in the sense that I kind of stumbled on it. It was a really small course – I think fifteen of us only doing film. So we had to take it in turns to have a go at different things and not many people wanted to edit, because none of us at the time understood how much you could give creatively. Most people wanted to direct, and I remember having a go at editing and somehow discovering that I was enjoying it enormously and people would respond to what I was doing suggesting I had a bit of a knack for it, and that obviously gave me satisfaction and because everyone was trying to direct I was lucky enough to have first pick to edit what was made. I edited my first two or three short films there, which were then the ones that allowed me into the Film School.

RC: and was the theory valuable at that point?

LZ: I think it was. Probably half of the time I was thinking 'God, why am I studying semiotics, it is really boring!' Or maybe thinking that some analysis or interpretation in film theory books felt really contrived and half of the time it had nothing to do with what the film-makers had in mind when they made the film. But I'm glad I went through that thinking process and I guess that overall I came away from that course feeling a stronger awareness of point of view. It sounds basic, but it was important to spend time thinking about it, both to be a good viewer and to develop a sense of responsibility as a film-maker.

RC: Were there people in your year group who were stimulating or some teachers?

LZ: Yes, I think I owe a lot to the course leader, who is still there now: Joost Hunnigher.[7] I think with his enthusiasm, he was a real inspiration for me. He taught me the first few things about editing – first not to get stuck into following rules and second to look at the material and see what it says, sometimes – and this often applied to student projects – what was intended on paper was not there; 'What can you get out of what you have?' he would say.

RC: and at that time did you drown yourself in movies – did you develop a taste for certain kinds – did you make discoveries through the films you saw?

LZ: I was trying to recollect what seminal films I saw, because they did make us see loads of things and that was the other amazing thing, as well as reading some books and studying psychoanalytic texts. One film that has always stayed with me, was Len Lye's '*The Colour Box*',[8] which was made in the 1930s at the GPO Film Unit. Its basically colour patterns and letters painted on celluloid and moving in sync with the music.

RC: Why was it fascinating at the time?

LZ: I think I had never seen anything like it! A moving painting, a work of art that made use of colours and rhythm. I think it was just a great discovery – suddenly seeing these colours dancing on the big screen to this music had completely blown me away.

I think I probably saw my first French New Wave films at PCL too. It was probably '*À Bout de souffle*'[9] that started making me think about editing – what you can do with it – how editing can affect something – how a point of view can be established – or how a film-maker can signal his/her presence to break the 'film as reality' illusion – that fascinated me as well.

RC: So would it have been more Godard than Truffaut?

LZ: Well, actually I saw more Truffaut than Godard – though I remember '*À Bout de souffle*' stayed with me very much I also fell in love with films like '*Jules et Jim*'.[10] Another seminal film, that I discovered later on even though it is by an Italian director, was '*The Battle of Algiers*'.[11] If I try to look at what there is in common I'm not quite sure, but I know that I'm generally driven by the passion of what something is about.

RC: Well I think we all have an eclectic list of favourite films if we are honest rather than one with a narrow logic.

LZ: Exactly! I used to wonder why my dad loved spaghetti westerns, I just wouldn't get it, I would find them so unappealing,

I guess I never sat and watched one properly until I grew up. Then one day I sat and watched '*Once Upon a Time in the West*',[12] and I fell in love with it. I think Sergio Leone is a master of film language – I love his use of sound.

There are a lot of films I love but there are also a lot of films I haven't seen. I am not a film buff and there is a side of me thinking that almost I want to be a little bit free from knowing what's been made. There's nothing worse than finding it difficult to shake of the influences that great film-makers can have on you. I find that knowing too much sometimes limits you, inhibits you, a little bit of naivety keeps ones work fresh.

RC: So have you held on to any of the other arts over the years?

LZ: Well I still take pictures, though not as much as I would like, and I keep having fantasies about getting back into music but now I think if I started playing again it would be percussion. I got inspired when I went to Cuba last year. I'd love to get back into studying piano but I think it is probably unlikely that I will.

RC: So in Cuba did you get a chance to play.

LZ: A bit – but mostly I was inspired by the music and I learned to dance salsa – realised a lot of my passions are connected to music and rhythm thankfully they do not all involve being stuck in a room on your own or in the company of one other person only. I know those things are what keep me happy, that keep me alive.

RC: How do you feel now about the relationship between growing up in Italy and Italian culture and cinema and its relationship to who you are now? Do you think there are things you tap into – or is that just subconscious?

LZ: Its difficult. I'm sure that where I grew up and the kind of culture I absorbed is affecting the person I am regardless of the fact that I've almost spent half of my life here now. It's a bit hidden in there, it maybe difficult to articulate it.

RC: What do you miss?

LZ: Apart from the basic things that everyone would know like the food and my family and the beauty of some places that are very accessible.

RC: I mean music is so rich in Italy – it always feel to me like more a part of life whereas here its mostly an activity – rather than something where the heart and soul are involved – its probably a romantic notion about Italy but . . .

LZ: Yes probably – I was thinking more something that was connected to your heart and how much you express your emotions – I would think that is what to me maybe distinguishes

'Englishness' from 'Italian-ness', the expression of what's in there – what's in your heart, passion and emotion.

RC: So by the time you got through the PCL course you had focussed on editing.

LZ: Yes, I didn't know how far I could go with it but I knew that I could close a door – put myself in a room with a whole load of rushes and I knew that I was (1) having fun and (2) I was getting something good out of it. At the time I was relying on other people telling me that, who appreciated what I was doing.

Tony Grisoni,[13] the screenwriter who was a student on the same course and was doing some part time teaching at the time, before he started writing scripts for Terry Gilliam, and Michael Winterbottom,[14] was a crucial source of encouragement to me. I owe a lot to him.

RC: With him did it develop your understanding of the relationship between editing and writing – the structure of narrative – the way stories are told.

LZ: I think a little bit, but because the films we were making at college were beginners films, it was hard to talk about writing and the production process, the writing was often very minimal! I think the writing often happened in the cutting room and I learnt a lot through that! I've learnt lots about structure and how to look at the heart of things.

RC: You always seemed very focussed – you gave that impression.

LZ: I know – its scary in the sense – because it is something that other people have commented on, but I do not feel it. Its interesting because I wouldn't be able to say that there was the point where everything felt or path felt so clear – it just organically developed. Obviously at the Film School where I met, what now I call 'the family', some of the fantastic people I still work with to this day, it all felt great – we had that nucleus of support and inspiration and basis for exchange of thoughts and ideas.

I've got a fantastic memory of that time, because I think we were trying to explore something that wasn't quite what we were directed to explore by some of the tutors, who maybe believed we should learn the conventions before we could experiment, but we encouraged each other to try things out, we believed in each other and the support drove us forward. It was an amazing platform for me and I think probably for my number one director-collaborator Lynne Ramsay[15] who I met in those years at the School. The minute we had some confirmation that we were onto something interesting we had the force to push things further.

RC: So at that time were there other people outside of the group who you found gave at least some kind of affirmation that what you were trying to do was worthwhile and legitimate or was that just reinforced from within?

LZ: We did find a lot of strength in each other – there wasn't a guru – but the one person in terms of editing I felt close to and I still do is Tom Priestley[16] – not for any specific reason but he taught me that, as far as editing is concerned, there was not one answer. He would come and see the work and he would never give THE solution and I appreciated that very much because it gave me confidence to find my own way.

RC: So when you came out of Film School was it Lynne's short that you did first?

LZ: I remember spending a couple of years cutting six or seven shorts when I came out. By that point I had cut Lynne's graduation film, '*Small Deaths*'[17] which had won a prize in Cannes. We knew that probably we would be making other things together. So in those two years I cut six or seven shorts of which two were directed by Lynne Ramsay one was '*Kill the Day*'[18] which I love – it is the least well known – and then '*Gasman*'[19] which won a prize in Cannes, so after those three shorts we could see the possibility of Lynne directing a feature and that we would probably all be together on that journey. Which is what happened. So '*Ratcatcher*'[20] was about two years after Film School. I remember saying to myself after Film School I don't want it to be more than two years before I get to do something really substantial and pretty much it was that. I said to myself if I have to wait longer I know I'll get frustrated and I'll end up changing direction or something.

RC: Reverting to type!

LZ: Working with Lynne was always a challenge – she has a very individual approach, to shooting that verges on the documentary. She likes to turn over a lot and gets inspired by unplanned events and spontaneous thoughts. On '*Ratcatcher*', which I cut in the old fashioned way – on film with a pic-sync and a Steenbeck – we ended up shooting a lot – we had a 22:1 ratio and working with many non-actors so every take – often was not the same so I think that was a difficult but great way to learn really – I mean a hard way to learn because suddenly you've got this mountain to climb and you've only been up a hill before. It felt like we had to work out how to do it sometimes but again knowing we could support each other through that that is what gave us strength – that is what made it possible.

RC: Were you left alone – without executives breathing down your necks?

LZ: Considering it was a first feature we were left relatively free to experiment – I just remember it being free and that we had the space to the point that it became really hard. I think we lost a lot of weight over the mountain we were climbing – I certainly did – physically like losing a stone in stress, but then I also have incredible memories of it – so we learned the hard way.

RC: and were you tough with each other?

LZ: We have a quite interesting relationship, me and her. We can be tough on each other, but I think because we ultimately have great respect for each other as well – well I definitely have for her – and I'm sure she has for me. I think what works for us and what we have developed is if one of us has doubts, like if we are trying to pursue something and we are trying to crack it and we often acknowledge that we have a different opinion, but we often know that we are in tune with things and how we respond to things and therefore if one of us feels something good is happening and the other one doesn't the interesting thing is that we keep searching, because we always have a sense that if one of us has a doubt maybe there is still something else to be found.

RC: Can you be specific in either film is there a part – is there a sequence you had a particular struggle with?

LZ: In '*Ratcatcher*' I can think of the opening sequence – meaning from the drowning of the boy to the introduction of the another boy – the film's main character. It was written and shot to be a bit more complex – than the way it ended up in the final cut of the film – well not complex but there were some details in the writing that were beautiful but did not help us in setting up the story. Also I remember we had problems with the footage because on the day we were shooting the canal scene we realised that one of the boys was so scared of water that he could hardly relax. Anyway it turned out to be a bit of a disaster and we felt we had on the one hand not enough good material to make a very important scene work and on the other a lot of beautiful footage with other elements that were not essential. We spent a lot of time working out how to present the first fifteen minutes of the film and our biggest lesson was pretty basic that less is more – so we took things out and gradually discovered that it worked much better. That was a particular sequence I know we worked on for a long time and had arguments over but we just kept exploring and exploring.

The first cut of '*Ratcatcher*' was over three hours long, and we were cutting on film. We often would film different versions off the Steenbeck, so that was our way of keeping track of the different cuts. I have to admit at one point we had such a big 'structure' crisis that we ended up importing a video copy of the cut into a digital system and trying some major restructuring of the film. We stripped the film right down to the bone – we did it very quickly and it was very beneficial for us to find out what we really missed. Lynne and Alwin together are lethal – they shoot such beautiful visuals that sometimes it is difficult to let them go!

What was fantastic however was that there was a lot of improvised material that came about during the shoot, which we incorporated in the first assembly and I still keep a VHS copy of it for myself. I'm very fond of it. For instance, what happened when they shot the little boy's funeral was that the period car, an old 1970s banger, that they used for the parents of the dead boy kept stalling and even when it stalled in the middle of a take Lynne never called cut. We ended up with this great long shot where these bereaved parents in their old car are meant to follow the hearse, their car stalls and all the friends and neighbours start pushing it behind the hearse. As it happens it did not end up in the final cut of the film, but there is a real beauty to theses things, and I would say, the biggest lesson I learnt from Lynne in a way, is just to look at anything, even the results of so called accidents and some real gems might pop out, never discard anything.

RC: That reminds me of Renoir's '*Partie de campagne*',[21] where the shoot was plagued with rain – and it was supposed to be a sunny film – in the end the film makes such eloquent use of the rain to change the mood and its what moves me most – that change of mood which was not in the script and yet they made use of it with a wonderful transition to the end sequence which cuts me to the quick every time I see it and that's the kind of accident of filming that Renoir loved to take advantage of. Its part of a wonderful opportunity to play.

LZ: and there are accidents that happen in the cutting room that sometimes are wonderful. I will always remember this in fact during '*Kill the Day*' which is the short film that was our first collaboration outside the film school with the same group of people. We were cutting that on 16mm film and Lynne was saying 'come on I want to learn how to use the Comp-editor', and she was fiddling with this machine to put a piece of film in correctly and she put it the wrong way up. It was this beautiful shot of two boys walking alongside a canal bank but the camera was recording their reflection, which appeared upside down. We ended up with an odd reflected image that was not upside down and we liked it so much that we decided to keep it like that in the final cut. It is difficult to admit it but sometimes wonderful things happen by accident.

RC: Changing the subject – how was the transition from the Steenbeck to the Avid?

LZ: I regard myself really lucky because at the time I started at Film School we were pretty much still cutting on film, so I learnt to cut the old fashioned way: cutting and splicing celluloid. When we got to make '*Ratcatcher*', my first feature as an editor, I was asked whether I wanted to cut it digitally or not. I did not feel I used digital systems with enough confidence at the time and I did not want to feel frustrated by the technicalities of it. Knowing that, Lynne and I opted for cheaper film equipment, a longer post production schedule and a lovely team of assistants. It was labour intensive, but I have no regrets and I felt much more in control, cutting on film.

Now that I know how to cut digitally it would be really hard to go back to cut on film – I would find that extremely – um – laborious, yet there is a beauty that goes with it and that's why I'm really glad that I learnt that way. That beauty is to do with the physicality of it; the simple fact that you don't have to sit in front of a computer all day – the laborious side of it forces you to take your time with it, the time it takes to rewind reels, find things and change them round or reassemble them goes back to our thinking process and computers often can do things faster than your brain can think of them.

On the other hand they do free the editor of the burden of doing dramatic changes, especially on things that partly work. When you would do it on film you knew it would be a big task and if there is something that works you would fear losing a bit of that – in actual fact you never do – you can always put things back as they were, it just takes more time. So there is an argument for and against that really. The computer makes you freer and that is wonderful, but it does tend to make you splice more shots together than necessary – I always try to remind myself not to cut too much.

I enjoy this freedom that the new technology allows you to have enormously but at the same time I find that projecting your film – watching your cuts projected in the theatre is not the same as watching a video projection. What you can do with sound is incomparable with what you could do when we were cutting sound on mag. Now if I have the choice I would like to have both – the computer and a print and have a pos-conform[22] and project it as the cut develops. Unfortunately a pos-conform is often the first thing to go when too much money is spent in the production of a film.

As I said I am really glad I learned the old-fashioned way because I think that affects the approach you have. That was something that Tom Priestley taught me – just watch and watch the rushes and don't dive in until you are ready and if you don't feel you're ready just keep watching them. I think with computers its too easy sometimes to just dive in and cut and then you realise you haven't really quite got in your head what you are trying to get out of the material, and film in a way kind of forced that on you – made you really think much more before you started your first assembly.

RC: I'd like to get your feelings about sound. Did you learn the value of sound gradually as you gained more editing experience?

LZ: I think I've always been aware of sound and worked with it a lot from the beginning – and talking about sound that means also silences. I'm very aware of it when I work definitely and its almost as if I build my own sound track in my head – as basic as that could be but I definitely think of it quite early on.

RC: With Lynne's films have you track-layed them?

LZ: The short films yes – we did everything without a sound editor and we enjoyed that tremendously so I would say that is a little bit of a trade mark for us now and then obviously the bigger the project the more people – and talented people we have incorporated in the team and the more 'sprouting' there is – the more kind of blossoming of ideas in a way.

RC: But I assume you don't just hand over when you've locked picture.

(loud sound of objects falling in another room)

LZ: Oops! Its probably some books falling off my bookshelf.

Oh yes – I definitely like to follow things through. I think you discover how the times you haven't had the chance to follow something through how that effects what you've done. So I like to see things through and know that you can incorporate other people but still work with them and new ideas that they might bring but also the basis of what you were thinking about when you were cutting your picture is there.

That applies to music as well – I'm discovering that music can spoil a lot of the work that has gone into a scene – I might make myself unpopular saying this, but there is often a tendency to use music as wallpaper and I am much more into intelligent use of sound. I like to think of sound a lot and yet its often about minimal sound, but that minimal sound is very important and specific.

RC: Do you think you have developed any habits in your editing?

LZ: I would say something that I stick to is the habit to cut things together and not look at them immediately I find it useful just to hold back from the temptation of watching back your cut until I've got something substantial to see. Some people find that quite unbelievable – maybe you are starting the assembly of a film and you get a call saying what are the rushes like and you comment on that and then how does the cut feel and sometimes I don't know – I don't want to know. Its almost like I am holding back – trying to be driven by my instinct and my understanding of what the material is about and the notes that I've been given, but trying not to overcrowd my head yet by looking at the scenes cut together until I've got quite a bit there to watch in context that is going to allow me to have a greater understanding of what works and what doesn't and why. Almost like trying to preserve the objectivity by not watching things over and over again too much.

RC: What do you do when you are not cutting a film?

LZ: I think I'm learning to adjust to the change of pace that goes with being freelance so when you are on a job you haven't got time for much else than the work and suddenly in between you've got a lot of time on your hands and you've got to learn to use this time in the best possible way. I travel a lot so that is fantastic and that makes me appreciate the patterns of the work. I spend time away from home – home being London. Apart from that catch up with life: films, music, exhibitions and friends of course.

RC: So was working with Stephen Frears[23] an entirely different kind of experience?

LZ: Well, let me think – it was a different experience in the sense that it was the first time I worked with a very established director on a feature length film and I was very excited about it.

Stephen however usually works with a regular editor: Mick Audsley[24] and I can appreciate what a regular relationship between editor and director can be about, because I have that myself – so suddenly stepping into someone else's shoes can be a little scary. It turned out really well in the end and I think there is something to be said for trying new collaborations every now and then – one might have to do more ground work, but the learning that comes out of that is often invaluable.

RC: What about the female point of view and working with a female director – is that significant or different?

LZ: There is a pride that goes with being in a male dominated industry. I also love the fact that the group of people that I started off with is mostly female. I am sure that it was something to do with our gender that made us connect and made us connect on some of the topics we wanted to talk about in our films. I have to say, however that editing is possibly the one specialisation in film where women have been given more access and that I believe is because an editor contributes a lot but does all the work locked in a dark room, behind the scenes – their contribution is not apparent.

RC: Are you comfortable to be in that position?

LZ: I'm actually quite comfortable with being behind the scenes. I think it suits me I am not the little girl who used to sing and dance in front of an audience as I did when I was seven! Having a rewarding relationship with my collaborators is what matters to me.

RC: Have you any idea what you would have done with your life if editing hadn't come along?

LZ: No. (laughs) I really don't – no, isn't that incredible! I don't think I do. I'm sure it would be a job in the creative field, but its been such a roller coaster with the kind of path that has been quite defined – I haven't even wandered and its just kind of been happening – yeah!

Notes

1. **Anna Negri** – Director/writer – *In the Beginning there was Underwear*, 1999.
2. *Dersu Usala* (1975), Akira Kurosawa (1910–98) – A magnificent and beautiful film set in Siberia and based on the true story of a Russian explorer.
3. *The Icicle Thieves* – **Maurizio Nichetti,** 1989.

4. ***The Bicycle Thieves*** – Vittorio De Sica, (1948 – co-incidentally the year Nichetti was born!).
5. **Polytechnic of Central London** – Now the University of Westminster.
6. **National Film and Television School** – Established in 1971, the UK's premier establishment for professional training in Media.
7. **Joost Hunnigher** – Internationally respected teacher and administrator of long standing.
8. ***The Colour Box*** (1935), Len Lye (1901–80). Born in New Zealand Lye became a prominent experimental film-maker often treating celluloid as raw material rather than as conventional 'film'.
9. ***À Bout de souffle*** – Jean-Luc Godard, edited by Cécile Ducigis, one of the prominent female editors who contributed greatly to the French New Wave, 1960.
10. ***Jules et Jim*** – François Truffaut, edited by Claudine Bouché, another of the women who cut for the rising stars of this period of French cinema, 1962.
11. ***The Battle of Algiers*** – Gillo Pontecorvo, 1965. Brilliant film evoking the struggle of Algeria for independence in the 1950s.
12. ***Once Upon a Time in the West*** – Sergio Leone from a story by Dario Argento and Bernardo Bertolucci, 1968. Famous opening sequence set at a remote railway station whilst a gang wait for a train – seems to play out in a rhythm that extends real time. Edited by Nino Baragli.
13. **Tony Grisoni** – Writer, e.g. *Weiser* (2001), Wojciek Marczewski.
14. **Terry Gilliam** – Worked with Grisoni on *Fear and Loathing in Las Vegas* 1998, **Michael Winterbottom** worked with Grisoni on *In This World*, 2002.
15. **Lynne Ramsay** – Graduated from NFTS in 1995 and won BAFTA for Most Promising Newcomer in 1999 with ***Ratcatcher***.
16. **Tom Priestley** – Cut for Karel Reisz, *Isadora*, John Boorman, *Deliverance* Roman Polanski, *Tess* and Michael Radford, *1984*, amongst others. Son of J B Priestley and one of the nicest people in the business.
17. ***Small Deaths*** – Jury prize at Cannes for best Short, 1996.
18. ***Kill the Day*** – Prize for Best European Short Film, 1996.
19. ***Gasman*** – Jury Prize at Cannes for best Short, 1997.
20. ***Ratcatcher*** – See above, 1999.
21. ***Partie de campagne*** – (1936 but not released until 1946), Jean Renoir – edited by Marguerite Renoir in the absence of the director – a minor masterpiece of exquisite construction.
22. **Pos-conform** – The process of match cutting a print of the rushes of a film as it is being cut digitally to allow for projection in the form it can best be judged.
23. **Stephen Frears** – Eminent director for whom Lucia cut *The Deal*, 2003, the story of the relationship between Tony Blair and Gordon Brown up to the election of the Labour government.
24. **Mick Audsley** – See interview in this book.

32 Gillies Mackinnon, Pia Di Ciaula and Roger Crittenden: A Conversation

Two weeks before lock-off on the film 'The Escapist' the director, Gillies Mackinnon and his editor, Pia Di Ciaula talked with me in their edit suite at De Lane Lea in London's Soho.

Pia Di Ciaula on set with Gillies Mackinnon (Courtesy of Pia Di Ciaula)

RC: It might be best Gillies if you could talk first about your feelings about the editing process.

GM: I'll do my best Roger. I think it's quite hard to talk about some things which are processes in film-making. That doesn't only apply to editing. Whenever I get into a situation where I have to talk about how do you work with actors or how do you visualise how to shoot a scene, or whatever it might be, I always feel as if you don't want to be too articulate, because if there's any sort of magical process at work you don't want to put too many names to it, you know.

I've been in a situation where I had to describe to a group of young film-makers, in a whole day session, trying to tell them in the morning what I do when I make a film. Then in the afternoon I had to demonstrate what I do, and I did everything opposite to what I had said. (Pia laughs.) So I got a bit of a lesson from that. I was quite stunned by the experience, you know. I bought a bottle of wine on the way home that night I remember.

At Film School[1] I spent a lot of time in the editing rooms. I thought that was very important background to be a director. In fact I don't understand how people can direct unless they have done that, because it's got to do with rhythm and in a way knowing what's necessary to shoot. To be there in a cutting room and to have to face up to the problems of all the inadequacies of material and try to be inventive. That whole process gives you a really good background so you know what's required when you are directing.

Actually when I first went to film school and I cut the first film I had I was so disorganised. We used to move from room to room you know, I wouldn't always get the same room.

RC: The mobile trim bin syndrome.

GM: I'm afraid it's worse than that Roger. I would never have wanted to say this until now but I had all my trims in one big plastic bag!

PC: We all did that!

GM: Oh did you, oh I'm so relieved, I used to walk around with all my trims bundled up together inside a plastic bag. Lots of time to experiment at film school. That was great. When I cut the film that was my graduation film, '*Passing Glory*'.[2] Well actually I didn't cut it, it was cut by David Barry, we had all the time in the world to cut that film. He was physically cutting it and I was there working with him and between the two of us we could go round and round the film and finally come to a conclusion. Which is not a luxury we have now of course. Now we have a certain amount of time and we have to pace ourselves, but then it wasn't like that and it was wonderful. Anyway film school was the last time I physically cut a film myself, which was the one in the plastic bag!

Since then I've worked with a variety of editors and the style is a little different every time. One thing I would say is that I think I've always worked with good editors. That's something I'm very grateful for, because working with a bad editor can be a nightmare.

I think it can be quite difficult for editors because they often have to take a position with a director. They have to be quite tactful and that becomes like they are walking on glass. It becomes very tense, you know. It's difficult for them to say what they really think sometimes. One of the good things working with Pia, is that she always says what she really thinks. She doesn't seem to have a problem with that! Sometimes she'll chew on it for a bit before it comes out, but it always comes out.

RC: Was that true from the start?

PC: I bit my tongue a few times on '*Regeneration*'.[3]

GM: I guess that was so in the first couple of weeks. I do remember that Pia was cutting in a style that I found too fast for the film. I didn't say very much really, but I'd recognised that there was a style employed that wasn't right for the film that was going to be made. That's all I said, and when I came back four or five days later it was just completely different. I know there was some process that Pia went through to get to that point. After that I felt that she completely got the right note on what I was doing.

RC: I think that Pia said that and what was implied was that she had to let the material speak to her and breathe. You said you'd come off doing Movies of the Week back to back.

PC: NBC!

RC: A kind of heavy rhythm.

GM: That was interesting that Pia was able to make the adjustment. Some people would not have been able to, they would have been thrown into a state of panic, probably, not really knowing what to do. What was miraculous about it was how completely she got the note.

PC: I guess once you hit that rhythm, because obviously I had to find a slower pace and rhythm within myself in order to do it. Then once you find it you know you can go from there.

RC: In a way it needs a sort of courage doesn't it? Letting some-thing breathe is in a way so much harder than just cutting from moment to moment that is moving it along.

PC: That's right, it was so different from anything I had done, because working for US networks they wanted to see every-one's reactions, really quickly. It was a different style and pace altogether.

* * * * * * * * * * * * *

RC: Do you, Gillies, see yourself as a European film-maker rather than a Hollywood film-maker. Can you see that distinction in your own attitude and style.

GM: I think probably European. I can sort of say that because I've had experience of working with the Americans you see. '*The Playboys*'[4] was financed by the Goldwyns, but it still had a mid-Atlantic feel. It had three American actors, playing Irish, but it wasn't an American film flat out. It had a European very quirky quality as well. So I learnt a lot about Hollywood on that film. I went through the test screening process etcetera. Then later I did a Touchstone film called '*A Simple Twist of Fate*'[5] with Steve Martin. Then I was working completely inside the Hollywood system. That was a gigantic learning curve. To find out what Hollywood is and not what we think Hollywood is. I lived and breathed it for that year.

RC: Was it uncomfortable for you?

GM: No, actually, I find that people assume that it would be, but if I look back on it I went into it in a very realistic way. I was-n't going in there with any illusions about what was happen-ing. It was Steve Martin's screenplay and he had asked me to do it because of '*The Playboys*'. To some extent we were quite close together creatively, which meant that the studio left us alone, to a large extent. They let us go and make the film. My impression when I look back on it was that I was making a film which was a little bit less personal than some of the other films I'd made. I was, maybe, making it more for Steve Martin than for myself although I think there's a lot of me in it as well.

  It was interesting on all levels to do. They were very gener-ous was the thing that I noticed, but the downside of that is that you start getting used to a lot of luxuries. You begin to think that is what you should have. I recognised that funny lit-tle horrible gnome growing up inside of me, and that's when

I decided to come back and do '*Small Faces*'[6] which is a low-budget film set in Glasgow. Creatively that was the right thing for me to do.

* * * * * * * * * * * * *

RC: Going through the whole process from film school onwards is there any sense in which the experience of editing feeds back into even the scripting of new projects.

GM: Oh yes definitely. I'm writing something just now, a prolonged first draft which is a more ambitious kind of a film really, a period film set in Scotland. When I was writing it before I started making '*The Escapist*' I think I was having real trouble being disciplined with myself, but after the experience of shooting this film which was so intense, when I came back and read it again, and boy I felt like a butcher. When I get into the cutting room then it makes me cautious in another way. I ask myself questions like will I cut this scene out. I think 'yeah, I think I probably will', so I don't write it, you know. Yeah, it definitely has a kick back in that way.

RC: Did you or do you have models of film-makers whose work you admire and who represent the kind of film-making you would prefer to aspire to?

GM: I've got a few, heroes if you like. I'm talking here about people like Tarkovsky, Klimov, Visconti, Fellini, Pasolini, Kurosawa, Bergman,[7] you know. So like I probably shouldn't say that, but you know it's the truth! These are the people who I think were really kind of geniuses in their way, and were very true and very real. I do think we are living in a time where we have a lot of very banal values being applied to cinema. There's a freedom in these films and I guess a lot of them really weren't made for very much money.

RC: They often had time but not money.

GM: That's true, Tarkovsky had all the time in the world.[8] I mean I think they were principally entertainers as film-makers, that's how I see it. It kind of irritates me when people keep talking about being artists. It's just a bit of self-flattery, actually, but I do think there are some artists in film-making.

RC: Do you two ever have conversations about other film-makers?

GM: Yes, we talk about other film-makers and other films, but we have slightly different tastes don't we. Pia will enjoy the more mainstream film and it's a problem for me. Pia can buy the ticket and . . .

PC: And I enjoy every minute of it . . .

GM: And I don't do that you see, I go in there with attitude!

(General laughter)

* * * * * * * * * * * * *

RC: What about the fact that the editing process begins during the shoot? Obviously an important part of the value of that is trust, isn't it. That you are getting another pair of eyes from the moment you start shooting, which then feeds back into how you feel it is going and what you shoot.

GM: Absolutely. This film that we just made because of certain script complications was being re-invented during the shooting. I had no time to sit in the cutting room during the shoot. This was a six-day-a-week shoot from six o'clock in the morning to about nine o'clock when I got home in the evening. I rarely was in the cutting room. Now with an editor who I didn't completely trust in that way, to cut it a bit like I would cut it, plus take a view, and add stuff in and try stuff. I am just basically confident that Pia will be doing a good job. By the end of the cut, there was a cut there of the whole story. It was a very good cut. It takes you quite far on (*in a working relationship*) to have that work happening, co-existing with the shooting. Plus Pia can call up the set and say there's something missing here or why don't you do that. If she says to me (aside) *and I didn't get you the wire shot, sorry* (laughter) if she says to me, I really need a shot of a barbed wire fence, I will try and get it. Even if I don't really understand why she wants it, that's fine we'll shoot it.

RC: You both have, in different ways a visual background. The relationship of image to storytelling is clearly crucial in what you've just said. There is a shot that you could get that will make a difference, because an editor could say there's a problem here and then you have to work out what might solve it. If the editor can go one step further and say if we had that particular image . . .

GM: No Pia will be very, very specific, about what it is we're missing.

RC: I understand from Pia that sound is very important to her in the process of cutting. Is that something that you value as well?

GM: Yeah, it is. Pia will always like create something to suggest at least where we are going, even if it's not what we finally have. She's very good on music too. She's very good on finding the right kind of music for a scene.

RC: I remember you both talking about the research for music on 'Hideous Kinky',[9] and all the listening you had to do.

GM/PC: Yeah!

GM: Big deal on 'Hideous Kinky' because we had to get stuff we could afford! For instance I'd let Pia listen to 'The Incredible String Band', which I had and she thought it was just terrible. In the end you did take a track and put it on there. It was not the kind of track I liked from the period, it sounded more like Cat Stevens,[10] but actually it really worked on the scene. Now I would never have made that connection, so that is great and it's in the film.

* * * * * * * * * * * * *

RC: I remember telling Pia that Dede Allen[11] was once asked what people should do who want to be editors, and she said surprisingly to her audience, 'Go to the theatre'. In this case it was New York, so it was 'go to Broadway, go to off-Broadway, go to off-off-Broadway – unless you're inside the way performance works you'll never be able to cut'. Is that something you have a dialogue about? You, Gillies, obviously have a sense whether a performance is working or not – you have to.

GM: I'm not sure I am answering your question or not, but Pia is sometimes sensitive to emotional qualities that I have missed. Does that make sense, Pia?

PC: Can you come up with an example?

GM: It seems very familiar, that you are seeing something that has touched you, and you try to retain that in the film, but I haven't valued it enough.

PC: Did I mention that Gillies gave me a script on 'Regeneration' that was just a sound script? He went through every scene and listed all the sound effects he heard. I've never received that from a director. So that's how important sound is to him. I still have that script, because I thought it was so unusual.

RC: Talking about Europe in general, you can't make generalisations, because there are so many different approaches to film across the continent.

GM: I think it is changing. I find that this American influx, starting up companies over here – a producer put it this way to me, it's like everyone woke up one morning and had this great idea, 'Let's make a commercial film!' This is such a pathetic interpretation of Hollywood and how it operates. The clichés that have been falling out of people's mouths these days, are appalling. They've read it in a book or seen it in a movie or they've picked it up from somebody. It's just not the way Hollywood operates. I find that when we adopt the Hollywood style it's kind of like really banal. We should stick to our own way of doing things, but obviously money has become so important. The accountants seem to make the basic decisions now.

As for the cutting room, I think I am very comfortable on set, shooting a film. I get my boots on in the morning. I put on my armour, and off I go. I fight all day long struggle, struggle, struggle against time, against the weather, whatever it might be, the problems you might face. There's never a moments respite, and I'm very comfortable with that you know, with that physically demanding process. It's physically coming at you the whole time. Then, when that ends and I go to the cutting room, I'm not as comfortable with the cutting room. That's why it's good to have an editor. My stamina is not the same as when I'm shooting. It's like I switch off a wee bit, because I can't think it through.

When I was wondering what to say to you Roger, I was remembering one thing. I don't know whether this is familiar to you or not Pia. When we come across a problem and it can't quite be solved, I will express a lot of frustration and be very irritable and leave.

PC: No!

GM: (laughs) I mean rather than sticking with it. Then I will come back the next day and Pia will often have found a completely different way of looking at it. It's not a conscious strategy on my part, but I think I – do I do that?

PC: You do it, but I'm very happy to continue on my own.

GM: There you go!

PC: Well, the problem is if someone's with you the whole time you almost have to go in their direction, and then you can't go off on tangents that you would when you are on your own.

RC: Yeah I know, and you're almost dependent on their energy.

PC: I know.

RC: Which has to filter through you.

PC: That's right and I just find that you end up taking a lot longer to get to the point. I mean I like working with you but it's also healthy to have some time on my own.

GM: I think that's definite. I can feel it myself. It's like you all get bogged down in things. Actually when I do walk away I can almost feel it in a tangible sense, that this is what Pia needs. For me to not be around and often the film will make a lot of progress when I do that.

PC: That's why I cant imagine getting all the material at wrap and starting cutting with a director in the room, for the whole time. I don't think you are getting the maximum out of the editor if you do that.

GM: There's also the issue of disagreement, and I think that can be a problem if there isn't a basic relationship between editor and director. I think what tends to happen is that sometimes Pia won't say that she disagrees but I know that she does.

PC: Well until it's locked anything can be changed!

GM: But usually she will tell me. In the end there's a moment comes when you recognise that whatever I felt or Pia felt before about what we were doing, if you find something better or something which is in advance of where you were before you drop it. I don't think we have a problem about disagreement, do we?

PC: No I think it's healthy.

RC: Actually it's essential isn't it?

PC: It is.

RC: Wouldn't you feel more uncomfortable if Pia agreed with everything?

PC: Oh yes I'll do that Gillies, you know, I'll do that, oh yes!

GM: Oh no, no, no – I wouldn't trust that in the first place. So there's no problem with disagreement. There's probably a problem with moods though! (laughs).

PC: How can you say that!

GM: No, I'm quite moody.

PC: You're not moody.

GM: Och, I'm not moody, okay I'm not moody. I made a mistake there.

PC: (Laughs).

GM: I think she's just being kind to me, really.

PC: No, I'm joking, but I'm also sensitive to maybe he's bored right, because maybe . . .

GM: Just because I'm snoring it doesn't mean I'm bored!

PC: No because it must be hard to sit in a room and watch somebody work, and not be hands on. I know I would find it frustrating.

GM: Well we have a process anyway of working. I feel I haven't backed off enough recently because it's getting near the end and I've got to be here and maybe that's a mistake. The process is looking at it, both of us making notes in our own notebook, Pia works, then we look at it again. Then every Friday we have a screening. We just watch the film without making notes. Maybe ask a few people along to get some feed back.

RC: At what point does watching the whole film as a habit, when does that start? Are you saying that once there is a complete cut you will always review the whole film?

GM: No we also identify particular sequences to work on.

RC: With this film or any of the other films have you to any extent thrown the structure in the air?

PC: Well we did that on '*Regeneration*' quite a bit. It starts with scene 25 then goes 7 to 11 and so on. This one as well, because it was a very linear script.

GM: No matter how much we refine that cut on this linear story, telling the story A to Z and no matter how many dramatic moments there were I always had this ultimate feeling of it being just not tense enough, you know. Then we started to experiment a little bit with time, and it seemed to create much more tension. The first time we ever did that I thought wow, this is really a different movie.

RC: Why do you think you have less stamina?

GM: In the cutting room? Maybe the word stamina isn't the right work, maybe it's concentration. It's like when I have a problem when I'm shooting I am totally relentless in solving that problem. Even when I think I've solved that problem I'm still working on it, to see if there's something I've missed. I work hundred per cent on the problems. I deal with the problems as they come up you know, bat them off! In the cutting room I don't have the same capacity mentally. I'll often want to go to sleep, no I mean really. It feels like the right thing for me to do rather than sit here and keep on thinking is to go to sleep and maybe I'll waken up with the solution. Seriously that's what happens with me.

RC: Of course the stamina with electronic editing is supposed to be harder to sustain that it was with film editing. Although it doesn't stop people staying glued to their Avid for hours and hours on end.

GM: Well, that's another issue by the way. Maybe that is related to it, because when we used to cut on film everything took a lot longer. It all happens so instantaneously now that if you are involved on any kind of a deeper level then you can't possibly catch up with what you are doing physically. So maybe that's why I either have to walk away or lie down there and go to sleep, for a wee while. I don't think your deeper feelings and the electronic medium are in rhythm with each other. Not for me anyway, Pia you know.

* * * * * * * * * * * * *

RC: That reminds me of Walter Murch's comments on how you work as an editor and the comparison between cutting on film and electronic non-linear editing. You know he did the re-cut of '*Touch of Evil*'[12] according to the memo sent to the studio by Orson Welles after they had removed him from the film and finished it without his involvement or agreement. Walter found himself sitting opposite Robert Wise[13] at some dinner so they said the first editor for Orson Welles meets the last, after his death. As I remember it from Walter, they ended up deciding that the way they cut was a combination of working from the end of a sequence to the beginning, mute with their eyes closed! Walter said that when he had to find a cut point on the Moviola he would close his eyes and hit the brake and if he stopped at the same frame twice he knew he'd got the rhythm right.

GM: The Zen of cutting.

RC: And the idea of watching a cut fast backwards on the Steenbeck actually told you something about the rhythm. You're ingesting it in a different way.

GM: That's like what they tell you at art school that you look at your painting in the mirror and you get to see it in it's true light, because everything gets so adjusted to what you are doing, angles and shapes and everything, but if you actually look at it in a mirror you see it afresh.

RC: Like drawing negative space.

GM: That's very interesting for me, because I do feel that taking out all issues of content that essentially its rhythm. You know its light and rhythm. That's what film-making is really. Including sound – light, dark, rhythm – light and shade, rhythm. You can apply that to everything, picture, sound, performance, everything. You can boil it down essentially to something so abstract that you can play it backwards and learn something from it. That I find very, very interesting.

GM: I have a certain kind of madness to so with ignoring continuity. I remember continuity and the costume designer at two o'clock in the morning on an ice rink in Edinburgh saying to me, Gillies you cannot do this, because of a list of things that have happened before. It's just absolutely in my mind that it's going to be this way and I don't care about the continuity. That is a kind of madness that overtakes me sometimes you know.

RC:　Presumably you carry that particular madness into the cutting. It might seem perverse but you will ignore continuity because you want to do something else.

GM:　It will never be the main thing in my mind. Even in the cutting room Pia will say to me well actually you can't do that. I never take that as a very serious sign that I can't do it. I don't know why that is, because in preparing a film I give a lot of attention to detail, about what will be in a scene. So at the same time I'm going against the grain. If Pia says to me there's a continuity problem I just never think that is going to be a reason for not doing it. You know I have actually with a certain amount of glee, presented things on screen with such glaring continuity errors that nobody has ever, ever mentioned.

RC:　Then I remember looking at certain scenes in '*Before the Revolution*'[14] the early Bertolucci, with Roberto Perpignani where there is no continuity of action at all. They were obviously playing. They had both absorbed the 'New Wave', and were enjoying that playing. But the rhythm is absolutely right. If you stopped at each cut you would say you can't cut from there to there, there is no match of continuity. People are standing, they are sitting, they are in a different place.

GM:　If the rhythm's right, if it is dramatic enough you know it's unlikely that anyone's going to be bothering or seeing that you know, but I think we are touching on something a little bit different. I think it's a little bit like the old masons who would build the perfect building, and put in a dud brick.

RC:　Or the Turkish carpet which must have a flaw.

GM:　I think there's a little bit of that, because I think that one of the greatest thrills I have when I sit with an audience is when I know that a big mistake is coming up. I get really, really excited. What do I love in the old movies by people like Pasolini; it's the mistake. It always touches me. When I see the bad camera move or the flaw, it always touches me. It really does. So maybe that's why I get the big thrill in my own film if there's something I know is wrong and I'm sitting with an audience, and it happens, and nobody throws anything at the screen. Nobody walks out.

RC: Are you saying that's something that film-makers can enjoy for themselves or do you think there's some value in imperfection?

GM: No I think it's a perversion!

PC: I don't think there's a value in putting in a mistake for the sake of having a mistake in the film.

GM: No Pia would get rid of the mistake. If she could, she would you know.

PC: I would go for performance. Continuity comes second. So I wouldn't change something if the performance was right.

GM: Pia will definitely be for the better performance, even if there is soft focus e.g. If other shots are worse for performance though being in focus.

RC: As Truffaut said if there's a judder in a tracking shot I can't do anything about it, then forget it, it doesn't matter.

GM: The thing is it makes visible the human hand. The flaw the mistake makes visible the human hand. It's no longer seamless illusion. I think that is part of what really touches me in a film like '*The Gospel According to Saint Matthew*'.[15] There is a number of times in that film where you can see the flawed hand of a human being. I like that because it seems as if the idea in commercial film-making is not to see the human hand. You see the face of the actor but you don't see the mind of the film-maker.

RC: That's true of what I feel about early Renoir. There's nothing perfect, but in a sense it's perfect. He hated the second take anyway, let alone worrying about flaws in the technique. That's part of the enjoyment. Part of a special pleasure.

GM: I suppose it's a personal thing. Maybe we can make too much of it.

RC: It maybe is a personal thing but its part of what is addressed in the relationship between editor and director, in terms of what matters.

GM: The thing is it only really touches you if it is a really beautiful film. If it were a banal film then it just would irritate you.

PC: Then all the mistakes jump out at you and put you off the film even more.

RC: So you've got to make something that's nearly perfect.

GM: If the microphone boom swung into the top of the shot in '*Bicycle Thieves*'[16] I wouldn't care.

PC: But *you* probably wouldn't even notice. *I* would notice.

GM: Yeah!

PC: It's true.

GM: Pia is very observant and she retains tremendous amounts of information, much more than I can. So when we go into the dubbing theatre and somebody asks a question Pia can backtrack to exactly where it was and what happened. Whereas when I've done something it tends to be gone.

PC: Yeah, well when you're in a mixing theatre and the dialogue editor has replaced a syllable, it just jumps out at me, because every word and every syllable is how I've cut it, and so if one thing is out of place I know.

GM: I think probably that very exacting discipline that Pia has is quite a good thing for me, because I drive myself very hard when I shoot a movie, but there is also that slightly cavalier part of me, that will just change things. It's part of what's exciting about it for me. I think that Pia's ability to notice things and also know what lies in the background is probably quite important for me.

RC: So you wouldn't want to cut your own films.

GM: No. I'm very, very glad that I spent time cutting my own films, but no I would not want to take that responsibility. I wouldn't want to be here when everything stops in my mind. I'd much rather go to sleep or walk away.

PC: Well sometimes you have to do that anyway. Even as an editor you have to walk away.

GM: But I also would want that other mind at work on the film, you see. It's not enough to be only my mind. Some days Pia will have an idea that I will develop; an idea that I would never have thought of. Or the other way round.

RC: On the other hand some of the people you say are your heroes did cut for themselves. Kurosawa for instance, apparently had food passed through a hatch, rather than have any human contact whilst cutting his own films.

GM: Well you can't knock Kurosawa. I think I can let the obsession go after shooting. I think I can pass it on. I'm glad to say. It's not that I don't still have the obsession, but you know I sort of carry it all myself when I'm shooting, with a lot of help from people of course, but everything is still my decision, whereas I don't feel that in the cutting room.

RC: So do you see your relationship say with your cinematographer as very different, than that with your editor.

GM: I'm not sure if it is really essentially different. The thing is that when I come up to shooting a film, what is going to happen on the set there, the world that is going to be created which is a very important thing for me. That is, we are building a world for the actor to walk into and believe and be that character, a world that the actor can trust. A lot of work goes into that and that comes from a lot of different people. As Andy Harris, who is the Production Designer that I often work with said – he once said to me after an incredible battle we had fought about trying to get something done well and on time – he said you know everything that I do is only just a place for the actors to walk in and act. I thought that was such a brilliant thing for a designer to say, because a lot of designers wouldn't say that. They're designing something its their design, but Andy really is only interested in building that place, which is not only his. It's something that comes from all of us. The same goes for the other contributors. By the time it gets to Pia, it's all accumulated.

RC: But by then you do have the clay that you have to make the film from, whereas the psychology of everything building up to it is different.

GM: But you would probably know what the visual sources are for the film.

PC: Yes because I do start early. When I know that I am doing a film I do get involved. For instance Gillies starts his own little black book on every film, and he will collect postcards, or little images or do cartoons or whatever that pertains to the film.

GM: Draw story-boards or take notes or anything; we're travelling along I see something, everything goes in the book.

PC: Or a colour.

RC: And you connect with that.

PC: I do, because then I can think about those images or just stories that Gillies tells me, while he's in pre-production and I read the drafts as they come in. I start thinking about styles of editing but until I get the footage, you can predict a certain direction but once you have the footage is when you can really get down to it.

GM: The visual thing that you put forward is probably quite interesting but I would go further than that, because I don't think that I approach film-making in a very intellectual way. I have no theatre background. My background is very visual, but working with actors is very important to me. I certainly don't come with a lot of theories, and a lot of intellectualisation, definitely not. What I try to do, maybe this is where it starts with the visual thing, is try to build this world. My approach to the film is more sensual, in the sense of how does it look, and especially the light the shade the rhythm. So I wouldn't sit here with Pia and rationalise what I've just seen in a very logical way. I'd be much more likely in an instinctive way to say, can't we just put that there.

RC: I do get a sense that Pia is not just inside the material but inside what she feels you feel about it. About the world you're creating. It's not just a surface reaction to the images themselves, it's about what they are supposed to be contributing to.

GM: I think that is actually something that I try to achieve all the way through. With actors also. The worst thing that I can do with an actor is intellectualise everything. For me it's the kiss of death. It's like you meet an actor, you go to a café. He's not sure about this and that. I'm not trying to persuade him, I'm just trying to get him to see what I see about it. A certain moment comes when it's almost like you pass something under the table and the actor takes it, and the actor passes something under the table and you take it. It's an invisible thing this, it doesn't happen. It's a token of trust. After that you can relax because you've given each other the tokens. It's the same working with others including the editor. If it isn't there you have a problem. Everything is a problem if you don't have that.

RC: But you are talking about a two-way thing.

GM: Absolutely. You've exchanged something and you can get inside each other's heads. If you can't do that you're always talking to a brick wall.

Notes

1. **Film School** – Gillies studied at the National Film and Television School in the 1980s.
2. *Passing Glory* – Graduation film set in Glasgow.
3. *Regeneration* – Gillies Mackinnon, based on the novel by Pat Barker, 1997.
4. *The Playboys* – Gillies Mackinnon, script by Shane Connaughton and Kerry Crabbe, 1992.
5. *A Simple Twist of Fate* – Gillies Mackinnon, 1994.
6. *Small Faces* – Gillies Mackinnon, 1996.
7. **Gillies' heroes** include **Elem Klimov (1933–2003)** – Russian director e.g. '*Come and See*' (1985), and '*Larisa*' (1980), a tribute to his wife the director Larisa Shepitko who was killed in a car accident.
8. **Tarkovsky** – Of course Gillies would agree that having all the time in the world was not much compensation for having to fight the authorities to even be allowed to make a film and when one was finished to have it shelved from distribution.

9. *Hideous Kinky* – Gillies Mackinnon, starring Kate Winslet, 1998.
10. **Cat Stevens** – Former folk singer who is now a Muslim activist as Yusef Islam.
11. **Dede Allen** – She made these remarks when addressing an audience of students at an American College.
12. *Touch of Evil* **(1958)** – Orson Welles. Restored according to Welles memo, which had survived in the Studio archives, by **Walter Murch** in 1998.
13. **Robert Wise** – Born 1914, editor, '*Citizen Kane*' (1941) and '*The Magnificent Ambersons*' (1942). Became director e.g. '*West Side Story*' (1961).
14. *Before the Revolution* – Bernardo Bertolucci, 1964.
15. *The Gospel According to Saint Matthew* – Pier Paolo Pasolini, 1964.
16. *Bicycle Thieves* – Vittorio De Sica, 1948.

Index

Index

Index

393

Index